Y0-CHV-882

Volume 2 of Russia and the South Pacific, 1696–1840
SOUTHERN AND EASTERN POLYNESIA

The second volume in Glynn Barratt's projected quartet on the naval, scientific, and social activities of the Imperial Russian Navy in the South Pacific, this book describes Russian activities in New Zealand, the Austral Islands, and Easter Island. These widely scattered areas were all visited by warships of the Russian navy and by companies of highly educated and observant officers and "gentlemen of science" in the early 1800s.

Barratt's annotated and careful translations of the visitors' eyewitness accounts provide fascinating, sometimes amusing, reading about the landfalls of the ships. The Russians' journals, reports, and drawings are collated with artefacts collected on the spot and with contemporaneous European data to produce a vivid picture of life and culture in these parts of the South Pacific in the early post-contact period.

Available in Soviet archives, many of the primary sources that Barratt has examined for this book until now have been almost completely ignored by Western scholars in spite of their importance in understanding the changes that took place in post-contact Oceania. These archival holdings, as described by the author, will be of major importance to those interested in the history and ethnohistory of southern and eastern Polynesia.

GLYNN BARRATT is a professor of Russian at Carleton University and the author of many books on Russia's naval and diplomatic history.

University of British Columbia Press
PACIFIC MARITIME STUDIES SERIES

Volume 2 of
Russia and the South Pacific
1696–1840

SOUTHERN
AND
EASTERN
POLYNESIA

Glynn Barratt

UNIVERSITY OF BRITISH COLUMBIA PRESS
Vancouver 1988

This book has been published with the help of a grant from the
Social Science Federation of Canada, using funds provided by
the Social Sciences and Humanities Research Council of
Canada.

Canadian Cataloguing in Publication Data

    Barratt, Glynn.
      Southern and eastern Polynesia

      (University of British Columbia Press
    Pacific maritime studies; 7)
      (Volume 2 of Russia and the South Pacific,
    1696–1840)
      Bibliography: p.
      Includes index.
      ISBN 0-7748-0305-3

      1. Polynesia–Relations–Soviet Union.
    2. Soviet Union– Relations–Polynesia.
    3. Polynesia–Discovery and exploration.
    4. Scientific expeditions–Polynesia–
    History–19th century. 5. Soviet Union–
    History, Naval. I. Title. II. Series.
    III. Series: Barratt, Glynn. Russia and
    the South Pacific, 1696–1840; v. 2.
    DU510.B37 1988   996   C88-091615-X

International Standard Book Number 0-7748-0305-3

Printed in Canada

P75894

Contents

Illustrations

1

Introduction

This is the second volume of my study with the general title *Russia and the South Pacific, 1696–1840*. The first volume, published by the University of British Columbia Press in 1988, surveyed the Russians' social, maritime, and scientific dealings in Australia during that period. The third will deal with Russian visits to, and study of, the Melanesian peoples and the Western Polynesian fringe, focusing principally upon Vanuatu, Fiji, Tuvalu (Ellice Islands), and Anuta. A fourth volume is planned, to cover Russian intercourse with the inhabitants and archipelagoes of Central Polynesia. Like Volume 1, *The Russians and Australia,* this is a survey; it cannot pretend to be a comprehensive treatment of a subject long neglected in the West: the early period of Russian interest and enterprise in Oceania, particularly its southern parts. Because it is a survey, I have chosen not to stray too far into the thickets of ethnology. The bulk of the material presented in my little study *Bellingshausen: A visit to New Zealand, 1820* (1979) is omitted here. Nor are the principal conclusions offered here those I arrived at in *Bellingshausen:* as I take the liberty of retranslating Russian narratives and journals into English, so I presume to change opinion on occasion, on the basis of new primary material that I have seen since 1980. I also emphasize the origins and later (post-1820) growth of Russian naval, mercantile, and scientific knowledge of New Zealand and the Maoris, as I did not do in my earlier work. Readers wishing for more details of the ethnographic records from the Bellingshausen visit to New Zealand are directed to my edition of *Queen Charlotte Sound, New Zealand: The Traditional and European Records* (Ottawa 1987). Other readers, with particular or even local interests, may benefit from the extensive bibliography which I include because of the broad nature of this book. Surveys will always raise more questions than they answer.

Russian knowledge of the peoples of the Great South Sea, or *Vostochnyi okean* (Eastern Ocean) as they called it, was considerable even in the early eighteenth century. Its foundation had been laid by the works of William Dampier (*New Voyage Round the World*, 1697) and Nicolaes Witsen (*Noord en Oost Tartarye* [North and East Tartary], 1692; 2d ed. 1705). By the early nineteenth century, Russians had contributed at least as much as Frenchmen, Americans, or Spaniards, though not as much as British subjects, to European knowledge of Polynesia. We in the West almost always overlook this. It is interesting that the recent growth of Soviet awareness of long-ago Russian naval dealings in the South Pacific Islands, caused by the Red Navy's new presence in that quarter of the globe, has no parallel in the West. It is as though we refuse to recognize that Soviet vessels are not Johnny-come-latelies on the South Pacific scene.

In the course of his Grand Embassy to Western Europe, Tsar Peter Alekseevich (Peter the Great) was for some days (August-September 1697) the guest of Nicolaes Witsen, the geographer, savant, and part-time minister for Muscovite affairs at Amsterdam, where he was Burgomeister. Peter was acquainted with Witsen's *Noord en Oost Tartarye*, which incorporated Russian as well as Dutch archival documents relating to the far Northeast of Asia and the Strait of Anian supposed by scholars of that era to separate the continents of Asia and America. That work offered woodcut drawings "illustrating" Abel Tasman's voyages of 1642–43 and 1644. Plate 28 of its Part 1, based on a crudely drawn original by Tasman's draughtsman, Isaak Gilseman, showed a Maori double canoe manned by stocky, muscular warriors. Thus was New Zealand brought into focus for the tsar and many other northern readers. On establishing his infant navy in 1696, Peter had entrusted Fedor Apraksin, its first Grand Admiral, with the direction of cartography. The Dutch and Apraksin were in contact by 1698. In this way the Russian Navy acquired its early knowledge of New Zealand, and it did its best throughout the century to gain such solid information as it could about the Great South Sea and its resources.

But that information was mainly derivative and academic. By the mid-1730s, the Imperial Academy of Sciences and not the Navy was responsible for the study of such places. More than once far-sighted naval officers proposed that Russian ships be sent from Kronstadt in the Baltic to the North Pacific Ocean, training companies of seamen, lending moral and material support to Russian outposts in the North Pacific basin, and assisting cossack economic enterprise in the remote Northeast of Asia. At least once, in 1786, a squadron very nearly made the voyage that would have brought it into South Pacific waters. It was another century, however, that witnessed the beginning (1803) of maritime connections between Slav and Polynesian and of Russian circumnavigation. By then the

Russian attitude toward the South Pacific Islanders, indeed toward the business of seaborne exploration, was completely fixed by Cook, who for half a century after his death was seen by the Russian naval officer as the model of a commander of a voyage of discovery and science.

Paradoxically, Cook reinforced the academic attitude that the Russians had adopted earlier toward the Islanders. He gave them the most sober, most factual descriptions of the Pacific islands, their topography, resources, climes, and people. Naval officers especially, many of whom had had professional connections with the British in the last third of the eighteenth century, both recognized Cook's eminence as a commander and were influenced by his scientific approach toward the business of discovery. His one worrisome appearance on the Russian Empire's easternmost extremity, at Unalaska Island in October 1778, made the government of Catherine II receptive to any factual accounts of a voyage to the North Pacific Ocean from the South. Knowledge was power, and both Russian sovereignty over the Aleutian Island chain and her portion of the North Pacific–China fur trade were perceived to be at stake. Russian awareness of South Pacific regions grew apace in the last years of the century, though mostly in the context of the North Pacific, of otter skins, and of a northern passage from Europe to the East.

Both the beginning of the Russian Navy's long-term but eventually unsuccessful effort to provision the North Pacific colonies and the beginning of the Russians' social, maritime, and scientific dealings with the Polynesian peoples are linked with the names of Ivan Fedorovich Kruzenshtern (1770–1846) and Iurii Fedorovich Lisianskii (1773–1839). Both officers spent a lengthy period (1794–99) as Russian Volunteers, undergoing useful practical training in the Royal Navy. Making use of their British contacts, they made their way to British India (1798–99), whence Lieutenant Kruzenshtern struggled on to China. In Canton, seat of the North Pacific fur trade that had sprung up after Cook's own men arrived there in 1780 with torn sea otter peltry from the Northwest Coast of North America, he made a systematic study of the Coast-to-China trade. He became the crucial link between Canton, the Russian Fleet, and the disputed Northwest Coast. In 1800 and again in 1802 he submitted to his government a plan to supply the Russian outposts from the Baltic Sea, to train whole companies of seamen, and to stake out a Russian claim in the Pacific seaborne fur trade. His ambition and persistence were rewarded: two suitable vessels were acquired in England in 1802 and renamed *Nadezhda* and *Neva*.

Commanded respectively by Kruzenshtern himself and by Lisianskii, they set sail from the Baltic Sea in August 1803, calling at Falmouth on their way to Oceania. In 1804 *Nadezhda*'s company made scientifically important contact with the people of the Taio-hae area of Nukuhiva Island in the Washington-Marquesas Group (7–17 May), before proceeding to the south shore of Hawaii Island (7–10 June), where their hopes of getting fresh provisions were dashed. *Neva* meanwhile looked in at Hangaroa Bay on Easter Island, before hastening to Taio-hae Bay and sailing with *Nadezhda* to the Hawaiian archipelago. From the modern ethnographic standpoint, the two ships passed a particularly fruitful week there, where Cook had worked and died (11–17 June). At Easter Island too, despite the natives' unexpected opposition to attempted landings, the young and well-trained company of officers and men undertook much ethnography and some hydrography. At Hanga-roa Bay, knives, scissors, mirrors, coins, and cloth were taken by the natives in exchange for local foodstuffs, woven artefacts, and other articles that were to form the basis of the Russians' ethnographical collection from that island—a collection still intact and on display in Leningrad. Like all their European predecessors from the Dutchman Jacob Roggeveen (1722) to Cook, Lisianskii's people made as accurate a study as they could of the Easter Islanders' tattooing, clothing, general physique, huts, small rush-mats, carving, and giant coastal statues. Twenty years after Cook's death at the Hawaiians' hands, the ambitious younger officer from Kronstadt bore in mind the emphases of his Pacific explorations, including certain scientific ones. It would have been extraordinary, in Lisianskii's and his officers' opinion, had any effort been neglected to extract the maximum scientific information from their stay on a coast where La Pérouse and Cook had laboured in their time. That sober zeal was undimmed twelve years later, when more young Russians came to Hanga-roa Bay aboard the *Riurik*.

> The problem of discovering a passage through the Arctic Ocean [wrote Rear-Admiral Nikolai Ivashintsev] had long preoccupied all the Maritime Powers; and Russia, for her part, had made more than one attempt to solve it both from landward and from seaward; but . . . protracted wars by land and sea had not allowed Russia to concern herself with scientific expeditions. Finally, with universal peace reigning over Europe, long-neglected academic questions once more provoked a general interest. One of the principal champions of science in the country at this time was Count Nikolai Petrovich Rumiantsev. At the beginning of 1815, Count Rumiantsev resolved to fit out at his own expense an expedition and . . . with this in view, a brig named *Riurik* was built in an Abo shipyard. She was of 180 tons, and command of her was given to Navy Lieutenant Otto E. Kotzebue, who had previously been a cadet in *Nadezhda* on her round-the-world voyage. Kotzebue had orders to occupy himself not only

with the main, Arctic object of the expedition, but also with geographical and scientific research in Oceania.

Kotzebue (1788–1846) sailed for Oceania in August 1815, accompanied by two foreign savants: the Danish naturalist Morten Wormskiöld (1783–1845) and the Franco-German naturalist-poet Adelbert von Chamisso. The latter added his account of *Riurik*'s call at Easter Island to the narrative written by Kotzebue's surgeon, Johann Friedrich Eschscholtz; the ship's artist, Ludovik Choris; and Kotzebue himself. As the artist dealt with Easter Island twice (1822, 1826), in texts accompanying his pictorial accounts of *Riurik*'s enterprise, we have five verbal descriptions of the visit of March 1816. Physical evidence, in the form of the artefacts collected on the island, complement the written record. This time the Russians landed despite an alarmingly hostile reception. Tense and hurried though it was, the visit gave Kotzebue, Chamisso, and Eschscholtz an opportunity that even Povalishin, second Lieutenant on *Neva,* had not had in 1804, to take a close look at the yelling Easter Islanders and at their works. It was not until the Russians reached Oahu eight months later and encountered Captain Alexander Adams, then commanding King Kamehameha's brig *Kahumanna,* that they learned the reason for the Easter Islanders' profound hostility. New Englanders aboard the schooner *Nancy* had abducted several islanders after the departure of *Neva,* with the intention of making slaves of them on the isolated Mas Afuera Island. Kotzebue and, in due course, Captain Frederick W. Beechey of HMS *Blossom,* witnessed the consequent native anger. Both officers contributed to the increasing mass of solid information on that bleakest of the Polynesian islands, Easter Island, building consciously on Cook's and Lisianskii's published data. In particular, they focused on the natives' body ornament, clothing, and wooden artefacts. Small figurines from Easter Island dating from the early nineteenth century remain in Leningrad's Museum of Ethnography today. They bear persuasive testimony to the vigour of a Polynesian culture that, within two generations, would be utterly destroyed by South American slave-traders and their allies.

Riurik was the last vessel to sail from the Baltic to the North Pacific Ocean's frozen rim without provoking the political unease in London that had always been expected of Madrid, which still viewed the Pacific as a Spanish *mare clausum.* The aims of science and empire were soon to be one in an age of peace and national rivalry. No one, declared Sir John Barrow, the indefatigable Secretary to the Admiralty Board, could reasonably argue that the Russian discovery of Kotzebue Sound on the remote northwestern tip of North America had no strategic or political significance. Had Kotzebue found the northern passage that his patron, Count Rumiantsev, and the officers of *Riurik* believed in, whatever purely scientific aims he had would have been quite beside the point. The search for Arctic passages was on again, ant it was clear that the Russians were not standing idle. At the urging of Barrow and his colleagues, Parliament promised large rewards to the discoverers of any such passages if they were British subjects. Thus began for Britain the golden age of Arctic exploration—the age of Scoresby, Franklin, Parry, and the Rosses. These efforts in turn provoked an even grander Russian Arctic undertaking, which was to benefit the study of South Pacific peoples, particularly the Polynesians.

By 1818 the Russians felt that the time had come for them to win laurels and political advantage from a scientific voyage of discovery in the tradition of Cook and Bougainville. Better yet, the Russian Naval Ministry would underwrite a double polar venture: two vessels, *Vostok* and *Mirnyi,* would probe the farthest South, where no European expedition had done any work whatever since Cook's return in 1775, while another two, *Otkrytie* and *Blagonamerennyi,* would press north in Kotzebue's wake, seeking some navigable link between Atlantic and Pacific waters. Thus began the planning of the Bellingshausen-Lazarev Antarctic Expedition (1819–21), in the course of which the Russians passed twelve days about Queen Charlotte Sound, New Zealand (28 May–9 June 1820), thence proceeding via Rapa in the Austral Islands' southernmost extremity toward the Tuamotu clusters and Tahiti. Like its Arctic counterpart, led with indifferent success by Captain Mikhail Vasil'ev, that Southern expedition was in essence an imperial response to mounting pressures, to which Englishmen and Russians alike had contributed since Cook's death. The shape and substance of these expeditions carried the stamp of Cook's activities of forty years before. Part of Cook's legacy, it may be emphasized, concerned the science of ethnology—a science newly born in Cook's own time and still in its infancy when Captain Faddei F. Bellingshausen and his second-in-command, Mikhail Lazarev, went south in 1819. Cook had received no orders to concern himself particularly with "curiosities," as ethnographica were then called, on his Pacific expeditions. Nonetheless, he and his officers and scientific gentlemen showed a keen, objective interest in the native peoples they met. Officially, the emphases of their studies fell on the naval sciences of hydrography and marine astronomy, and on the twin natural sciences of zoology and botany. In fact, they made a study of the peoples they encountered, sketching, observing, and collecting conscientiously across the breadth of Oceania. So potent an example was not lost on Kruzenshtern in 1802, nor was it lost on Bellingshausen and his principal assistant, the astronomer Ivan Mikhailovich Simonov (1794–1855) in 1820.

Bellingshausen's orders, which arrived in four sets, were precise in few respects, for by its nature the Southern enterprise was such that its development could not well be determined in advance by a committee. As "Divisional Commander," he was merely told to overlook no area of scientific interest. Whenever feasible, his officers were to assist his German naturalists in their work. This turned out to be unnecessary, as the naturalists literally missed the boat! Thus he was at liberty to read the scientific sections of his orders as he chose; and as Cook and Kruzenshtern had done, he chose to read them in a way that favoured a study of the South Pacific Islanders. Large quantities of broken iron, buttons, gimlets, beads, scissors and knives, as well as cloth and other things cheaply and readily obtainable from Kronstadt or St. Petersburg, were stowed for later use in large-scale barter. Here the Russians were more fortunate than Cook. *Vostok* and *Mirnyi* were larger and roomier than the Englishman's vessels had been, *Vostok* at 907 tons and *Mirnyi* at 530. Bellingshausen left for South Pacific waters and his meetings with the Maoris and the Rapa Islanders with larger stores of manufactured articles for barter than his predecessors had enjoyed. From the start matters augured well for would-be students of Pacific ethnographica. And when the German scientists failed to join the expedition, Simonov's and Bellingshausen's interest in native peoples grew in significance.

The Russians were received with hospitality and warmth in New South Wales when, in April 1820, they concluded the initial phase of their Antarctic work and stopped there for rest and fresh supplies. Refreshed and well provisioned by the Governor, Lachlan Macquarie, they set sail for Rapa Island, which Vancouver had discovered almost thirty years before (1791) but where no landing had been made. As his instructions bade him, Bellingshausen steered from Port Jackson (Sydney) on a course to clear Three Kings' Islands on the northern tip of New Zealand. Shortly after, however, uncooperative elements compelled him to make for Cook's Queen Charlotte Sound (Totaranui) in New Zealand. That sheltered area was reached on 28 May and, using Cook's charts, the Russians moved southwest until they sighted Long and Motuara Islands. As Lisianskii had deliberately retraced Cook's footsteps on the shore of Ka'awaloa in Hawaii in 1804, so Bellingshausen now came to Cook's Ship Cove, Cannibal Cove, and Hippah Island. Being perfectly familiar with Cook's and his subordinates' descriptions of the place from almost fifty years before, *Vostok*'s and *Mirnyi*'s officers prepared briskly for a session of comparative ethnography. For Maori studies, the results were of the highest value. Russian eyewitness accounts are offered in this volume to the English-speaking public for the first time in a scientific context.

As observed, the Russians' consciousness of the New Zealanders had antedated their awareness of any other South Pacific people, thanks to Tsar Peter ı's Dutch connections and preoccupations. That awareness had intermittently been animated in the intervening years; and, again, chance—not design—had been the catalyst of interest. It was fortuitous, for instance, that Lieutenant Kruzenshtern should as a consequence of temperament and circumstance in 1805 have shown so keen an interest in Tasman's tracks along New Zealand's coasts in December 1642. The Russian public was unprepared for the kind of learned papers that he published on this subject. And it was purely by chance that Captain Golovnin encountered an astute Maori chief while at Cape Town in the spring of 1808—Matara, a young *ariki* of the North Island Ngapuhi tribe, who spoke English as fluently as he himself did! Furthermore, a meeting between Russians from the ship *Suvorov* and a group of Maori chiefs at Parramatta, New South Wales, six years later could hardly have been foreseen by either party. The impact that such meetings made on educated Russians should not be exaggerated, however. After all, their accounts were published in service journals with a modest readership; nor were they considered more than glosses on the narratives of Cook and other visitors to *Novaia Zelandia*. It was in this respect that Bellingshausen's visit and its later published record were distinct. At last the Russians had a store of first-hand, primary materials with which to work.

The journals, letters, logs, and published narratives of *Vostok*'s and *Mirnyi*'s people were well complemented by the artefacts taken to Russia in the early fall of 1822 and by the illustrative evidence provided by *Vostok*'s artist, Pavel Nikolaevich Mikhailov, whose large portfolio remains in Leningrad today. Taken together, the evidence of Cook and Bellingshausen throws a crucial light on the position in the Sounds. Because Queen Charlotte Sound was the nexus of communication (peaceable and otherwise) between New Zealand's two main islands, the Russian data are important for the study of inter-island trade and commerce in the early 1800s. Bellingshausen's was the only European expedition of that period to work among the Maori of the South Island. The absence of all other written records and the virtual extinction of traditions that might tell us anything about the *hapu* (group) that Bellingshausen met lend particular significance to Russian eyewitness accounts; and it is fortunate indeed that six narratives have survived, as well as drawings by Mikhailov and "1820" artefacts in the Soviet collections on New Zealand. Many of the latter show by their carving styles that although they were offered to the Russians at Queen Charlotte Sound, they had been made in distant regions of New Zealand. Russian evidence also provides us with a glimpse of Cook's Ship Cove, Cannibal Cove, and Hippah Island as they were before the musket-wielding warriors of Chief Te Rauparaha and Atiawa fell like wolves upon the weaker Southern fold. By 1828 the little group that Bellingshausen had encountered had been scattered or destroyed.

The places dealt with in this volume lay off the beaten track of Russian oceanic shipping in the nineteenth century. Kamchatka-bound or Sitka-bound, most Russian vessels that entered the Pacific took a route far to the north of Australasia, especially after 1820, and a good distance from Easter Island or the Australs. Not surprisingly, those ships that did inspect the southerly and easterly extremities of Polynesia were on scientific missions (like the *Riurik, Vostok,* and *Mirnyi*) or at least on a multi-purpose voyage with a major scientific element (like the *Neva*). This very fact reveals the value of the evidence for Rapa, Easter Island, and New Zealand in the period concerned. Russian officers and seamen who were chosen to participate in voyages like those of Kotzebue, Bellingshausen, or Lisianskii were, by temperament and training, the most likely to be sound observers and recorders of their surroundings. Although numerous Russian merchantmen called at Oahu in the later nineteenth century, few of their officers made contributions to Hawaiian studies half as useful as those of Lisianskii, Chamisso, or Kotzebue of the period from 1804 to 1817. Remote and isolated though New Zealand, Easter Island, and the Australs were, the Russian Navy's competent Pacific service drew the maximum advantage from its opportunities to visit them, thereby enriching Polynesian studies today.

Among the many individuals to whom I am indebted for assistance or advice are the following, to whom I now express my gratitude: David R. Simmons of Auckland, Michael Trotter of Christchurch, and Patrick Waddington of Wellington, New Zealand; Nikolai A. Butinov, Tamara K. Shafranovskaia, and Rudolf F. Its of the Peter-the-Great Museum of Ethnography, N.N. Miklukho-Maklai Institute of Anthropology and Ethnography of the Soviet Academy of Sciences in Leningrad; A.S. Gur'ianov, Director of the Main Library and Museum, Kazan' State University; I.G. Grigor'eva, Director of the International Exchange Division, Saltykov-Shchedrin Public Library, Leningrad; Daniel D. Tumarkin of the Institute of Ethnography in Moscow; L.I. Senchura, Secretary to the All-Union Geographical Society of the USSR; and Richard A. Pierce of Queen's University, Kingston, Ontario. I wish also to acknowledge my indebtedness to Sirje Annist of Eesti NSV Riikliik Ajaloomuuseum, Tallin, Estonian SSR; Roger Rose of the Bernice P. Bishop Museum, Honolulu; Lydia Black of Providence, Rhode Island and Fairbanks, Alaska; and

Marvin Falk, Polar Collections Librarian at the Elmer E. Rasmuson Library, University of Alaska in Fairbanks. I also thank for their assistance of various kinds the directors or academic secretaries of the following institutions: the Central Naval Museum in Leningrad (TsVMM); the Central State Naval Archive of the USSR (TsGAVMF); the Central State Historical Archive of the Estonian Republic in Tartu (TsGIAE), the Mitchell Library, Sydney; the State Archives Office of New South Wales, also in Sydney; and the Hocken Library, Dunedin, New Zealand. Finally, I thank the Social Sciences and Humanities Research Council of Canada and the University of Illinois at Urbana-Champaign for enabling me to undertake research while on leave from my own institution, Carleton University in Ottawa.

Part One

EASTER ISLAND

1

PREPARATIONS FOR A VOYAGE

What the Russians knew of Easter Island in the eighteenth century was
drawn from Dutch and British sources that described the hurried visits of
Jacob Roggeveen in 1722 and Cook in 1774. Those published texts included *Carl Friedrich Behrens Reise durch die Süd-Länder und um die
Welt* (Frankfurt and Leipzig 1737); a second edition thereof and a French
version or paraphrase entitled *Histoire de l'Expédition de trois Vaisseaux
... aux Terres Australes en MDCCXXI* (Paris); a work entitled
Tweejaarige Reyze rondom de Wereld... (Dordrecht 1728), apparently
published by Joannes van Braam on the basis of Admiral Roggeveen's
narrative, which was as factually sound as Behrens's was fanciful;
Cook's *Voyage Towards the South Pole and Round the World* (London
1777), together with assorted French and German versions, the most
popular in Russia being Jean Baptiste Suard's *Voyage au pôle austral ...
en 1772, 1773, 1774 et 1775, écrit par Jacques Cook* (Paris 1778); and
George Forster's *Voyage Round the World* (London 1777; 2 vols.). All
these accounts were also readily accessible to Russians with the proper
language skills in such voyage compilations as Charles de Brosses's or
Alexander Dalrymple's. Like Englishmen and Frenchmen of the period,
the Russians had no knowledge of the Spanish naval visit to the island under *Capitan* González in 1770.

Russian interest in Roggeveen's discoveries was marginal until the last
years of the eighteenth century; even then, neither Roggeveen's nor Behrens's narratives made much impression on the wider reading public,
which had more recent and more striking travel literature to amuse it and

to stimulate their imagination. It was essentially the Admiralty that finally examined the primary accounts of South Pacific exploration undertaken almost eighty years before. It did so not as a result of any new preoccupation with Easter Island (*Ostrov Paskhi*) in particular, but with the Russians' *North* Pacific needs and interests in mind. An awareness of the commercial and strategic implications of Captain Cook's last expedition (1776–80) had been growing in high government circles in St. Petersburg. By the mid-1780s, the Russian Naval Staff had ceased considering the South Pacific islands in solely an academic light and as an area without relevance to Russia's future needs. It was impossible to overlook the huge potential of the North Pacific fur trade or the threat already posed by foreign mariners to Russian interests in the Aleutian Islands and along the Northwest Coast of North America.[1] In this context, Russian government officials and the Empress Catherine herself became receptive to accounts of any European voyages across the Great South Sea.

It fell to Loggin I. Golenishchev-Kutuzov (1769–1845), a precocious young official in the Admiralty College, which his own father had headed in the reign of Paul I, to render Cook's second and final *Voyages* in Russian. Kutuzov translated not from the 1777 London edition of *A Voyage Towards the South Pole*, but rather from J.B.L. Suard's *Voyage au pôle austral et autour du monde*. Nevertheless, he gave his countrymen their first clear impression, in their own language, of Easter Island's physical conditions, native populace, and "mysteries," as well as of the British seamen's dealings with the islanders ashore. He was competent and intelligent, and annotated Suard's text with commentaries that reveal the scientific nature of his own Pacific interests. *Puteshestvie v iuzhnoi polovine zemnago shara i vokrug onago, uchinennoe v prodolzhenie 1772, 73, 74 i 75 godov . . . (A Voyage in the Southern Hemisphere of the Globe and Around it, Performed in the Years 1772–75 . . .)* appeared, belatedly, in 1796–1800. Printed by the Naval Cadet Corps, the work was in six parts, the last a collection of twenty-six illustrations and maps. The Easter Island passage (12–14 March 1774) appeared in Part 3 (1798) and offered material from both Cook and George Forster, the latter being in quotation marks. Part 5 also dealt with Easter Island: it was a translation of Johann Reinhold Forster's *Observations Made during a Voyage Round the World . . .* (London 1778); Forster had spent more time ashore on Easter Island than Cook himself. From the beginning, however, Russian consciousness of Easter Island developed within a North Pacific context—and was largely overshadowed by a growing awareness of other islands closer to the Northwest Coast and its peltry: the Hawaiian archipelago.

When Cook anchored at Unalaska Island with *Discovery* and *Resolution* in October 1778, Catherine II had for fifteen years deliberately not supported the cossack hunter-traders in the Aleutians in a significant way. At most, she had awarded gold medallions and noble rank to certain merchants based in the remote Northeast, Kamchatka, or Okhotsk.[2] Catherine was unwilling to provoke either the Spanish or, especially, the British by assertiveness in North Pacific waters that could lead to confrontation and retreat. It was thus natural that officials in Siberia had, since the mid-1770s, been troubled by reports of foreign naval expeditions in the North Pacific, near Kamchatka, or advancing on the Northwest Coast of North America or the Aleutian Islands.[3] Their alarm increased in 1776, when Russian agents sent reports that Spanish vessels, which had earlier been in a latitude of 55° N, were to press further north and west.[4]

News that *Discovery* and *Resolution* had put in at Petropavlovsk-in-Kamchatka twice, in May and August 1779, after much probing in an area tacitly claimed by Russia, led to action by imperial officialdom. Heavy artillery were painfully dragged overland to Petropavlovsk from Irkutsk and other centres in Siberia.[5] The empress and those officials responsible for defending Russian interests so far away now examined the implications of Cook's sudden appearances and the activity of his subordinates. They sought reliable accounts of the *Adventure-Resolution* expedition of 1772–75 and sought to obtain data on Cook's final voyage. Suddenly, the Russian government was eager for accounts of *any* voyages into the North Pacific Ocean from the south. Russian knowledge of the Sandwich Islands and other distant parts increased apace.[6]

In 1779, some of the better-educated men in *Resolution* and *Discovery* thought of entering the North Pacific (Coast-to-China) fur trade on their own account. Others considered seeking British or American or even Russian backing for their venture, and less-educated ones simply fled in a boat at Canton.[7] On their return to Europe, the more imaginative responded to the challenge of unemployment by developing and selling their North Pacific schemes.[8] Two members of Cook's final expedition in particular, Lieutenant James Trevenen (1760–90) and John Ledyard (1751–89), the Connecticut marine who had established the first contact between Russian and American in the Pacific while on Unalaska Island,[9] clung to their memories of profits made in China, where a single good sea otter skin originally acquired for a hatchet could be sold for sixty dollars.[10] Driven by visions of prosperity, both men took their North Pacific projects to Russia. The marine met with frustration. He was not allowed to walk across Siberia to Bering Strait, the Northwest Coast, Virginia, and home, as he intended. Nor did he manage to attach himself to Captain Joseph Billings, also formerly with *Discovery* and now successfully exploiting his connection with the famous Cook.[11] He did, however, spend some time at the St. Petersburg Academy of Sciences with Peter Simon Pallas, the distinguished Russo-German botanist, and passed on to him much information about natural resources and conditions on the Northwest Coast and the Sandwich Islands. For Trevenen, Russian service brought professional advancement but an early and heroic death in battle during the Russo-Swedish War in 1790 aboard a Russian warship. First, however, he played a crucial role in making the government aware of the Hawaiian archipelago and its potential use to Russia in the far Northeast and East.

Trevenen found himself on half-pay and intolerably idle when he returned to Britain. He considered investing in a commercial enterprise in New South Wales or in North America, but was thwarted by the City and by agents of the Admiralty.[12] It was then that "his ardent mind embraced the World as his country, and he formed a Plan."[13] The plan was offered to the minister plenipotentiary for Russia to Great Britain, Count Semeon R. Vorontsov (1744–1832). Count Vorontsov, a lifelong Anglophile, "saw its merits and transmitted it to his mistress, then on her journey to Cheronese [the newly-conquered Crimea]." It was essentially a commercial plan, but it was versatile and echoed an assertive note struck by the empress in a recent edict, of 22 December 1786.[14] Vexed by the "poaching and encroachments" in the "Eastern Sea" of an increasing number of British shipmasters, notably Captain James R. Hanna of the brig *Sea Otter*,[15] Catherine had heeded the urgings of Count Alexander R. Vorontsov, President of the Commerce College, and adopted a far firmer policy than previously. To Russia, she declared, "must belong the American Coast from 55°21′ , extending northward . . . all islands situated near the mainland and extending westward in a chain, as well as . . . the Kuril Islands of Japan."[16] Approving of Trevenen's frank allusions both to warships and to growing trade, she offered him fine prospects in the Russian Fleet (1787), and he subsequently left for Russia with his North Pacific project.[17]

Trevenen's plan prefigured that adopted in the fall of 1802, when, after long debate, the Russian government sent two ships, *Nadezhda* and *Neva*, from Kronstadt in the Baltic Sea to Russia's North Pacific outposts. The two vessels paused in Brazil before "proceeding to some . . . islands in the South Sea [the Marquesas and Hawaiian Islands]," and they returned by way of China and South Africa. They carried a cargo of the sort envisaged by Trevenen almost twenty years before, besides 300,000 roubles' worth of gifts for the Mikado of Japan, where an attempt was made to open trade.[18] The venture also served as "a nursery for seamen." The only aspect of *Nadezhda*'s and *Neva*'s Pacific venture that Trevenen did not foresee was the scientific one, but he was right in thinking that Catherine was more concerned with power than with philosophy.

Political developments in Europe led the empress to abandon the Trevenen project, and its author discovered on arriving in St. Petersburg that the imperial authorities had been considering not one but two or three such naval ventures, none of which came to fruition. All involved a rest-and-victualling pause at the Hawaiian archipelago. This is apparent from the sailing orders given, only weeks before Trevenen's arrival on the scene, to Captain Grigorii Ivanovich Mulovskii, commander of a four-ship naval squadron setting out for the Pacific. A bastard son of Count Ivan G. Chernyshev, minister of the marine, Captain Mulovskii was a well-trained officer and was fully capable of following instructions that reflected the experience of Cook.[19] His squadron consisted of two larger vessels, *Kolmogor* (600 tons) and *Solovki* (530 tons), and two smaller ones, *Sokol* and *Turukhtan* (approximately 450 tons apiece), and was supposedly about to sail on a voyage of discovery and commerce. In reality, it was intended as an armed deterrent to threats against Russian interests both from New Spain and from American and British seaborne traders.[20] "The Admiralty College," read the empress's edict, "shall without delay send from the Baltic Sea ships armed like those employed by Captain Cook ... together with two small armed sloops. The latter shall be Navy craft or otherwise, as the College may think best."[21]

Mindful of reports that Captain Hanna's pioneering cruise had lasted only seven weeks but resulted in a haul of sea otter and other skins that had produced a $20,000 profit,[22] and under great pressure from the Commerce College and the Court, the Admiralty College took prompt action. A committee was established to decide on routes, revictualling points, and rendezvous in the Pacific. Among the works that this committee consulted was the recent French translation of Cook's final *Voyage* (*Troisième voyage de Cook ... en 1776, 1777, 1778, 1779 et 1780*, Paris: Hôtel de Thou 1785) by Jean-Nicolas Demeunier (1751–1814). It offered evidence that the Hawaiian archipelago was a suitable revictualling point for Russian vessels on their way from South America to the Pacific's northern rim. The productivity, luxuriance, sweet springs, and pleasant climate of Hawaii were persuasively described. Accordingly Captain Mulovskii was instructed that his ships should rendezvous in Hawaii. When in his judgment all was ready, two vessels were to start on an extensive survey of the Kuril Islands, Sakhalin, and the Amur River's mouth, while the others made directly for Nootka Sound. All of North America north of 55°N would be annexed to Russia, and iron crests marked with the year would be left at certain spots.[23]

Although Mulovskii's expedition was cancelled at the last minute, his instructions are replete with interest from the perspective of Hawaiian studies. They reflect the influence of an Anglo-Russian maritime entente that was already old during the infancy of Peter the Great, the creator of a modern Russian fleet,[24] and positively venerable when Mulovskii served as a Russian Volunteer aboard British warships (1769–71).[25] The Admiralty College, the instructions emphasize, was quite willing to benefit from English experience where long-range and protracted expeditions were concerned. What could be borrowed to advantage—for example, maps, new optical equipment, or "a stove for the distilling of sea water into pure"—should be borrowed.[26] Furthermore, Mulovskii's orders clearly show that an understanding of a major problem with all Russian efforts to maintain some naval presence in Kamchatka, Okhotsk, and the settlements on the Aleutian Islands: lacking dockyards and a suitably located source of foodstuffs in those distant parts, the Russian government had to keep sending ships around the world at great expense.[27] Either the Navy had to obtain proper facilities for constructing and repairing ships, and find a way to feed men on inhospitable Pacific shores and islands, or the Crown had to bear the burden of maintaining its authority over such great distances. In either case, it was important to have friendly ports of call along the routes to Petropavlovsk and the Northwest Coast from European Russia. The link between Hawaii and provisionment of cossack hunter-traders in the North was already firm in naval minds. Russians would continue to look upon Hawaii as a mid-Pacific food source of political significance to her activities in the North Pacific basin.

In an age when English was not usually learned by the nobility in Russia, it was passably read by many younger naval officers. This was to some extent a consequence of professional connections with the British.[28] A total mastery of English was unnecessary, however, if one merely wished to read the *Voyages* of Captain Cook to learn a little of the place where he had died. The *Voyages* were accessible in French and, by the early 1800s, in Russian.[29] Loggin Golenishchev-Kutuzov, for example, translated Cook's second and final *Voyage* into stylish Russian prose, although style appeared to concern him more than literal precision.[30] The significance of these grand Russian versions of Cook's *Voyages* was doubtless lessened by the industry of French translators like Demeunier and further undermined by their belated publication. Nonetheless, they combined with English, French, and other versions to spread some knowledge of Cook's work, and incidentally of the Hawaiian Islands, among a wide and quickly growing Russian readership. Cook's star rose in the Russian naval firmament in 1805–10 as a result.[31] Ten years later the brightest and most promising officers had not ceased to revere the name of Cook and to regard his former comrades George Vancouver and Matthew Flinders with a measure of the same respect.[32]

The accounts of Cook and his associates concerning the resources and potential of Hawaii had a deep effect on government officials and naval officers who were already aware, in the late 1780s, of the economic promise of the East. Among the former were Count Semeon R. Vorontsov and Count Nikolai P. Rumiantsev (1754–1826), later Chancellor of Russia and a powerful supporter of the Russian North Pacific enterprise in all its forms. Among the latter were two, Lieutenants Ivan F. Kruzenshtern (in German, von Krusenstern) and Iurii F. Lisianskii, who had personally been to the East Indies to assess that trade potential for themselves.

THE KRUZENSHTERN-LISIANSKII EXPEDITION

The Kruzenshtern-Lisianskii expedition of 1803–6, in the course of which a company of Russian seamen first encountered the Easter Islanders, stemmed from Kruzenshtern's journey to Canton in 1798–99 and his reports on its position as the main mart of the North Pacific fur trade. His journey itself was a consequence of his naval service as a Russian Volunteer with the British (1793–97).[33] It is clear from his introductory remarks to the St. Petersburg edition (1809) of his *Voyage Round the World in 1803, 1804, 1805, and 1806 . . . in the Ships "Nadezhda" and "Neva"* that his "British period" had been a stimulating one:

> While serving with the English fleet during the revolutionary war of 1793–99, my attention was both caught and held by the significance of the English trade with the East Indies and China. It seemed to me quite possible that Russia too could take some part in the seaborne trade with China and the Indies . . . And there was little doubt that she would benefit from doing so despite her lack of establishments in those parts. The problem was that . . . few but Englishmen, and even few of those, had any real knowledge of the Eastern Seas. So I resolved to go to India myself. Count Vorontsov, then Russian ambassador in London, soon arranged the necessary passage for me and, early in 1797, I proceeded on an English warship to the Cape of Good Hope and from there, in a frigate, to India.

During their period of secondment to the Royal Navy, Kruzenshtern and Lisianskii were based at Halifax, Nova Scotia, but passed at least a third of their time simply travelling, observing, and absorbing new impressions.[34] Short of ready cash, they travelled cheaply, sallying from a British port when possible, remaining by and large in friendly, English-speaking territory.[35] Antigua, Bermuda, Barbados, Maryland, the Carolinas, and Virginia were areas on which both they and later Russian Volunteers largely focused their attention.[36] All were regions populated by the Negroes brought from Africa as slaves for general plantation work. Lisianskii in Antigua and Kruzenshtern in prosperous Barbados made studies of the later-eighteenth-century colonial administrations that they saw in action, and reflected on the workings of the local slave-based commerce.[37] British planters of the Caribbean colonies seemed prosperous with few exceptions, but the value of the West Indies to England, Kruzenshtern already knew, was fairly modest in comparison with that of the East Indies. Such reflections brought to mind the fact that Russia, too, had colonies on islands far removed from her commercial and population centres. Her possessions on the North Pacific rim had proved unable to support themselves, still less export some useful crop. Lisianskii wondered if administrative practices, at least, might be adapted from British models. Both he and Kruzenshtern wrote sound reports to their government on the administration, trade, and commerce of the British Caribbean colonies. In doing so, they paid particular attention to the Negro, noting down what they had seen with objectivity.[38] Their reports augured well for the scientific aspect of any voyage with which either was to be professionally linked. So too did Lisianskii's growing liking for zoology and botany, sciences that he pursued when opportunity arose on the mainland of America and on Antigua, and that he would certainly have taken further if a bout of yellow fever had not forced him to return to Halifax (1795).[39]

Three years after their departure from St. Petersburg, Kruzenshtern, Lisianskii, and their comrade Lieutenant Andrei Baskakov all returned to London from America.[40] They wasted no time before approaching the ambassador, Count Semeon R. Vorontsov, with plans for further travel east. Lisianskii was not destined to go further than South Africa that year: a fresh attack of yellow fever while at Cape Town forced him to remain there several months. He put his misfortune to good scientific use, botanizing on the veld, forming large, well-ordered shell and bone collections, and also moving further toward the study of the life style, beliefs, and customs of assorted peoples—what today we term ethnography.[41] Meanwhile Kruzenshtern pressed on to China, sick and nearly insolvent.

He reached Canton in November 1798, via Bengal and Penang, after a three-month cruise aboard a British man-of-war and much discomfort. Kruzenshtern immediately launched himself into a study of the workings of the China trade—and more particularly of its North Pacific seaborne branch. The latter was a branch from which his countrymen were totally excluded, thanks to maritime incompetence, a lack of ships and seamen, the absence of charts and pilots at Okhotsk and Kamchatka, and, above all, a lack of knowledge about a huge and growing market.[42]

> During my sojourn at Canton in 1798–99, a small craft of about 100 tons, commanded by an Englishman, arrived there from the North-west Coast of North America. She had been fitted out in Macao, the venture had not taken more than five months, and the cargo which consisted entirely of furs was sold for 60,000 piastres. My countrymen, I knew, conducted a considerable trade in furs with China ... but were obliged to take the peltry to Okhotsk, and thence to Kiakhta overland. Two years or more were thereby lost and (as I also knew) several vessels and their rich cargoes were lost even crossing from the islands of the Eastern Sea. It seemed to me that profits would decidedly be greater if we Russians took our goods straight to Canton from the Aleutians or the Coast... And, on my passage home from China, I composed a memoir to that effect, which I intended to present to the minister of commerce.[43]

Kruzenshtern's return to European Russia in 1800 coincided with the climax of several power struggles in St. Petersburg that caused a fractured government to dismiss his project from its thoughts.[44] It was a galling interlude for him, symbolic of the pettymindedness and tyranny that characterized the reign of Paul I. After Paul was murdered, however, an efficient naval officer of liberal persuasions, Admiral Nikolai S. Mordvinov, was appointed minister of the marine,[45] and Kruzenshtern's project was approved in only slightly altered form.[46]

The central element in Kruzenshtern's design, as in Trevenen's, was that vessels would be sent from Kronstadt in the Baltic to the Northwest Coast of North America, where they would barter with the Indians for otter skins. They would then proceed to China, to sell some skins and purchase Chinese wares before returning to the Baltic Sea. Although his plan owed much to those of earlier men, its final version of 1802 contained a scientific element and a probability of contact with Pacific Islanders[47] that were absent from those of Trevenen and Mulovskii.

It was not until 7 August 1802 that Kruzenshtern was formally appointed to command an expedition that, he gathered, was expected to depart that season.[48] Such a schedule was quite unrealistic: ships had not even been found, and in the best of circumstances they could not have left until late September. Admiral Mordvinov supported Kruzenshtern's protest against rushing an important and expensive undertaking. Departure

was delayed by one full year.[49] Kruzenshtern then turned to the selection
of his officers and men. He had the time and inclination to choose carefully. Without exception, the lieutenants he picked had already given evidence of high ability and, more significantly from the standpoint of ethnography, of scientific bent.[50] Several officers later made a real contribution to Hawaiian studies, by describing and/or drawing what they saw
along the Kona Coast in 1804 or by collecting artefacts. Among them
were Second Lieutenant Petr Povalishin of *Neva* and Fourth Lieutenant
Ermolai Levenshtern of *Nadezhda*.[51] The choice of scientists was promising too, from the ethnographic perspective. Within a month of being
named commander, Kruzenshtern argued successfully for the appointment of an eminent zoologist and botanist, Wilhelm-Gottlieb Tilesius von
Tilenau (1769–1857), whom Baron Hans von Manteufel of Prussia had
recommended to the Russian government.[52] Kruzenshtern's strategy was
first and foremost to ensure that the Crown and the Directors of the powerful, monopolistic Russian-American Company would fully back his
venture. That assured, he could develop other technical and scientific
aspects of his project, specifically those suggested by the voyages of
Cook.

Lisianskii and a shipwright named Razumov, meanwhile, were looking
out for vessels suited to a long and multi-purpose expedition of the sort
intended. They found them on the River Thames.[53] *Leander,* built in London in the spring of 1800, was a 432-ton sloop. *Thames* was a recently
built ship of 370 tons, only a trifle heavier than Cook's *Endeavour* but
without the reinforcement and the massive, blunt construction of the
Whitby collier. Lisianskii bought the two vessels for cash and had them
modified internally, at the expense of the imperial exchequer. The purchase price of £17,000 was high and so was the cost of alterations, but
the two ships served the Russians as well as he expected and far better
than the Company's critics would admit.[54] *Leander* was renamed
Nadezhda (Hope), and *Thames* became *Neva*. They made eleven knots or
better on the crossing to the Continent, and docked at Kronstadt on 5 June
1803.

Kruzenshtern meanwhile was adjusting to another piece of news, this
time delivered by Rumiantsev in his role as minister of commerce.
Nadezhda, he was told, would face more tasks in the Pacific and the East
than had originally been envisaged. She would undertake both scientific
and commercial missions and would also take a personal acquaintance of
the tsar, Nikolai Petrovich Rezanov (1764–1807), an important court official and the chief administrator of the Company, as Russian envoy to
Japan.[55] *Nadezhda* and *Neva* would part in mid-Pacific and Lisianskii
would enjoy his own command for many months. Both he and

Kruzenshtern, however, would remain under surveillance by the Company: Fedor I. Shemelin and Nikolai I. Korobitsyn, each a *prikazchik* (clerk or factor) in the Company's employ, were appointed to *Nadezhda* and *Neva* respectively. There were to be future complications. Both were shrewd and able men, highly regarded by the Company. Neither, however, had a positive opinion of the Navy or its officers. They were of merchant antecedents and were perfectly aware of the Navy's condescending attitude towards themselves and other servants of the Company, especially in the Pacific and America.

While *Nadezhda* and *Neva* were fitting out at Kronstadt, Kruzenshtern discovered what he could about Rezanov and his diplomatic mission. Twelve months earlier, he learned, the tsar had asked Rezanov to reorganize the Senate's First Department on less oligarchic lines. But even while Rezanov had been doing so, he had been fostering various plans for the Pacific and the East, including Kruzenshtern's. His interest in the Pacific and the Coast-to-China fur trade rested squarely on his marriage to a daughter of the wealthiest and most successful of the fur traders based in Kamchatka, Grigorii I. Shelikhov. As Shelikhov's son-in-law, he had inherited a valuable block of shares in the Shelikhov company, from which the present Company had emerged and which he effectively controlled. Still, there had been no thought of his examining in person the remote Pacific settlements that he had read about for years in the Company reports.[56] As an important functionary, as the virtual controller of the Company, and as a man in frequent contact with the emperor, he had enough to keep him busy in St. Petersburg. Then, in November 1802 his wife died and he entered a decline. With kindly motives, Alexander I sent him off as Russian envoy to Japan. *Nadezhda*'s sailing was convenient and timely.

Rezanov's presence in the Kruzenshtern-Lisianskii expedition in the dual role of envoy and influential Company official was symbolic of a coming confrontation between Company and Navy in the North Pacific basin. Fundamentally it was a question of confused authority. Upon arriving in Japan or in the North Pacific settlements, Rezanov the grandee would command. Meanwhile, the officers and men of *Nadezhda* and *Neva* regarded Kruzenshtern alone as their commander and Rezanov as an arrogant and interfering passenger.[57] As if to increase the likelihood of trouble on the voyage out, captain and envoy had their own sets of instructions, and while Kruzenshtern's was composed by Admiral Mordvinov's naval staff in consultation with Rumiantsev's, Rezanov's was drafted at the ministry of commerce on behalf of Alexander, who signed a formal document addressed to the Mikado of Japan.[58]

At first the blurred lines of authority actually seemed to assist the preparation of the expedition. They made it almost certain that whatever was regarded by the Company or Navy as conducive to the expedition's ultimate success would be provided by one government department or another. This phenomenon was reinforced by the participation in the venture of a trading enterprise and the Academies of Sciences and Arts. The Company sent fine maps and monographs, including the *Voyages* of Cook, Vancouver, Bougainville, and others; the Admiralty College sent brand new rigging; goods arrived from Prussia, Saxony, and Switzerland, and scientific instruments were checked at the Academy of Sciences. Even the tsar showed passing interest, by travelling to Kronstadt in his carriage to inspect the quays where, day by day, Lisianskii was overseeing the stowing of great quantities of foodstuffs, naval stores, Company goods, trinkets, and instruments.[59]

Kruzenshtern had named Lisianskii as his second-in-command because he knew him to be "zealous in the service" and a thoroughly accomplished officer.[60] In his "inferior commissioned officers," he also looked for steadiness of temper and a first-class service record. Makar' I. Ratamov, whom he took as first lieutenant of *Nadezhda,* had commanded ships of war for fifteen years. Second Lieutenant Fedor A. Romberg had won success while with the frigate *Narva,* Petr Golovachev, third lieutenant, while based at Kronstadt. Fourth Lieutenant Ermolai E. Levenshtern (in German, von Loewenstern) had served successfully with Admiral F. Ushakov, once Nelson's ally and bugbear, in the eastern Mediterranean.[61] Like Romberg, he was well read, widely travelled, and distinguished by a ceaseless curiosity. To the extent that he was able, Kruzenshtern excluded malcontents and men of limited horizons. If he emphasized the virtues of "attachment and obedience" in members of his company, it was with Captain Bligh's experience in mind.[62] *Nadezhda* would also be serving for three years as the maritime laboratory and office of her scientific gentlemen: Tilesius von Tilenau, naturalist; Johann Caspar Hörner, Swiss astronomer; and Karl von Espenberg, surgeon-zoologist.[63] On Kruzenshtern's instructions, extra clothes and even mattresses were issued to all members of both crews. It was his object to establish an esprit de corps by handsome pay, good food, and kindness, and with Company assistance to ensure that the new Pacific branch of naval service would be special and exclusive, with an enviable promise of advancement.

Even such practical measures to minimize tensions between lower deck and quarter-deck, however, proved ineffectual against the problem presented by Rezanov and, by late July, his five-man retinue. Rezanov's books and paintings, mirrors, trunks and models, wine, servants' supplies, and many gifts for the Mikado were continuing to pile up on the quay despite the fact that *Nadezhda*'s sailing date had come. "I was in the roadstead," Kruzenshtern records, "but effects were still arriving, which I was not a little puzzled how to stow."[64] In fact, the captain had been very vexed by the appointment of Rezanov not only as envoy to Japan but as leader of the entire mission in an ill-defined and ambiguous sense. Rezanov's coming had deprived him and Lisianskii of a certain sum of money and, potentially, of some fame. When *Nadezhda* and *Neva* at last left the roadstead, on 4 August 1803, the wind promptly swung to the west, again delaying their departure. Nerves were strained even further.

THE ETHNOGRAPHIC IMPULSE

Kruzenshtern's great achievement was turning what had started as a mercantile-cum-diplomatic scheme into a scientific venture of importance to the educated world. This much is clear from a statement of intention that the Company directors issued in connection with the coming expedition on 29 July 1802, immediately after an extraordinary meeting of the stockholders and board at which the pros and cons of Kruzenshtern's revised Pacific plan were considered.[65]

> The provisioning of the American colonies for several years at one go would decrease the volume of goods passing through the port of Okhotsk. This in itself would lower the very considerable cost of overland transport, while still protecting the whole of Iakutsk Province from want... Secondly, our Company might well succeed in establishing a lucrative trade in furs at Canton, gaining the upper hand over other nations. On the return voyage, we might even attempt to trade in the settlements of foreigners' East Indies companies, e.g., Calcutta, Bengal, and Batavia... in due course bringing sugar, coffee, indigo, and other goods straight to St. Petersburg.[66]

No mention here of academic challenges, no breath even of strictly naval science, let alone study of animals and men! And yet less than a month after he was named commander of the expedition, Kruzenshtern had gained von Tilenau. That success, for which he owed much to Rumiantsev and his links with the Academy of Sciences and nothing whatsoever to Rezanov, was symbolic of his determination that no scientific chance be lost.[67]

It was the direct involvement of Rumiantsev and the court in the coming expedition that enabled Kruzenshtern to challenge the directors' heavy emphasis on the commercial aspect of his mission in another, more decisive way. Originally, the directors had proposed to send two graduates of the St. Petersburg Commercial Institution with *Nadezhda* and *Neva,* to write reports on trade conditions in the East and the Pacific.[68] Insisting pragmatically on the dangers of an overcrowded vessel, Kruzenshtern used all his leverage to have these graduates replaced by one astronomer. Hörner was eventually named, offered a contract, and accepted in *Nadezhda*—to the lasting benefit of Polynesian studies.[69]

For many years after his death in 1779, the Russians saw Cook as the principal example of the leader of a voyage of discovery.[70] For both Lisianskii and Kruzenshtern, he was "the great Cook," whose determinations of position were so accurate that a chronometer could be adjusted to them, whose relations with his men had been unfailingly humane.[71] Cook's influence permeated Kruzenshtern's earlier life, and his expeditions were the model for those of the ambitious Russian officer. Cook had emphasized the scientific. George Forster and Joseph Banks had been zoologists and botanists. Astronomy had been regarded as essential for its own sake. Cook himself had shown an interest in native artefacts and in the languages, beliefs, and social life of other peoples, such as the Hawaiians, even though he lacked instructions on the matter and was certainly not under pressure to concern himself at length with ethnographica. He had collected representative pre-contact artefacts, many of them in Leningrad today, from the Hawaiian archipelago.[72] His outlook was, to say the least, conducive to the infant science that we now know as ethnography.

Cook's example was certainly not lost on Kruzenshtern. In April 1803 he was named a corresponding member of the St. Petersburg Academy of Sciences. The honour was both an act of faith in an important individual who had not yet published a single learned paper and, on another level, an expression of the link between his enterprise and the Academy. That bond had earlier been formed by the Academy's readiness to check or lend equipment, to advise on any scientific points, to draft instructions in zoology, botany and even mineralogy for the benefit of expedition members.[73] The Company directors had no choice but to accept the situation and acknowledge that the voyage of *Nadezhda* and *Neva* was gaining major academic and political significance. Kruzenshtern's instructions from the Company, dated 29 May 1803, contained the following crucial lines:

> All that you learn from your observations or otherwise acquire during your voyage which has significance for natural history, geography, navigation, or any other science, you will unfailingly submit to the

Company together with any maps or descriptions that may have been made. We think it superfluous to go into detail in these matters, having learned of your zeal in this regard.[74]

The "zealous" Kruzenshtern was thus given full liberty not only to insist upon but also to construe the broadly scientific aspects of his orders. As Cook had done, he chose to read his orders in a way that favoured study of the native peoples he met along the way, though not at the expense of naval sciences. On his insistence, broken iron hoops, beads, mirrors, nails, knives, and cloth, all in considerable quantities, were stowed aboard *Nadezhda* and *Neva* for barter in the North and South Pacific. Lacking recent information, he misjudged the wants and tastes of the Hawaiians and did not take on sufficient red material or extra canvas. It is significant, however, that he meant to draw the maximum advantage from a brief pause in Hawaii, through judicious choice of trade goods and subordinates. As he expressed it, "I wished to fill the spare room in my ship with such men as might contribute to the advancement of the sciences; for it seemed to me that our long-awaited sojourn in the Southern Hemisphere, and the tasks of philosophy itself, must surely offer useful employment for them all."[75]

Kruzenshtern did not deliberately seek out men who seemed more likely to collaborate in any ethnographic effort than the mass of their contemporaries in the Navy. Nonetheless, such men did accompany him to Hawaii and the East, thanks to careful criteria for their selection and the nature of their own earlier training in the arts of observation and description. Long expected to be accurate in seaborne measurement and reckoning of any kind, always conservative in guesswork, and above all thorough when surveying the unusual or unfamiliar, such men were likely to make useful contributions to Pacific and American ethnography.

So too with the astronomer, the surgeons, and the other scientists aboard *Nadezhda* and *Neva:* though not ethnographers by training, they were accustomed to the discipline of scrutiny and were well able to apply it to descriptions of Pacific islanders. Such is evident from both their journals and their later published works.[76]

Political considerations, chance, and long delays conspired to enhance the growing ethnographic promise of the Kruzenshtern-Lisianskii expedition. The St. Petersburg Academy of Arts placed two young draughtsmen at the Company's disposal in the spring of 1803, and the more senior of them, Stepan Kurliandtsev, was accepted as the expedition's artist. Then in August, as the two ships were revictualling carefully in Copenhagen roads in preparation for the North Atlantic crossing, came a greater stroke of fortune from the viewpoint of ethnography: the arrival of the versatile young German surgeon, Georg Heinrich Langsdorf (1774–1852).

Langsdorf had belatedly arrived at Copenhagen in the hope that, although Tilesius von Tilenau and Hörner had been formally appointed to the Russian expedition, he might be taken on as well.[77] Rezanov was impressed by the young naturalist's energy and by his willingness to go without a salary. There could be no doubt that Langsdorf was well qualified to join the expedition: he was a protégé of Johann Friedrich Blumenbach, the anthropologist and physiologist whose student he had been at Göttingen, and he had lately worked in Lisbon, always in the very highest medical and social circles.[78] He was welcomed as Rezanov's private secretary. Of the significance of his arrival for Pacific anthropology, suffice it to note that Blumenbach, the father and most eminent practitioner of craniology, was personally friendly with Sir Joseph Banks and had delivered public lectures on the voyages of Cook at Göttingen.[79] In sum, all smiled on the ethnographic impulse that was the joint legacy of Kruzenshtern and Cook to Russia's navy at the turn of a new century.

THE VOYAGE

After stops at Copenhagen and at Falmouth on the southwest tip of England, where the hulls of *Nadezhda* and *Neva* were inspected by their carpenters and instruments were brought by road from London, Kruzenshtern set sail for Brazil. One further stop was made, at Teneriffe. The Russians made their way from Santa Cruz to the Marquesas archipelago by way of Santa Catarina Island, north of Rio de Janeiro, in the winter months of 1803–4. Almost immediately after their departure from the port of Santa Cruz, where fresh supplies were purchased, Kruzenshtern imposed a strict and rigorous routine on the companies of both ships. Henceforth nothing but disaster was to halt the clockwork rounds of testing, sampling, reckoning, and measurement that now engrossed the energies of Hörner and the German naturalists. Reckonings of latitude and longitude; checking of compasses and other instruments; testings of air and water temperature, humidity, ship's headway, and water content; and botanizing—all proceeded under many watchful eyes, but not Rezanov's. The envoy remained below and out of sight. He had been vexed by the abuse with which the senior lieutenants had met his clumsy efforts to exert his authority over the ship.[80]

Nadezhda and *Neva* sailed together along the coast of Patagonia, among schools of whales and with clouds of stormy petrels overhead.[81] The winds were high but, undeterred, von Tilenau and Langsdorf pressed ahead with their experiments on "ocean fluorescence,"[82] made a study of the floating seaweed islands (*Macrocystis pirifera*) that were later to concern both Captain V.M. Golovnin and Captain F.F. Bellingshausen (in *Kamchatka* and *Vostok* respectively),[83] and, by late February 1804, began to read up on the place where the expedition would be pausing: Easter Island. "Kruzenshtern wished to spend one day at Easter Island, to check chronometers and discover what had happened to the goats, sheep, and swine left there by La Pérouse."[84] By 26 February, both vessels were south of the notorious Cape Horn, with killer whales in their wake. Storms then erupted, but on 3 March *Nadezhda* and *Neva* entered the South Pacific Ocean from the east. Amid rejoicing, scientific work and shipboard routines were carried on: neither Lisianskii nor Kruzenshtern lost the slightest opportunity to make a physical experiment, conduct hydrography, or exercise both officers and men in other ways. The parallel of Cape Victoria was passed on 22 March.

Slightly after this Kruzenshtern, to the concealed disappointment of his officers and his gentlemen of science, decided not to call at Easter Island after all but to proceed to Nukuhiva in the Washington-Marquesas Group. Lisianskii, however, was still at liberty to go there to revictual and to investigate whatever interested him. The pleasure that *Neva*'s people experienced on learning this was hardly diminished by the storms that broke again after 30 March and lasted a week.[85]

EASTER ISLAND

Neva was separated from *Nadezhda* in a thick fog on 24 March 1804, more than a thousand miles to the west of Valparaiso in Chile.[86] In the unfrequented wastes of the Pacific, this had a sobering effect upon *Neva*'s whole company. A gale on 28–29 March convinced them that their anxiety was well founded. Enormous seas and the unlikelihood of any assistance led Lisianskii, a man of decidedly anti-ecclesiastic attitudes, to reflect upon Divinity and Providence at sea.[87] At length, he made for Easter Island, the rendezvous agreed upon in the event of separation. By 1 April, *Neva* was in 39°S, 99°W and in an area where Etienne Marchand had claimed to have sighted land in 1791.[88] The weather moderated in the first ten days of April, and as the ship's motion became slight, Lisianskii and his men prepared to meet the Polynesians. While the smiths brought up the forge and made large nails, chisels, knives, and axes to barter with the Easter Islanders for fresh supplies, Lisianskii and his two lieutenants, Povalishin and Arbuzov, took a fresh look at the literature they had on the island, consisting of Cook's, Forster's, and La Pérouse's published works. Of Roggeveen's seminal visit in the *Arend* in 1722 or that of Capitan Gonzalez y Haedo in 1770 Lisianskii's men knew nothing.[89] This was most unfortunate, as a little knowledge of the Easter Islanders' first contacts with Europeans, represented by the Dutch and Spanish, would have allowed the Russians to understand various aspects of their own tension-filled visit. It is essential that *we* consider the Russian visit in the context of those earlier encounters.

When he sighted Easter Island on Easter Sunday 1722, Dutch Admiral Jacob Roggeveen at first took it for "Davis Land," which had allegedly been seen 500 leagues due west of Copiapo by the English privateer Edward Davis.[90] The eminent historian of Easter Island, Alfred Métraux, has observed: "History affords few examples of an indifference to equal that shown in 1687 by the privateer Edward Davis when... he sighted a sandy beach behind which were silhouetted high mountains [in the South Pacific west of Chile]. He immediately swung his ship round on to an easterly course towards Peruvian waters, without making the slightest effort to find out whether he was the victim of an optical illusion or the discoverer of a new country. This 'Davis Land'... confirmed the cosmographers of the period in their conviction that a continent existed in those regions which formed, as it were, a counterbalance to Asia and Europe."[91] Not even Russian captains in the early 1800s were untouched by the continuing necessity to lay to rest the myth of "Davis Land" or to establish its position, once for all.[92] As Roggeveen drew near the unexpected island to his west, however, its appearance grew less and less like anything described by Davis. Next morning, a native came on board in the most casual and friendly manner, strolled about the *Arend,* touched her rigging, and in general behaved with great composure. Soon, three dozen other Easter Islanders were on the deck, laughing and shouting. It was not long before they stole seamen's caps and a linen tablecloth, afterwards plunging unhesitatingly into the sea. These first petty thefts began a trend in European-Easter Islander relations that survived the centuries. Annoyed but not yet angry, the Dutch resolved to land that same day, to barter, reclaim their property, survey, and reconnoitre. Natives massed along the beach as the historic moment approached. Were they hostile? Hospitable? The Dutch could not be sure, so incoherent and conflicting were the signals being sent: "While some made gestures of friendship and seemed delighted by the visit, others wore a hostile expression and picked up stones. This marked contrast characterized the natives' attitude on the occasion of every subsequent European landing on the island."[92] Among these Europeans were the Russians, first in *Neva* in 1804, then in *Riurik* in 1816. *Neva*'s men were received with the same baffling, confusing gestures that the Dutch had seen a century before.

Roggeveen landed with 134 armed seamen and cautiously advanced over the rocks along the shore of Easter Island's northern rim (Te Pito

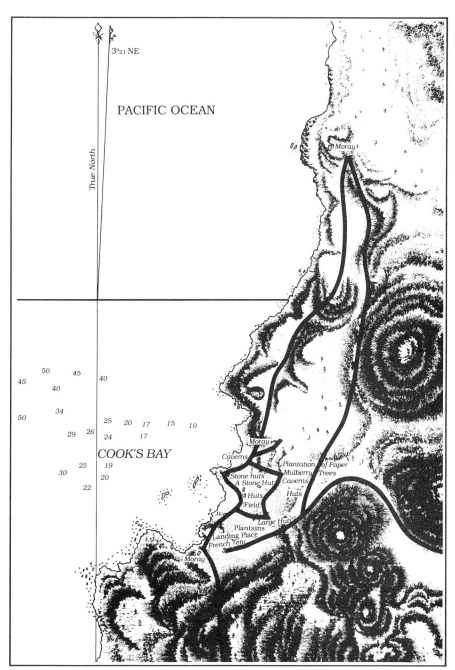

3°21′NE

True North

PACIFIC OCEAN

Moray

50   45
45   40
         40
50   34
              25   20   17   15   10
         29 26   24   17
         COOK'S BAY   Moray
                                  Cavems
              25   19   Plantation of Paper
         30   20   Stone huts   Mulberry Trees
              22   A Stone Hut   Cavems
                            Huts   Huts
                            Field
                                  Large Hut
                              Plantains
                            Landing Place
                         French Ten
                              Moray

Map 1 Hanga-roa Bay and the adjacent coast of Easter Island, adapted from La Pérouse, *Voyage* , for the English-language edition of *Voyage Round the World... Charts and Plates to La Pérouse's Voyage* (London: Robinson 1798), engraved by Neele, printed as Plate 10

Kura). None of the reed bundles or craft of small planks "sewn" together that they had seen the day before were now in evidence. Nor was the eerie silence broken till, in Roggeveen's own words, "to our great astonishment and without any expectation, there were heard four to five musket-shots and behind us with a loud shout 'it's time, it's time, fire!!' whereupon... more than thirty muskets were let off, and the Indians, being completely surprised and frightened by this, fled, leaving behind 10 to 12 dead, besides the wounded."[93]

An islander had tried to pull a musket from a sailor by the muzzle, with resulting death and destruction. Soon the natives returned, timid and humble, and presented Roggeveen with little standards as a token of respect. The Dutch were tense and ill at ease, but trade began: Dutch linens for hens, edible roots, bananas, sugar cane.[94] Glancing at little huts made of branches, neck and ear ornaments, tattooing that produced the same effect as deep blue paint, and huge stone idols, the Dutch quickly retired to their boats.[95] They were puzzled by the giant images before which fires burned and which the natives plainly worshipped. ("We could not comprehend how it was possible that these people, who are devoid of heavy thick timber for making any machines, as well as strong ropes, had nevertheless been able to erect such images, which were fully 30 feet high."[96] The stone statues (*moai*), for which Easter Island has been famous ever since, in fact weighed less than their dimensions suggested, being of tufa cut from the side of an extinct volcano (Rano Raraku). It is commonly accepted that they were raised as monuments to dead chieftains or other persons of importance, facing little inland courts and with their backs toward the ocean.[97] Some were eighty feet high, others even shorter than a man. They were still there when *Neva* arrived in 1804.

Roggeveen's discovery produced no interest in Europe. The search for "Davis Land" went on, however, and eventually Spain sent warships to annex the island Roggeveen had seen. There were no murders in the course of Felipe Gonzalez y Haedo's intensive six-day stay in 1770, but again there was pilfering, tension, and misunderstanding. Girls openly offered themselves to Spanish seamen; Spanish morals were offended. Large crosses were raised on the Poike Hills; the islanders ignored them, then coveted the precious timber.[98] Cook arrived in 1774. Again the islanders were gay and threatening, lighthearted and outrageously dishonest in their barter. They put stones in the bags of sweet potato they offered the British. Native women offered sex for trifling gifts with the approval of their menfolk. And again blood was shed.[99]

The experience of the Dutch, Spanish, and British was repeated by La Pérouse in 1786. A cultivated and humane aristocrat, the Frenchman could not bring himself to kill a man for stolen caps or handkerchiefs. For want of any better policy, he simply laughed at native stratagems to rob him of his goods.[100] The Easter Islanders of course took full advantage of this windfall and, mocking him, took what they could. While maidens led the seamen on, men picked their pockets. Looting worsened as the visit drew to a close, and as a last resort the French fired blank cartridges. Despite the turmoil, La Pérouse made an intelligent and fairly comprehensive survey of the island and its populace, and Lisianskii had a copy of his narrative, as well as Cook's, aboard *Neva*.

The inhabitants of Rapanui (Easter Island) had been absolutely isolated from the rest of Polynesia since the arrival circa 1200 AD of their semi-legendary king, Hotu-matu'a, and his followers from the Marquesas Islands. The early nineteenth-century Russian accounts illuminate various aspects of their culture, which was soon to be destroyed.[101] The significance of the brief but lucid evidence of 1804 is made plain by Chamisso and Kotzebue, who reported that few of the great *moai* noted by Lisianskii were still intact and upright twelve years later.[102] Civil war among the islanders led to more destruction, to be touched upon by Russia's most distinguished anthropologist, N.N. Miklukho-Maklai.[103] Lisianskii's narrative illuminates seven areas of native life and culture: weaving or plaiting, husbandry, tattooing, navigation, house construction, and *moai*.

"NEVA" AT EASTER ISLAND: FIRST CONTACT, 16–20 APRIL 1804

The Russians first caught sight of Easter Island at 11 AM on 16 April, from approximately forty miles away. Lisianskii steered WNW towards Katiki Volcano and modern-day Cape Roggeveen, on the island's eastern edge. By 5:00 PM he was close enough to observe not only numerous *moai* round its shores but also massive terraced platforms made of stone. Some *moai* were 12 or 15 feet in height and about 600 feet long. They had apparently been stood along the terraces, or *ahu*. Light was fading as the Russians trained their telescopes on Easter Island's cliffs, but they could see, behind the barren stony beaches, rising grasslands on the slopes of dead volcanoes. It was harsh yet green, fertile yet treeless. Winds were squally and the air was hazy, so, with night at hand, Lisianskii had the topsails reefed and stood out from the shore. Small gulls circled above in shrieking clouds.[104]

> Easter Island has too often been pictured in the grimmest light. A bare island, a field of volcanic stones, an unproductive tract of land ... By what strange freak did a brilliant civilization manage to develop this supposedly barren rock? In reality, Easter Island's arid appearance is deceptive. Roggeveen considered it so fertile that he

dubbed it an "earthly paradise." M. de La Pérouse's gardener was
delighted with the nature of the soil... Then as now, the slopes of
the volcanoes were green meadows; along the shore one could see a
succession of gardens and banana plantations. Trees alone were lacking.[105]

Lisianskii's people soon saw what this lack of standing timber meant:
stunted shrubs and twisted branches made canoe building a taxing business. They saw the fruit trees for themselves within a day, however, and
were in due course offered plantains and bananas, sweet potatoes, sugar
cane, and yams.[106]

The next morning found *Neva* twelve miles east of the Poike Hills. As
the wind was now northwesterly, it was simple to proceed along the island's southern shore, past Hotuiti and the cliffs of Vaihu toward the
South Cape and the slopes of Rano Kao (see Map 2). By 8:00 AM *Neva*
weathered the cape, passing due south of "two large rocks," one
strikingly similar to an imposing ship with her main topgallant sail set.
These were Motu Kaokao and, below it, Motu-nui, "Birdmen's Island."
Interestingly, the Russians make no mention of the village of Orongo,
then still standing in the lee of Rano Kao and the centre of the local bird-
man cult. All telescopes were trained due north, towards Cook Bay or
Hanga-roa.

> The island's greatest religious festival, the only one concerning
> which circumstantial details survive, was that of the bird-man, in-
> timately linked with the cult of the god Makemake. The long mystic
> drama enacted every year on the Orongo cliffs not only was of great
> religious significance, but also profoundly affected the island's social
> life. The aim of these rites... was the discovery and possession of
> the first egg laid by the *manu-tara* (*Sterna hirundo*), the sooty tern,
> on the islet of Motu-nui... The egg was the incarnation of the god
> Makemake and the tangible expression of religious and social forces
> of great intensity.[107]

All early European visitors to Easter Island came into contact with one
aspect or another of the complex and, to them, mysterious or foolish cult
of the bird-man (*tangata-manu*). The Spaniards in 1770 saw native
"signatures" on a document that were in fact stylized birds seen on Island petroglyphs.[108] The Russians left with humanoid yet birdlike
statuettes whose true significance they did not understand.[109] More were
acquired for St. Petersburg's collection in the later nineteenth century.[110]
These statuettes showed protruding ribs and vertebrae, an emaciated face,

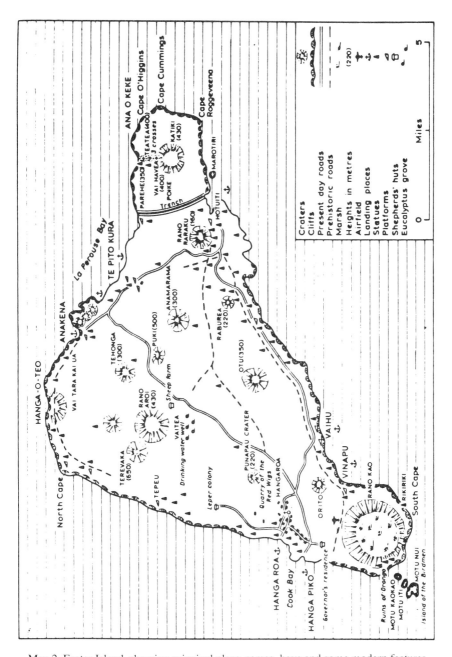

Map 2 Easter Island, showing principal place-names, bays and some modern features

and a birdlike beak known as *moai kavakava;* they formed a link between the bird-man cult and ancestor worship.

As they coasted west below the island's southern cliffs and drew parallel with the extinct Otu Volcano, the Russians were struck by certain aspects of the sanctuary platform and associated statues: "Towards the middle stood two large black statues, one twice the size of the other; yet it appeared as if both were intended to form but one monument, as they were contiguous to each other and enclosed within the same mound."[111]

They saw other *moai* on the west and north coasts of the island, but did not remark upon their blackness. This suggests that the *ahu* south of Otu crater boasted images of basalt, not tufa.[112] Thirty years earlier and perhaps three miles to the west, near Vaihu, Cook's men had gazed at comparable mausoleum statues.[113] Lisianskii saw four images at Hanga-roa in one day and others in succeeding days. Only some were broken. Most were of tufa, showing heavy human features: "Volcanic tufa is a sort of earth bound by the presence of fragments and nodules of stone. It is friable and easily carved. The modern sculptors consider this material easier to work than wood. With nothing but an axe they cut out a large block of tufa in a day ... The first point is to establish the real weight of these statues. This has been greatly exaggerated."[114] Lisianskii's observations are as significant for what they leave unstated as for what they confirm. There is, for instance, clear mention of the cylinders or "hats" brought from Punapau crater, which once surmounted many images. (The Dutch mistook them for baskets full of small white stones; the islanders termed them *pukao*.)[115] There are, however, no references to the images' facial expressions or to fires at their bases—alas, the Russians spent no time ashore and had no chance to study them.

Neva stood three miles off Cook Bay, on the west coast of the island, by 9:30 AM on 17 April. The imposing images there much resembled those described by La Pérouse and stood where Hanga-roa settlement remains today. Lisianskii had proposed to anchor there, but the winds were unco-operative. Since he was to rendezvous with Kruzenshtern, however, he had to remain a day or two offshore. "Accordingly, on the 18th, we again ranged along the eastern side of the island, and found it as pleasant as it appeared the day before. The middle of it is much lower than its extremities; and a few huts are dispersed here and there amongst the fruit trees, of which, however, there was no great plenty. We kept so near the coast that we could easily distinguish the natives following the ship along the beach."[116]

The lower central stretch of coast was necessarily Te Pito Kura, or La Pérouse Bay. The huts were by the shore to the east of Anakena craters, where a quarry was in use. The fruit trees were banana and/or plantain. The natives were members of a different tribe, or *mata*, from those who had observed *Neva* as she passed Hanga-roa. Copper-skinned and "naked" they might be, but the men now following *Neva* were the immediate adherents of the king (*ariki-mau*) of the island, a descendant of the great Hotu-matu'a's eldest son, Tu'u-maheke. Those whom Povalishin was to meet off Hanga-roa on 21 April were a different and more or less unfriendly group, descendants of Chief Miru.[117] Few natives could have been ignorant of the Russians' presence by the second afternoon. Passing up the island's eastern coastline for the second time, the Russians saw five monuments. One had four great images, another three, another two. Two other groups seemed to be population centres in the east: the area "contained a greater number of inhabitants, and seemed better cultivated, than any other spot we had yet seen."[118] Assuming that Lisianskii was enumerating *ahu* from east to west as he returned to Cook Bay, this busy, cultivated area was necessarily Orongo, centre of the bird-man cult. Lisianskii made no mention of "huts" in connection with this pair of villages, but, significantly, commented that the place was "steep" and "craggy." Geologically, the whole locality was made of "stone, resembling slate or limestone, lying in horizontal strata."[119] Relatively recent archaeology has shown that "the houses of Orongo, forty-six in number, were built of schistous slabs modelled after the thatched huts which the worshippers had originally erected."[120] Also visible were broken images with their *pukao* ("hats") still atop shattered heads. As Lisianskii put it, "We also observed numerous heaps of stone, covered with something white at the top; respecting which I could form no satisfactory conjecture."[121] As so often was the case, he was following in the mental footsteps of Cook and La Pérouse.[122]

There was much to do and see. The strong northwesterly and a complete absence of harbours, however, deprived the visitors of quiet nights at anchor. White-capped waves and roaring surf promised no respite. Next morning, 19 April, there was a heavy swell. Light breezes sometimes died away entirely as, undeterred by heavy rain, Lisianskii took *Neva* along the north shore once again. Four *ahu* were spotted, one with three, two with two, and one with one stone image. Altogether, the Russians noted twenty-five or thirty statues standing and in good repair. Passing La Pérouse Bay for the second time, they saw that many fires had been lit. Perhaps without sufficient reason, they supposed them "to be signals of invitation on shore." Lisianskii would have anchored where La Pérouse's *Boussole* and *Astrolabe* had paused had he regarded it as safe, but a report from Povalishin, who had rowed in with the jolly boat to test the current off Te Pito Kura, changed his mind. He steered west and past North Cape.[123]

So unsettled was the weather on 20 April that it was impossible to examine the north shore of the island. Lisianskii made for Cook Bay, hoping to anchor at last, but conditions grew far worse. Not until 8:00 AM on the 21st did *Neva* reach the bay, where, to the officers' annoyance and the men's frustration, an immense, ponderous swell again made anchoring impossible. Determined to leave some indication of his visit so that Kruzenshtern would know that those in *Neva* were well and following the plan, Lisianskii had recourse to Povalishin and the jolly boat again:

> I dispatched Lieutenant Povalishin in the jolly boat with knives, small pieces of iron, empty bottles, and some printed linens. His orders were to go as near the shore as the surf would permit and distribute the above-mentioned articles to the natives who, without doubt, would swim off to him. At the same time, I recommended him to examine the bay and to try the surroundings, but without attempting to land.[124]

LIEUTENANT PETR POVALISHIN'S CALL AT HANGA-ROA,
21 APRIL 1804

Lisianskii's movements off Easter Island were guided by La Pérouse. He brought *Neva* toward Cook Bay with the intention of dropping anchor in twenty-four fathoms of water or at five cable-lengths from shore, as the Frenchman had suggested. By bringing the sandy beach to bear SE and by losing sight of the two large rocks near the bay's southern extremity, Lisianskii brought his ship into the depth that La Pérouse had recommended. Thus *Neva* was less than half a mile offshore when Povalishin left her, at approximately 9:00 AM. Though small, that distance was sufficient to prevent the Easter Islanders from coming out to her once Povalishin had established that the Russians meant no harm. Such was the miserable state to which their art of navigation had been reduced for want of wood and constant practice.[125]

Povalishin and his party moved slowly, taking soundings as they worked their way toward the surf: ten fathoms were sounded at one and a half cable-lengths. The shore was sketched. The watching islanders became impatient, especially when they saw that Povalishin was not keen to face the pounding surf. Southwesterlies worked the surface to a heavy swell. The natives, estimated at about five hundred, waved and yelled. One can sympathize with the young lieutenant's caution if one examines the sketch made of the landing of *Riurik*'s boats at the same spot twelve

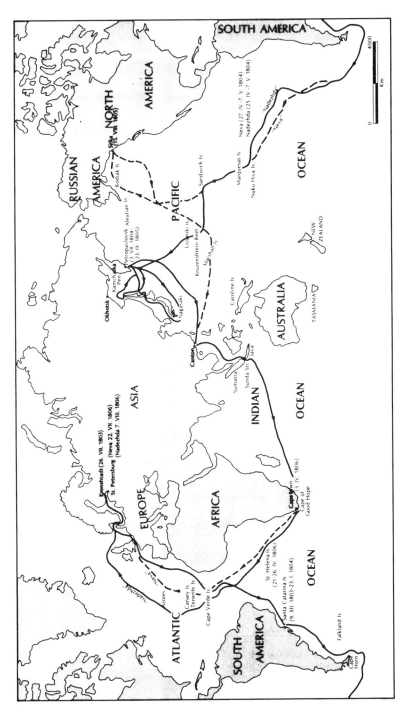

Map 3 Voyage of Kruzenshtern and Lisianskii on the *Nadezhda* and *Neva*, 1803-6

years later.[126] Kotzebue's artist, Ludovik (or Louis) Choris (1795–1828), presented a sombre scene of jumbled boulders, choppy waves, and islanders massing ashore (*Vue de l'Isle de Pâques*). At last some thirty men swam through the surf to Povalishin who, most prudently, repeated the word *teeo* (or *taio*), Tahitian for "a friend," while motioning them to climb into his launch one at a time. All guns were loaded. What ensued was watched via telescope from *Neva* by Nikolai I. Korobitsyn, a Russian-American Company clerk (*prikazchik*) and a sensible observer of the Easter island scene.[127] Korobitsyn's journal showed up in a Leningrad second-hand bookstore in 1940 and, thanks to the prompt action of Professor E.I. Gleiber, its Director, was acquired by the Russian All-Union Geographical Society, in whose possession it remains today.[128] Because Korobitsyn met Povalishin and his men on their return to *Neva,* his account of the Easter Island visit is a precious complement to the official narrative left by Lisianskii. Korobitsyn was a man of merchant antecedents, hard-headed and with an eye for the illuminating detail:

> Not one of them came empty-handed, but every one had something with him some of the product of the island: bananas, plantains, sugar cane, potatoes, and roots of yams. But they would not give these things to the Russians before they themselves had received gifts such as knives, scissors, little mirrors, printed linen kerchiefs, and chain lockets made of Russian coins. Most of all, they liked knives and, having received one, would excitedly return for more. The last of the islanders... received a bottle stopped with white resin, containing a note for the information of the *Nadezhda...* Mr. Povalishin completed the distribution of the presents and returned on board ship at 2:00 PM. According to his report on the external appearance of the islanders, all those who swam up... were of ordinary stature, shapely, and of sound constitution.[129]

In addition to the goods mentioned above, the Russians left "copper money, strung upon wire" and "several mustard bottles, with small pieces of wood fastened to them, upon which the name of our ship was written."[130] The language barrier caused problems for them, but they had established first contact and the barter, though quite limited, was satisfactory. Within an hour, the jolly boat was full of plantains, or bananas, sugar cane, and sweet potatoes, and the islanders were offering their clothing and woven artefacts. Among the articles obtained by Povalishin and brought by him to Russia was an elegantly made rush-mat on which one native reached his boat.[131] In Povalishin's view, this native—who appeared to be sixty years old and who brought out sweet potatoes from a plaited bag—had previously encountered a European vessel. He alone had long hair and wore a bushy beard, and the sight of Europeans did not trouble him.

The evidence of Povalishin and his men regarding native numbers, dress, and body ornament is supplemented by the evidence of those who watched from *Neva* with first-rate telescopes. The general opinion at the time was that five hundred were gathered on the shore, including children. Many men were "stoutly built, and tall, some of them being six feet high."[132] "With regard to complexion and colour of skin, they differed very little from Europeans."[133] Because their clothing was so scanty and they spent much time in the sun, their skin was rather reddish, as though sunburned. The "extraordinary large ears which reach down to the shoulders" described by Cook (that is, with lobes widely perforated and stretched by the insertion of some heavy ornament of shark vertebra or wood) were not seen by the Russians.[134] Possibly the style was fading in the late 1700s. Far more probably, the Russians simply failed to observe distended lobes.[135]

Like all their European predecessors, the Russians were struck unfavourably by the Easter Islanders' tattooing. "On their faces," wrote Korobitsyn, "they had scars incised with blue pigment."[136] Lisianskii reported that most tattooing was on the face and hands or arms.[137] Regrettably, no sketches of the patterns, geometric forms, or animal motifs employed in 1804 were made. Russian evidence is quite specific on the natives' hairstyles. Hair was cut a little at the front and often worn "in the manner of a *toupée*." Men went "cropped and beardless."[138] Excessive hairiness was viewed as ugly by the Easter Islanders, and also by the Nukuhivans shortly after.[139] Some men had their hair in a topknot. Interestingly, the Russians make no mention of the many forms of headgear that Easter Islanders were said to have been fond of in the eighteenth century—cock-feather diadems, reed helmets with a fine feather mosaic, women's hats of wickerwork, and so forth.[140] Nor, apparently, were natives desperate to get the Russian seamen's caps. Of course, the opportunities for getting them were slight; and La Pérouse's men, on the other hand, had been ashore for hours at a stretch.

The Easter Islanders did not go naked. They had "pieces of papyrus hanging from a belt or a grass rope in front and back to cover their secret parts."[141] The "papyrus" was, in fact, beaten bark of paper mulberry (*Broussonetia papyrifera*), which was successfully cultivated despite Easter Island's cold sea winds. The strips were well soaked in water and pounded with a wooden mallet; but unlike the other Polynesian peoples, the Easter Islanders did not join bark pieces together just by beating them, preferring instead to sew squares together with bone needles. Povalishin saw evidence of this. "Amongst the crowd were some who constantly waved square pieces of white and striped cloth, about the size of a pocket-handkerchief."[142] The stripes would have been made by dyes based upon turmeric, red earth, *Solanum nigrum* juice, and other substances. (The blueness of the islanders' facial tattoos likewise resulted from the application of *Solanum nigrum* juice, well mixed with *ti* stems.) No doubt thoughts of scraping paper mulberry's hard surface with an iron knife instead of obsidian contributed to the islanders' rejoicing at getting the Russian implements. One striking feature of the visit was the inconspicuous and guarded female presence: not for Povalishin's men the sexual advances that had once delighted Englishmen and Frenchmen, Dutch and Spaniards. Many of the men standing at Cook Bay wore "a kind of short cloak, or piece of cloth, suspended from the shoulders and scarcely covering the thighs." The Russians had arrived in southern autumn, and while cloaks possibly were used for an aesthetic purpose, they served mainly for warmth. How well the natives coped with cool conditions is apparent from their offering the Russians sugar cane, sweet potatoes, and bananas. (Near the Te Peu *ahu,* notes Métraux, the lava crust is split, producing cavities which Easter Islanders have long used as sunken gardens. There, where the cold winds cannot reach, a hothouse atmosphere has prevailed for centuries.)[143] In general, the Russians recognized how well the natives had adapted to their isolated home. Good health was evident, at least among the men. Lisianskii drew the obvious conclusion: that the island diet was, despite Cook's suggestion, adequate: "If they have no animals, as is said, they are nevertheless plentifully supplied with substitutes which, if not so substantial, are at least equally nourishing."[144] No cripples, deformities, or skin diseases were reported by Povalishin. Korobitsyn looked vainly for a trace of cattle raising on the island, and it is striking that the islanders brought out no hens to barter, even though they had quite a number.[145]

Povalishin's men could see the native houses behind the beach, in the vicinity of modern-day Hanga-roa. They were not impressed, though there were some large houses:

> The houses, or rather huts, of these tribes are made of reeds and look like large overturned boats. They are 100 feet or more in length, between 15 and 20 feet wide, and not more than 12 feet high. The entrances or doorways to these huts are at the edge of the elevation on which they are situated and are not spacious, being only three to four feet high. Between ten and twenty families are house in each of these huts, which are intended to offer protection to the dwellers against storms, rains, and the heat of the sun.[146]

Later material has been incorporated in this description: the visitors of 1804 had no way of knowing how many families lived in any hut. Still, the passage is interesting, especially in apposition to Lisianskii's narrative. Some houses, Lisianskii wrote, stood quite separately; but occasionally two or three huddled together. Doors were conical in form and not rectangular, and houses seemed devoid of windows. "Every house was planted round with bananas and sugar-canes." Today, the ground plan of such structures can be seen at Hanga-roa. Basalt curbs set in an oval or ellipse mark the sites of Povalishin's "overturned boats." The Russians were correct to speak of reeds, although these—in overlapping mats or bundles—merely covered fragile *ti* frames.[147] The "elevation" was a platform of boulders filled with stones and scoria. Some houses were 250 feet or longer; a major axis of 100 feet was not unusual.[148] In sum, the Russian evidence suggests that Easter Island dwellings had remained unchanged since the visit of Roggeveen. Where Lisianskii speaks of upturned longboats, Bouman speaks of "Greenland sloops turned upside down."[149] Lath-and-reed construction, low conical door, missing windows, mats of split, plaited banana leaves—all testified to the survival of the classical techniques in 1804.

The Russians saw no boats of the variety described by La Pérouse: plank craft with slender booms attached to the flat gunwale, prow and poop shaped like a duck's bill, six or seven feet long. They were surprised by this, and wrongly surmised that such canoes had simply vanished in recent times. They thought that Easter Islanders had lost the daring on the high seas characteristic of other Polynesians: "When they were desired to go to the ship, they expressed by signs that it was too far; which proves, as do also the rush-mats which everyone had to assist him in swimming, that the boats seen by La Pérouse do not at present exist on the island."[150] Kotzebue saw such craft at Hanga-roa in 1816 and Beechey in 1826, and they are known to have survived a little longer yet. The rush-mats used while swimming, on the other hand, were excellently made and much admired by the Russians. Lisianskii comments on the plaited bag and mat that Povalishin had acquired from the old man with the bushy beard: "The first, which was fifteen inches long and ten wide, was made of hard grass in a very masterly manner. The second, which was four feet and a half long, and fifteen inches and a half broad, consisted of sugar cane, plaited with rushes; and in point of workmanship, was scarcely inferior to any thing of the kind made in Europe."

Povalishin did his best to estimate the sizes of the images that he could see beyond the surf, comparing them with human forms. Four were relatively close, with one broken and shortened by half. The other three appeared about thirteen feet tall, with the cylinder or "hat" on top accounting for a quarter of this.[151] In general, the evidence of 1804 was that the Easter Island culture had been only slightly altered by previous European visits. Russian iron tools were prized and recognized immediately for superior utility. There is no evidence, however, that the iron tools that Cook or La Pérouse had left behind changed traditional technology. The absence of women while *Neva* remained offshore, which the Russians attributed to jealousy or fear, may have been connected with negative experience during earlier European visits. It is probable, however, that if Russian seamen had gone ashore, certain women would have striven to seduce them with their charms, commanding a higher price because of their previous unavailability. All other European mariners had been enticed by smiles and alluring demonstrations encouraged by the local men.[152] Years later, the *Riurik*'s men were not similarly regaled, the native women even standing "at a great distance" from shore,[153] but this can be explained by the violence committed by the Yankee trader *Nancy* in 1808, particularly the New Englanders' abduction of ten women and a dozen men after a bloody clash.[154]

Neva's jolly boat returned at 2:00 PM, bringing supplies, small artefacts, and information, but no water. Had a landing been made, Lisianskii would immediately have investigated La Pérouse's contention that the Easter Islanders drank sea water and so had no need of reservoirs, rock pits, or tanks. Lisianskii was extremely skeptical of this.[155] After coasting once again along the north shore of the island, he sailed for Nukuhiva in the Washington-Marquesas Group. In the days preceding his departure, fires ashore burned in many places. Were these fires truly invitations? As they left, the Russians wondered if perhaps they were connected with religious practices or if the islanders were simply cooking. ("From the many fires regularly lit at nine o'clock, it may be inferred that victuals are prepared here in the open air, and that nine o'clock is the accustomed hour for a general meal.")[156]

Lisianskii was adept at lunar distances and conscientious where astronomy and all dependent calculations were concerned. At Easter Island, he showed his professional abilities, correcting Cook's co-ordinates of 1774 and even challenging the hero's modest population estimate of seven hundred:

> Captain Cook places Easter Island in latitude 27°5'36''S, and longitude 109°46'20''W; but by my observations, the middle of it proved to be 27°9'23''S, and 190°25'20''W... I know not how to account for this difference of latitude, unless by supposing that this celebrated navigator calculated his to some point lying to the northward of the

middle of the island. His estimate also of the population of the island
. . . from six to seven hundred, appears to me a little strange. When I
consider the number of persons who assembled in the bay on the approach of our boat, and the many habitations which I observed round
the coast, I think I may safely assert that the island contains at least
fifteen hundred inhabitants.[157]

The estimate was good. Within ten years of the Peruvian slave-traders'
first attack on the island (1862), however, the island population had
shrunk to the figure named by Cook. By 1935, it was 456. Today it is
around 800. Blows delivered by the Chileans, Peruvians, New Englanders, and others in the nineteenth century produced a wound that has not
healed.[158]

INTRODUCING EASTER ISLAND TO THE RUSSIANS, 1806–16

The return of *Nadezhda* and *Neva* to Kronstadt in August 1806 produced
considerable interest among the educated public. Hoping to draw maximum advantage and prestige from the expedition's mixed results,[159] the
Russian-American Company board had Chinese wares and South Pacific
artefacts put on display in a building that the board itself rented on Gorokhovaia (Harrach) Street in St. Petersburg. The exhibition was extremely
well attended.[160] Almost certainly some artefacts from Easter Island were
among the Polynesian sub-collection.

Some time after this, Lisianskii ordered that such artefacts should go to
the St. Petersburg Imperial Public Library or, in accordance with his previous instructions from the Naval Ministry regarding all materials acquired on his voyage, to the Admiralty Department's museum.[161] Povalishin offered artefacts to that museum at the same time. Hoping for better
care and presentation of such artefacts, the Imperial Library transferred
most of the Polynesian articles collected by *Neva* in 1804–5 to the
Rumiantsev Museum of Ethnography in Moscow.[162] The Admiralty in its
turn, in 1827–29, donated most or all its Polynesian artefacts to the
Kunstkammer of the Academy of Sciences.[163] Deplorably, the documents
relating to the transfer have been lost.[164] We may confidently state, then,
that Easter Island artefacts reached Russia with *Neva* in 1806 and were
dispersed in later years. Some quite possibly remained in private hands.[165]

Lisianskii's *Voyage* was the chief organ by which the Russian public
learned of the Easter Island visit. There was potentially great interest:
both Cook's and La Pérouse's observations on a place that was "exotic"
had after all been translated (or perhaps well paraphrased) into Russian.[166]

Forster too was widely known, and his remarks on Easter Island's giant statues, long-eared natives, and mysteriously barren air had contributed toward the Russians' interest in it.[167]

Lisianskii was profoundly disappointed and annoyed when an official of the Admiralty, Apollon Nikol'skii, rejected his account of the *Neva*'s Pacific venture with a note to the effect that it was awkwardly composed and, "in its present state at least, could not be printed to the credit of the Navy."[168] Other senior officials, he was told, had also questioned the necessity of his composing his account at all, since Kruzenshtern was known to be producing one.[169] The tone and content of Nikol'skii's letter led Lisianskii, rightly, to believe himself the victim of political intrigue. He retired from the Russian Navy in February 1809, despite being only thirty-six years old and having a first-rate service record.[170] Though discouraged by the Admiralty, he persisted in producing his own account, based on his journals, of the voyage of *Neva*. A struggle followed for possession of the nine plates of engravings that, by oversight, had earlier been ordered by the Admiralty and completed. Finally, the government agreed to print a hundred copies of the nine plates for itself, and fifty for Lisianskii's use. It had been suggested earlier that twelve hundred copies be produced.[171] Despite government harassment and his own fatigue, Lisianskii at last had his *Voyage* printed, at a cost to him of almost 19,000 roubles. It appeared in St. Petersburg in April 1812. If the sum was large, the timing was deplorable: the country was preoccupied with war, particularly with Napoleon's invasion of the Western Russian Provinces. Moscow burned. At about this time, Lisianskii realized he was a lost pawn in an escalating struggle between agents of the Navy and the Company for full control of the Company's board and possessions in the North Pacific basin.[172]

Puteshestvie vokrug sveta v 1803, 4, 5 i 1806 godakh... na korable Neva appeared in two small volumes without illustrations. Also published in 1812 was the accompanying atlas *Sobranie kart i risunkov ... (Collection of Maps and Drawings...)*, with detailed and elegant drawings of Polynesian artefacts by Lisianskii himself. The "Easter Island" passage appeared in Chapter 4 of Volume 1, on pages 82–99. Both text and illustrations were warmly received by the savants who had accompanied the Kruzenshtern-Lisianskii expedition, notably by Georg Heinrich Langsdorf (whose *Bemerkungen auf eine Reise um die Welt* appeared that same year in Frankfurt-am-Main), Tilesius von Tilenau, Espenberg, and Hörner. Such men were not involved in Navy-Company contentions, were interested in objectivity, and were also aware of Lisianskii's good connections with the Court and with the tsar's family.[173] The fact remained, however, that the book had not been published at a good time. Sales dragged.

Lisianskii's English translation of his work appeared in London in 1814. Its publication, by Booth and Company, was a symptom of an upturn in the English public's interest in seaborne exploration, especially in regions of potential economic value. Growing British consciousness of Russia's trading and imperial ambitions in the North Pacific also boosted sales, and the book did very well.[174] Extremely favourable notices at length made an impression on the Russian Admiralty; belatedly and grudgingly, it gave Lisianskii 12,517 roubles to defray his early publication costs, leaving him 6,000 roubles out of pocket.[175] Vindicated but disgusted, he resolved to have no further dealings with officialdom and bought an estate far from the capital, where, far from ships and naval bureaucrats, his life acquired a much smoother rhythm.[176]

Lisianskii's narratives and the *Neva*'s brief visit made Easter Island more real to the Russian public. They also proved that Russia could contribute to opening Oceania to European science. Although Povalishin had not gone ashore, he had disproved the foolish notion that the islanders were herculean people, twelve feet high, as Roggeveen apparently believed.[177] He had also described the dwellings, appearance, products, great stone images, tattooing, dress, and conduct of those islanders. His descriptions satisfied even Langsdorf, who, the very week Lisianskii was closing on the island from the east, had been expecting to examine it himself. Kruzenshtern's change of plans and the unfavourable winds that had sent *Nadezhda* on a course far from the island, on her way to Nukuhiva and Kamchatka, were a major disappointment to the crew: "Captain von Krusenstern had previously agreed with Captain Lisianskii that, in case of a separation, Easter Island should be the place of rendezvous; and thither, therefore, the attention of the whole crew was immediately directed. We sought out all the accounts of former navigators by whom it had been visited, and studied them assiduously, so that our curiosity was in the end extremely excited."[178]

La Pérouse had left goats, sheep and hogs, orange and lemon trees, cotton plants, dozens of seeds, and other things on Easter Island. Langsdorf and his companions in *Nadezhda* were impatient to discover whether these gifts had been preserved or thrown away. The Russians la mented that they could not "visit so interesting a spot and examine the truth."[179] A single day ashore, moreover, would have altered Johann Caspar Hörner's mind about the Easter Islanders' habit of drinking sea water. This they did, so he contended in a paper on the properties of sea water that finally appeared in the spring of 1820,[180] since the island's springs had vanished during the great volcanic movements of the eighteenth century. Such erroneous comments kept the memory of Easter Island fresh in Russian minds.

APPROACH BY THE "RIURIK" TO EASTER ISLAND, MARCH 1816

The next Russian company to visit Easter Island was that of Count N.P. Rumiantsev's 180-ton fir brig, the *Riurik,* whose voyage took her to Concepcion Bay in Chile, the Tuamotus, the Carolines, and onto Kamchatka.[181] Besides his two lieutenants, Gleb Shishmarev and Ivan Zakharin, Otto von Kotzebue had with him a first-rate surgeon and zoologist, Johann Friedrich Eschscholtz (1793—1831), and Adelbert von Chamisso (1781–1838), an internationally celebrated writer and savant.[182] *Riurik*'s brief call at Easter Island gained historical and ethnographic value from the presence of such men, especially when their narratives are taken together with the pen sketches and aquarelles made by Ludovik (in Russian, Loggin Andreevich) Choris or Khoris, *Riurik*'s talented artist.[183] In particular, Choris's view of Cook Bay, Easter Island, first published in *Vues et paysages des régions équinoxiales* (Paris 1826, Plate ix) with an accompanying 500-word "explanatory text," bolsters the value of the Chamisso and Kotzebue narratives of 1821.

Kotzebue's narrative was an official one, and was therefore sober, even circumspect in tone, though a love of local colour and the sweeping phrase shines through. Chamisso and Choris were freer to express themselves at the conclusion of their Arctic and Pacific wanderings, but both had a good deal to lose by casting shadows on the expedition's image of success and skilful management and by antagonizing Count Rumiantsev and his Admiralty friends. In 1820 Choris was a young man with a fortune still to make. He was careful to maintain correctly cordial relations with the count's naval adviser and his own potential patron, Kruzenshtern, for seven years after *Riurik*'s return, even advising him of his progress in Paris (1821–22) toward printing a first volume of drawings from the expedition: *Voyage pittoresque autour du monde* (Paris 1822).[184] Chamisso, too, could not afford to aggravate Kotzebue's older friends. Western historians have often overlooked this fact, contending that "unhampered by political considerations," Chamisso had "perfect liberty to say the whole truth about everything."[185] He did express his displeasure with the form in which his comments as the expedition's naturalist, *Bemerkungen und Ansichten,* were published in the third volume of Kotzebue's narrative of 1821.[186] The point, however, is that his account appeared as a section of the government-approved *Entdeckungs-Reise in die Südsee und nach der Berings-strasse* (Weimar 1821). Not until 1836 was his *Tagebuch*, or diary, of 1815–18 published.[187] Happily, it threw fresh light on *Riurik*'s short stop at Hanga-roa more than twenty years before, and at the same time gave faces and expressions to her men (whom Kotzebue had referred to just by name).

> First Lieutenant Gleb Semenovich Shishmarev, a friend of the captain's and, as an officer, his senior; speaking Russian only; with a face serenely beaming, like a full moon, agreeable to behold; of a robust, healthy constitution; a man who has *not* forgotten how to laugh. Second Lieutenant Ivan Iakovlevich Zakharin, sickly, irritable, but kindhearted; understands a little French and Italian. The Ship's Surgeon, a scientist and entomologist, Ivan Ivanovich Eschscholtz, a young doctor from Dorpat, pretty reserved but as true and noble as gold. The painter, Loggin ("Ludwig") Andreevich Choris, by origin a German who, though even then very young, had already accompanied Marshall von Bieberstein on an expedition into the Caucasus as his draughtsman ... Assistant pilot Khromchenko, a very good-natured, hard-working lad.[188]

Taken together, the evidence of Chamisso, Choris, and Kotzebue gives a full picture of the *Riurik*'s visit to Easter Island and contributes to Polynesian history and ethnohistory as well as to the Russian Navy's record in those seas.[189]

Because he was determined to be hydrographically correct, it took Kotzebue more than three weeks to reach the island from Concepcion Bay, though winds were generally favourable. Once again, "Davis Land" was an important factor in delay. *Riurik* passed the area where it was still supposed to lie (27°20'S, 88°04'W) on 16–17 March. No land was seen. On the 20th, in longitude 95°35'W, the vain search was abandoned. Kotzebue shifted course towards the southwest, hoping to chance on another dot of land shown on his map, called "Wareham Rocks." This too he could not find, although it had been marked by Aaron Arrowsmith (1750–1823) with great precision on his annotated global chart (London 1794). Not till 25 March did land appear in the barren and forbidding form of Sala-y-Gomez, a remote and empty islet that the independent Chileans would soon claim. By Kotzebue's reckoning, it lay in 26°36'15''S, 105°34'28'''W, and was less than one mile long. Scattered grey rocks gave the place an air of "melancholy ruin." Almost certain that the "Wareham Rocks" were near, Kotzebue spent another futile day searching for other land due west, then altered course for Easter Island.[190] It was sighted on 28 March at 3:00 AM, just fifteen miles off. Dawn brought its eastern edge, Ana o Keke and Poike, clearly into view. Excitement rose aboard the brig: the very knowledge that a South Pacific people would be met, wrote Chamisso, made it "a day of joy."[191]

Like Cook and Lisianskii before him, Kotzebue coasted west towards the South Cape, weathered Motu-nui and the two adjacent islets (only a pair had been spotted by *Neva*),[192] and arrived off Cook Bay hoping either to anchor immediately or at least to make prompt contact with the natives. Smoke rose from the Hanga-roa area, and the Russians thought it was to let the inhabitants of the interior know a ship was near. Telescopes were trained along the coast:

> Easter Island rises majestically out of the waves in a triangular form, swelling into pyramidical mountains. It represents in miniature the regular large lines of Owhyee [Hawaii]. It appears to be covered everywhere with the liveliest green: the ground, even on the steepest declivities of the mountains, is divided into regular fields, which are distinguished by various lively colours, and many of which are covered with yellow blossoms. We... believe we distinguished on the southeast coast, by the aid of our telescopes, some of the colossal statues which have excited so much admiration.[193]

The images observed between Vaihu and Hotuiti were doubtless among those seen from the *Neva* in 1804. Even today remains are numerous along that stretch of coast. The "regular fields" observed in 1816 were "divided" from each other by the loose stone barriers produced by earth clearance. The paper-mulberry and certain other plants easily damaged by the wind were, in this period, protected by a low wall of unmortared stone. Chamisso bears witness to the regular arrangement of the natives' fields and, by inference, to widespread husbandry.[194] The latter was demonstrated to Chamisso that very day, when a considerable quantity of taro, banana, sugar cane, and yams were offered to the Russians.

Riurik was perhaps half a mile offshore when two canoes set out toward her. Both were paddled by two men. There were no sails:

> The structure of the canoes, of which we saw several, and which will hold only two persons, corresponds exactly with those mentioned by La Pérouse; they are from five to six feet long and about one foot in breadth, made of narrow boards joined together, and furnished on both sides with an outrigger. La Pérouse's opinion is that the islanders, for want of wood, will soon be quite at a loss for boats, but he is mistaken: it is true we did not discover a single tree on this island, but they build their canoes of driftwood, which the current brings in great quantities from the coast of America.[195]

Kotzebue had himself seen driftwood on the southeast coastline. It remained abundant through the nineteenth century, as we know from the bizarre boatbuilding overseen in the 1860s by the missionary Eugène Eyraud.[196] Chamisso records the number of canoes as three. ("Two canoes—we saw only three in all—each containing two men, approached with signs of friendship, but without venturing near the ship.")[197] As these craft approached the Russians scanned the coast in vain for the four images Lisianskii had observed. They were not there.

The two craft stopped some distance from the brig; only then did Kotzebue realize that their four occupants were scared. Approaching *Riurik* "with fear and distrust," they showed the Russians roots, but would not risk closer contact. Kotzebue had his longboat lowered and Lieutenant Shishmarev set out on a repetition of Povalishin's probe of 1804. First, he sounded with a lead line, the brig remaining under sail lest he find better anchorage; then he attempted to make contact with the natives. But the two canoes at once pulled off towards the shore, where crowds watched. Shishmarev, too, approached the shore. Judging the distance from the longboat to the brig sufficient for their safety, several men plunged through the surf "laden with taro roots, yams, and banana fruits, which they readily exchanged for little pieces of iron hoops."[198] Then things turned sour. As in the past, the Easter Islanders' behaviour confused their visitors. Some shouted; others were silent. Some exchanged their foodstuffs for Russian iron peaceably; others were belligerent from the beginning and tried to steal some article of worth. The Russians' muskets were primed. Shishmarev lost his patience with one native, and to deter the others, as Kotzebue puts it coolly, "from being infected by his bad example, we fired some small shot at him, which, however, did not prevent them from practising their thievish arts."[199] "A deceit," adds Chamisso, "was severely punished."[200] The report of muskets was heard ashore, where by now at least a hundred islanders had gathered round the only solid shelter on the open rock. This structure was a watchtower called a *tupa*. Eight or nine feet high, it was made of unmortared stone and was used for spotting sea turtles. Fishermen's or watchmen's quarters were attached to or below the tower proper.[201] Things looked ominous when shortly afterwards a second boat was lowered from the *Riurik*.

LIEUTENANT SHISHMAREV'S LANDING AT HANGA-ROA,
28 MARCH 1816

We know the precise spot where *Riurik*'s people landed. The brig anchored where *Neva* had before her, with the sandy bay 45°SE and two large boulders hidden by the southern point. The remains of the *tupa*

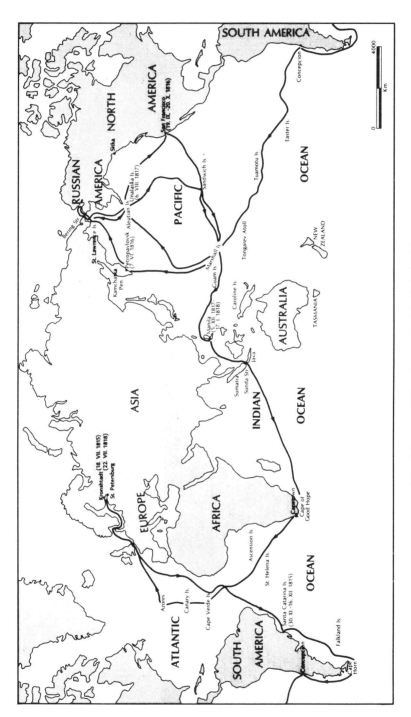

Map 4 Voyage of Kotzebue on the *Riurik*, 1815-18

drawn by Choris still stand today. Less easily determined is the mood in which the two well-armed Russian parties rowed for shore. Did they think the recent gunfire would simply be forgotten by their hosts? Certainly not. And yet they looked for friendly barter. Here is Kotzebue:

> As it was my intention to land, I had two boats manned for the purpose, and we left the *Riurik,* seventeen in number, at three o'clock in the afternoon. A great number of savages had assembled on the beach; they cried and capered, and made the most singular motions, and seemed to await our arrival with impatience; but as they had chosen for their rendezvous the only place where the surf would permit our landing, we could not venture to leave our boats before they had made room, which they could in no wise be persuaded to do. Amidst laughing and joking, they obliged us to put off from the shore, and even pursued us in the water; but this did not seem dangerous as they were all unarmed. We had scarcely left the shore when hundreds swam round our boats, who exchanged banana fruits and sugar cane for old iron; at the same time making an intolerable noise.[202]

They were, adds Chamisso, "friendly, noisy, impatient, and disorderly." As the Russian boats approached and they felt themselves increasingly threatened, "everyone ran about. Signs of peace, threats, stone throwing, shots, testimonies of friendship, were all exchanged."[203] In short, a chaos of confused and contradictory approaches. Only one thing was quite plain: the Easter Islanders felt comfortable enough to barter if the boats remained offshore but would not permit a landing.

Kotzebue's evidence supports Lisianskii regarding the natives' superb knowledge of the island coast. They knew where visitors must land. Stretches of sea, identified by landmarks or particular stone images, were named and studied over generations.[204] Summer had ended when *Riurik* arrived at Hanga-roa, and most likely so had the local tunny fishing. The fishing nets with which *ature* (tunny-bait) and other little fish were caught were soon offered for Russian iron wares.[205] These nets were made of paper-mulberry fibre, the material the islanders used to make the ropes for hauling *moai* to their sites. They wanted knives more than anything else in exchange for nets or roots or fruit.

The Russians would not be dissuaded from landing. Despite the stones thrown at them by the spectators on or in front of the *tupa,* they opened fire once again, pulled hard, and reached the shore. Scrambling quickly over the rocks, they pointed their guns at those rushing to surround them and still emitting "awful shouts." It was clear that Kotzebue's people were unwelcome and the natives very tense: "They had painted their faces red, white, and black, which gave them a terrific appearance, danced with the most ridiculous motions and contortions of the body, making such a terrible noise that we were obliged to halloo in each other's ears to understand what we said. . . In order to disperse them, and to get some room, I had knives thrown among them; but notwithstanding this I felt a stone strike my hat. I again gave orders to fire, and this at length enabled me to get on shore."[206]

The Russians soon realized that the islanders were armed: stones lay everywhere and they were marvellously skilful marksmen. Seamen reeled from the blows and anger flared. The pointlessness of trying to establish trade with such men became apparent. Kotzebue planned retreat, but even that seemed dangerous. More musket fire gave the Russians a chance to scramble back to sea; imprecations, hissing balls, and well-aimed stones filled the air. To gain another few seconds, seamen flung more bits of iron-hoop behind them as they retreated.

Understandably, Kotzebue's comments on the islanders are terse. He was disgusted and bewildered. Although he correctly concluded that other Europeans had preceded him and committed acts of violence on the island, his remarks on, for example, an Eastern Polynesian version of the *haka* ("ridiculous motions and contortions of the body") compare most unfavourably with those of Simonov and Bellingshausen on the Maori wardance (1820). His final observations on the islanders' appearance were: "They are all tattooed; and those who are so over the whole body have the appearance of chiefs. We saw here the stuff made of the bark of trees which is manufactured on most of the South Sea Islands, for some of the men wore short cloaks of it; and the women, who stood at a great distance, were entirely wrapped in it."[207]

True, Kotzebue provides us with interesting information: that bark stuffs were abundant, that the body area tattooed seemed to reflect a social status, and that black and white as well as red colouring substances were painted on the face in order to terrify. (Beechey saw the same colours in 1826 and was reminded of European clowns.)[208] Still, the material is not very rich. By contrast, Chamisso says of his brief stay at Easter Island:

> The bluish broad-lined tattooing, which exactly follows the direction of the muscle, has a very pleasing effect on the brown ground of their skin. There seems to be no want of bast stuffs. White or yellow mantles of it are very general. Fresh wreathes of leaves are worn in their hair, which is cut at different lengths. Headdresses of black feathers are more rare; we observed several ornamental necklaces

which were adorned in the middle with a polished shell (*Patella*). We met with no inelegant, disfiguring ornaments. Some old men had their pierced and extended ear-lappets tied together, drawn again through the hole, and thus not very perceptible. The fore-teeth were frequently broken off ... We saw only a few women. They had painted their faces dark red, were without either beauty or grace, and seemed to be without consideration among the men.[209]

Though brief, these are the observations of a genuine savant. One must admire Chamisso's sharp sight and cool behaviour in an awkward situation. In his narrative there is no echo of alarm or stress. Suffice it here to make a few remarks about a passage that could serve as the basis for a chapter on the Easter Islanders' material and social culture in the early 1800s.

Chamisso saw the colourful results of *ti* stem and *poporo* juice mixed into deep blue charcoal and of turmeric-based dye. Also classical were the head ornaments: leaf wreathes and cock-feather headdresses, both brought to Easter Island from the Marquesas and seen by Kruzenshtern in 1804 at Taio-hae Bay on Nukuhiva. One such headdress remains in the Peter-the-Great Museum of Ethnography in Leningrad to this day.[210] Apparently, the custom of widely perforating ear lobes and inserting heavy ornaments was on the wane by 1816. Chamisso makes no mention of the ancient *rei-miro* (wooden crescent) or *tahonga* (wooden "heart"), symbols of wealth and status in the earliest post-contact times,[211] but the ornaments he observed were of traditional and even ancient style. The Dutch had seen with some contempt polished mother-of-pearl neck ornaments in 1722, and initially supposed them to be silver.[212] Like their predecessors, the Russians of 1816 saw certain young men whose skin tone was appreciably lighter than others'.[213] In Chamisso's view, the "situation of the islanders" had somewhat improved since Cook's visit. On the other hand, stone images had vanished and at least one European ship had spread alarm.

The Russians saw no evidence of want. They were offered an abundance of bananas, yams, sugar cane, and sweet potatoes, and they saw well-cultivated plots over the hills at Hanga-roa. La Pérouse's seeds seemed not to have prospered, nor were sheep or hogs or cattle to be seen. Indeed, flesh was much valued by the islanders. "A fowl was offered to us for a large knife, but was taken away again when we refused the bargain; a proof how much they value these animals, and how few they have of them."[214] Only those foodstuffs listed by Cook, La Pérouse, and Lisianskii were seen on the island; nor were the native houses different in any way. The only obvious difference in 1816 was that many statues had vanished or been broken, victims of the civil strife that raged on Easter Island in the first years of the century.

WITHDRAWAL AND REFLECTION, 1816–17

Riurik's two boats returned from shore laden with foodstuffs, artefacts, and not a few round stones flung at them. The Russians were frustrated and annoyed by their reception but, like La Pérouse, saw the pointlessness of revenge. No bones were broken, though severe bruises were sustained by two or three unlucky seamen. The brig was under sail by 7:00 PM.[215]

Choris added some touches to his view of Cook Bay while his memory was fresh, and made additions to his diary. The view was a particularly useful exercise for him, for he was soon depicting other Russian landings in the South Pacific: at "Rumiantsev Island" (Tikei in the Eastern Tuamotus) and Penrhyn or Tongareva in the Northern Cooks.[216] The text accompanying his excellent Easter Island view, which the Parisian lithographers Noël Ainé et Cie. did credit to when they were entrusted with it in 1821,[217] adds useful information to Chamisso's account. Most cultivated fields of Easter Island were divided from each other by straight walls (*clôtures en ligne droite*). The yellow colour was due to masses of flowers, not a crop; and the *Broussonetia papyrifera* of the island was relatively stunted (*ne s'élève qu'à la hauteur d'un arbrisseau*). Some Russians managed to take a few steps ashore and noted the exactness of La Pérouse's description. The islanders had dyed their cloaks various shades of yellow and orange. Only two females were spotted, one suckling a baby. A single club was seen (*un seul homme armé d'une massue*), despite earlier mariners' reports of other weaponry.

The reason for the islanders' hostility towards the *Riurik* was clarified at Honolulu, where the Russians spent three weeks later that year.[218] The informant was King Kamehameha I's English-born shipmaster, Alexander Adams. At the time of Kotzebue's visit to Oahu, Adams commanded the royal brig *Kahumanna* (ex-*Forester* of London).[219] He told the Russians about a call made at Easter Island by the New England schooner *Nancy* in 1805. (The correct year was 1808, but many of Adams's details were wrong.) The American captain, whose name Adams did not reveal, had been hunting seals at Mas Afuera Island to the west of Santiago, Chile, but was unsuccessful for want of crew. The captain had gone to Easter Island to abduct some men and women in order to take them to Mas Afuera to begin a private colony. *Nancy* sailed into Cook Bay: "The combat is said to have been bloody... and twelve men and ten women fell into the merciless hands of the Americans. Upon this, the poor creatures were carried on board, fettered for the first three days, and not released till they were out of sight of land. The first use they made of their liberty was that the men jumped overboard; and the women, who attempted to follow them, were prevented only by force."[220] The men dived when he tried to recapture them, and drowned; the women were taken to Mas Afuera. Adams himself had attempted unsuccessfully to land on Easter Island not long afterwards; the natives were furiously hostile. Nor had they welcomed Captain Winship of the trader *Albatross* when he had called "in 1809."

Adams's sometimes inaccurate account of the atrocity was further "modified" in third-hand Russian versions. Choris, for instance, gave the year of the onslaught as 1800, and the *Nancy*'s port as New London.[221] More recently, both Soviet and Western writers have supposed that Captain Adams committed the atrocity himself and for that reason did not give the raider's name to Kotzebue during their discussion of 13 December 1816.[222] The story the Russians heard at Honolulu shows how likely facts then were to be distorted by Pacific shipmasters and how Russo-American connections in the North Pacific basin were evolving in the early 1800s.[223] To illustrate the latter: the Easter Island raider of 1808 was Captain J. Crocker. His ship, *Nancy,* was old and worn—she had been sighted by Vancouver off Niihau in the Hawaiian Islands fourteen years before.[224] Crocker was hard-driving and ruthless. As captain of the *Hancock,* he had visited the Russian settlement of Sitka in May 1799, where his men mutinied.[225] He thought it best to limit his contact with the Russians and be gone, but his activities were all reported to Chief Manager Baranov. Five years later, he was again in Oceania, visiting Kosrae in the Carolines. His comments and his reckoning of its position were available to Russians long before Lütke took *Seniavin* there in 1827.[226] As for Adams, he and *Riurik*'s officers had mutual acquaintances at Sitka.

When it was published in 1821, Kotzebue's *Voyage of Discovery* informed the Russian public of an outrage perpetrated on Easter Island thirteen years before. It was "a crime that foreshadowed the fate awaiting the rest of the island's population half a century later."[227]

2

THE RUSSIAN TEXTS

GEORG HEINRICH LANGSDORF, 1804

Nothing further of note occurred until 24 March, when there arose a powerful NNW wind, which prevailed till the end of that month. It was on this day that, to our very great concern, we were separated from our companion on this voyage, the *Neva,* in a thick and persistent mist.[1] Captain von Krusenstern had earlier agreed with Captain Lisiansky that in the event of separation Easter Island should be our place of rendezvous.[2] The attention of our whole company was, accordingly, now bent towards that island; and, fetching out all the accounts of previous mariners by whom Easter Island had been visited, we studied them with diligence.[3] The result was that, after a while, we had provoked our curiosity and were extremely keen to see the island in question, to compare its present state with what others had seen. In particular, we wanted to find out if the gifts left for the natives there by the unfortunate La Pérouse had been cared for and preserved, so as to contribute to their comfort and happiness.[4] These presents had been goats, sheep, hogs, orange and lemon trees, cotton plants, Turkish corn,[5] and a quantity of seeds of different sorts. Unluckily for us, contrary winds joined together with other and very particular circumstances[6] to oblige Captain Krusenstern finally to give up his intention of calling there, even though we were now within five hundred sea miles of the place. The latest accounts we have of it are thus derived from the voyages of Captains Cook and Forster,[7] or from La Pérouse's venture. I cannot refrain here from taking note of a passage in a work describing the original discovery of this island. The passage illustrates, in the brightest tones, that propensity to the fabulous which was pervasive in accounts left by the explorers of those times.[8]

These savages do not go naked, but cover themselves in a variety of cotton cloth. The most remarkable thing about them is long ears, which they regard as a mark of beauty. Some individuals have apertures so large in the ears that a man's hand could easily be passed through. To this point, at least, my narrative will be believed, since it contains nothing very uncommon. But I must here add that these savages are of more than gigantic build, the men being twice as large and twice as tall as the very biggest people in our own land.[9] Most stand twelve feet high, so that, incredible though it may seem, we could easily have passed between their legs without stooping. These people were also, however, very well proportioned. Each might have been taken for a Hercules. The women were shorter than the men, standing no more than ten or eleven feet tall. I must suppose that most who read this will disbelieve what I assert and regard this as a poetical creation; but I do declare that I have written nothing more than the strict truth and further assert that, when these people are examined minutely, they will be found to be as I here describe: of a size and stature quite extraordinary.

Let us now refer to Captain Forster's testimony. He observes, "We did not find among these people a single one who could well be called tall, and they were extremely lean, too. The women are small and of slight build."[10] Such are the contrary accounts of different voyagers. It was a matter of great regret to us that we could not visit so interesting a place to examine the truth for ourselves. But we were now being carried daily into a warmer zone, by very turbulent winds.[11]

NIKOLAI I. KOROBITSYN, APRIL 1804

On the night of 12 March,[12] the wind being high but the skies cloudy, we were separated from *Nadezhda;* at dawn next day, we could not even spot her on the horizon. Until the 14th we tacked in various directions in an effort to find her.[13] Even though the horizon had cleared by that day, however, we could not sight *Nadezhda.* It was therefore decided to set a course northwest towards the Pacific or South Sea Islands, and we in fact held that course until 4 April.

At 10:00 AM that morning, we caught sight of Easter Island thirty-five Italian miles off to the NNW. At 3:00 PM that same day, we fired a single round from each of our guns in order to clean them out. Then, as a precautionary measure, we reloaded them all with cannonballs.[15] We hove to at 9:00 PM, being within about five miles of Easter Island.[16]

We tacked about near and around the island from the 5th to the 9th of

April, waiting for *Nadezhda*. In the course of this five-day period of tacking near Easter Island, we saw crowds of natives assembled on the shores and running along in an effort to keep abreast of our ship. We could see quite plainly that none of them wore clothing.[17]

At 1:00 PM on the afternoon of 9 April, we sent a launch ashore with Lieutenant Povalishin, our second mate, and four armed seamen, to investigate the layout of the coast and to leave a few gifts behind for the islanders, as a token of this Russian visit.[18] When Lieutenant Povalishin came with his launch to within one and a half cable-lengths of the shore, however, he could see absolutely no way of effecting a landing on account of the rocky bottom and powerful surf. And so, not reaching the actual shoreline, he was obliged to let go a drag hook. By then, a crowd of perhaps five hundred natives had gathered right by the shore and were making all manner of gestures to try to induce the party in our launch to land.[19] But, for the reasons already given, the Russians were unable to satisfy the islanders' desire. Lieutenant Povalishin now made signs to the islanders that they should not fear to swim out to the boat, and simultaneously waved so they could see various presents that he had brought for them. As soon as the natives caught sight of these, they plunged into the sea and about twenty of them swam through the surf and up to the launch.[20] Not one came out empty-handed: every man carried island produce with him—bananas, plantains,[21] sugar cane, potatoes,[22] and yam roots. They would not surrender these to the Russians, though, till they themselves had been handed such gifts as knives, scissors, little mirrors, printed linen kerchiefs, or chain lockets made of Russian coins.[23] They liked the knives best of all and, having secured one, would return excitedly for another. The last of the islanders to remain received, in addition to such gifts from Lieutenant Povalishin, a bottle with a white resin stopper containing a note for the information of *Nadezhda,* in case she should put in a later appearance. One must doubt, however, if that bottle stayed intact in the islanders' hands, or could have done so until such time as the ship might have arrived. Being unacquainted with their language, we of course had no way of explaining to them except by signs exactly what we wanted, that is, that they were expected to keep the bottle and surrender it to the *Nadezhda*. Povalishin completed his distribution of presents and returned on board ship at 2:00 PM.

According to Lieutenant Povalishin's report on the outward appearance of these islanders, all who swam out to the ship's launch were of middling stature, well built, and of sound constitution.[24] They differed very little from Europeans in complexion and skin tones, but because they went naked, they had sunburnt bodies of a rather red hue.[25] Scars were incised on their faces and coloured with blue pigment. Their hair, worn in the manner of a *toupée,* was cut a little in front and dark blond. In general, though, there seems to be nothing very remarkable about their build or about any part of their body. And yet we read in Captain Cook's account of these people that they have extraordinarily large ear lobes, reaching down to the shoulders. This turned out to be quite untrue, for what we saw was at complete variance with such a description.[26] As for their countenance, all uncivilized peoples have severe ones.

These natives' clothing consists of merely two pieces of papyrus hanging from a belt or a grass rope front and back, to cover the private parts.[27] They possess no other garments,[28] nor means for adorning themselves. As for the houses or, more accurately, the huts of these tribes, they are made of reeds and somewhat resemble large upturned boats. They are one hundred feet or more long, between fifteen and twenty feet in breadth, and no more than twelve feet high. The entrances or doorways to these huts are at the edge of the elevation on which they stand and certainly not very large, being from three to four feet high.[29] Each of these huts houses ten or twenty families and offers protection to the inhabitants against storms, rain, and the sun's heat.[30] As we were unable to land on the island, it is impossible to give a detailed description of these natives' character, manners, or customs.

Easter Island is very pleasantly situated, of medium elevation, and produces a good impression on the voyager.[31] No plants but banana trees and plantain bushes were to be seen, though.[32] Along the coast, on small elevations,[33] we spotted a considerable number of stone monuments of human likeness, carved from the waist and wearing top hats one quarter their own height.[34] We could see nothing else very remarkable about this island. Cattle are not raised there.[35] It has a circumference of about thirty Italian miles but lacks bays or roadsteads where a ship might conveniently anchor. Nor is there any suitable spot where rowed boats might beach, on account of the very rocky bottom. According to our astronomical observations, this island lies in latitude 27°S, longitude 109°30'W.[36] We left Easter Island at 6:00 PM on the afternoon of the 9th of April, setting a course for the Marquesas Islands and using the NE trade wind.

ARCHPRIEST GEDEON

From 1 March on, our voyage continued quietly until the 12th. On that day, however, a thick mist separated us from the *Nadezhda,* keeping us apart right till the Marquesas Islands. On 4 April, at 11:00 AM, we spotted Easter Island at a distance from us of thirty Italian miles. In view of the proximity of the shore, we lay to all that night. Then we spent four days sailing round the island, waiting for *Nadezhda.*

Shores covered by a pleasant verdure, well laid out plantations of banana and sugar cane not far from native dwellings, a considerable crowd of people, and other things induced feelings of great delight in us—especially after our seventy-day sea crossing.[37] But it was dangerous to drop anchor here, for lack of a good harbour, and so like modern Tantaluses we were forced to desire and to feast only with our eyes on what we could not have. Not one of the natives came out to our ship. This was, of course, for want of craft.[38]

Having approached the island's southern tip on 9 April and moved to within three *versts*[39] of the shore, we backed the top mainsail and sent Lieutenant and Chevalier Povalishin ashore in the yawl with five armed men. He gave the natives various gifts and also a sealed bottle containing a note to be handed to the ship *Nadezhda* when she should reach the island. One hour later, Lieutenant Povalishin returned, bringing with him a few potatoes, sweet potatoes, yams, bananas, and sugar cane sticks that he had acquired from the islanders in exchange for the proffered gifts.[40] The good quality of the former foodstuffs and the succulence of the latter demonstrated the soil's fertility.

Where Lieutenant Povalishin put in, the island is elevated, with several high hills in the interior from whose summits the land slopes with an even protuberance towards the sea. There are no woods. The natives are naked and swarthy but well shaped and even stout in the body. They have black hair. Some have long ears, others have designs on the body; others again have their faces smeared with paint. Not far from the shore in many places of the island stand those high stone monuments which Mr. La Pérouse and Mr. Delangle, his comrade and fellow-traveller, considered to be ancient memorials to the dead because they had seen around them many human bones.[41] Those celebrated mariners landed on this island in April 1786.

At 6:00 PM, we set a course for the Marquesas Islands.

IURII F. LISIANSKII, 1812 TEXT

16 April.   Since we had begun to meet with squalls right from midnight and the weather seemed changeable, I hove to at 3:00 AM and so remained until 7:00 AM. We then got under way again even though the horizon was covered with clouds. And at 11:00 AM we caught sight of Easter Island, lying directly facing us.[42] Taking a course from the south to northwest, *Neva* came up to the eastern extremity of the island at about 5:00 PM. No sooner had we approached the first rock among those that lie by the island's southern tip than squalls sprang up from the north and the shores were lost in gloom.[43] Therefore, having turned away eastwards, we reefed up for the night. Even before we had reached Easter Island, we had seen quantities of small birds, resembling doves, only a little smaller.[44] We had deduced from this that we must be near the island.

17 April.   When morning came, we saw the coast twelve miles to our west. At 8:00 AM, with a northwesterly wind, we moved towards the island's southern extremity, where two rocks lie.[45] One of these is of very remarkable appearance and, from afar, resembles a ship with her main topgallant set: our navigator[46] took it for the ship *Nadezhda*. Passing these rocks, we met numerous strands of grass.

From the eastern side, Easter Island struck me as very pleasant. It is covered with verdure in many places. We saw several rows[47] of banana trees, skilfully planted out, and bushes beside which there had to be dwellings, for we noted smoke there this morning as we had the previous evening.[48] Very nearly right in the centre of the eastern shore stand two high black statues, one of which seemed twice as tall as the other.[49] In my opinion, they comprise a single monument, for they stand very near each other and both are surrounded by one palisade.[50]

The southern part of the island is extremely craggy and made of a rock that, from a distance, resembles slate lying in horizontal strata. Verdure was visible at the top of a cliff face. Getting round the island's southern point, I drifted westward till noon, then approached the west coast to within three miles. From this position, the anchorage revealed itself to me, with a heavy surf on the shore beyond.[51] There too we observed a few trees and four black idols, of which three were high but the fourth seemed broken off halfway up. These idols stand right by the shoreline and bear a great resemblance to the monuments described in La Pérouse's *Voyage*.[52] I would have anchored on this day had I not feared westerly winds that make this situation a very risky one. A light breeze was blowing by now from NNW, but rain clouds would sometimes gather and it seemed to me, on this basis, that the weather was very unstable.

Not finding our consort here, I decided to wait here for a few days and meanwhile to occupy myself with a survey of the shores, generally becoming better acquainted with this place which certainly merits attention. To that end, I twice worked back to the eastern part of the island. We passed along it at a distance of some five kilometres, weathering the eastern point at about midday. But then the clouds that had started to appear since early morning finally broke, and rain poured down, with a variable wind. Because I did not want to lose my last bearings, I moved some seven miles offshore and there hove to.

18 April.   The middle of the eastern part of Easter Island is lower than its extremities.[53] Here and there, it is covered with plants, by which stand native dwellings. So close to the shore were we that the people who had gathered out of curiosity were quite plainly visible. Some of them ran along the shore after us, but others climbed up onto rock piles.[54] At about nine o'clock, smoke appeared from many places, and I concluded that the islanders prepare a meal for themselves at this hour.

The cliff is surmounted by five monuments on this side. We had observed the first one as soon as we rounded the island's southern point. It consists of four statues. The second group is a little further on and consists of three idols. A third follows, that same which we had seen the evening before. The fourth and fifth stand nearer to the eastern cape.[55] By the last two groups there are far more dwellings than elsewhere and the foot of a hill is encircled by plants. There, indeed, we were presented with the spectacle of a very extensive plantation of what looked like bananas, and other plantings of which some appeared to be sugar cane.[56] Though the wind was blowing from the NW, quite a heavy surf still broke along the shore. I observed only one sandy spot, but even that was strewn about with so many rocks that it could not serve as an anchorage or landing point. Many stones lay right along the shore: we took some of them for sitting people. In other places these stones formed large piles, on the top of which something white was visible. No doubt, they had been heaped up by the natives on purpose and have some significance.[57] The people themselves seemed to be naked and of dark colouring. As for animals, we saw not a single one.

Today a quantity of flying fish appeared around our ship. Up to now, I have seen only three varieties of sea bird: a tropical one, the wild species that I mentioned earlier, and a black one that resembled the second both in appearance and in flight but was a shade bigger.[58]

When the sun set, a perfect calm ensued, which obliged us to remain for the night nine miles to the north of the east cape.

19 April.   At dawn a gentle southerly wind sprang up, with a large southwesterly swell. Sighting the shores of the island, we set our course along the northern one.[59] It was my intention to pass along it as closely as we had along the eastern coast; but the faint wind and calms, accompanied by rains, did not permit me to do so. However, our greatest distance from the shore was not more than five miles and we could closely examine not only the capes and other features that comprise the principal object of voyagers' descriptions, but also plantations and dwellings. This portion of Easter Island is less heavily populated than is the eastern part.[60]

Between the northern and eastern capes we noted four monuments, of which the first stood in the centre and consisted of a single statue; the second and third were composed of two statues each, and the fourth of three. On approaching these monuments, we saw that the natives had laid fires in various places, which continued to burn till evening. Perhaps this was an invitation to us to come to the shore. Finding no suitable place to anchor, however, I was pursuing my course to westward.[61]

Meanwhile, our boat was sent off to make observations of the current. No current was found, even though we were constantly encountering strands of floating grass. I ordered some of these to be fished up and found that one was overgrown with coral, another had little pieces of red coral and shells by its root, and a third, broken off at the middle, was full of sparks which upon close examination proved to be tiny living creatures.[62]

20 April. The night was rainy. The weather continuing bad, I was not disposed to stand at anchor this day, deciding rather to move past the west shore of the island. Shortly after noon, there was a calm, but at 3:00 PM a light breeze sprang up, with the aid of which the ship made two knots. Then darkness fell. At about 6:00 I moved to the south, and stayed there till the following morning. A persistent swell from the SW produced considerable agitation of the water all along the island's west coast, where we observed numerous fires and various plants. It must be concluded that this part of the island is just as heavily populated as the eastern one. Rain fell all night, with variable winds from the north and south.

21 April. As soon as the sun rose, we steered towards the shore, but gusty winds and the dark clouds that we had so often met with here obliged us twice to heave to before 8:00 AM. At about 9:00, though, the sky cleared and the ship moved up to Cook Bay.[63] Still, the wind was from the SW and I could not decide to drop anchor here. But, in order not to leave this island without having left *some* sign for the *Nadezhda,* in the event of her arriving after us, I sent off Lieutenant Povalishin in the boat. Taking with him a certain number of knives, some printed linen,[64] some bottles, and other things, he could distribute them all among the islanders, at the same time attempting to look over the position and measure the depth of water without actually landing. The boat returned to the ship at 2:00 PM with a few bananas, sweet potatoes, yams, and some sugar cane. Having drawn level with the east cape again, we set a course for the Marquesas Islands.

Description of Easter Island

Easter Island was discovered by the Dutch navigator Roggeveen in the year 1722. I do not propose to enter into the details of the history of its discovery, since a great deal has already been written about it. I here adduce only those things that I myself witnessed.[65]

We sighted the island when more than forty miles off, even though the horizon was not completely clear. It would seem that in clear weather it would be possible to sight it from sixty miles away. The first thing we saw was a hill with a hillock to its right, away to WNW.[66] On covering ten miles, we lost the hillock from view but saw two small elevations to the left, which in due course fused with the aforementioned hill. Having sailed fairly close right round this island, I nowhere found a place where a ship could stand at anchor. The shores are steep and craggy everywhere except where there are two little bays on the east side of the island, by the southern point, and on the northern side before one reaches the northern cape.[67]

The so-called Cook Bay, whither my boat was sent off, is apparently the best place for a landing; but even that place is dangerous in westerly and southwesterly winds. For the swell is then so heavy that one cannot place much trust in anchors, especially right by the shore itself. When one and a quarter miles out from the surf, we found a depth of 60 *sazhen,* hard stone bottom.[68] When one and a half cables[69] offshore, Povalishin found a depth of 10 *sazhen;* when three cable-lengths out, he found a depth of 16 *sazhen;* when four cables out,[70] he measured a depth of 24 *sazhen.*[71] As La Pérouse writes that one can drop anchor in 24 *sazhen* of water, it follows that this he did when five cables' length[72] from the shore. One can boldly approach this bay from any direction, with regard only to the wind; nor can one mistake the place of anchorage, since there is a little sandy beach opposite it but everywhere else, from the northern cape to the southern,[73] it is rocky.

The natives of this island are not so poor as they are said to be by the mariners who preceded us there. If they lack cattle, which I cannot positively affirm to be the case, not having been ashore there, they are at least well supplied with many nourishing and nutritious plants. And though their dwellings cannot compare with Europeans', still they are fairly good. In appearance, these dwellings resemble elongated barrows or boats turned upside down. Some houses stand alone, others in twos or threes. No windows were visible to us, but the doors are made in the middle of the structure and are small and conical. Around each dwelling is a field, planted with bananas and sugar cane. Along the shores are a quantity of statues, faithfully depicted in La Pérouse's *Voyage.* Carved from stone, they offer a very crude representation of a human head with a covering of cylindrical shape. In addition, we noted many heaps of stones with small blackish or white spots on the top. It seems that they also serve in place of some sort of monument.[74]

According to our observations, the natives light fires always at about 9:00 PM. One may conclude that at this time they prepare food for themselves outside their houses and also take a meal. It is extraordinary that the people of Easter Island should—as many mariners relate—lack water, since they can furnish themselves with it quite easily during the rains, which are frequent throughout the year.[75] In the West Indies there are many islands with neither rivers nor springs. Yet their inhabitants, as I myself witnessed,[76] dig large pits in the ground and there collect sufficient rain water in the winter to supply their needs without difficulty for the rest of the year. La Pérouse assures us that the natives of Easter Island, which we describe, are accustomed to drink sea water and so do not trouble about obtaining fresh water.[77]

On drawing near to Cook Bay, we caught sight of many islanders. Having spotted our boat, they all immediately rushed to a small sandy spit and awaited its approach with the utmost impatience, expressing their joy with yells and making signs to show the best place to land. Seeing that the boat had stopped, some thirty men at once threw themselves into the water and swam out to it, regardless of the high surf. Povalishin several times repeated the word *tio,* which means "friend" in their language,[78] then indicated that they should swim right up to his boat, but one man at a time and not all together. First of all, he presented a bottle containing a letter from me to Kruzenshtern, explaining to the natives by signs that they should show it to another ship like ours, when she approached the island. Then he presented each man with five-kopek pieces on little chains, which the islanders instantly put round their necks, also with pieces of linen, mustard bottles with little pieces of wood tied to them, on which was written the word "Neva," and some knives. These last presents were far more welcome to the natives than all the other articles.[79] I much regretted that I had not sent them more, especially when I later learned that an old man of perhaps sixty had swum out to the boat and, having with him a little grass bag full of cooked sweet potato, earnestly requested a knife in exchange. Still, having received some of the kopeks that I had ordered threaded on wire like earrings, and some pieces of linen, he had been perfectly content. He had returned to shore, leaving the seamen not only some sugar cane and the bag of potato, but even the mat woven from reeds on which, in place of a craft, he had reached our boat. Perhaps the old man had had occasion to meet Europeans more than once in his lifetime. He alone, at all events, had long hair and wore a small, dark grey beard. All the rest were cropped, dark-haired, and beardless.[80] Every man had a clump of reeds with which, it seemed, he could support himself in the water. Our seamen drew their attention to the *Neva* by gestures, but the natives merely expressed their great regret that they could not go out so far. From this fact, as from the use of clumps of reed and mats for swimming, it would seem to follow that those craft mentioned by La Pérouse[81] were now no longer in use on Easter Island.

Povalishin thinks that there were about five hundred persons on the shore at this time, including some little children. He was so busy with his guests swimming out to the boat that he did not manage to determine if these were all men ashore, or whether women too were of their number. Many of the natives were covered from neck to knees by some sort of cloak, and others held pieces of white or motley cloth the size of an ordinary kerchief, which they constantly waved.[82] According to Povalishin and all who were with him, the islanders resembled Southern Europeans, sunburnt from exposure, in their dark orange face and skin tones. Narrow lines had been drawn on their face, nose, neck, and arms. Their ears were of ordinary size, their bodily build was sound, and they were occasionally as tall as six feet.[83] The boat stood so near the shore that our people were quite able to examine a few dwellings and the stones from which the closest monuments or statues had been formed. According to Povalishin, the latter were about thirteen feet in height. One quarter of the total was accounted for by the cylinder that is placed on the statues' heads.[84]

I cannot give an accurate judgment of these islanders' manufactures, but certainly the little bag and the mat given to Povalishin by the old man merit some attention. The former is fifteen inches long and very skilfully woven from grasses; the latter is about 4¾ feet long and 15½ inches wide.[85] In the centre of the mat are placed sugar cane stems woven round with rushes. The lace with which the mat has been reinforced, and of which the little bag's handles are formed, although also of grass, is in no way inferior in point of neatness to flax. Indeed, from the outset we mistook it for flaxen cord.[86]

Cook places Easter Island in latitude 27°06′S, longitude 109°46′W. By my reckonings, however, its centre lies in 27°09′23″S, longitude 109°25′20″W.[87] The latitude of the southern cape seemed to us 27°13′24″, and the longitude 109°30′41″W. Nor are we in agreement with Cook with regard to the population of this island. I myself did not go ashore, but let us bear in mind that 500 persons, having spotted our ship, immediately assembled from the locality. Should we not conclude that the same might have occurred at the other settlements on the isle? Besides, when circumnavigating the island we counted twenty-three houses that stood near the shores. Supposing that this was only half of the total number of structures, and that some forty people live in each, one reaches the number 1,840 persons. So in my view there must be at the very least one and a half thousand natives on Easter Island.[88]

Apart from small trees growing sparsely here and there, we saw no timber but banana trees, with which or with other sorts of edible plant, I estimate, one twentieth part of the island's area has been planted. All other places, even the summits of the hills, are covered with a low-growing grass and offer a most attractive sight from the sea. During our passage round the island, several azimuth bearings were taken which, by the readings of two different compasses,[89] indicated a mean variation of the magnetic needle of 6°12′00′′E.

Early in the morning of the next day, we were twelve miles to the eastward of the shore;[90] and at eight, with the wind at northwest, we approached the southern point, which is remarkable for two large rocks, one of which so strikingly resembles a ship with her main topgallant sail set[91] that, upon first perceiving it, one of my people mistook it for *Nadejda*.

The eastern part of Easter Island is very pleasant. It is covered with verdure, and many spots of it appeared to be planted with bananas. Towards the middle stood two large black statues,[92] one twice the size of the other; yet it appeared as if both were intended to form but one monument, as they were contiguous to each other and enclosed within the same mound. The south side of the island is craggy and steep, composed of a stone, resembling slate or limestone, lying in horizontal strata, the upper surface covered with grass.[93]

After getting round the south point, I steered towards the west side of the island; and when at the distance of about three miles, I recognized Cook's Bay, against the shores of which a heavy swell broke. Not far from the beach we observed four statues, three of which were very tall; the other appeared to have been broken down, so as to have lost half its height.[94] They bore a great resemblance to the monuments described by La Pérouse, in the voyage in which this navigator so unfortunately perished.[95]

I had intended at first to anchor in Cook's Bay; but the weather being unsettled, I was apprehensive of westerly winds, which would have rendered it very unsafe. As we had seen nothing of the *Nadejda* since our separation, I resolved to wait at this island a few days, in the hope of her rejoining us, and to take a slight survey of the place.[96] Accordingly, on the 18th, we again ranged along the eastern side of the island, and found it as pleasant as it appeared the day before.[97] The middle of it is much lower than its extremities; and a few huts are dispersed here and there amongst the fruit trees, of which, however, there were no great plenty. We kept so near the coast that we could easily distinguish the natives following the ship along the beach. They were entirely naked, and of a dark copper colour. In coasting it this time, we observed five monuments. The first, which consisted of four statues, presented itself to view as soon as we had passed the south end of the island;[98] the second had three; the third was the one we had seen the day before; and at no great distance from the eastern point stood the fourth and fifth. The neighbourhood of the two last-mentioned monuments contained a greater number of habitations and seemed better cultivated than any other spot we had yet seen.[99] We also observed numerous heaps of stone, covered with something white at the top; respecting which I could form no satisfactory conjecture.[100]

Though the wind was at northwest, the surf broke rather heavily against the shore, along the whole extent of which I could not discover a single anchorage. At sunset the wind died away, and left us nine miles to the northward of the east point. During the day, we were surrounded by flying fish[101] and different sea birds.

On the 19th we had light breezes and a heavy swell from the southwest. At daylight we took our course along the northern shore. I at first proposed passing it as near as possible, but was prevented doing so by the frequent calms and rain; the ship, however, was never further distant than five miles, so that we could clearly distinguish all the points and remarkable places. This side of the island appeared to be but thinly inhabited. I saw four monuments: the first of which consisted of one statue only;[102] the second and third of two each; and the fourth of three. On our approaching nearer, fires were lighted in different places by the inhabitants, and were kept burning till sunset. We supposed these to be signals of invitation on shore;[102] but as no good landing place was found, I continued lying to westward. In the meantime my jolly boat, which had been despatched to try the current, returned, but discovered nothing worthy of remark.

On the 20th the weather was so unsettled that I could not prosecute my survey along the northern side of the island, and therefore attempted that of the west, though with no greater success, from being becalmed.

The next morning the weather was so squally that I could not reach Cook's Bay till eight o'clock. I wished to have dropped anchor there, but the heavy southwest swell prevented me. Determined, however, to leave some indication on the island by which the *Nadejda*, in case of her touching there, might trace us, I despatched Lieutenant Powalishin in the jolly boat, with knives, small pieces of iron,[104] empty bottles, and some printed linens. His orders were to go as near the shore as the surf would permit, and distribute the abovementioned articles to the natives who, without doubt, would swim off to him. At the same time, I recommended him to examine the bay and try the soundings, but without attempting to land.[105] At two in the afternoon he returned, and brought some plantains, bananas, sweet potatoes, yams, and sugar cane.[106] Everything being thus executed according to my wish, I only waited to get another view of the north side of the island; and, having succeeded in this, at six o'clock we set sail for the Marquesas, with the satisfaction of having surveyed one of the most curious spots in the world.[107]

It appeared to me that the inhabitants of this island are not so poor in provisions as former navigators have asserted them to be. If they have no animals, as is said,[108] they are nevertheless plentifully supplied with substitutes, which, if not so substantial, are at least equally nourishing. Their houses, though greatly inferior to ours, appear to be sufficiently commodious for a people living in a state of nature; they resemble, in form, our longboats turned upside down. Some of them stand separately, and others two or three together. The door was of a conical form; but I did not observe any windows. Every house was planted round with bananas and sugar canes.[109]

The shore is encompassed by monuments,[110] very correctly described by La Pérouse.[111] They are built of stone, with a rude representation, on the top of each figure, of a human head surmounted with a cylinder.

From the many fires, regularly lighted about nine o'clock, it may be inferred that victuals are prepared here in the open air,[112] and that nine o'clock is the accustomed hour for a general meal.

That the inhabitants of this island should have no fresh water, as is related by some navigators,[113] is to me a matter of surprise; because, during the rainy season, they might easily supply themselves with it in tanks, so common throughout the West India islands: but, if it be true, as La Pérouse informs us, that they drink sea water, like the Albatrosses of Cape Horn,[114] they have no need of this article.

When lying to, near Cook's Bay, we saw a great number of people who, on perceiving our boat, swam off to meet it, expressing their joy with a loud noise, and pointing out with their hands the best place for landing. Finding, however, that the boat did not intend to land, thirty of them forced themselves through a very heavy surf, and joined it. Mr. Powalishin uttered, repeatedly, the word *teeo* (friend), and made signs that they should come to him, one at a time. To the first of his visitors he gave a sealed bottle, with a letter in it to Captain Kruzenstern, requesting, by signs, that it might be delivered to a ship as large as ours, if such should arrive there.[115] Afterwards he distributed among them knives, Russian copper money, strung upon wire, to be worn round the neck, some pieces of printed linen, and lastly several mustard bottles, with small pieces of wood fastened to them, upon which the name of our ship was written. The knives were received with great eagerness by the islanders;[116] and I was very sorry that I sent so few, as an old islander of sixty, who came after the rest and presented Mr. Powalishin with a bag made of grass filled with sweet potatoes, solicited one in the most earnest manner: there were, however, none left, and he only received some copper earrings and a few other trifles; but with these the poor old man was so satisfied, that he left with Mr. Powalishin all he had, including the rush-mat, which he used in support for swimming.

To judge from the behaviour of this man, he must have seen Europeans before.[117] He was the only one who had long hair on the head, and a bushy brown beard; the rest were all cropped and beardless. When they were desired to go to the ship, they expressed by signs that it was too far; which proves, as also do the rush-mats, which every one had to assist him in swimming,[118] that the boats seen by La Pérouse do not at present exist on the island.[119]

Lieutenant Powalishin thinks that there were about five hundred persons on shore near him, including children. Being very busy with his visitors, he did not observe if there were any women amongst them; but he saw that many of them had a kind of short cloak, or piece of cloth, suspended from the shoulders and scarcely covering the thighs.[120] Amongst the crowd were some who constantly waved square pieces of white and striped cloth, of the size of a pocket handkerchief. From what he and all who were with him in the boat observed, it appears that these islanders are stoutly built and tall, some of them being six feet, and of a colour resembling a sunburnt European. Those that swam to him had their faces and hands tattooed, which was all that was remarkable in their appearance.

From the description which Mr. Powalishin gave me of what he saw, I know not how to reconcile myself to the tremendous large ears mentioned by Mr. Forster, who represents them as hanging down upon the shoulders and having holes perforated in them through which five fingers may be thrust.[121] Mr. Powalishin assured me that this was not the case with those of the islanders who visited him, whose ears were no longer than ours. If, therefore, any of this long-eared race still remained on the island, they did not, in this instance, make their appearance; probably, however, the fashion of expanding the ears here is now at an end.[122]

Our boat was so near the shore that the houses and monuments of the bay were distinctly seen. The monuments were built of stone and appeared to be about thirteen feet high, a fourth part of which height was taken up by the cylinder placed on the head of each figure.[123]

I cannot well judge of the handicraft of these islanders; but the bag and mat of the old man are deserving of notice. The first, which was fifteen inches long and ten wide, was made of hard grass in a very masterly manner. The second, which was four and a half feet long and fifteen inches and a half broad, consisted of sugar cane platted over with rushes; and, in point of workmanship, was scarcely inferior to anything of the kind made in Europe.[124]

Captain Cook places Easter Island in latitude 27°5′36″S and longitude 109°46′20″W; but, by my observations, the middle of it proved to be 27°9′23′′S and 109°25′20′′W. On the 13th and 15th of the present month,[125] I took thirty lunar distances, and brought the calculation by our chronometers to the time of our making land. I know not how to account for this difference of latitude, unless by supposing that this celebrated navigator calculated his to some point lying to the northward of the middle of the island.[126] His estimate also of the population of the island, which he says is from six to seven hundred,[127] appears to me a little strange. When I consider the number of persons that assembled in the bay on the approach of our boat, and the many habitations which I observed round the coast, I think I may safely assert that the island contains at least fifteen hundred inhabitants.[128]

During our stay here, we found the variation of the compass to be 6°12′E.[129]

ADELBERT VON CHAMISSO, 1821

Easter Island rises majestically out of the waves in the shape of a triangle, swelling into pyramidical mountains. In miniature, it represents the grand, regular lines of O-Waihi [Hawaii]. Everywhere it appeared to us covered with the brightest green. Even on the steepest slopes of the hills, the ground was divided into regular fields,[130] distinguished by assorted lively hues; and many were full of yellow blossoms.[131] We gazed in wonder at this volcanic earth, strewn with stone, which is so celebrated for its want of wood and water.[132]

We believe that on the south coast we made out, through telescopes, some of those colossal structures that have occasioned so much amazement. In Cook's Bay on the west coast, however, where we stood at anchor, those busts which once distinguished the landing-place and which Lisianskoy had observed, were no longer to be found.[133]

Two canoes (we saw only three in all on the island), each with a crew of three men, came out with signs of welcome but did not venture too close to the ship. Many natives swam round our boat, which was put off to sound the water, and began to barter with it.[134] The deceitfulness of one of these traders was severely punished.[135] With a view to making a landing, we next put another boat off. A large crowd awaited us ashore, peaceable, joyous, shouting, impatient, childlike, and, finally, disorderly. It is not for us to decide, with La Pérouse, if these childish people are deserving of pity or if they are in fact more disorderly than their brethren.[136] It is certain, however, that this circumstance does render communication with them the more difficult. We approached the strand. Everyone ran about, yelling and rejoicing: and marks of peace, threats,

stone throwing, and shots,[137] and more testimonies of amity were exchanged. Finally, the swimmers ventured to come out to us in numbers,
barter began and was conducted with correctness. All of them, repeating
the cry of *Hoë! Hoë!*, sought knives or iron, for which they offered us in
exchange fruit, roots, or very neat fishing nets.[138] We went ashore for a
moment.

These people, who had been represented as so ugly, seemed to us of attractive countenance and pleasant and expressive physiognomy, with
well-built, slender, and sound physique; nor did their old age appear to be
accompanied by illness.The eye of the artist rejoiced to gaze upon a more
beautiful nature than the bathing places of Europe, which had been his
only school, had afforded him.[139] The bluish broad-lined tattooing, exactly
following the direction of the muscle,[140] has a most pleasing effect against
the brown background of their skin. There would seem to be no want of
bast material. White or yellow cloaks of it are quite general.[141] Fresh
wreathes of leaves were worn in their hair, which was cut longer or
shorter. Headdresses of black feathers are rarer. We observed a few
neatly made necklaces embellished at the centre by a polished shell
(*Patella*).[142] We encountered no unattractive, disfiguring ornaments. The
pierced and extended earlobes of certain old men had been tied together,
then drawn back through the aperture, so they were not greatly in evidence.[143] Front teeth were often broken off. Some young men struck us by
the far lighter colour of their skin.[144] We saw only a few women, and these
had their faces painted dark red,[145] lacked grace and beauty, and moreover
appeared to enjoy no consideration among the men. One of these women
had an infant at the breast. We restrain ourselves from drawing any conclusion, on this basis, regarding the proportion of representatives of the
two sexes.[146]

If we compare the reports of Cook, La Pérouse, and Lisianskoy with
our own experience, we are brought to the supposition that the Easter Island population has increased and that the islanders' situation has improved. But we were unable to determine whether or not the generous intent of the philanthropic Louis xvi, who sent these natives our domestic
animals, useful plants, and fruit trees with La Pérouse, has been successfully realized. We must doubt it, for we saw only the products indicated
in Cook: bananas, sugar cane, roots, and very small hens.[147]

As we weighed anchor in the evening, life-giving clouds rested on the
island's heights.

We have since learned the probable reason for the doubtful reception
we received at Easter Island, and we have had reason to blush for ourselves who call these people savages.[148]

JOHANN FRIEDRICH ESCHSCHOLTZ

On Easter Island, we could not see anywhere along the west coast any of those numerous statues described by all previous voyagers who had visited the place.[149] Only one pedestal seemed to remain.[150] On the southeastern shore we saw four black upright blocks which, though the sighting was from afar, must be supposed to have been statues.[151] Of the pierced and stretched ear lobes, which were at one time the common fashion here, we saw only a single instance, on an old islander.[152] The stone on that part of the shore where we landed was an ancient brown lava.[153] The tattooing of the face consisted mostly of a single stripe, running all round, near which were a number of round spots at regular distances from one another.[154] Some individuals had the face completely tattooed, only a few reddish places remaining to indicate the skin colour. And the lips of all we saw were dyed either black or blue.[155] Many persons had been punctured and thickly marked with black dots right from the instep to the knee.[156] The only domestic animal we saw was a single fowl.

The inhabitants of the Penrhyn Islands, by contrast, were not tattooed ... As on Easter Island, iron appeared to be called *Hoio*.[157]

LUDOVIK CHORIS, 1822 TEXT[158]

On 16/28 March, early in the morning, we encountered Easter Island, or Vaihiou. On its northern coasts we saw areas that seemed to be covered with trees, but these were probably only banana trees.[159] Soon, with the aid of binoculars, we spotted the monuments of which Cook and La Pérouse have spoken; and then we discovered smoke rising in several places. We were moving slowly, so that we did not reach Cook's Bay till midday.

Two fragile canoes with outriggers,[160] each carrying two men, advanced towards us. The men made signs to us and shouted loudly while pointing to the land and holding up fishing-nets in their hands. But despite all our invitations, they refused to come any nearer and soon went on their way back.

A boat was now immediately put off to sound the bay and find an anchorage. The natives had gathered in a great crowd on the shore meanwhile; and many threw themselves into the water, bringing out bananas, yams, and sugar cane that they exchanged for iron. They did not think much of the trinkets they were offered. One islander, having received a pair of scissors that were the price of the bananas he had in his hand, fled without leaving his wares. He was called back in vain. The man's companions, who surrounded our boat, appeared even to be mocking our people, so that finally the officer commanding that launch[161] was obliged to fire on the fugitive. The latter cast down his fruit and hurried ashore, and his comrades followed suit.

The island's appearance was rather arid, indeed; still, it struck us as less miserable than it had Cook and La Pérouse. All the slopes of the elevations had been divided into fields and planted with different kinds of vegetation, whose various colours produced a very pleasant effect.[162] No doubt these natives owe to the benevolence of the French expedition led by La Pérouse several of the useful plants that they cultivate today. On all sides, men could be seen running along the shore. Most were naked, but some wore varieties of yellow or white mantles of different sizes.[163]

Just as soon as we had dropped anchor, two boats containing twenty-two armed men headed for the shore.[164] But we were still approaching it when natives began to throw stones at us. Some men yelled while others made threatening gestures. The shore was soon covered by at least six hundred men, who had the air of meaning to oppose our disembarkation. We fired a few shots with powder, and large numbers of the natives hid themselves behind rocks. But as soon as the noise had passed, and when they recognized that no one had been harmed, they came out of their hiding places, laughing and mocking us. It was not reasonable to take revenge on jokes played by these great children; and so, as we still had the very keenest desire to have some communication with them, it was necessary to attempt to draw them to us. They refused to permit us to go amongst them. We therefore showed the islanders tools made of iron.[165] The boldest of them jumped into the water and brought us fruit. They did not cease, however, to show every sign of fear. In the end, though, when they perceived that they would be paid well for their fruit, they agreed to barter their nets and a small chicken in exchange for our iron. They returned to shore when their stocks were exhausted. We now made signs to them that they should move away from the shoreline. They understood us perfectly, and we in fact landed. All the same, it was plain that these people were not well disposed towards us, and so we stayed ashore barely five minutes. Besides, the undertow was very strong and our boats might have run into danger.

We did not see on the shore of the bay those statues of which voyagers who preceded us here had spoken. Nor, with the exception of a structure seven feet high made of small stones, into which it was possible to climb by way of an opening made in the side, did we observe anything remarkable. Nothing indicated that the structure in question was a human habitation.[166] To the right of our landing place and some two hundred paces back from the sealine, there rose a great number of pillars, three to four feet high, formed of a single rock, and each surmounted by a white-coloured stone.[167]

Among the throng of natives who now covered the shore and whose number had slowly crept up to nine hundred, we made out only two women. One solitary man had a club in the shape of a spatula, embellished with carvings[168]... It was useless to insist upon visiting this island in spite of the inhabitants' own wishes; and so, at sunset, we made sail.

LUDOVIK CHORIS, 1826 TEXT

The surface of Vaihou, named Easter Island by the Europeans, rises into rounded slopes which in turn rest against pyramid-shaped mountains. In appearance, this island situated at so great a distance from all other land pleases the eye by its fresh verdure. We believed that we saw, even on the steep hillsides, cultivated fields that were separated by straight enclosures.[169] The diversity of their hues produced the most pleasant effect, indeed, and it was possible to make out many beautiful flowers of a yellow colour.[170]

This singular island lacks running water; not a single tree grows there.[171] As for the paper-mulberry, it grows no higher than a little bush, but it provides the natives with the raw material for their clothing. Their body is tattooed. They cultivate sugar cane, bananas, taro, potatoes, and other rootcrops.[172]

All the navigators who had traversed the Pacific Ocean had been well received by these islanders, and we hoped to be, too. A pair of canoes came out in front of us but kept their distance. The men in them watched us mistrustfully, even while offering us roots from a distance. Our ship's launch and a boat then headed for the island. A considerable crowd awaited us ashore, and there were demonstrations of delight and such yelling that we could not hear one another. We wanted to disembark; they opposed us, repulsed us, pursued us right in the water—without great danger for us, because they are unarmed. We moved off from the shore, and they followed us out, swimming, and offered to exchange roots for pieces of iron. But the band still ashore now assailed us with a hail of stones. We fired at them from our rifles. The natives surrounding us moved off. We disembarked, and the islanders instantly surrounded us again. They were daubed with red, white, and black, which gave them a terrible appearance; they made a frightful racket.[173] We advance; they once more throw stones at us. We disperse them with shots, then take a few steps across the island, recognizing the exactness of the description left by La Pérouse.

Convinced now that the natives absolutely refused to receive us, we left them, leaving knives, scissors, and other articles for them, and regained the ship. Most of these savages went naked but some had white, yellow, or orange cloaks. We saw only one man armed with a club, and we spotted only two women, one of them feeding an infant.

We afterwards learned the reason for the strange behaviour of these islanders, who, it transpired, had already driven off other navigators. In 1800, a rogue commanding an American vessel from New London took advantage of the friendly reception he had had at the island to abduct several natives of both sexes, meaning to transport them to Juan Fernandez Island and there put them to work preparing sealskins. His hopes were deceived. After three days, when these unfortunates had been unbound, they all cast themselves into the ocean.[174]

OTTO VON KOTZEBUE

The island was reached on 28 March: by three o'clock that morning we were within fifteen miles of it and at dawn we saw it distinctly before us. Having doubled its southern point,[175] we steered along the west coast, no great distance, to Cook's Bay. There we noted columns of smoke rising—probably a signal to the inhabitants of the interior of the country that a ship was approaching.[176] At noon, when we were quite close to Cook's Bay, we observed two craft paddling out towards us, each manned by a couple of islanders only.[177] I was in great hopes that these people, who had placed so much trust in La Pérouse, would accord us the same cordial reception. But this, to my great surprise, was by no means the case. The natives approached us with fear and mistrust till within gunshot, then showed us some roots from that distance; but they could by no means be induced to come nearer than that to the ship.

The structure of these craft, of which we saw several and which held only two persons each, precisely corresponded with those which La Pérouse mentions. They are from five to six feet long[178] and about a foot in breadth, and are equipped on both sides with an outrigger.[179] It was La Pérouse's opinion that these islanders must soon be without boats, for want of timber, but he was wrong here. It is true that we did not find a single large tree on the island, but the natives construct their craft from driftwood, which is brought by the ocean current from the American coast in some quantity.

The bottom in many parts of Cook's Bay proving very poor, I sent Lieutenant Shishmarev to discover a more suitable place to anchor, with the aid of a sounding lead. Meanwhile I kept the *Riurik* under sail. The islanders, who had hitherto been following the ship, conversing loudly and apparently in the best of humours, hastened off to the shore when they saw our boat putting off. This surprised me the more because the Easter Islanders had earlier placed so much confidence in mariners. It was only the ship, however, that seemed to alarm them. As soon as our boat neared the shoreline, a number of natives swam out to it, laden with taro roots, yams, and bananas, all of which they willingly bartered for little bits of old iron hoop. Some men dealt honestly, others with cunning, and one even made an attempt to get something by force. Lest the rest be infected by his bad example, we fired small shot at this man, which, however, did not prevent them from practising their thievery.[180]

Receiving a signal from our boat to the effect that they had found a good anchorage, I made a couple of tacks and reached the spot, dropping anchor in twenty-two fathoms, fine sandy bottom. A sandy bay bore S45°E from us, two rocks being now concealed behind the larger bay's southern cape.[181] Our boat returned, no islanders venturing to pursue it back. Since it was my intention to make a landing, I next had two boats readied for that purpose and we set out from *Riurik,* seventeen in number, at three o'clock in the afternoon.

A considerable crowd of natives had assembled on the beach by now, and were crying and capering about with the most singular motions. They seemed to be awaiting our arrival with impatience. As they had selected for the rendezvous the only spot where the surf allowed a landing, however, we could not venture to leave our boats till they had made room for us—which they could simply not be persuaded to do. While still laughing and joking, they in effect obliged us to put off from shore, even pursuing us in the water. They were all unarmed,[182] though, so this did not seem dangerous to us. But we had scarcely left the shore before hundreds were swimming round our boats, exchanging bananas and sugar cane for old iron and, since all spoke at once with the greatest animation, creating an awful racket. Some individuals appeared to be wits, as general and loud laughter broke out now and then.

Spectators on shore, at last wearying of this scene, now amused themselves by pelting us with stones, to which I quickly put an end with a few musket shots. But by this means I also lost my gay company in the water, gained the landing place, and managed hastily to put some of my seamen ashore. Hardly had the natives perceived *this* development before they encircled us with yet greater importunity. They had painted their faces red, white, and black[183] so acquiring a terrible appearance, and danced with the most ludicrous movements and bodily contortions. At the same time, they created such a noise that we were obliged to shout into each other's ears to understand what was said. I can well imagine the impression this made of necessity on Lieutenant Shishmarev, who saw these natives for the first time and thought himself surrounded by so many monkeys. For, though I had been previously acquainted with the South Sea Islanders, this scene surpassed all my ideas, too.[184] To scatter the natives and to get more space, I had some knives thrown amongst them. Despite this, however, I felt a stone strike my hat. I gave orders to fire, and this at length permitted me to get ashore.

My first business there was to search for the large and remarkable statues on the beach which both Cook and La Pérouse had seen there. Look though I might, however, I discovered only a broken pile of stones lying close to an uninjured pedestal; not a single trace remained of all the rest. The mistrustful conduct of these islanders led me to suppose that Europeans had had a quarrel with them, avenging themselves by smashing these statues. It also struck me as very odd that, amidst all the great bustle ashore and in the water, we had not spotted a single woman: earlier voyagers had complained often of the women's importunities here. This confirmed me in the opinion that Europeans must have committed excesses here lately.

Being quite convinced that the islanders would not, in fact, permit us to enter their country, we made an attempt to retreat to the boats, which were, in any case, unsafe in the high surf.[185] But even now we found ourselves forced to protect ourselves from their advances by several musket shots, nor would they leave us in peace until they heard the balls hissing about their ears. We gave them more iron, then hurried back to *Riurik* as our stay could only be lost time, under such circumstances, and every hour was precious to me.

The natives seem all to be of medium stature but well made, mostly with copper skin though a few are tolerably pale. They all have tattoos, and those who are tattooed over the whole body have certainly the appearance of chiefs. We observed the material that is manufactured from the bark of trees, which is produced on most of the South Sea Islands. Some men wore short cloaks made of it, and the women, who stood at a distance, were entirely wrapped in it.[186] To judge by the vivacity of these people, they are quite content with their situation. They probably do not want for food, for they brought out to us a considerable supply of bananas, yams, sugar cane, and sweet potatoes. Nor do they neglect agriculture: we saw hillsides near the bay which were covered by fields. These, with their variegated greens, afforded a most pleasant sight. The seeds that La Pérouse left for these islanders, though, have probably failed. The natives brought us none of the fruits in question. We also looked in vain for the sheep and swine that he left here.[187] One fowl was offered to us for a large knife, and was taken back again when the deal was declined, which would seem to prove how highly they value such animals and how few they have.[188]

The dwellings of these people are exactly as described by La Pérouse, and the long house marked on his map still stands, as well as the stone hut on the shore.[189] It is my belief that, apart from the disappearance of the remarkable statues, nothing much has changed here since the time of his visit. We saw only two statues after we had doubled the south point, and they were of little consequence. As we departed from Easter Island, its natives once again pelted us with stones, hurling them after us with shrieks. I was glad to find that, by seven o'clock, we were all back on *Riurik* with no broken bones and under full sail.

Information that explains the hostile behaviour of these islanders was afterwards given to me, at the Sandwich Islands, by Captain Alexander Adams. I now pass it on to the reader. Adams, an Englishman by birth, was in 1816 commanding the brig *Kahumanna,* the property of the King of the Sandwich Islands, and had earlier served in the same brig when she had been known as *Forester,* of London. He had then been second to Captain Piccort or Piggot, who had sold the brig to the king.[190] According to Adams, the master of the schooner *Nancy,* from New London in America (whose name Adams did not vouchsafe to me), had in the year 1805 busied himself at the island of Massafuero [Mas a Fuero], hunting the kind of seal known in Russia as *kotik* (sea-cat). The skin of the animal fetches a good price on the Chinese market, so Americans attempt to discover its haunts in every part of the world. This animal had been discovered accidentally and immediately hunted in Massafuero, a hitherto uninhabited island to the west of Juan Fernandez, where criminals are sent from Chile. As the island offered no safe anchorage, however, the schooner was obliged to remain under sail; and as the master had not enough men to be able to employ some in the seal hunt, he decided to make for Easter Island and there abduct some men and women. He thought he would carry them to Massafuero and there establish a colony that could continue the seal hunting. In accordance with this evil plan, he landed at Cook's Bay and in fact attempted to seize a number of the natives.

The struggle is said to have been bloody, for the brave islanders defended themselves with valour; but they were at last forced to yield to the Europeans' terrible weapons and twelve men and ten women fell into the hands of the merciless Americans. These wretched creatures were forthwith carried on board and fettered. Not till three days later, when they were out of sight of all land, were they released. The first use they made of their restored liberty was to leap overboard. The men succeeded, the women were only restrained from following them by brute force. The master hove to, in hopes that the natives would return to the schooner for refuge when the waves threatened to overcome their strength; but he soon enough saw how mistaken he was in this calculation, for the islanders, who had been accustomed to the water since infancy, did not think it quite impossible—despite the three days' passage—to reach their native land. At all events, they preferred dying in the ocean to leading a miserable life of captivity. Having disputed the point some time, some swam off in the direction of Easter Island while others, who had not agreed on the right course, swam off to the north. Enraged by this unexpected heroism, the master now sent a boat after the natives; but the boat came back empty after many vain efforts, as the swimmers always dived at its approach, and the ocean compassionately received them into its bosom. At last, the master left the native men to their fate, bringing the women to the island. He is reputed to have made numerous subsequent attempts to abduct people from Easter Island.[191]

Adams had heard this tale from the master himself, which was very likely the reason why he declined to mention the name. He also assured me that he himself had visited Easter Island in 1806, but had been unable to land because of the natives' hostility. He added that the *Albatross,* commanded by Captain Winship, had met the same fate in the year 1809.[192]

My instructions required me to visit Pitcairn Island and thence proceed west to 137°.[193] As our passage from Kronstadt to Chile had taken longer than had been calculated in our planning, however, I found myself now obliged to take the shortest possible course to Kamchatka.

3

THE SCIENTIFIC LEGACY

GENERAL OBSERVATIONS

Lisianskii spent five days (17–21 April 1804) sailing around or standing hard by Easter Island, but did not attempt to land. Kotzebue landed on 28 March 1816, but was gone within the day.[1] It is not surprising, under these circumstances, that the Russians undertook less science and learned less about the place than their predecessors Cook (13–18 March 1774) and La Pérouse (8–10 April 1786). Nevertheless, the Russians did contribute to contemporary European knowledge of the island and its people, in ethnography, cartography, and—more modestly—in mineralogy and botany. What could be done afloat was done: the coasts were sounded, bays were charted, elevations measured, villages described, and statues drawn. Brief though it was, Lieutenant Povalishin's surf-sprayed barter session with the islanders in Hanga-roa Bay produced a detailed report on the sights and sounds ashore, of which Lisianskii took maximum advantage in his *Voyage*. He was a first-rate draughtsman, as the Polynesian artefacts depicted in the Atlas accompanying the 1812 (St. Petersburg) edition of his *Voyage* well attest;[2] and so were Navigator Vasilii S. Khromchenko, Surgeon Johann Friedrich Eschscholtz (1793–1831), and of course the artist Ludovik Choris (1795–1828), all of *Riurik*.[3] Fedor I. Shubert (1758–1825), astronomer at the Academy of Sciences, had provided help for naval officers in higher mathematics and marine astronomy at the Admiralty's request.[4] Another Academician, Aleksandr F. Sevast'ianov (1771–1824), was the author of *Instructions in the Area of Zoological Science*,[5] one copy of which went with *Neva;* and other well-known scientists (M.V. Severgin, T.A. Smelovskii) likewise furnished her with papers to assist with mineralogy and botany in the Pacific or the

North.[6] All the experience acquired from the voyage of *Nadezhda* and *Neva* (1803–6) went into scientific orders for the *Riurik*. In addition, the *Instructions for the Astronomical and Physical Departments* of the Kotzebue venture were draughted by the Swiss mathematician who had served as the *Nadezhda*'s astronomer in the Pacific, Johann Caspar Hörner.[7] Those instructions covered practical surveying, calculus, refractions; use of wind gauges, hygrometers, the Six-thermometer and other instruments; and the principles of meteorology, "solar reckoning," and magnetic variations.[8] Kotzebue and his people were specifically enjoined, on their departure from the Baltic, "to measure *everything measurable*."[9] Kotzebue was as conscious of those orders, when he called at Easter Island on his passage to the Tuamotu Archipelago from Chile, as his passenger Chamisso was aware of a great obligation to the academic world. Perhaps, although he was younger than Chamisso by seven years, Kotzebue could not feel "a joy just like a child's" as Easter Island came in view.[10] He was by temperament controlled and dry. But he could hope to build on Cook's and La Pérouse's work in that locality, as three years later Bellingshausen hoped to complement—if not improve upon—Cook's work in the Antarctic seas.[11] That men like Bellingshausen, Kruzenshtern, and Kotzebue should so consciously be complementing Cook's Pacific work in 1804–27 was a scientifically significant result of Anglo-Russian naval contacts as well as an alliance in the struggle with Napoleonic France.[12]

It was, of course, to find a navigable passage through the Arctic from Pacific to Atlantic tidal waters that Kotzebue sailed in 1815, in *Riurik,* in the employ of Count N.P. Rumiantsev.[13] "Universal peace finally reigning over Europe," as the eminent hydrographer-historian Admiral Nikolai A. Ivashintsev put it at the time of Kotzebue's death in 1847, "long neglected scientific problems once again provoked general interest . . . Lt. Kotzebue had instructions to employ himself not only on the main objective of the venture [to the north of Bering Strait] but also with important geographical and scientific work in Oceania."[14] To help him, Chamisso, Eschscholtz, and Morten Wormskiöld, a Danish naturalist, were appointed to the expedition.[15] Thus, a failure to discover any sea route back to Europe through the Arctic might be compensated for by mid or North Pacific exploration and research. Kruzenshtern expressed it thus when introducing Kotzebue's *Voyage* to a Russian readership in June 1818:

> Supposing that the wished-for discovery of a connection between the two seas should not be made, still a number of significant advantages would accrue from the voyage to science, navigation in particular. . .

Two crossings of the entire South Sea, in quite different directions, would assuredly contribute not a little towards the extension of our knowledge of that great ocean, as well as of the natives of the very numerous isles that are strewn across it. And a rich harvest of articles of natural history could also be anticipated, since the Count had appointed an able naturalist [Chamisso] as well as a ship's surgeon, to the expedition. The imminent venture was thus of the highest importance to the sciences.[16]

Kotzebue's plan to explore Easter Island was defeated by the islanders' hostility, which stemmed, as we have seen, from crimes committed by the Yankee sealer *Nancy*. Other visitors since 1808, including Captain Nathan Winship of the *Albatross*,[17] had met with a similar reception from the islanders. It is regrettable that Lisianskii had not attempted to land, especially as *Neva* called at Hanga-roa Bay before the *Nancy*. The ethnographic data collected during Kotzebue's visit cannot justly be compared with those of Cook or La Pérouse, but they are important nonetheless. The Russian narratives, complemented by Choris's neglected aquarelles and Captain Frederick W. Beechey's text of 1831, deserve more notice from ethnology. The leading Easter Island specialists of recent times (Walter Knoche, Henri Lavachéry, Alfred Métraux) would have done better to rely upon original editions of the Russian texts in question instead of, in the case of Kotzebue, depending on the work of Hannibal E. Lloyd (1771–1847).[18] It is ridiculous that primary material in Russian should be viewed by anthropologists, historians, and others in the West as less accessible than French or German ones.

ETHNOGRAPHY

Health, Food, and Diet

All Russian texts concur that the Easter Islanders were strong and healthy: "well built, and of sound constitution" (Korobitsyn); "their bodily build was sound" (Lisianskii); "well built, slender, sound physique" (Chamisso). Cook had arrived at Easter Island in 1774, with the remarks of Roggeveen and C.H. Behrens in mind.[19] As he perused the 1739 version of Behrens's notoriously unreliable account of the Dutch visit of 1722,[20] translated into English in Alexander Dalrymple's *Collection* (Volume 2),[21] he saw references to twelve-foot native giants on Easter Island's shores. Later he noted with some asperity that he "did not see a Man . . . that measured Six feet."[22] The islanders were, he says, "in general a very slender race but very Nimble and Active." J.R. Forster agreed: "slender limbed, of the common size between 5 & 6 foot."[23] Lisianskii's people believed that they saw some men at Hanga-roa who were "as tall as six feet." Neither men nor women appeared in the least undernourished. They were strong swimmers, capable—even without reed supports—of circling around visiting boats for extended periods and simultaneously bartering or chatting. Archaeology confirms that on average the islanders were a relatively tall Polynesian people.[24] "Their old age," adds Chamisso, did not "appear to be accompanied by illness." The Russians noted neither yaws nor signs of any other illnesses.[25] In general, they thought the natives handsome, well proportioned, and well nourished. Lisianskii believed that their health was not adversely affected by a lack of drinking water, and noted that "one twentieth part of the island's area was under cultivation."

In 1774, the British had considered the Easter Islanders darker-skinned than the men of the Society Islands.[26] Lisianskii found them "of dark colouring" or, in his English text, "of a dark copper colour," but Povalishin thought they resembled "Southern Europeans, sunburnt from exposure" and saw something "dark orange" in their skin tone. Both Chamisso and Kotzebue, however, observed at least two overall skin tones in 1816. The majority were "of a copper colour" (Kotzebue); but some individuals were "tolerably white" or at least had skin of a "far lighter colour" (Chamisso). It did not seem to the Russians, though, that there were persons of two different races on Easter Island—and in this, they were right.[27] Even so, their texts reflect bemusement that hair of various shades should be seen among so isolated a group of Polynesians. According to Korobitsyn, "their hair, worn in the manner of a *toupée,* was cut a little in front and dark blond." By *toupée,* Korobitsyn presumably meant a *pukao* or topknot tied over the crown, as observed by the Dutch in 1722.[28] But Lisianskii painted a different picture. Most of the islanders, he noted in agreement with Cook, were dark-haired and beardless. Brown hair was also seen at Hanga-roa. One member of the Gonzalez expedition of 1770 said he had seen "chestnut-coloured" hair, and even hair "tending to red or a cinnamon tint."[29] Korobitsyn confirmed this without indicating that bleaching had been used. No Russian text, in fact, alludes to bleaching techniques, though all refer to body painting.

On the basis of shore observation only, Lisianskii thought that at least two square miles of land must be under cultivation in 1804. This area was covered with "banana trees... or other sorts of edible plant." La Pérouse had seen more of the island in 1786, but had offered a comparable figure: "scarcely a tenth part."[30] This cultivated ground was, to judge by the Russian evidence, around numerous coasts but especially at

Hanga-roa, Vinapu, south of Rano-Raraku, and east of Ovahe Bay on the northern shore. Plantations appear to have been numerous and well maintained despite the lack of walls or of fencing to contain them. Fruit trees might look sparse from the sea, but the Russians were supplied with good amounts of plantains and bananas. On both visits, they were given ample sugar cane and sweet potato (*kumara*). Choris shows, in his *Vue de l'Ile de Pâques,* that hillsides near Hanga-roa had been cleared of boulders in the past, the stones being piled onto elongated heaps or semi-walls. The labour needed must have been considerable.[31]

As *Neva* approached the island from the south and east, Lisianskii noted "rows of banana trees, skilfully planted out." Next day (18 April), he spotted "a very extensive plantation of what looked like bananas." Bananas were at once offered by the islanders in barter and seemed to be plentiful, although the islanders, to the Russians' disapproval, did not release the fruit till they had first received their bits of iron hoop. Like sugar cane, they were to be seen "around each dwelling." Bananas evidently flourished on the west coast of the island in the early 1800s, as today.[32] Sugar cane (*toa*), which the Russians likewise purchased in some quantity in 1804 and 1816, was a staple in the islanders' diet. Lisianskii believed the bulrush-mat swimming supports he saw in use at Hanga-roa had been plaited round a central core of *toa* stems. He was most probably correct.[33]

Russian evidence confirms the importance of the sweet potato (*Ipomoea batatas*) in the Easter Island diet. In 1804, as in Roggeveen's time, it was eaten every day and took the place of bread;[34] no barter session was without it and the Russians, recognizing its nutritious properties, were glad to take it cooked or raw. The incident of 21 April 1804 when Lieutenant Povalishin was offered "a little grass bag full of cooked sweet potato" faithfully echoed one of 15 March 1774.[35]

Yams too were offered to both *Neva* and *Riurik*, but taro does not figure in the 1804 accounts. No Russian text mentions the gourd (*Lagenaria vulgaris*), although both the Spaniards and Cook had noted it.[36] The Russians, however, did not step inside any Easter Island house, where calabashes and containers were invariably kept.

Of the Polynesians' three domesticated animals, only fowl were brought to Easter Island from the West, or else they alone survived to the time of Roggeveen's visit. Cook and La Pérouse both suggest that these were scarce by the eighteenth century,[37] and Kotzebue indicates that the scarcity was worse in the early 1800s. A single bird was offered for a large knife, then removed when Kotzebue's agent balked at the exchange. Chamisso acquired an Easter Island fishnet, but the Russian texts lack any material about native fishing skills. Doubtless the Russians' very presence caused the postponement of whatever fishing the natives might have planned at such a season.[38]

Like their European predecessors, the Russians attempted to estimate the total population of Easter Island on the basis of the native groups observed around the coasts. Lisianskii thought Cook's and J.R. Forster's estimates of 600–900 far too low.[39] Povalishin thought that at least 500 persons had welcomed him in Hanga-roa Bay. True, *Neva*'s four-day manoeuvres round the island had given the populace ample time to assemble at Hanga-roa (assuming that internal political arrangements made such mass movement to that spot feasible), but Lisianskii was right to assume that "other settlements" might have produced comparable crowds under the same circumstances. His arguments were questionable, but his final guess—1,500 to 1,840—was good. Chamisso, too, believed that even La Pérouse's estimate of 2,000 was much nearer the mark than Cook's 600.[40] Moreover, it was evident to him that the population had increased between 1804 and 1816. He thought that this was probably linked to an improvement in the islanders' overall "situation," by which he no doubt meant food supply.[41] Kotzebue and Choris similarly believed that the Easter Islanders' numbers had risen since the 1770s. *Riurik*'s artist claimed that 900 persons were on the shore at Hanga-roa, only two of them women.[42] Such a fact, if true, lends support to La Pérouse's figure; for even with the disproportion between the sexes to which many earlier visitors had alluded,[43] it hardly suggests a total of less than 2,000–3,000 people.

Body Ornament and Clothing

Tattooing was widespread at the time of the Russian visits. "Scars were incised on their faces and coloured with blue pigment" (Korobitsyn); "Narrow lines had been drawn on their face, nose, neck, and arms" (Lisianskii). These lines were sometimes very narrow; at other times broad. Chamisso saw "bluish, broad-lined tattooing, exactly following the direction of the muscle." The proportion of the body tattooed varied very greatly from one individual to another. In Kotzebue's view, a full tattoo had social connotations and implied rank and influence: heavily tattooed men "had the appearance of chiefs." By far the most useful data on the subject are those provided by Eschscholtz and Choris. The former, a trained surgeon, took a professional interest in the skin and was highly observant besides. The latter left an illustration of a tattooed Easter Islander that has been criticized as "inaccurate in many details" by Métraux (*Ethnology of Easter Island,* p. 240) but that is important because of the scarcity of such drawings made by William Hodges, Cook's artist in 1774, and by later visitors to Easter Island.[44]

Eschscholtz refers to a "single stripe" running around the face, with a number of adjacent "round spots at regular distances from one another." Ancient images made of bulrushes and tightly wrapped in *tapa,* two of which are held by the Peabody Museum at Cambridge, Massachusetts, show several such bands or stripes—if one interprets Eschscholtz's phrase to mean running across or behind the cheeks.[45] More probably, however, he meant curving across the upper forehead just below the hair-line, continuing down the temples, and turning back at eye level towards the ears, a traditional design known as *retu* and observed by the French ethnologist Henri Lavachéry as late as 1931.[46] As for the "round spots," they were the *humu* or *puraki* that ran below and along such stripes; Beechey's people saw them at Hanga-roa and considered them "arched lines" on the forehead.[47] The Russians did not record parallel lines on the forehead; but the rows of dots by the hairline, also observed by Linton Palmer's informants in the 1850s, were complemented by tattooed triangles on the cheeks and upper face.[48] Choris's depiction of such triangular patches is echoed in the 1841 atlas accompanying Du Petit-Thouars's *Voyage.*[49] The blue tone noted by the Russians was caused by skin action on the traditional mix of *Solanum nigrum* juice and charred leaves of the *ti* tree, which is now almost gone from the island. We learn from Eschscholtz that lips, too, were tattooed blue or black; and Lisianskii and Choris concur that narrow bands went round the neck, like a necklace. Several nineteenth-century visitors noted such blue bands, which were of pre-European origin.[50]

Choris had little time to make rough sketches while *Riurik*'s people were ashore or while islanders were near him, either in canoes or in the water, but he was a highly skilled artist and did not need much. Like his Hawaiian work of 1816, his Easter Island record has been severely criticized.[51] In my view, his Polynesian illustrations have been underrated. While it is undeniable that the Easter Islander shown in *Habitans de l'Ile de Pâques* is crudely drawn and that the lithography of 1821–22 was not good,[52] Choris cannot reasonably be supposed to have invented such major features of local tattooing as bold slanting bands across the arms and thighs or perpendicular parallel lines along the shins; nor are the parallel bands shown on the native's lower leg without support in the literature.[53] The absence of tattooing on the Easter Island woman clad in a substantial waistcloth, which had also been observed by the Dutch in 1722[54] substantiates Cook's suggestion that the island's females were only lightly marked.[55]

On the other hand, Chamisso saw women whose faces had been

"painted dark red." George Forster had noted in 1774 that women at Hanga-roa "painted the whole face with a reddish brown ruddle"; and according to the later witness, Father Eugène Eyraud, red was the sole colour that Easter Island women generally used.[56] Choris and Kotzebue agree that in 1816 many men painted their faces red, white, and black. The red dye, obtained from pulverized tuff, and yellow or orange dye made from turmeric, had been used in addition to a shell-lime-based substance or unoxidized tuff that gave the required white colour.[57]

Russian evidence suggests that the custom of extending the ear lobes was less common in the early 1800s than in the previous century. Korobitsyn saw no ear lobes that reached down to the shoulders, and Lisianskii saw no ears that were not "of ordinary size." No huge apertures were seen. Chamisso did spot "pierced and extended ear lobes" on some old men, but noted that they had so been tied and pulled back through the aperture that "they were not greatly in evidence," which meant that they could have easily been missed from a distance. Eschscholtz saw only one old man with such disfigured lobes, despite looking out for them. These data are confirmed by Beechey (1825) and Eyraud (1866).[58] The Russians do not mention ear plugs such as eighteenth-century seamen had seen.[59]

Hairstyles, on the other hand, had hardly changed at all since Roggeveen's visit. In 1804, Korobitsyn saw big topknots (*pukao*) and was reminded of *toupées*. Men on the island continued to cut their hair a little in front with obsidian knives. In 1816 one man caught Lisianskii's attention because of his long hair and grey beard. "All the rest were cropped, dark haired, and beardless." The Russian evidence suggests that the hair was not bleached or otherwise artificially coloured.

The Russian narratives indicate that the personal ornaments seen by eighteenth-century visitors had changed little by 1804–16. Chamisso listed three types: fresh-cut wreaths of leaves for the head, polished shells (*repu reva*) suspended by cords, and black feather headdresses. Leaf wreaths were still worn by girls in the 1870s[60] and were evidently more commonly worn by men in former times. Chamisso remarked that black feather headdresses (made from cock-feathers and much prized) were far less common than usual. The flat shell necklace was suspended from a cord of human hair or vegetable-fibre thread. None of the figures depicted by Choris appears to wear any ornament, nor did Kotzebue refer to any at all.[61] The Russian texts make clear, however, that the islanders much appreciated ornaments such as five-kopek coins on little chains, which they "instantly put round their necks" (Lisianskii, 1812 text). Choris reported (1822) that "they did not think much of trinkets" in general, preferring iron or European cloth and clothing. Among the classical Easter Island ornaments not mentioned by the Russians are the *rei-miro,* the carved wooden pendant, and the wooden ball (*tahonga*).[62]

When we consider Easter Island clothing, we are struck by the general insistence that cloaks made of paper mulberry were fairly numerous and often used. "Many," wrote Lisianskii, "were covered from neck to knees by some sort of cloak." "Many," he added for the benefit of British readers of his 1814 text, "had a kind of short cloak, or piece of cloth, suspended from the shoulders and scarcely covering the thighs." Furthermore, many men waved pieces of white or dyed tapa, and many women were "entirely wrapped in it." Yet in 1774 Cook's people had been struck by the stunted and unpromising appearance of the paper mulberry (*Broussonetia papyrifera*) plants they saw. It was a "poor and weak" variety, "and not above 2½ feet high at most" in the southwest of the island;[63] "the same Sort of Cloth Plant as at the other isles but not much."[64] Choris confirms, in his 1826 text, that in 1816 the island's paper mulberry grew "no higher than a little bush." But it is clear from the Kotzebue narrative that tapa was relatively abundant at the time. Far from suffering from the cold, the islanders had adequate supplies of *kahu.*

These *kahu* cloaks were of varying lengths. Some fell from the shoulders to the upper thigh, others to the shin. Women sometimes wore cloaks in addition to thick waistcloths in colder periods, and so looked "entirely wrapped" in tapa. The *kahu* was apparently worn over both shoulders and tied at the front or over one shoulder with a side knot. La Pérouse, Pierre Loti, and other observers record that the cloak was usually worn over the right shoulder,[65] but Choris's *Habitans de l'Ile de Pâques* shows the opposite. The Russians saw many cloaks dyed orange or yellow with turmeric. In general, men wore cloaks less commonly than women, but did wear a bunch of grass suspended from a string and tied round the waist. They did not wear a *maro* (loin cloth) of one piece of bark-cloth but were not, despite their describers' loose use of the term "naked," completely uncovered. At least two figures waving (or wearing draped over the arm?) three-foot-long strips of tapa, at the centre of Choris's *Vue de l'Ile de Pâques,* wear the traditional grass bunch over the genitals. Korobitsyn records, however, that in 1804 some men covered their private parts not with grass but with "two pieces of papyrus hanging from a belt." Cook had seen a perineal band consisting of "a slip of cloth betwixt their legs, each end of which is fastened to a cord or belt."[66] Lisianskii records that the strips of tapa that the islanders "constantly waved" at his people were the size of a kerchief, "white or motley." Perhaps they were such "slips of cloth" or perineal bands, removed with the object of better attracting the foreigners' attention. In any event, they were single strips of beaten bark, or *kohiti,* not yet widened by being sewn to other strips: the approximate length, three feet, corresponds well with Choris's remark about the height of the island *mahute: à la hauteur d'un arbrisseau.*[67]

As in former times, the Easter Islanders in 1804–16 prized the cloth and clothing brought by Europeans and did their best to obtain as much as possible of both by regular barter or by deceit. Russian *naboika,* or printed linen, appealed to them greatly and was, with iron, a major item in trade. Although the Russians had read their Cook and La Pérouse, and were ready to satisfy the islanders' desire for clothing, they did not speculate in print about its cause.[68]

Wooden Artefacts in Leningrad

Lisianskii was not especially encouraged by the Company to concern himself with "curiosities" in the Pacific.[69] He, like Kruzenshtern, was ordered to present the Company with all that he might "learn or gain from observations on the voyage . . . of significance for natural history . . . or other sciences,"[70] but he was not instructed to collect native artefacts. Lisianskii, however, was predisposed to read his orders in a way that favoured the study of native peoples in Oceania once he had met all provisioning requirements and basic service duties.[71] While in South Africa in 1797 en route to British India, and very likely in the Caribbean also two years previously, he had complemented his scientific activities by learning all he could about the Negro,[72] and in 1804 he began collecting artefacts in Polynesia.[73] In his journal from *Neva,* Company clerk Nikolai Korobitsyn makes the illuminating charge that his captain was not only too intent upon collecting artefacts—in the Marquesas and Hawaii, for example—but also took advantage of others' efforts in building his collection.[74] "The islanders [at Taio-hae Bay, Nukuhiva] gave him various objects of that country which, in his greed, Lisianskii appropriated as his own property." This charge has been solidly refuted by Lisianskii's Soviet biographer, E. Shteinberg, on the bases of the objects' worthlessness to a commercial company, Lisianskii's right to order barter in the way most likely to ensure ample purchases of foodstuffs for his people, and, especially, his scientific motive in collecting them.[75] It is significant, however, that captains like Lisianskii were indeed in a position to embellish their collections of Pacific artefacts, all sailing orders notwithstanding. And as Shteinberg remarks elsewhere in connection with Hawaii's Kona Coast, "not a few local rarities were, in fact, taken in besides the provisions. The ethnographic collection started by Lisianskii even during his . . . voyages of 1792–95 were still further enriched."[76] The artefacts

Lisianskii had acquired while a Russian Volunteer aboard HMS *L'Oiseau* and other British warships were unquestionably his.

It is not known how many artefacts, if any, Lisianskii or Povalishin carried away from Hanga-roa Bay on 21 April 1804. It is certain that trade took place, and the fact that rarities are not referred to in the Russian texts by no means demonstrates that none were taken. Also, quite a few Hawaiian artefacts, it seems, were thrown deliberately overboard "as useless and cumbersome" once their purchasers had lost their early interest in them."[77] It is apparent that the same could have happened to other Pacific artefacts during the voyage of *Neva*. Other articles were doubtless lost elsewhere, as was usual immediately after distant voyages by Russians and others.[78] Finally, when Lisianskii later directed that Pacific artefacts in his charge be deposited with the St. Petersburg Imperial Public Library or with the Admiralty Department's museum, Povalishin also submitted other artefacts to the museum.[79] He, if anyone, might have had Easter Island objects in his possession in 1806–9. The artefacts on display at the Public Library (now the N.N. Saltykov-Shchedrin Public Library in Leningrad) were transferred, with Lisianskii's full approval, to the Rumiantsev Public Museum in Moscow in 1826. There they formed the core of an "Ethnographic Cabinet" from which emerged the Dashkov Ethnographic Museum in 1867. "The basis of the Cabinet was formed by the ethnographical collections of Count N.P. Rumiantsev, which, at the time of their transfer to Moscow, had consisted of 163 display items, about 400 objects in all, most material culture of the Pacific Islanders, North America (Alaska), or Japan. These had been assembled, on Count Rumiantsev's instructions, during the round-the-world expedition of Kruzenshtern and Lisianskii."[80] Any Easter Island artefacts sent to Moscow from St. Petersburg—that is, from *Neva*'s store—were among those lost in the turmoil of the Great Patriotic War.[81]

Even a cursory attempt to determine the provenance of Easter Island artefacts that have survived to the present, and that Soviet museum authorities claim have been in Russia since the early 1800s, reveals that soon after *Neva*'s return to Kronstadt on 4 August 1806, her artefact collections were split up and subsequently moved about St. Petersburg.[82] It is clear that some artefacts were taken from *Neva* and put with others from *Nadezhda* for a public exhibition of Pacific and Chinese artefacts held, in September 1806, in a building rented by the Russian-American Company on Gorokhovaia (Harrach) Street, in the city centre.[83] Others went to the Admiralty Department's museum.[84] A third group went to the *Kunstkammer* of the Academy of Sciences.[85] This last was accompanied by an inventory drawn up by Lisianskii himself, who continued to be actively interested in Oceanic artefacts until his death.[86] The inventory did not mention anything from Easter Island.

The Russian texts do not mention collecting on the shore of Hanga-roa Bay during Kotzebue's visit in 1816. Such silence, however, proves nothing. For instance, although *Riurik* left Hawaii that same year with assorted artefacts, some of which remained in Moscow till the present century,[87] the Soviet ethnologist Iuliia M. Likhtenberg points out that we have practically no information on that score from Kotzebue.[88] There are few passages in his *Voyage* of the sort found in his description of a visit to Kamehameha's court at Kailua on 24 November 1816 ("one of his ministers presented me with a collar of coloured feathers.")[89] Was the boat party from *Riurik* ashore in Hanga-roa long enough to pick up artefacts? We know that Chamisso had time to spot an unfamiliar plant among the boulders and pick it for later inspection in his cabin.[90] Did the islanders have artefacts at hand, ready for barter, when the Russians came ashore? We cannot say positively, but it is noteworthy that Nathan Winship of the *Albatross,* and other Yankee masters who looked in hurriedly at Hanga-roa in the years preceding *Riurik's* arrival, carried Hawaiian artefacts to North America for sale from at least 1805. And when HMS *Blossom* (Captain F.W. Beechey) reached that bay in 1825, the Easter Islanders immediately offered fruit and wooden figurines. "Bananas, yams, potatoes, sugar cane, nets, idols, &c, were offered for sale, and some were even thrown into the boat, leaving their visitors to make what return they chose."[91] Such actions most probably induced earlier European visitors to leave the islanders more goods of the kind they wanted: clothes and iron.

The Peter-the-Great Museum of the N.N. Miklukho-Maklai Institute of Anthropology and Ethnography (MAE) in Leningrad holds three wooden artefacts that its inventory asserts were from Easter Island and were presented to the *Kunstkammer,* MAE's predecessor, in 1827–28.[92] They are all in collection 736 and are claimed to have gone to the *Kunstkammer* from the Admiralty Museum.[93] This was the Muzei Admiralteiskago Departamenta Morskago Ministerstva, into which went curios brought to Russia by servants of the Navy.[94] Regrettably, all original documents relating to the transfer of artefacts from that museum to the Academy, a process that continued from 1826 until 1830, are now missing.[95] Several factors, however, substantiate the Soviet assertion that objects in MAE's collection 736 were indeed brought back "by the first Russian mariners to visit the South Pacific Ocean"[96] and therefore predate 1828. Much work has been done, in connection with Leningrad's Hawaiian artefacts, by Adrienne Kaeppler.[97] The following discussion deals with the three pre-1828 Easter Island statuettes or figurines: Peter-the-Great Museum's items 736-203, -204, and -205.

First, all three artefacts were carved with obsidian (*mataa*) from Mount Orito or with a basalt adze (*maea-toki*) from La Pérouse Bay, not with implements of European origin.[98] This suggests an early nineteenth-century or older date of manufacture. Second, a number of the Marquesan artefacts whose numbering at MAE (736-175, -177, -178, -182, -184) indicates that they pre-dated 1828, have been satisfactorily identified by L.G. Rozina, a former associate of that institution, with illustrations on Plate 1 of Lisianskii's 1812 *Atlas*.[99] Third, other Marquesan and some Hawaiian artefacts also collected by Lisianskii in 1804 but long kept in collection 750 in the Peter-the-Great Museum, may be so identified on the basis of illustrations in that same *Atlas;*[100] an 1807 inventory still held in the Leningrad Section of the Archive of the Academy of Sciences of the USSR (LOAAN);[101] and, most convincingly, Lisianskii's own handwriting on certain labels that were once attached to the appropriate artefacts from Nukuhiva or the Kona Coast of Hawaii, but were removed in 1903 and stuck on to a new inventory of collection 750 by the ethnographer and archivist E.I. Petri.[102] Fourth, Petri also began work on a new inventory for collection 736, the draft of which indicates that some artefacts still had their 1807 labels attached.[103] It is noteworthy that labels now on Petri's 1903 inventory of MAE's collection 750 clearly show that the collection presented to the *Kunstkammer* by Lisianskii was originally far larger than the modern collection, with twenty-three artefacts; item 750-17, for example, was "Lisjansky No. 76."[104] It is true that we lack incontrovertible evidence that the Easter Island objects were sent from the Admiralty Museum to the *Kunstkammer* in 1827–28 or had been in the Academy's keeping since 1806–7, but there is little doubt that they date from the early 1800s. No other artefacts in either collection 736 or 750 appear to have been acquired by Russian naval officers from other mariners, from residents of Pacific outposts, or from museums, as Easter Island artefacts certainly were acquired by Miklukho-Maklai and Vladimir V. Sviatlovskii in 1871 and 1908.[105] And even if the Easter Island figurines in collection 736 were not acquired by Lisianskii or Kotzebue, their pre-1828 origin is practically certain.

What, then, are Leningrad's old Easter Island carvings? They are a *tangata-manu,* or bird-man image combining the head of a bird with an emaciated human body; a *moai kavakava,* a male wooden image with emaciated body and elongated head; and a grotesque *moai paapaa,* or female image.[106]

At the time of the Russian visits to Easter Island, the annual feast of the bird-man, held at Orongo on the southwest point, was extremely important to the natives, and had been for many generations. The rites were not only associated with the cult of the greatest island god, Makemake, but were also endowed with special social significance, since notions of prestige and economic privilege were all connected with them. Ostensibly, the purpose of the ceremony, which took place in southern summer, was to obtain the first egg of the *manu-tara* (sooty tern, *Sterna fuscata*). Servants (*hopu*) of the chiefs searched for it on Motu-nui islet. The chief whose servant obtained the coveted first egg also gained the title of bird-man, which, surrounded with tapus, brought its temporary holder material advantages and huge moral-cum-religious benefits. The far-reaching significance of this cult in pre-contact Easter Island is obvious from the extensive relics at Orongo and from the frequent use of bird and bird-man motifs in all forms of Easter Island art—tablets, wooden images, and petroglyphs. Orongo village, which lay in the narrow ridge separating the ocean from Rano-kao crater lake, was filled with people during the feast but deserted when the Russians passed.[107] On its rocks and in its caves, the image of the bird-headed god was carved more than one hundred and fifty times. Wooden images such as that acquired by the Russians are rare, however. The bird-man image (MAE's 736-204) illustrates the extent to which conventional motifs were imposed upon all Easter Island wood carving. First published by Walter Lehmann ("Essai d'une monographie bibliographique sur l'Ile de Pâques," *Anthropos,* vol. 2, p. 260, 1907), it was again brought to the notice of Western ethnologists in 1935 by the French scholar Stephen Chauvet.[108] It stands 33.5 cm high, with a beak almost 8 cm long, and is on semi-permanent public display in the Peter-the-Great Museum's Australia and Oceania Hall.

The male image (*moai kavakava*), No. 736–203, shows all the standard characteristics of that form of ancient carving: disproportionately large and elongated head; eyeballs made of polyhedral obsidian pieces; long ears, protruding larynx, and prominent ribs and spinal column.[109] It too stands 33 cm high and is of dark, polished wood. Artifact 736–205, which the Soviet authorities describe as a *moai-miro* (wood image) rather than *moai paapaa* (flat image), no doubt in recognition of the several unusual features of the piece,[110] seems to fall between the categories of female and grotesque *moai*. Both forms belong to the ancient repertoire of the Easter Island carvers.[111]

Like that of the great stone statues, the significance of such images is now unknown. Clearly they had ritual use and importance, but the details have vanished with the demise of the priestly class in the 1862 slave raids by the Peruvians.[112] Clearly, some images were taken out during feasts by men who danced with them, and many were kept wrapped in tapa. It is now commonly accepted that the wooden images with cadaverous ribcages were intended to represent the spirits of the dead.[113] Small wooden images seem to have been used in every part of Polynesia as temporary tabernacles for the gods and/or ancestral spirits; examples from Tahiti and New Zealand support the possible function of the Leningrad *moai* discussed here.[114]

As a group, these three wooden *moai* show the finest craftsmanship, which is natural, given the time of acquisition. As A. Métraux puts it, "figures not carved for sale" were characterized by "elegance of outline and by a vigorous style . . . expressive of an art with a long tradition."[115]

Other Aspects of Material Culture

The Russian texts and Choris's three "Easter Island plates" (1822, pl. 9; 1826, pls. 10–11) also give data on four areas of material culture hitherto neglected in this survey: dwellings and stone structures containing chambers; canoe making; the manufacture of woven or plaited articles; and weaponry. Although the data are brief, they belie William J. Thomson's remark that Lisianskii and Kotzebue made such hurried calls at Easter Island that "their journals afford little information."[116]

In 1804 and 1816, the Russians saw at Hanga-roa thatched houses of the classical type: "made of reeds and somewhat resembling large upturned boats" (Korobitsyn). They recognized these as communal dwellings. Some were one hundred feet or more in length, up to twenty feet wide, and some twelve feet from ground to ridgepole. The largest Cook had seen in 1774 were sixty feet long, nine feet high at the centre, and approximately the same in breadth,[117] while the French had in 1786 seen a huge community house three hundred feet long, large enough to shelter at least two hundred persons.[118] It is plain that Easter Island frame houses varied greatly in size, depending on their functions. Lisianskii was reminded of both upturned boats and "elongated barrows." The houses did not stand in organized patterns. Their entrances were from three to four feet high and "at the edge of the elevation on which they stand" (Korobitsyn). Cook and Wales had estimated these doors (*papare*) to be a mere two feet high, but also found them "conical" and "made in the middle of the structure," as did Lisianskii and Povalishin through English telescopes. Many huts were surrounded by sugar cane plots or banana trees; and a number, to judge by Korobitsyn's phrasing, struck the Russians as large enough to house "ten or twenty families." "The long house marked on La Pérouse's map," noted Kotzebue, still stood, "together with the stone hut on the shore." This was an assembly house (*hare nui*) being constructed near Hanga-roa when La Pérouse arrived; it was inspected and scrupulously described by the engineer Bernizet.[119] Kotzebue had the Frenchman's work open before him in *Riurik*'s wardroom.

The "stone hut" was probably the structure depicted at the centre of

Choris's *Vue de l'Ile de Pâques* and described by Choris himself as seven feet high, made of small rocks, and containing a chamber accessible through a side opening. This was a *tupa,* or turtle watchtower, corresponding to the structure described by George Forster as a heap of stones "piled up into a little hillock, which had one steep perpendicular side, where a hole went underground."[120] The British were denied access to the place,[121] which Bernizet later supposed to be a repository for stores and prized possessions.[122] Choris did not depict the *tapu* pillars that stood about six hundred feet from the shoreline and a little south of the Russians' landing place. He observed, though, that they were numerous, about four feet high, and had a "paving-stone" (in French, *dalle*) placed on top and painted white. These cairns, as Cook and La Pérouse had rightly inferred, were ordinary symbols for *tapu.*[123] Four feet was almost their maximum height, judging by nineteenth-century evidence.[124]

Russian evidence for the Easter Island canoe is more precious and controversial than for land structures. Choris's two drawings, in particular, have provoked discussion.[125] In 1804 the Russians saw no craft whatsoever on or near Easter Island, which led Lisianskii to suppose that canoes of the sort seen by La Pérouse "were no longer in use." In 1816 *Riurik* was met by two canoes, each containing two (Kotzebue and Choris) or three (Chamisso) men. These craft were exactly like those seen by the French, except that some had double outriggers, or balancers on both sides. They were "from five to six feet long, and about a foot in breadth, made of narrow boards joined together" (Kotzebue). Gonzalez's people had spoken in similar terms of "narrow boards," and La Pérouse had seen canoes of similar length:[126] canoe-builders were as conservative on Easter Island as in other parts of Polynesia.

Choris's sketches, Figures 1 and 2 of Plate 10 in *Vues et Paysages* (1826), indicate that both ends of canoes seen in 1816 were extended, resembling narrow bowsprits. James Hornell estimated that these projections were some fifteen inches long.[127] One of the canoes drawn by Choris (Fig. 1) has a double outrigger of thin booms resting horizontally on the gunwales and lending support to two slender floats. Alfred Métraux's contention that the craft in question probably lacked a double outrigger—that is, that the representation was inaccurate—must be tempered by Kotzebue's text.[128] Choris wrote independently of his former captain while in Paris in 1820–22, and Kotzebue had in any case seen the canoes with his own eyes. They were, he stated, "furnished on both sides with an outrigger." The statement is unambiguous. Métraux's skepticism with regard to Choris's work is further undermined by his remarks in connection with Figure 2 of plate 10, showing a craft to whose outrigger booms are tied horseshoe-shaped frames. Even in 1934 a few islanders recalled that such rod frames had been lashed to the booms as supports for nets or fishing lines; and Métraux himself refers to just such a "contrivance" put, according to Hornell, on the sterns of canoes at Takatoto in the Tuamotu Archipelago.[129] In his 1912 study *Easter Island: The Rapanui Speech and the Peopling of Southeast Polynesia*, the linguist and ethnologist William Churchill demonstrated convincingly the many linguistic affiliations between Easter Islanders and natives of "the Paumotu."[130] It is indeed possible that Choris gave a wrong impression of the angle at which the booms were set athwart the canoe in question; and it is true, as Métraux observes, that the Easter Islanders would hardly have installed nonfunctional floats on their craft, wood being so scarce. The fact remains, however, that Choris was a professional artist, and his accuracy could have been criticized by men who had been with him aboard *Riurik*, if such criticism had been justified. Métraux himself makes a further point that undercuts his rejection of Choris's evidence: "it would not be surprising for a native to think of attaching a second outrigger to compensate for the inefficiency of a single float too slender to insure the balance of the boat."[131] Easter Island craft were unseaworthy in the later eighteenth century, and the natives were constantly wary of being capsized.[132]

In 1804 Povalishin traded some pieces of material and coin earrings for a "little grass bag full of cooked sweet potato." It was fifteen inches in length, excellently woven, and very like baskets in which the British had been given food thirty years before.[133] Lisianskii's phrasing indicates that the basket was made not of bulrushes but rather of material stripped from the banana trunk sheath. The technique of making such containers was used even in modern times.[134] The mat also acquired by *Neva,* "about 4 and three-quarters feet long and 15½ inches wide" and made of "rushes" woven around central sugar cane stems, was obviously a *pora* raft of the type seen by numerous European voyagers and developed to compensate for the island's notorious shortage of timber.[135] The length specified by the Russians corresponds with Plate 44 in Aubert Du Petit-Thouars' *Voyage autour du monde* (1841), where a *pora* reaches from the ground to a native's chin. Choris and Chamisso made clear that "very neat fishing nets" were stowed in *Riurik;* neither, regrettably, provided details.

Lastly, we turn to the weapon referred to by Choris (1826 text) as a club (*une massue*) and depicted by him in Figure 4 of Plate 10 of the *Vues et paysages*. It was evidently the only manufactured weapon observed by the Russians on Easter Island. The principal armament there was still, as in earlier times, small stones. The club was certainly a short wooden one, *paoa,* of the sort used in hand-to-hand fighting and described by Thomson as resembling the Maori *patu* or *mere,* "except that they were invariably made of wood."[136] It shows several anomalous and odd features, however. First, *paoa* in the major collections do not show as distinctly rounded an upper "head" or as long a "neck."[137] Second, they lack such extensive carving as that on the lower face of Figure 4. Third, they invariably—unless furnished with lizard-head handles—have more heavily carved humanoid faces on the handle and show lines to represent hair. The carving on Choris's club is unique. A few remarks may be ventured on the matter of its reliability as ethnographic evidence and on the processes of representation in 1816–21.

It is unlikely that Choris handled the club ashore: neither time nor circumstance permitted it. It is possible that he sketched what he could see of the club on the spot, and that the head remained unfinished in the absence of the article itself or of proper notes. The head was presumably being held and so was hidden. It is also conceivable that the weapon was just being manufactured and that the humanoid face had yet to be more fully carved (though in this case the elaborate linear and rectangular carving below seems rather odd and premature). At any rate, we know that Choris took his portfolio to Paris in the early weeks of 1819 and that the lithography for *Voyage pittoresque* was done, under the control of Noël Aîné et Cie., by half-a-dozen different craftsmen of varying skill.[138] "Since it was impossible to know in advance the number of pages of text that would make up the work," as Choris observed in his introduction of 1822, "the author had materials relating to each particular land printed separately. Each of these parts had its own title . . . and pagination, so that, at the conclusion of the work, they might be arranged in a way corresponding with the dates of the voyage." In short, Choris had in mind a series of pamphlets that could be combined ultimately to form a book. Because of *Riurik*'s route, Easter Island was among the first illustrations and remained that way in the book's organization. Through Chamisso, now back in Berlin, Choris had acquired a number of influential friends in Paris, including the zoologist Georges Léopold Cuvier (1769–1832) and the Prussian botanist Karl-Sigismund Kunth (1788–1850). Both collaborated on the *Voyage pittoresque*, providing commentaries on the natural science that Choris depicted. Other friends and collaborators, such as the younger zoologist Achille Valenciennes (1794–1863) and the journalist and traveller Jean-Baptiste-Benoît Eyriès (1767–1846), a founder-member of the French Geographical Society and Choris's general editor in 1820–22, were found independently. Through his painting masters François Gérard (1770–1837) and Jean-Baptiste Régnault (1754–1829),[139] Choris had by 1821 made contact with the Noël family of land- and seascape painters and lithographers. Alexis Nicolas Noël (1792–1871), whose *Voyage pittoresque en France et en Allemagne* had won critical acclaim in 1818–19, took a particular interest in Choris's project, which in some ways echoed his French and German one.[140] In 1821 he hired Auguste-André Bovet (1799–1864), the Swiss engraver who had only recently introduced the lithographic process to Geneva, to work on Choris's *Vue de l'Ile de Pâques*.[141] For the lithographing of the first two bulletins of the embryonic *Vues et paysages* in 1821, however, Choris, Noël, and Eyriès turned to other men. Plates 10 and 11 of the bulletin entitled *Ile de Pâques ou Vaihiou, et Ile Rumanzoff* (the two Easter Island plates) went to Langlumé of Paris.

Langlumé was a prolific worker, best known to Choris's mentors (who were followers of the cool Neoclassical school of Jacques-Louis David) for his lithographs based on mythological subjects by Prud'hon.[142] He had no known sympathy for ethnographic or exotically scientific themes and worked, rather quickly, on commission.[143] The Easter Island plates of 1821–22 were not among his best. It is, however, very unlikely that a man with such a reputation to protect would simply have produced ornamental variations on Choris's theme, a simple wooden club. We have to conclude that Choris made the best of an unfavourable situation, drew such aspects of the *paoa* as he could at Hanga-roa, and then left his study incomplete.

Botany

Riurik brought two distinguished botanists to Easter Island: Adelbert von Chamisso and Morten Wormskiöld. Johann Friedrich Eschscholtz, the ship's surgeon, also had botanical interests, although zoology was closer to his heart.[144] So, too, in a professional way, did Choris as artist: both *Voyage pittoresque autour du monde* (1822) and *Vues et Paysages* (1826) contain correctly drawn and detailed Pacific island flora.[145] Unlike Eschscholtz and the youthful painter Choris, though, both Chamisso and Wormskiöld, a Danish naval officer with much experience of field work in Greenland and Northern Norway, had arrived in the Pacific with instructions to concern themselves specifically with plants. Chamisso received no "sailing orders" from the expedition's sponsor, Count Rumiantsev, and studied what he chose in the realm of zoology and botany; his Pacific botanizing of 1816–17 bore out any expectations the Count may have had of him.[146] Morten Wormskiöld, a highly able natural historian who was to pass more than two years in Kamchatka (1816–18), had orders from the Danish government.[147] Here is Kruzenshtern:

> Since a rich harvest of naturalia was to be expected, the Count had appointed a competent naturalist to accompany the expedition. The

forthcoming venture was, in fact, of the greatest importance to science... Dr. Ledebour, then professor of natural history at the University of Dorpat, had originally been chosen as the naturalist on the expedition, and he had himself proposed as his assistant Dr. Eschscholtz, who was at the same time to serve as ship's surgeon. But because Dr. Ledebour's health prevented him from realizing his wish to voyage, Mr. A. von Chamisso of Berlin went as naturalist in his stead, having been recommended by Professors Rudolph and Lichtenstein... Though lack of space made it impossible to engage another gentleman of science for the undertaking, Count Rumiantsev could not resist the wishes of the learned Dane, Mr. von Wormskiöld, to sail also: he desired no salary, only the payment of his basic living expenses.[148]

Chamisso and Wormskiöld joined *Riurik* in Copenhagen in August 1815 and collaborated occasionally, in friendly fashion, over the next eleven months.[149] Wormskiöld kept a full diary throughout his Pacific crossing of 1816, sending letters at intervals to a respected Danish botanist, Jens W. Hornemann.[150] On the basis of these, Dr. Hornemann placed a series of short articles in the Copenhagen literary journal *Dansk Literatur-Tidende* in 1816–18.[151] Wormskiöld's activities with the Russians in Oceania are scarcely touched upon in published works, and his *Riurik* journal has never appeared in print.[152] Chamisso's *Tagebuch*, on the other hand, has been available in printed form since 1836[153] and complements his more circumspect and sober *Bemerkungen und Ansichten* of 1819–21.[154]

Chamisso and, probably, Wormskiöld, landed near Hanga-roa village at 3:00 PM on 28 March 1816. (Kotzebue wrote that seventeen men put off in two boats, but Choris's *Vue de l'Ile de Pâques* shows nineteen, including six non-rowers who presumably were officers and savants.[155] At least one of *Riurik*'s officers would have remained aboard during this landing; this officer, illustrated by Choris, was Lieutenant Ivan Zakharin. Both Shishmarev and Kotzebue went ashore. Thus, four of the six men landing were non-naval gentlemen, and a process of elimination tells us that they were Eschscholtz, Chamisso, Choris, and Wormskiöld.)[156] The naturalists had been at sea for three weeks and had seen little of scientific interest since leaving Talcaguano in Chile.[157] After reading up on Easter Island they were anxious to verify what La Pérouse's people and the Forsters had observed where flora, fauna, and the natives were concerned.[158]

We have seen that a few minutes after they landed, the Russians were pelted with stones by the Easter Islanders. Despite such danger and the wish to observe the attackers and their artefacts, Chamisso managed to spot and collect at least two plants growing on Hanga-roa's shoreline: a wild celery, *Apium graveolens* L., and a star thistle, *Centaurea apula* Lam.[159] He kept both in his handkerchief and took them back to the ship for pressing in a blotting-paper book.[160]

Chamisso left St. Petersburg for Berlin in early winter 1818, taking with him a large portion of his botanical collection from the *Riurik*'s voyage. Like Choris, he maintained a correct correspondence with Kruzenshtern but felt no urge to return to Russia. In Berlin he was received with royal honours and appointed Curator of the city's well-financed Botanical Garden, which, like the new Friedrich Wilhelm University, seemed to celebrate freedom regained. After a decade, Berlin in 1815 was free of French occupation forces, and the Botanical Garden itself had lately undergone a renaissance, thanks to the energy of Karl Ludwig Willdenow (1765–1812), whose famous herbarium included more than 20,000 specimens.[161] Chamisso brought his Pacific herbarium to a collection that had grown from donations by the greatest French and German travellers: Bonpland, La Billardière, Humboldt, and Klein. His fortune did not end at that. He very soon established contact with a range of fine collaborators, men like Georg Friedrich Kaulfuss (1773–1830), George Bentham (1800–84), and the publisher-botanist Diedrich Franz von Schlechtendal (1794–1866.) Even in 1823, Schlechtendal was planning to publish his *Linnaea: Ein Journal für die Botanik*, the first volume of which came out in 1826. Chamisso's material was precisely what the publisher required. From their collaboration sprang a comprehensive listing and description of the plants brought to Berlin from the *Riurik*'s Pacific expedition. That major work, which treated plants by family and genus, had the general title *De Plantis expeditione speculatoria Romanzoffiana observatis: Rationem dicunt Adalbertus de Chamisso et Diedericus de Schlechtendal*. Chamisso justly observed in his introduction to the work that Easter Island was not celebrated for the wealth of its flora, but was rather infamous for its poverty thereof (*Insula Paschatis ... silvis denudata, pauperie Florae infamis*), and that circumstances had not favoured *his* collecting (*vix in aridum posuimus pedem, gentes enim minaces nos arcuere.*)[162] Still, he was able to offer the learned world material on two little-known plants.

He provided a full description of the member of the family Umbelliferae (parsley) that he noted, sailors were wont to refer to as a nostrum or medicinal plant: wild celery, *Apium graveolens* L.[163] It was most likely of interest to *Riurik*'s seamen and to Dr. Eschscholtz, as well as to the foreign botanist. Chamisso had with him on board the basic botanical results of Cook's second voyage, notably the two Forsters' joint effort, *Caracteres generum Plantarum, quas in Itinere ad Insulas maris austra-*

lis Collegerunt... annis 1772–1775 (London 1775), and George Forster's subsequent commentary, *De Plantibus esculentis Insularum Oceani
Australis commentatio botanica* (Berlin 1786). He therefore recognized
that the celery in question had appeared in that useful little handbook and
so was not a fresh discovery.[164] Conversely, Forster had not given all the
data he himself could now provide. The *Apium* growing at Hanga-roa was
perhaps two feet high, branching above, with broadly triangular leaves.[165]

Starting in 1826, several noted botanists completely described one or
other plant family represented in the Chamisso herbarium in Prussia.
George Bentham, nephew and secretary of the eminent philosopher
Jeremy Bentham, described the mints.[166] Kaulfuss took on the *Filices* and
soon extended his project to include all members of that genus.[167] Thistles
were offered to a youthful German botanist, Christian Friedrich Lessing,
who accordingly presented information on *Centaurea apula* L. (Compositae) from Easter Island.[168] By coincidence, his publication was
delayed by a botanizing journey that he made to Central Norway, where
his route crossed that taken by Wormskiöld in 1807.[169] He too built upon
his work with Chamisso, to write a survey of *Compositae* in general:
Synopsis generum Compositarum (Berlin 1832).

Chamisso's Easter Island thistle had a violet head, and differed little
from thistles in Chile. It too was already known to the scientific community, as *Calcitrapa patibilcensis,* but was now botanically described at
some length for the first time.[170] Preoccupied by the implications of his
discovery in 1819 of metagenesis in the subclass *Salpae,* Chamisso paid
little attention, in the last part of his life, to his plants from Oceania.
Sadly, all were lost during World War II.[171]

Hydrography

The official plans and objectives of the round-the-world expedition undertaken by Kruzenshtern and Lisianskii changed several times between
July 1802 and August 1803,[172] and again early in 1804, when Kruzenshtern finally arrived in the Pacific.[173] Initially, the emphasis of the
venture was purely economic. Diplomatic and political objectives were
added at the tsar's behest, and so Ambassador Rezanov gained a berth
aboard *Nadezhda,* to her captain's pique.[174] From the outset, however,
Kruzenshtern meant to emphasize the expedition's maritime and
scientific aspects. Academically inclined, he was elected a corresponding
member of St. Petersburg's Academy of Sciences on 25 April 1803,[175] and
for two years actively prepared for scientific and investigative work in
Oceania. Part of his course of preparation was historical hydrography.
Nadezhda and *Neva* were to traverse those southern waters where the later

eighteenth-century cartographers still placed the misty "Davis Land" that had allegedly been sighted by the *Batchelor's Delight* sometime in 1687,[176] as well as half-a-dozen other islands that the Portuguese or Spanish had supposedly observed due west of Chile. Busy though he was, in 1803 Kruzenshtern studied the available charts, intending to maximize the benefit to the naval sciences of any route he might follow from Cape Horn to the Polynesian Islands.[177]

As it turned out, Kruzenshtern was obliged to abandon his plans for exploration in the South Pacific Ocean. Russian-American Company cargo was required in Kamchatka and he wished to make delivery and move on to Japan before September.[178] According to the Soviet historian V.V. Nevskii, "Originally, Kruzenshtern had intended to devote the summer of 1804 to geographical investigations in Oceania; but he had aboard a cargo for the colonies ... and decided not to call at Easter Island but to take the *Nadezhda* straight to the Marquesas Islands."[179] By now, however, he had made a study of the "Davis Land problem." A tireless and methodical researcher, he made full use of the ship's library—provided by the Academy, the Admiralty, and even the Company for his use— even as *Nadezhda* crossed the South Pacific. This is clear from the publication dates of his learned articles in the St. Petersburg periodical *Tekhnologicheskii Zhurnal*, then controlled by the Academy. One of them, published early in 1806, analysed Dutch records of Abel Tasman's movements around Van Diemen's Land in 1642.[180] Both the preparatory work and the drafting of the paper were undertaken at sea—a virtuoso demonstration of his power of concentration. Kruzenshtern's reflections of the matter of "Davis Land," as reported by William Dampier and Davis's surgeon, Lionel Wafer, also found their way into the same journal, in whose pages there was in 1804–6 a public debate about Davis and his alleged discovery. Suffice it here to mention a most sensible contribution, entitled "Regarding the Existence of Kruzenshtern's 'Davis Land'," from the astronomer Fedor Ivanovich Shubert (1758–1825).[181] Recently named head of the St. Petersburg Observatory, Shubert was a personal acquaintance of Kruzenshtern and the author of a seminal *Guide to Astronomical Observations for Determining Latitude and Longitude* (1803), copies of which went with *Nadezhda* and *Neva* to Oceania.[182] With Kruzenshtern's hearty collaboration, Shubert subsequently offered courses in astronomy for naval officers about to leave on distant voyages and published the *Maritime Calendar* (*Morskoi mesiatseslov*), which more than once referred to Davis, Easter Island, and associated cartographic problems in the years 1813–20.[183]

The Pacific crossings of *Nadezhda* and *Neva* in 1804–5 enabled the Russians to develop theoretical and practical expertise never before seen in their naval service: in hydrography, geodesy, and meteorology. Kruzenshtern paid heed to the "Orders with Regard to Mineralogy and Theory of the Earth" drafted for him in 1803 by the Academician Mikhail V. Severgin.[184] He and others published much useful material in 1812.[185] Meteorological observations were made in the South Pacific Ocean from *Nadezhda* and *Neva* that, in terms of both procedure and completeness, complemented observations made that very season (1804) in Siberia.[186] Kruzenshtern's tables, like Johann Caspar Hörner's, were early models of their kind and set an admirable precedent for later Russian publications based on Pacific voyages.[187] It is impossible, however, to examine either Kruzenshtern's *Voyage Round the World* (1809–12) or the accounts of his subordinates and not be conscious that he saw hydrography as the queen of sciences for all seafaring men of every age. He himself was among the greatest nineteenth-century hydrographers and was recognized as such throughout the educated world before his death.[188]

It was not a coincidence that the years 1804–8 saw huge advances in hydrography, marine astronomy, and scientific training in the Russian Fleet. When they visited Easter Island in 1804, Lisianskii's people depended, first, on foreign printed guides and, second, on recent handbooks on surveying and hydrography by Admiral Gavriil A. Sarychev and Academician P.Ia. Gamaleia.[189] Later on, Gamaleia's *Theory and Practice of Navigation* (St. P., 1806–8) showed the fruits of the *Nadezhda*'s and *Neva*'s experiences. In particular, Part 3 had thirty tables to assist in calculating geographical position and no less than eighteen sections on planetary movements, the use of modern instruments and guides, mathematics, and "the arts of navigation." Such progress was paralleled at Kronstadt and other naval centres by advances in cartography itself. Here too a vital role was played by Kruzenshtern, who as captain of a ship in Oceania in 1804 had depended on the atlases and charts of Aaron Arrowsmith drawn in another century.[190] By 1807 Kruzenshtern was fully conscious of the need for what became his magnum opus: *An Atlas of the South Sea*, published in 1823–26 at State expense, with appendices added in 1826–36).[191]

Kruzenshtern had both the duty and the pleasure of collecting materials for his new *Atlas* and rectifying the errors in charts of the Pacific used by all navies in 1808–38. Accordingly, he wanted the *Riurik* to sail into latitude 27°S from South America, to search for "Davis Land." There, if anywhere, he had surmised in 1804, it must exist.[192] Kotzebue duly steered from Concepcion, Chile, to latitude 27°20'S, longitude 88°4'W and thence due west, "in the neighbourhood where Davis's Land is supposed to lie." He persisted in vain for five days (16–20 March 1816), reaching longitude 95°35'W. It was neither the first nor the last time that Russian seamen hunted such chimerical and isolated specks in the immense Pacific wastes due west of Chile: even sensible Lisianskii had in late March 1804 hoped to sight an unknown land in latitude 39°20'S, longitude 98°42'W.[193] There, in 1791, Captain Etienne Marchand of the merchantman *Solide* had seen a flock of birds "never known to fly far from shore."[194] No land was found, however.

The maps aboard *Riurik,* including Aaron Arrowsmith's,[195] showed other rocky outcrops in the ocean. Wareham's Rocks were among them, and Kotzebue vainly sought them also in the area of latitude 26°30'S, longitude 100°W. Tropical birds raised his hopes more than once, but in the end nothing was found.[196] *Riurik* moved west towards Sala-y-Gomez, a barren island some two hundred miles east of Easter Island, sighting it at 10:00 AM on 25 March 1816

The Russians approached Sala-y-Gomez cautiously from the south, and were depressed by its bleak and melancholy air. It was inhabited only by sea birds and its points were lashed by the surf. Involuntarily the visitors scanned both reefs and rocks for signs of broken ships. Such abundance of birds' eggs, Chamisso reflected, "would have sufficed but too adequately to protract the castaway's wretched existence, caught on barren rocks between the ocean and the sky."[197] By Vasilii S. Khromchenko's reckoning, the island's centre lay in latitude 26°36'15''S, longitude 105°34'28''W.[198] Kruzenshtern later accepted Kotzebue's opinion that Wareham's Rocks did not exist and had been confused with Sala-y-Gomez. Since 1815 he had been on "sick leave" from active duty and lived at his estate of Ass in Estonia while working on his *Atlas of the South Sea.* He analysed the cartographic data received from Kotzebue in 1818 together with other materials, "and so, sorting out materials by their degree of reliability, he [Kruzenshtern] step by step introduced strict order into chaos."[199]

The general chart of Easter Island made from *Neva* in 1804 and headed "Rogeven [Roggeveen] or Easter Island, Described by the Ship *Neva* in the Year 1804" was published in Lisianskii's *Sobranie kart i risunkov* (St. P. 1812) without more specific attribution. Together with three views of the island from the SE and ESE at ranges of 40–24 miles, it was reproduced in the N.V. Dumitrashko edition of the 1812 *Puteshestvie vokrug sveta...* (Moscow 1947). Elevation contours were an advance over eighteenth-century work, as the principal volcanic masses well indicated. In cartographic style, the chart is similar to the better known Nukuhivan work of May 1804 (reproduced in green tint by the London printer John Booth in 1814),[200] and so was probably based on Lisianskii's surveying and penmanship.

Neither Lisianskii's nor Kotzebue's surveying around Easter Island,

however, had hydrographic significance equal to Kruzenshtern's collation of the data of Kotzebue and earlier captains on Sala-y-Gomez Island.
Specifically, Kruzenshtern rid modern maps of "Wareham's Rocks" and
produced the evidence that should also have rid them (but did not until the
1840s) of "Gwyn Rock." He pointed out the near certainty that the
Americans had actually sighted Sala-y-Gomez, not another outcrop
("Gwyn"),[201] and incidentally observed that Captain Gomez had placed
his island 8' further north and 8' further east than had the Russians. Despite his personal friendship with the cartographer-admiral Espinosa,
whom he met in London,[202] Kruzenshtern had a poor opinion of Spanish
navigation and the resulting South Sea charts.[203] Arriving back in Berlin in
1819, Chamisso wasted no time before examining Kruzenshtern's *Contributions to Hydrography* (Leipzig 1819), especially as they related to Pacific areas that he himself had lately visited. He was pleased with what he
read about the Carolines, the Radak Chain, and Easter Island and the outcrops to its east.[204]

Part Two

NEW ZEALAND

Introductory Remarks

Russian knowledge of New Zealand and the Maori dates from the late seventeenth century. New Zealand was the first region of Polynesia of which the Russians had authoritative data, all collected from the Dutch. The Dutch material was complemented in the later eighteenth century by primary accounts of Captain James Cook's several visits to that country and his lengthy stays within Queen Charlotte Sound. In 1808 and 1814, the first Russian encounters with the Maori took place at Cape Town and Sydney. Though the officers of the *Diana* and *Suvorov* found the Maoris from the Bay of Islands (Matara, Ruatara, Hongi Hika, and others) intellectually quick and very friendly, they could not think of them other than as recent and potential cannibals. The reports of Cook and his associates, published in German, French, and Russian, reinforced this association. Nonetheless, a Russian expedition led by Captain F.F. Bellingshausen paid a visit to Queen Charlotte Sound in 1820, using Cook's charts and accounts. It proved to be most important from the standpoint of ethnology, and was useful for the visitors as well, who were amply supplied with food.

4

EARLIER RUSSIAN KNOWLEDGE OF NEW ZEALAND, 1692–1814

Peter I founded a modern Russian navy in 1696 and entrusted Fedor M. Apraksin, its first Grand Admiral, with directing both "inner coasts hydrography" and cartography and with gathering maps.[1] Thus the Russian Navy in its infancy acquired a knowledge of New Zealand and the Maoris. This knowledge came from the work of the Dutchmen Abel Janszoon Tasman and Franchoijs Jacobszoon Visscher, his chief associate during the crucial voyage of the *Heemskerck* and *Zeehaan* to New Zealand in the latter part of 1642,[2] as described by other Dutchmen in the late 1600s, Dirck Rembrantszoon Nierop and Nicolaes Witsen.[3] Peter knew of Nierop's abbreviated summary of a presumably authentic copy of Tasman's journal, kept aboard the *Heemskerck* in 1642–43,[4] though not till twenty years after its appearance in Amsterdam in 1674.[5] His principal informant, however, was Witsen, both where Tasman and New Zealand were concerned and, in a far more sweeping way, about the peoples, resources, and sea-going canoes of Oceania. For like the tsar, Witsen was deeply interested in the arts and sciences of navigation in the East and in the Great South Sea.[6] By the late 1680s the tsar was certainly acquainted with Witsen's careful and authoritative study, *Aeloude en Hedendaegsche Scheepsbouw en Bestier* ... (*Ancient and Modern Shipbuilding and Management*..., Amsterdam: Commelijn, Broer & Appelaer 1671, 560 pages). Chapter 16 of that work, entitled "Indian Craft," offered materials and detailed illustrations of the craft of the Mariana Islanders and other Oceanic peoples, though not of Maori canoes.[7] An able scholar and geographer, Witsen thus brought Spanish and Portuguese primary sources to the notice of the Russians for the first time.

Witsen was born in 1641 of a wealthy family with naval interests but legal antecedents. He accompanied his father to Great Britain in his sixteenth year (1656), was well received by the Lord Protector, Oliver Cromwell, and ever after moved comfortably in academic as well as socially exalted circles.[8] By 1664 he was in Moscow as a member of a diplomatic mission from the Dutch States General, and he later acted as the "unofficial minister for Muscovite affairs" in Amsterdam.[9] Witsen had both mercantile and scientific interests in the northeastern parts of Asia (at that time the Dutch were still the only Europeans with permission to conduct a modest trade at Nagasaki), and followed cossack progress on the northern edge of "Tartary" as best he could. In 1692, he completed *Noord en Oost Tartarye* (*North and East Tartary*). It was based in part upon his Muscovite journals and materials more recently obtained from Russian agents of the Dutch, and in part on Dutch, Spanish, and Portuguese accounts of distant voyages.[10] The tsar, being very interested in discovery and navigation and in the problem of the "Strait of Anian" (which supposedly separated North America from Northeast Asia), had a solid working knowledge of this work. Not surprisingly, perhaps, Witsen had sent him and his co-ruler and half-sister, Sofia, a copy of the handsome first edition. The Dutchman was conscious of the great potential value of this link and kept it strong by many diplomatic, maritime, and other forms of service for the Russians in the Netherlands.[11] Peter was grateful for Witsen's book, which brought the Maori to his notice and to that of many other northern readers.[12]

Passages from *Aeloude en Hedendaegsche Scheepsbouw* and *Noord en Oost Tartarye* dealt with Pacific navigation and Maori canoe building and other crafts witnessed by Tasman and his men.

> In the East Indies and throughout the New World, one sees in general use craft carved out of tree trunks and known as cano or canoe. Large or small, according to the size of the tree, they are made from hollowed or burned out trunks, then spread outwards with struts. These craft are propelled by means of paddles and seldom carry sails. Cargo is simply placed on their bottom, but because they are never ballasted as such, these canoes overturn easily. They have no rudder, being steered by a long oar from the stern.[13]

An accompanying plate (37) illustrates four varieties of "East Indian" (Pacific or Indonesian) canoe, and another plate shows a double canoe from Guam.

The natives of Zeelandia Nova have deep, carrying voices, blow on musical instruments that sound like Moorish trumpets. . . and row their craft with paddles. They are of middling height, coarse in appearance, the skin tone being between brown and yellow, and have black hair tied up straight on top of the head, sometimes with a large white feather stuck in. Their craft, illustrated here, consist of two long and narrow outrigger canoes connected by boards or some other arrangement, so that, seated, they can look down at the water between the hulls. The paddles are about a fathom long and narrow, coming to a point. These people are very skilful in manoeuvring these craft. As for clothing, some wear mats, a few wear material, and most are naked from the waist up. They use long blunt pikes for weapons, as well as short heavy clubs made of wood.[14]

This is taken from an account of events in or near Golden Bay, New Zealand, on 18–19 December 1642, immediately before an attack by the Maori that left five Dutchmen dead.[15] The plate alluded to by Witsen, Plate 28 of Part 1 of *Noord en Oost Tartary,* is headed: *"Vaartuig en Gedaante der Inwooners van Zeelandia Nova" ("Craft and Appearance of the Inhabitants of New Zealand").* It was certainly examined by the Russians and, as an important illustration in the development of European perceptions of the Maori, elicited these comments from the New Zealand historian and bibliographer E.H. McCormick: "To the reader ignorant of Dutch, clearest evidence of Witsen's familiarity with Tasman's journals is found in illustrations based on the crude drawings of Isaak Gilseman, artist-draughtsman of the 1642–43 expedition. Of five that can be so identified in Witsen, there is one . . . that depicts a double canoe manned by Maoris of stocky, muscular build and in the distance a wild, somewhat forbidding landscape."[16] Peter read Dutch quite well but was doubtless attracted by Witsen's reworkings of Isaak Gilseman's drawings.[17] Witsen refers to Tasman's movements of 5–8 January 1643 near Three Kings' Islands thus:

At thirty degrees in Nova Zeelandia the people were tall, carried clubs and sticks as weapons, and cultivated land was observed along the shoreline. Along here is the passage into the South Sea. The natives came aboard, were offered gifts, and in return gave a small fishing line with mother-of-pearl hook. . . One finds coconuts here, and roots, and bananas, that may be had in exchange for nails, which these people prize highly. There were also many hogs. The people are primitive but kindly: their houses are unadorned and they sleep on bark mats on the earthen floor. There are no signs of religion.[18]

It is significant that, essentially as a result of the strong Russo-Dutch connections that existed by 1670, the tsar had access to such primary and secondary materials. Witsen, for his part, saw no reason why the Russians should not know and honour Dutch accomplishments at sea: he was a patriot as well as a scholar.

Peter's Grand Embassy to Western Europe in 1697–98 gave him ample opportunity to gather more useful information. He arrived in Amsterdam on 16 August, was received with proper pomp, and met his host, Witsen, who was Amsterdam's respected burgomaster.[19] The next day he visited the City Hall at 2:00 PM.[20] So well did matters go that when he left he presented twenty golden pieces to the officials who had shown him around.[21] What pleased the tsar so much about the place? There were assorted scientific instruments, objets d'art, and handsome globes (including one by the respected local firm of Willem Blaeu that embodied Tasman's data from the voyages of 1642–44);[22] and it is reasonable to suppose that these were of interest to him. But the main tourist attraction of the City Hall was not above the ground but on it: a double hemisphere set in the floor, incorporating data from the 1642 voyage of *Heemskerck* and *Zeehaan* to Australasia.[23] Historical geographers now recognize that the two hemispheres derived from an original Blaeu drawing of approximately 1648.[24] Though far from new when Peter came, the floor was still in good repair and was stimulating to one with his interests.[25]

While in Amsterdam, Peter gave orders for the acquisition of assorted Dutch materials. More were purchased or donated in the next decade. Many travelled to St. Petersburg in 1705–10 with Russians who had undergone practical training in the Netherlands under the watchful eye of Rear-Admiral Cornelius Cruys (1657–1727), whom the tsar himself had hired.[26] The Russians' knowledge of the Maoris, slight though it was, thus predated their knowledge of other Polynesians by at least one generation.

RUSSIAN PURCHASES OF FOREIGN PRINTED WORKS AND GLOBES

There are several extant globes and maps by the Amsterdam firm of Willem Janszoon Blaeu that incorporated data from Tasman's voyages of 1642–44 within a few years of their completion. One is a world map that, from internal inscriptions, could have been printed in 1648.[27] A copy was at the St. Petersburg Academy of Sciences by 1733.[28] Several globes made in 1648–56 under the direction of Joan Blaeu, the founder's son, show "Zeelandia Nova": the Blaeus had access to charts and probably also to journals of the Dutch East India Company explorers.[29] The company's globes, too, enriched the St. Petersburg Academy's collections by the time of Peter's daughter, Empress Elizabeth (1741–61). Little had been written of the Dutch finds in the far South by the mid-seventeenth century, but, unlike the Spanish, the Dutch do not seem to have tried to conceal from rival nations what their compatriots had learned. Dutch cartographers were given access to the Company's materials, and the city of Amsterdam as well as various merchants gave atlases or globes to foreign princes whom they saw as potent friends or friends-to-be.[30] The Soviet Academy of Sciences, descendant of the post-Petrine Imperial Academy and the inheritor of its collections, holds a copy of the first book to describe—in a fanciful but sprightly manner—Tasman's dealings with the Maoris in 1642–43, *De Nieuwe en Onbekende Weereld* by Arnoldus Montanus (1671).[31] "Stronger on human appeal than geographical detail," Andrew Sharp observes coolly, "it does not seem to have had much effect in making Tasman's discoveries more widely known."[32] Documentation now in Leningrad, however, does not prove that the Montanus narrative was already in St. Petersburg in early times. The same, regrettably, is true of Leningrad's copy of Dirck Rembrantszoon van Nierop's *Eenige Oefeningen* (Amsterdam 1674), the second part of which contained a vital "kort Verhael" that derived from Tasman's journal.[33] On the other hand, we know that certain early eighteenth-century collections—Witsen's *Noord en Oost Tartary*, François Valentijn's *Oud en Nieuw Oost-Indien* (1724–26), and Francois Coréal's *Voyages ... aux Indes Occidentales* (Amsterdam 1722)[34]—were in St. Petersburg within a few years after Peter's death in 1725.[35] Perhaps the Gilseman-Witsen drawing of a Maori canoe was the first representation of New Zealand ever published, but the Valentijn compendium, the "secular harvest of a lifetime" spent as minister of God in Indonesia,[36] offered the Russian reader five New Zealand views, including one showing the bloody incident in Murderers' or Golden Bay.[37] The Coréal account of Tasman's voyage up the west coast of New Zealand was written in the language most accessible to educated Russians of the age. Few in St. Petersburg were troubled by the fact that, though arrestingly presented in the first person, that narrative had practically been lifted from the Nierop text of 1674 as rendered by an English translator and annotator, John J. Narborough, in 1694.[38]

Of maps showing a portion of New Zealand that were held by the St. Petersburg Academy of Sciences and/or the Admiralty College in the late 1750s, two are noteworthy: those drawn by François Valentijn for *Oud en Nieuw Oost-Indien* and by the French cartographer-polemicist Philippe Buache (1754). The two belonged to different schools and eras of cartography: whereas Valentijn showed with some precision the indented coast (between "De Zuyt Baey" and "3 Koningen Eyland") that Tasman and his company had actually followed up the west coast of New

Zealand, the Buache representation of the Southern Hemisphere was essentially an imaginative flight.[39] Buache embodied French mid-century cartography at its most dangerous and unprofessional:

> Despite the reforms of Guillaume Delisle at the start of the century, French geographers reverted to conceptions popularized by Sanson. They magnified Australia-Austrialia, joining it to New Guinea and Tasmania... But the mapping of New Zealand was even more fantastic, with a hypothetical east coast continued diagonally across the southern seas to the tip of South America... Buache was one of the offenders. In 1754 he showed New Zealand as a projection of that Southern Land so many people still believed in.[40]

The Buache map was not questioned in St. Petersburg. Buache was a respected name at the Academy and he was known as the successor to Delisle, *premier géographe du roi*. Peter had been acquainted with Delisle, even granting him extended audiences while in Paris in 1717;[41] another active member of that family of mapmakers, Joseph-Nicolas, had spent two decades in St. Petersburg itself, lending his personal authority to other men's mistakes. Another brother, Louis Delisle de la Croyère, had won fame at the price of an early death on Vitus Bering's second venture in the far Northeast of Asia.[42] Thus, in the holdings of Admiralty College and the Academy alike, misconceptions about New Zealand were reinforced over decades as a result of French indifference to facts, entrenched reputations, and the Russians' inability to ascertain the truth for themselves.[43] Wholly dependent upon foreign maps and lacking either companies or vessels fit to venture to the far side of the globe (even a plan to send two ships to Madagascar and Bengal, drafted by Admiral G. Wilster in December 1723, had proven impractical, though Russian squadrons had at least reached the Aegean in the seventies),[44] an ailing Admiralty College was forced to make great efforts to acquire recent charts from foreign sources. Its agents did their best in London, Paris, and the Netherlands to acquire the soundest charts that could be had of distant seas and shores, and by the seventies they had a powerful supporter at the Admiralty College in the eminent hydrographer Admiral A.I. Nagaev (1704–81). Nagaev gathered charts of distant waters in a scientific spirit, without regard for the Russians' lack of trading or strategic interests in, say, the Great South Sea.[45] Nevertheless, for some quarters of the globe trustworthy maps could not be bought by Russian agents. The Russian government had to acquire copies of compendia, translations of original accounts, and, above all, *Voyages* in the Pacific in both recent and not so recent times.

It was convenient that as the century progressed the need to purchase such materials abroad decreased. When Peter, in June 1721, despatched the scholarly librarian Johann-Daniel Schumacher (1696–1761) to buy such volumes in the Netherlands, France, Germany, and England (and to study in passing the arrangements in the leading foreign libraries),[46] there had been no possibility of turning to a bookseller or publisher in Russia instead. Matters were different within twenty years: 1741 saw the appearance of Schumacher's two-volume listing of the young Russian academy's holdings,[47] and a set of catalogues of these came out over the next three years.[48] Items based on Nierop were included. The Academy sold foreign volumes to the public.[49] By the sixties, more than thirty booksellers competed in St. Petersburg and Moscow, both importing foreign travel literature and producing listings (*rospisi*) that now enable us to study the development of Russian knowledge of the South Sea in that period.[50] Among compendia of voyages (in extract for the most part) that reflected Tasman's enterprise of 1642–43, were Antoine François Prévost d'Exiles' *Histoire générale des Voyages* (Paris 1753), Charles de Brosses's *Histoire des Navigations aux Terres Australes* (Paris 1756), and Alexander Dalrymple's *Account of the Discoveries Made in the South Pacifick Ocean* (London 1767) and *Historical Collection* (1771).[51] All continued to be sold into the late 1700s by such booksellers as I.P. Glazunov, I.Ia. Veitbrekht, and Christian Rüdiger.

CAPTAIN COOK'S VOYAGES AND RUSSIAN KNOWLEDGE
OF NEW ZEALAND

Accounts of Cook's discoveries in the *Endeavour* were available to Russians by 1771, and to the Magra and the Hawkesworth-Cook accounts of that year was added Sydney Parkinson's in 1773. Extracts from Joseph Banks's *Voyage Round the World*, published anonymously in 1771, and from his summary of Cook's recent discoveries found their way into the Russian periodical *Kalendar', ili Mesiatsoslov geograficheskoi* in 1773,[52] accompanied by a curious engraving of the Southern Hemisphere by Nikolai Zubkov.[53] Because of the Anglo-Russian naval entente in the eighteenth century, a group of Russian Volunteers was in London and was aware of such events.[54] Also, Englishmen and Scots were in the Russian naval service, ready to pass on such news which able Russian officers now wished to read in the original.[55]

    The second and third voyages of Cook seized the attention of a swelling Russian readership and of the Russian government. When Cook reached Unaslaska Island with *Discovery* and *Resolution* in 1778, Catherine II had for many years deliberately not supported the cossack enterprise in the Aleutians.[56] The news of the British ships' appearance was reported to the government by Governor Magnus von Behm from Bol'sheretsk and provoked concern.[57] Concern led to action at word that the British had put in at Petropavlovsk-in-Kamchatka in May and August 1779 and were probing energetically in an area claimed tacitly by Russia. More artillery was painfully transported overland to Petropavlovsk; and the government at last paid heed to accounts of Cook's great voyages and to the matter of acquiring and/or translating recent, relevant material.[58] Thus, thanks to Cook, Russian knowledge and awareness of South Pacific islands grew significantly in the mid-1780s and continued to expand into the early nineteenth century.[59]

It is not clear whether Catherine herself believed the British had arrived at Petropavlovsk with imperialist designs, as Siberian officials V.I. Shmalev, F.N. Klichka had asserted in despatches to the capital.[60] In any case, she hid any doubts she may have had about the motives of the Cook-Clerke expedition, but at once took steps to learn all that she could about the expedition's movements and results.[61] Work was accelerated on the translation into Russian of the London (1777) text of the *Adventure-Resolution* expedition, known as *Puteshestvie k iuzhnomu poliusu*, and on the purchasing of materials in English, German, French, or Dutch. No item in the European press escaped the Admiralty College's attention: all were noted, clipped, collated.[62] Under these circumstances, facts about New Zealand reached Russia in the eighties, in the works of Rickman (1781), Zimmermann (1781), and Ellis (1782).[63] Heinrich Zimmermann's was the first account of Cook's third voyage to appear on the Continent, and it soon found its way across the Baltic German Provinces to Reval and St. Petersburg.[64]

Loggin Ivanovich Golenishchev-Kutuzov translated Cook's second and last *Voyages* into Russian. He had inherited both maritime and literary interests from his father. Ivan Logginovich had written sentimental letters à la Fenelon and translated Voltaire.[65] Neither father nor son regarded literal precision in translating a foreign text worth the sacrifice of elegance. The son chose not to work from Cook's own text, turning instead to the mellifluous French version by J.B.L. Suard, *Voyage dans l'hémisphère Australe... fait pendant les années 1772–1775* (Paris 1778). Suard's volumes contained fine maps by Hodges and Johann Reinhold Forster's *Observations*, but they were not correct translations in the modern understanding of that word. Great similarities exist between the 1777 text and that produced, after a series of delays, by Golenishchev-Kutuzov (1796–1800). In tone, however, the Russian text is altogether independent of both the French and the English narratives. Nevertheless, Part 1 of *Puteshestvie v iuzhnoi polovine zemnago shara i vokrug onago*

(St. P. 1796) was, among other things, a crucial contribution to Russian knowledge of Oceania that developed during the last years of the century. It offered colourful, authoritative scenes of Maori life and brought Queen Charlotte Sound and Dusky Bay before the eyes of an educated readership.[66]

Part 1 of *Puteshestvie* had fourteen chapters. Half of these (3–9) dealt with the *Resolution*'s and *Adventure*'s visit to New Zealand from March to June 1773.[67] Excluding commentary from Furneaux's sojourn in Van Diemen's Land, in Chapter 7, this amounted to 147 full pages of text—by far the largest piece of writing on New Zealand that had yet come out in Russian. Nor was illustrative or pictorial material neglected: four large maps embellished the translation, one an elegant representation of Dusky Bay ("Karta Zaliva Diuski v Novoi Zelandii, 1773 goda"). The work also broke new ground for Russian publishing, as it resulted from a combined effort of Admiralty draughtsmen, the Academy of Sciences (which actually printed later portions of the six-part *Puteshestvie*), and printers at the Naval Cadet Corps, where Kutuzov had his office.[68] Part 5 of the work was published in 1800. It was a version of Johann Reinhold Forster's *Observations made During a Voyage round the World, on Physical Geography, Natural History, and Ethic Philosophy*, and it contributed greatly to the Russians' perception of New Zealand.[69] Now ethnography, hydrography, and maritime astronomy were complemented by zoology and botany, and even by geology and physics. Few more erudite or multifaceted presenters of the Polynesian world could have been found than the elder Forster.[70] Kutuzov's myriad professional connections with St. Petersburg were but an incidental bonus.[71] The twenty-six fine illustrations and maps, including the single portrait of the celebrated "Captain Kuk" by "E. Koshkin," that formed the sixth part of Kutuzov's *Puteshestvie* were re-engraved from London originals, many by Cook's artist, Hodges. They did not disgrace the young translator's work.

Here, to illustrate the images of New Zealand that filtered through Suard's text to the Russians in the 1790s, are two extracts from that work, under the headings: "6 April 1773" and "29 May 1773." The Anglo-Maori encounters they describe enlivened Cook's long stay in Queen Charlotte Sound—the sound that Russians themselves wished to visit more than any other in May 1820:

Returning to the ship towards evening, we caught sight of a Zealander with two women. They appeared in the NE extremity of an islet which, for that reason, I now called Indian's Island. We would have passed by without noticing them had the man not hailed us with a yell. He was standing on a rock, a club in his hand, and behind him, nearer the bush, stood the two women, each with a spear. Their faces were dark olive in colour, their hair black and curly, smeared with oil and covered with a red powder . . . We said to them, in the language of Otahiti, *Taio-Hare* ("Come here, friend!"). The man was perceptibly nervous as our launch drew near, but he remained on the spot and did not budge. Finally, I got out of the launch with a sheet of white paper in my hand and, going up to him, embraced him and gave him some nails, gimlets, and other trifles that I happened to have on me. This calmed him and pretty soon both women approached us. We chatted for half an hour, without understanding each other.

Thirty Zealanders visited us, bringing with them much fish, which we exchanged for nails, etc. I took one of them to Motuara Island and showed him the potatoes earlier planted there by Mr. Fannen of *Adventure*. It is clear that the plant will take. The Zealander was so pleased that he began to cut the grass around the potato plants. Then we took him to the other kitchen gardens . . . Among the natives who had come to see us were several women, with tattooed lips coloured dark blue and cheeks covered with some dark red substance made of red chalk and oil . . . Having obtained her husband's consent, a woman was free to agree to satisfy the shameful desires of our own men, for one large nail, or a shirt, or some other gift. Many women in fact gave themselves over to this disgusting debauchery, but did so with revulsion, and would not have satisfied the newcomers' lusts were it not for their own husbands' power over them and threats. Our men observed their tears without pity, and paid no heed to their moanings.[72]

The long delays and gentle pace of Kutuzov's work contrasted greatly with the urgency with which it had been set in motion. This was a commentary on the diligence of the French translators, Jean-Baptiste Suard and Jean-Nicolas Demeunier, who had many followers in Russia.[73] The significance of the Kutuzov *Puteshestvie,* in summary, was diminished by the work of the French translators and by their belated publication. Nonetheless, it did spread interest about New Zealand and its cannibal inhabitants among a wider Russian readership. So too did other works published in Russian as the century drew to its end; Mikhail Verevkin's paraphrase of Antoine Prévost d'Exiles' *Histoire générale des Voyages* (*Istoriia o stranstviiakh voobshche* . . . of 1787, of which Part 21 dealt with Cook),[74] and, more important, Joachim Heinrich Campe's Russian version of his own *Sammlung interessanter Reisebeschreibung für die Jugend* (1786–90).[75] Campe (1746–1818) based the fourth part of his book, describing Cook's first voyage to the Great South Sea, on Hawkesworth.[76] Printed by Rüdiger and Klaudius in Moscow in 1798, his *Sobranie* (*Collection*) once again brought Cook's earliest visit to New Zealand to the Russians' notice at the very time when Suard and Kutuzov were amusing them with pictures from the second voyage.[77] Together, these works gave St. Petersburg the impression that New Zealanders were a dangerous and brutal race, albeit cultured after a fashion and inhabiting a country rich in food.[78] This attitude persisted for at least a century.[79]

KRUZENSHTERN'S ASSESSMENT OF THE TASMAN VOYAGE, 1806

"In 1800 and 1802, Lieutenant Kruzenshtern submitted to the Admiralty College a plan to send ships with supplies via Cape Horn to Russian America. . . . The vessels *Leander* and *Thames* were duly bought in England for some £17,000 and renamed *Nadezhda* and *Neva*. Captained by Kruzenshtern and Yury Lisyansky, they left Kronstadt in 1803."[80] Although commercially and diplomatically the voyage of *Nadezhda* and *Neva* was a failure, it was successful as a naval training exercise, and as a scientific venture it was brilliantly managed and obtained results of permanent worth.[81] Kruzenshtern was a scholar by temperament, and *Nadezhda* left the Baltic with the finest scientific library that ever sailed on any Russian ship.[82] While at sea in 1804–5, he found the energy and time to make an academic study of the major Dutch transoceanic crossings and discoveries from Tasman's day to Roggeveen's. It was as though *Nadezhda*'s intersection of the Pacific routes of Dutchmen of another century, and Kruzenshtern's uncomfortable awareness of how completely unreliable the Pacific charts were, released in the captain a powerful hydrographic impulse. The work he began in 1804 would preoccupy him for twenty years.[83]

Kruzenshtern's paper, "Tasman's Discoveries," appeared in the Academy of Sciences' periodical, *Tekhnologicheskii Zhurnal*, in 1806.[84] Not content with the ten pages it contained on the manoeuvres of *Heemskerck* and *Zeehaan* up the west coast of New Zealand, he sent in a closely wrought "Continuation." It appeared that same year,[85] lifting Russian cartography to new heights.

According to Kruzenshtern, Tasman visited two spots on 17 and 18 December 1642. Dalrymple, after all, had given in his *Historical Collection* (1771; 2: 70–74) two views, one from "Murderers' Bay," the other from "Abel Tasman Bay." Why, asked Kruzenshtern, should the former be identified with Cook's "Blind Bay"? The extant evidence suggested that it was actually Cook's unnamed discovery of 1773, that is, a bay six miles east of Cape Farewell. And Tasman's "Abel Tasman Bay" was, in reality, "Blind Bay." Modern historical cartography confirms the reasoning.[86]

Imperfect though his sources were, Kruzenshtern was also certain that the Dutch had pressed some way along Cook Strait (or "Zeehaan Bay") on 19–20 December 1642.[87] Later researchers, such as J.E. Heeres and R.P. Meyjes, have concurred.[88] To view the so-called Huydecoper Chart of a portion of New Zealand reproduced by Andrew Sharp in 1968[89] is to appreciate that soundness of the Kruzenshtern approach to a particularly complex problem.

Turning next to Cook's Cape Egmont, Kruzenshtern spoke on behalf of its most probable discoverers, the Dutch. "I would suggest," he writes, "that Cape Pieter Boreel lies in Latitude $39°23'20''$S, Longitude $174°12'29''$E, resting on observations made by Cook, and corrected by Astronomer Wales, to fix their Cape Egmont."[90] In conclusion, Kruzenshtern gives "Tasman's Journal of his Voyage, Presented in Tabular Form." It is exemplary in its simplicity and clarity.

Profound hydrographer and cautious scholar though he was, however, Kruzenshtern was not immune to the more human side of François Valentijn's account as he received it via Dalrymple's *Historical Collection*. And indeed it would be wrong to summarize his "Tasman articles" of 1806 without alluding to his eloquent transcription of the narrative describing how the Dutch were clubbed to death in Golden Bay.[91] The transcription is omitted here: references to attacking savages, colliding craft, and bloodied clubs and pikes are all too uniform and could easily have been imagined over time. What is significant is Kruzenshtern's own paragraph of commentary at its end:

> I have here included a full account of that unhappy event, so somewhat overstepping the bounds of my own subject, but I could not refrain from depicting, in all its clarity, the barbaric character of the New Zealanders. Tasman was the first European to reach New Zealand, so those *children of nature* had not yet been spoiled by Enlightened Europe. Yet how did they act? Not in the least provoked, they fell upon unarmed Europeans and killed them . . . And the conduct of New Zealanders towards all Europeans who have visited them, and evinced more goodness than they could reciprocate, has always been malicious. The avaricious murder of Marion and his people, as also of the men in Adventure Bay, inspires horror against such savages.[92]

Kruzenshtern's words were remembered by the people of the sloops *Vostok* and *Mirnyi* as they approached New Zealand in the early part of winter in 1820.[93]

CAPTAIN VASILII M. GOLOVNIN AND "PRINCE MATARA," 1808

Lisianskii brought *Neva* safely to Kronstadt on 5 August 1806, two weeks before *Nadezhda* arrived.[94] Within six weeks she was again being prepared for a voyage to the North Pacific settlements, for the directors of the Russian-American Company were, like the government, disposed to view the Kruzenshtern-Lisianskii expedition as an overall success. *Neva* sailed from Kronstadt on 19 October with a cargo of supplies for Sitka (Novo-Arkhangel'sk), under Fleet-Lieutenant Leontii Adrianovich Hagemeister (in Russian, Gagemeister, 1780–1833).[95] In 1806 the Napoleonic Wars produced a fluid situation on the Continent, and it was considered prudent to despatch a Russian warship to escort her. The 305-ton sloop *Diana,* mounting 16 guns, was chosen for the mission. Ninety feet from stem to stern, she had been built two years before on the River Svir' and was a fine command for her young captain, Vasilii Mikhailovich Golovnin (1776–1831).[96] It was impossible, however, to ready her for a North Pacific venture as quickly as the Company required, and *Neva* sailed alone. *Neva* became the first Russian vessel in Australia (June 1807). *Diana* also made her way alone from Kronstadt roadstead when at length Lieutenant Golovnin received permission to proceed on 25 July 1807. "In place of ballast, as much as 6,000 *poods* of various supplies, such as rigging and iron for Kamchatka and Okhotsk, were stowed in her hold."[97] She was, however, anything but a transport, being armed with 14 new six-pounders, eight-pound carronades, and falconets of modern type. Moreover, Golovnin took orders from the Naval Ministry, represented by the nationalistic Admiral Pavel V. Chichagov, not from the Company's Main Board.[98]

Like Kruzenshtern, Lisianskii, and Gagemeister, Golovnin had served in British warships as a Russian Volunteer.[99] In the process, he had become aware of Russia's Asian and Pacific opportunities. His service contacts with the British were particularly close. As an orphaned adolescent, he had fallen under James Trevenen's influence when both served in the ship *Ne Tron' Menia.* Lieutenant Trevenen, one of several of Cook's young officers who successfully exploited this association by serving in the Russian Baltic Fleet, led Golovnin to master English and read Cook's *Voyages* in the original.[100] Golovnin served under Collingwood and Nelson (1802–5), seeing action in *Plantagenet, Ville de Paris,* and *Prince of Wales* against the French. Like Kruzenshtern a decade earlier, he studied the colonial administration of the Caribbean Islands that he visited, did well in battle, and requested an extension of his secondment, agreeing to go unpaid.[101] Within one month of his return to Baltic duty in August 1806, he was appointed to *Diana,* with sailing orders for Okhotsk and Petropavlovsk. As his second-in-command, he selected P.I. Rikord (1776–1855). His crew of fifty-five men and three young officers had a vessel that could easily have carried twice the number.[102]

Golovnin was almost caught in the Continental War at the start of his voyage: he was present at the British fleet's blockade of Copenhagen and bombardment of the Danish fort of Kronberg. Cannonballs fell in the water nearby, and a drifting, blazing ship threatened to set the sloop afire. Watched from Nelson's flagship but unhindered, Golovnin went on his way to Helsingör and Portsmouth roads. Copenhagen set the tone for his whole voyage.[103]

Britain and Russia were at peace in mid-September 1807; but the meaning of the pact of Tilsit had been obvious for weeks. In the event, the Russian company was well received at Portsmouth; nor was there any difficulty when Golovnin suddenly decided to sail on 1 November. Shortly afterwards, news of a break between the Russian and the British courts was published. British Admiralty orders to detain *Diana* went to stations where she might put in for food and water. The orders also cancelled the papers lately issued to her captain in London, guaranteeing her a safe, unhindered passage through all regions where the British writ then ran. Golovnin crossed the equator on 20 December and reached Santa Catarina Island in Brazil on 10 January 1808. The Portuguese authorities were friendly, and *Diana* and her well-rested company headed south. They rounded Cape Horn on 12 February, but now the weather turned violent. For thirteen days and nights, the Russians fought to make a mile of headway westward, but the elements prevailed. Golovnin set course for South Africa. On the morning of 21 April 1808, *Diana* entered Simon's Bay by Cape Town. She was boarded that same hour, and her people were arrested and removed by jolly boat. Armed British sailors stayed aboard for some time.

As commander, Golovnin was asked to undertake on behalf of himself and his company neither to break the peace and order of the colony nor to attempt to flee.[104] Placing his confidence in the official British pass in his possession and despatching formal protests, he unwillingly agreed. He was thereafter treated poorly by the British commander, Admiral Bertie, and detained for thirteen months. He would certainly have stayed in Cape Town longer still, had anger not impelled him to make a bold escape during a squall on 16 May 1809. Insulted by demands that his subordinates reduce their rations and aware that his sloop had not been mentioned in despatches sent from London, he ordered the *Diana*'s cables cut and took flight.[105]

Among the ships also in Simon's Bay during *Diana*'s stay, were vessels bound for Australasia from Great Britain. One of these was a transport, *Porpoise*, taking female felons out to Sydney and a Maori, Matara, via Sydney to his native Bay of Islands. Matara was a son of Chief Te Pahi (1760?–1809) of the Ngapuhi tribe at Kerikeri.[106] Golovnin was introduced to him and to his escort and companion, a modest Scottish doctor named McMillin; because the chief spoke English well enough, the Russian was able to have quite a lengthy conversation with his fellow-visitor. McMillin gave the Russians information about Maori relations with the British traders since the mid-1790s—whalers, sealers, flax and timber gatherers, and others—based at Sydney.[107] Governor Philip Gidley King, the Russian gathered, had a personal and long-term interest in stimulating Anglo-Maori contact. He was friendly with Te Pahi, who, together with Matara and three other sons, had gone to Sydney on the transport *Buffalo* in November 1805. Te Pahi, said McMillin, had been generously entertained by King, who found him decent and intelligent; had met the leading residents of New South Wales, notably the Reverend Samuel Marsden and the rich Captain Macarthur; and had gone back to New Zealand with many gifts in March 1806. Matara and at least one other Maori, however, had expressed the wish to voyage on to England after spending more time in Sydney, and the governor acceded to his wish.[108] Passage was afterwards arranged aboard a whaler bound for London.

Matara was the second young Maori visitor to gain official recognition in England. Like Moehanga, who had sailed from New Zealand twelve months earlier with Dr. John Savage aboard another whaler, *Ferret*, he was Ngapuhi.[109] But unlike Moehanga, whose tales of the marvels he had seen would be dismissed by his compatriots as ravings, he was indisputably of chiefly rank. His gifts from George III and English noblemen, philanthropists, and others were not appropriated, like the low-born Moehanga's, by his betters. Even Ruatara's visit to Great Britain in July and August 1809 was not similarly blessed by royal favour.[110] An intelligent young chief of status, in the best of health, and with generally Anglophilic attitudes, Matara was a vital messenger from London to the powerful Ngapuhi tribe. Golovnin had had some experience of Anglo-native dealings when he visited Jamaica and the Leeward Islands. He was curious about a Maori chief, and so invited him to dine aboard *Diana*.

The doctor, Mr. McMillin, was a modest, civil, sensible man. The prince was eighteen years old, small in stature but stately. His face had a European set to it and was dark violet in colour, with none of the facial designs tattooed for the sake of ornament according to the custom of savage peoples. He was lively and gay, and understood practically everything said in ordinary English conversation, though he spoke it very incorrectly and pronounced it even worse... Matara had two wives, to whom he was very much attached. On his departing, his father had given him detailed instructions as to what to study among the Europeans and what to adopt from them. It seemed to us that he had considerable natural abilities and many of his observations gave no indication whatever that he was a savage from New Zealand and uneducated.

Strolling on the shore with Lieutenant Rikord, he found a copper crest from a soldier's pouch. The glitter of the thing had caught his eye. Picking it up, he said to Mr. Rikord, "It's unlikely that whoever lost this would have found it himself, so I shall not consider it theft to take it." Having made this remark, he pocketed it... I myself showed him a sea-chart on which were marked the Cape of Good Hope, New Holland, and New Zealand. He immediately pointed with his finger to the tract he would have to cross, indicating Port Jackson and Norfolk Island, where his transport was to go before calling at the Bay of Islands. When I showed him our route to Kamchatka, he commented that Russia (doubtless taking Kamchatka for the whole of Russia) was even further from England than was New Zealand. But hearing from us that one could cross to Russia from England in a week, he asked: then why did we not go there via England? ...

The King of England had made this prince a chevalier of an order instituted or, more accurately, invented for native rulers: the Order of Amity. To the father [Te Pahi] he had sent a rich cap and mantle as crown and robes. Besides, there was sent a quantity of various useful gifts—utensils, clothing, etc. These were packed into chests marked: "To King Te Pahi from King George." The son had likewise received valuable gifts whilst in England.[111]

Diana carried several books relating to New Zealand, and these were put out for Matara's entertainment. One volume, very likely a Cook *Voyage* with illustrations by Hodges or Parkinson, had representations of a Maori man and woman. Matara did not think them accurate. His preoccupation with weaponry showed in one remark, *"tewha-tewha"*, alluding to a hatchetlike cudgel of New Zealand. Had the Russians understood it, they might have suspected his peaceful aims upon returning. Golovnin found spoken Maori "quick and abrupt but not unpleasant to the ear."

Te Pahi, Marsden's would-be helper, was confused by raiding whalers at the Bay of Islands with Te Puhi and mistakenly murdered in revenge for Europeans killed in the ship *Boyd* in 1810.[112] Te Pahi's sons also became involved in the affair when the captain of the vessel that had first learned of the massacre, the *Ann,* promptly implicated "Prince Mattarra," "lately arrived from England . . . the principal leader."[113] News of Matara's alleged role in the grim affair reached St. Petersburg after a long delay. After another period of captivity, this time by Japanese officials in the Kuril Islands and Hokkaido, Golovnin discovered

> how that savage had thoroughly repaid the friendship shown him by the English government. In perfidious fashion, he had gained possession of two whalers belonging to that nation and slaughtered all the English in them, leaving alive only two or three Englishwomen who saved themselves by a daring flight, swimming across to another English vessel which arrived there after a while. A similar fate was being prepared for this brig, but the women saved her. It is said that the English government has despatched an expedition to punish this ungrateful villain for his perfidy.[114]

Thus was intelligence swiftly replaced in the Russian image of the Maori by "perfidy." Both Cook and Kruzenshtern had alluded to this. Matara reinforced this impression at a time when another might have been fairer.[115]

PETR A. ZAGORSKII, ANDRÉ THOUIN, AND
NEW ZEALAND FLAX, 1810

No Maori appears to have visited St. Petersburg before the end of the Napoleonic Wars. Many New Zealand plants and animals, however, arrived there in the early 1800s, where they stimulated interest in theories of propagation, population movement, and comparative zoology. Because no Russian vessels visited New Zealand, Russian scientists depended for their source materials on French and British institutions. Both New Zealand and Australian plant specimens were bartered in some numbers in this period, and in St. Petersburg, as elsewhere in Europe, they enlarged public and private herbaria significantly.[116] Various departments of St. Petersburg's Academy of Sciences subscribed to foreign publications and scrutinized them for relevant material.

One Russian who evinced a special interest in Australasian flora in the early 1800s was Petr Andreevich Zagorskii (1764–1846).[117] An anatomist and founder of the first Russian college of anatomy, he had many links with foreign scientists. He worked for a long time at the Admiralty Hospital, had many Navy friends, and corresponded indefatigably.[118] Among his correspondents were Jacques-Julien de La Billardière (1755–1834), who had sailed on the search for La Pérouse (1791–93) and written *Novae Hollandiae Plantarum Specimen* (1804–6), and the distinguished botanist André Thouin (1747–1824).[119] Thouin, head of the Jardin des Plantes in Paris, had a lively interest in the naturalization of exotic Southern plants, on which he presented lecture courses. He believed that the New Zealand flax (*Phormium tenax*) could be successfully grown in Northern Europe and conducted long, controlled experiments (as did La Billardière) to substantiate this. Zagorskii read his 1803 article on the subject with keen appreciation,[120] then reported on it in *Tekhnologicheskii Zhurnal*. Through no fault of his, it was printed only after two full years, in 1810.[121]

> New Zealand flax is a long-lived plant of the lily family. From a fleshy, knobbed root, many branches push out; and from these come bunches of nine or ten leaves, each some four feet long, two inches wide, and sharp-tipped... One pod of this plant, sent to France in December 1800, was lacking small fibrous roots and had suffered, when being brought from England, from cold damp air. It was planted in an orangery, in a fresh bed beneath which a stove was lit and daily refueled, so that the heat in one area of the bed touched on 47 Réaumur... Despite all this, the plant suffered no damage but to the contrary, grew in lively style and flowered.

Thouin had supposed that *Phormium tenax* would grow in France and be profitable. Zagorskii saw no reason why it should be excluded from the Southern parts of Russia, where the temperature range was like that of parts of New Zealand.

SUVOROV'S OFFICERS AND MAORI "KINGS" AT PARRAMATTA, 1814

For three more years, conditions in Europe made it impolitic for the directors of the Russian-American Company to risk a valuable shipment to the North Pacific settlements. At length, the colonies' extreme need of supplies and naval stores could be left unmet no longer. Lieutenant Mikhail Petrovich Lazarev sailed with the French-built ship *Suvorov,* 330 tons, in mid-October 1813, arriving in Rio de Janeiro with an English merchant convoy six months later.[122] From Brazil, *Suvorov* made for New South Wales and reached Port Jackson on 25 August. Her arrival was a triumph: she brought news of Blücher's move on Paris in despatches from the British ambassador at Rio, Lord Strangford, to Governor Lachlan Macquarie.[123] There was singing in the streets and, that same day, a *Sydney Gazette Extraordinary*.[124] Lieutenant Lazarev and company were all *personae gratae* in the colony, and not merely as bearers of good news. Governor Macquarie had warm memories of Kronstadt, where, on a journey home from India by way of Muscovy, he had been well received by Russian naval officers in 1807.[125] Both Lazarev and his second-in-command Lieutenant Semeon Unkovskii had spent time in British warships, spoke English, and were polished patriots.[126]

Suvorov's people availed themselves of the hospitality and open friendliness of their hosts in New South Wales. They rode out to Parramatta on mounts offered by George Johnston, the man who had arrested Captain Bligh.[127] There Samuel Marsden was attentive to Unkovskii and his comrade Pavel Povalo-Shveikovskii, though he was preoccupied with preparations for his first New Zealand visit.[128] There too another group of Russians encountered the Maori, represented by "two kings" who arrived aboard the small brig *Active* in the same week as *Suvorov,* on 22 August 1814.[129]

The chiefs met by the Russians were, like Matara and Te Pahi, to whom they were related, from the Bay of Islands and came at Marsden's summons to assist him in his missionary effort in their native land. "One of them spoke some English," notes Unkovskii, referring to Ruatara (1787?–1815), who had passed two months in London in 1809 before returning in the convict vessel *Ann* to New South Wales.[130] Very probably, the second "king" encountered in Reverend Marsden's house was Hongi Hika. Also in the colony that winter, but perhaps not met by the Russians, were Korokoro, Tuhi, and Tuhi's younger brother, plus at least three Maori servants.[131] All accompanied Reverend Marsden in the *Active,* which he had purchased, when she sailed for the Bay of Islands. They arrived safely on 22 December 1814.[132]

5

THE RUSSIANS IN NEW ZEALAND

THE BELLINGSHAUSEN VISIT TO NEW ZEALAND, 1820:
PREPARATIONS

Suvorov was the last vessel to sail from the Baltic Sea to Oceania and back without provoking wary interest, if not unease, in British Admiralty circles. With the return of peace to Europe, the search for the elusive Northern Passage to the Orient resumed; and Kotzebue lost little time in taking *Riurik,* the brig purchased and fitted out by Count N.P. Rumiantsev, then the Chancellor of Russia, through the Bering Strait and north into the giant bay named after him (Zund Kotzebue—Kotzebue Sound).[1] Now, in another age of peaceful rivalry, "the aims of science and of empire were essentially one and the same. Knowledge was power."[2]

None, argued John Barrow, Secretary to the Admiralty Board in London, could suggest that even Kotzebue's qualified success on the remote northwestern tip of North America had no strategic or political significance; for had *Riurik* in fact sighted the navigable passage through the ice that Count Rumiantsev and her officers believed in, then such scientific objects as the Russians might have had would have been quite beside the point. "It would," wrote Barrow testily, "be somewhat mortifying if a naval power of but yesterday were to complete a discovery in the nineteenth century which was so happily commenced by Englishmen in the sixteenth."[3] The House of Commons concurred, and duly offered a large reward to the British ship and company that could discover the passage. The golden age of British Arctic exploration thus began. But just as Kotzebue's Arctic explorations spurred the British to renewed efforts in the North, giving employment to distinguished officers who might otherwise have been unemployed,[4] so those efforts provoked the even grander Russian expedition linked today with Captain Bellingshausen's name.

The time had come, it was agreed in March 1818, for Russians to win laurels and political advantage from a scientific voyage of discovery in the tradition of Cook and Bougainville.[5] Not to realize the capital accrued through Kotzebue's recent voyage to the Arctic was unthinkable. Because the Russian Navy lacked enough ships to undertake a set of distant expeditions,[6] it adopted the notion of a double polar expedition in mid-November 1818.[7] While two ships sought a navigable passage in the North linking Pacific and Atlantic waters, another squadron would investigate the furthest South, where no European expedition had done any work since Cook's return in 1775. In Antarctica Russians might match and complement the work of Cook, with which a Russian readership had been familiar since 1800 thanks to Loggin Golenishchev-Kutuzov's version of Jean-Baptiste Suard's *Voyage au Pôle Austral*.[8] The Bellingshausen-Lazarev Antarctic Expedition of 1819–21, in the course of which the sloop *Vostok* (*East*) and the reconfigured transport *Mirnyi* (*Peaceful*) passed twelve days about Queen Charlotte Sound (28 May–9 June 1820),[9] thus stemmed from and developed the political, professional, and scientific tendencies that marked the Russians' naval activities in the North Pacific basin. Russia's two-pronged polar enterprise—*Vostok* and *Mirnyi* to the furthest South, *Otkrytie* and *Blagonamerennyi* through the Bering Strait and northward[10]—was an imperial reaction to mounting international pressures.[11]

The shape of the double expedition showed the influence of Cook, Kotzebue, and Vancouver. The legacy of Cook's Pacific voyages was both scientific and naval. It was preserved by Russian officers like Bellingshausen (1778-1852), who were born too late to have encountered such Cook subordinates as James Trevenen, Joseph Billings, and John Ledyard.[12] Cook's spirit went with Bellingshausen to New Zealand. As Cook had taken an interest in Maori artefacts, customs, language, and beliefs, so also did Bellingshausen when he arrived in late May 1820—with Cook's chart open before him—by the wooded shores of Motuara Island in Queen Charlotte Sound.[13]

Cook had received no orders to concern himself with ethnographica. His purposes in sailing in *Endeavour* were to follow Venus's predicted transit from Tahiti, to discover southern lands if possible, and to complete a grand botanical design. Nonetheless, both he and Joseph Banks, his rich and well-born passenger, showed a lively and objective interest in all the native peoples they encountered, as they did during the second and third voyages. Officially, the emphasis fell first upon discovery and the naval sciences of hydrography and marine astronomy, then on the natural sciences of zoology and botany.[14] In fact, however, Cook and his people made as close and full a study of the Maoris as time allowed, collecting, sketching, interviewing, and in the process taking an infant science forward.[15] This example was not lost on Kruzenshtern in 1802–4, nor was it overlooked during the lengthy preparations for the polar expeditions to be led by Captains Faddei F. Bellingshausen to the South and Mikhail Vasil'ev to the North.[16]

From the beginning, Kruzenshtern took an informed and influential interest in the proposed Antarctic venture, drafting lengthy memoranda on the matter at the invitation of the Minister of the Marine, de Traversay.[17] Well respected, he was in 1818 in a position to renew Cook's scientific legacy in a Russian context, and he did so with a will. Naval bureaucracy, however, embodied by the idle, French-born minister, recalled Cook's voyages in terms of breadfruit, birds, and Forsters first, charting second, and curio collecting third. Kruzenshtern's opinions were overridden. Invitations to participate in the Antarctic and Pacific expedition went to two young German botanists named Karl-Heinrich Mertens (1796–1853) and Gustav Kunze (1793–1851).[18] Cook, after all, had had the Forsters in his company, and Kruzenshtern himself had had Tilesius von Tilenau, Georg Heinrich Langsdorf, and—for good measure—a surgeon, Dr. Espenberg, with much knowledge of plants and pharmacology. Why should the pattern, broadly sanctioned by European maritime tradition, now be broken? Mertens, who had recently studied medicine at Halle and was evidently versatile, and Kunze, who was about to defend an intimidating Leipzig dissertation (*De Dysphagia commentatio pathologica*),[19] were to report to Copenhagen and board *Vostok* in Denmark as she sailed from the Continent. Marquis de Traversay's officials at the Admiralty, meanwhile, adjusted gracelessly to personnel realities. Bellingshausen would command the southern squadron, but only because both Captain V.M. Golovnin and Captain Makar' I. Ratmanov were unavailable.[20] This development was a happy one for New Zealand and Pacific studies. Ratmanov was a good sea officer and ardent patriot, but as a scientific officer he was inferior not only to Bellingshausen but to all the latter's young lieutenants in *Vostok* (Ivan Ignat'ev, Arkadii Leskov, and the future Decembrist Konstantin P. Torson).[21] Many years before he was named to *Vostok,* moreover, Bellingshausen had gained a reputation for reliability at sea that was thereafter to link him with Pacific exploration and Cook. In the Baltic as commander of the frigate *Mel'pomena* (1809–10), then as captain of the *Flora* and *Minerva* on the Black Sea station, he engaged for months in taxing hydrographic work and showed much coolness under pressure. He was a rear-admiral by 1826. "It would," writes Hunter Christie, "be invidious to compare Cook and Bellingshausen. Cook has well been called incomparable; but no pioneer ever found a worthier disciple and successor."[22]

Mikhail Petrovich Lazarev was named to *Mirnyi* at Bellingshausen's recommendation. Both men had already seen the South Pacific Ocean. Both were first-rate navigators. Both proceeded, with the Admiralty's blessing, to select their own lieutenants, specialists, and lower decks.[23] It was predictable, no doubt, that the able companies they selected included young men of literary bent as well as scientific skill. Among the memoirists to whom we turn for useful sketches of the Bellingshausen visit to New Zealand are Nikolai Galkin of Kazan', *Mirnyi*'s surgeon;[24] Midshipman Pavel Mikhailovich Novosil'skii, also of that ship;[25] and *Vostok*'s astronomer, Ivan Mikhailovich Simonov (1794–1855). Possessed of enormous curiosity, the latter was truly a one-man scientific corps in Oceania, adept in physics and ethnology as well as in astronomy, geodesy, and—to a point—linguistics.[26]

Born beside the sea in Astrakhan, Simonov showed precocious skill in mathematics. At fifteen, he entered the newly instituted University of Kazan' and impressed all his teachers; by 1816 he was serving as extraordinary professor in its Faculty of Sciences and lecturing on theory of numbers. His appointment to *Vostok* on secondment marked the onset of the major intellectual and physical adventure of his life.[27] He returned with crammed journals and stores of Polynesian artefacts, certain of which are still in Kazan' today.[28] He was in due course named a corresponding member of the St. Petersburg Academy of Sciences, then in 1846 appointed to succeed the mathematician N.I. Lobachevskii as *rektor* of the university with which he was connected all his working life, Kazan'.[29]

Like Dr. Galkin, who was the director of Kazan's *Gimnaziia* (Secondary School) by 1830 and in contact with his former comrade Simonov, Midshipman Novosil'skii typified by his ability and range of interests the younger Russian chosen for the South Pacific venture. A graduate of the Imperial Naval Cadet Corps, he returned to it in 1822 as an instructor in astronomy and higher mathematics. Three years later, he transferred to the Ministry of Public Education. He pursued a comfortable dry-land career but maintained an active interest in polar and Pacific exploration.[30]

Bellingshausen's sailing and related scientific orders arrived in four sets and were precise in most respects. He and his people were to enter the Pacific by a certain route within a certain season, and work towards the furthest South.[31] But because the Bellingshausen enterprise was on a mission of discovery, certain elements could not be determined in advance by a committee. Many passages in its commander's final orders were, accordingly, sweeping and imprecise. Wherever possible, for instance, all his officers were to engage in scientific work; nor was this work to be invariably nautical in application or in emphasis. *Vostok*'s and *Mirnyi*'s lieutenants would assist Mertens and Kunze as they could. Bellingshausen himself was to "pass over nothing new, useful, or curious" in his narrative, and this applied "not only to matters bearing upon naval science, but also in the broader sense, relating to matters that might widen any area of knowledge."[32] He was, in short, to take note of all and anything of interest to him—with the full knowledge that his journals would be read, perhaps before he could redraft and polish them, by his superiors! Small wonder that his prose was cool and sober regardless of the subject matter: he was ever navigating between the Scylla and Charybdis of frivolity and tedium. (At any rate, he had three years in which to polish the observations he made, often at night and in discomfort, on the far side of the globe, before submitting ten full notebooks to the government in April 1824.)[33] Like Kruzenshtern but unlike Kotzebue, Bellingshausen had considerable liberty both to construe and to insist upon the strictly scientific portions of his orders as he wished. As had Cook and Kruzenshtern, he chose to read them in a way that favoured the study of all native peoples he met, though not at the expense of naval science.

Bellingshausen was a Baltic German officer, like Kruzenshtern, Hagemeister, Kotzebue, Lütke, Wrangel, Levenshtern, and others. He had always been alive to ethnic, cultural, and temperamental differences between individuals and peoples, between Slavs and Germans, Ests and Baltic gentry. In 1803–6 he had met non-European peoples in Japan, Kamchatka, Oceania, and South America, and he had studied them with an objective eye. *Vostok*'s astronomer, as we have seen, was always ready to support whatever ethnographic impulses his captain might evince in the Pacific; and the latter made it clear, when he arrived in the Baltic from the south of Russia in May 1819, that ethnography was high on the agenda. Stocks of broken iron hoops, buttons and gimlets, beads, scissors and knives, assorted cloths, and other things that could be readily and cheaply had were stowed for large-scale barter in the South Pacific Ocean.[34] Here, Bellingshausen was more fortunate than Cook had been: *Vostok* and *Mirnyi* were larger craft than Cook's. *Vostok* was a vessel of 900 tons and *Mirnyi,* a roomy 535-ton transport.[35] Then, in July 1819, Mertens and Kunze failed to keep their rendezvous with Bellingshausen. The significance of Simonov's and others' unemotional and solid interest in native peoples grew accordingly. There was to be no Russian Jacquinot or Lottin on the Southern expedition to insist on birds or insect life. All seemed to smile on the ethnographic impulse that was the legacy of Cook and Kruzenshtern.

Vostok and *Mirnyi* sailed from Kronstadt in July 1819 and made for Portsmouth, where they anchored on the 29th near the Russian sloop *Kamchatka* (Captain V.M. Golovnin). Troughton sextants, Dolland telescopes, and Arnold chronometers were bought in London,[36] and a meeting was arranged with the now venerable Joseph Banks. The Russians sailed for Rio de Janeiro four weeks later in the highest spirits. In Brazil too, where *Vostok* and *Mirnyi* were escorted for days by Sir Thomas Hardy's squadron, all went excellently. To their newly purchased scientific instruments (and British charts and tinned pea soup) the Russians added wine and freshly killed beef.[37] At last, they set their course due south. South Georgia Island was sighted on 27 December. Cook having surveyed the northern shores of Willis Island, Bellingshausen promptly moved along its south.[38] Next came work in the South Sandwich Group. Again the charting was exemplary. By late January 1820, Bellingshausen was within twenty-five miles of what is now called Princess Martha Land. He turned aside. On 18 February he could see an enormous icecap. This was Antarctica, and fold by fold it stretched on out of sight. The Russians then proceeded east, remaining south of 60°S for one-quarter of its circuit round the globe. At last, on 10 April 1820, *Vostok* dropped anchor in Port Jackson (Sydney), followed shortly by *Mirnyi*.[39]

The Russians were extremely well received in New South Wales, where Lazarev, who had already visited with *Suvorov* in 1814 and was remembered by colonial officials, served as general interpreter. They were impressed by the potential of the colony.[40] Refreshed and well provisioned for a winter cruise about the Tuamotu (Paumotu) Archipelago, where, as Andrew Sharp has shown, he sighted Angatau, Nihiru, Katiu, Fakarava, Matahiva and assorted other atolls,[41] Bellingshausen left Port Jackson on 8 May. As his instructions bade him, he set a course that would enable him to clear Three Kings' Islands on the north tip of New Zealand. Winter winds are fickle and unhelpful in the Tasman Sea for the mariner intent on making Rapa from the latitude of Sydney. Day by day, *Vostok* and *Mirnyi* struggled north but drifted east towards New Zealand. Then on 18–19 May both were hustled further eastward by a storm. Orders were issued for a rendezvous in Cook's Queen Charlotte Sound.[42] Both secure and convenient for watering and revictualing, the sound spared Bellingshausen's people a long, exhausting trial as they beat up north-by-west. Helped by winds and currents from the 27th on, the Russians fixed Cape Koamaru (41°5'10''S latitude, 174°23'46''E longitude), then "tacked boldly, relying on the special chart of Queen Charlotte Sound prepared on Captain Cook's first voyage."[43]

THE RUSSIAN VISIT TO QUEEN CHARLOTTE SOUND: AN OVERVIEW

Bellingshausen dropped anchor at 4:00 PM on 28 May. His first New Zealand anchorage, in nine fathoms, was south of Little Waikawa Bay and west of Motuara Island. A "fenced-in" settlement or village site was

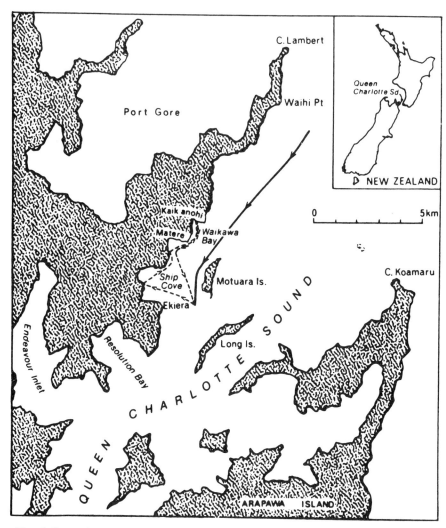

Map 5 Queen Charlotte Sound, New Zealand, showing Russian naval movements of May-June 1820

spotted in Little Waikawa Bay, and shortly after two canoes came from there, containing sixteen and twenty-three men. The canoes had open carving with snail patterns at the prow, a representation of a human head with tongue protruding, and shell (mother-of-pearl) eyes. Men of rank were heavily tattooed. One man stood and delivered a speech in a sonorous voice, gesticulating; the Russians responded by waving white kerchiefs and making "signs of peace." The Maori chief was then induced to board *Vostok,* which he did very nervously; he was presented with beads, cloth, a small knife, and a mirror, and asked to obtain fresh fish (*he ika*). The atmosphere was friendly but tense.[44]

The Maoris returned to shore and darkness fell. Because *Mirnyi* had not succeeded in entering the sound but was still under full sail outside, lamps were hoisted on *Vostok* and false fires were burned at intervals during the night. *Mirnyi* managed to join *Vostok* off Motuara Island by midnight. Sentries were posted on both ships with loaded guns, lest the cannibalistic Maoris attempted a raid in the darkness. At 9:00 AM the next day, both vessels moved to another position, whence Motuara's west point bore N 16°E, and the southern headland of Cook's Ship Cove bore S 37°W. *Vostok* now lay within a few yards of Cook's anchorage of May 1773.[45] Even as the Russians were tacking into this safer position, two Maori canoes came out and followed them. As soon as *Vostok* was motionless, seven *pood* or 250 pounds of fresh fish were taken from the Maoris in exchange for European goods. The chief was invited to dine in *Vostok* and ate with appetite but disliked wine. The additional gift of a well polished axe (*toki*) delighted him. Other Maoris also enjoyed Russian biscuits and gruel, but one cup of rum sufficed for them all. The meal over, the Maoris sat in two rows facing each other on *Vostok*'s quarterdeck and sang. One man intoned, then the rest caught up the air. The expeditionary artist, Pavel Nikolaevich Mikhailov (1780–1840), at this point made a detailed study of the chief, whom he had sketched earlier in a rough, preliminary way.[46] A graduate of St. Petersburg's Academy of Arts, Mikhailov had orders to sketch "all noteworthy places visited, and to portray native peoples and their dress."[47] He duly drew the village visible in Little Waikawa Bay, as it is called today,[48] as well as several other Maoris in his immediate vicinity on 29–30 May. The chief, meanwhile, encouraged the Russians to land, offering them women, no doubt hoping to acquire more European wares.

Next morning (30 May), Maoris visited both Russian ships, the old chief dining with Lazarev. While pulling ropes with the Russian seamen aboard *Mirnyi,* one Maori fell heavily to the deck. The incident caused mirth and led to an impromptu presentation of a *haka*. The people of *Vostok* could not see this action dance, which was recorded by Midshipman Novosil'skii of *Mirnyi*. That same morning, Bellingshausen and a group of officers landed at Ship Cove, where the song of thousands of birds re-echoed like pianos accompanied by flutes. A stream of sweet water was found and promptly exploited. Finally, on 31 May, the Russians landed in force, taking two cutters mounting swivel guns and many hand arms. The landing point was in the first cove north of Ship Cove, modern-day Cannibal Cove. (On his 1770 chart of the Sound, which Bellingshausen used, Cook had given the name Cannibal Cove to modern-day Little Waikawa Bay, but the confusion did not trouble the Russians much, as they were too busy to notice.)[49] The chief received his guests politely and, together with his wife and pretty daughter, was presented with another batch of gifts. This time, however, the Russians had the best of the exchange, for Bellingshausen was presented with a handsome cloak with double *taniko* borders.[50] Proceeding north by cutter, they landed next at the Little Waikawa Bay village, entering by a wicket in a seven-foot-high palisade. Crossing a cobblestone-edged stream by a wooden beam, the Russian party made its way into a chief's house supported by three rows of posts. The central rows were carved and coloured red. Fine mats covered the ground and pikes hung on the walls. The Maoris were civil and hospitable. Again, women were offered—and declined. Again goods were exchanged, the chief giving a ceremonial or chiefly paddle (*hoe*) for a good-sized piece of bright red cloth.[51] Together with several weapons also acquired on that day, the paddle remains in Leningrad's Peter-the-Great Museum of Ethnography, on semi-permanent display.

Returning to the sloops, the Russian cutters coasted south from Matere, towards Motuara's west side. Spotting cultivated plots fairly high up on a headland, Bellingshausen made a further stop. The plots contained potatoes, and the Russians saw a long row of baskets holding more. These were plants successfully propagated from English potatoes left by Mr. Fannen of *Adventure*. Bellingshausen rightly reckoned that potatoes and settled agriculture were a central element in Maori life, and that nomadic ways had been ended in the sound by the arrival of Europeans. It was evident from hybrid clothing (half-coats with sleeves of flax sewn on, jerseylike garments) that at least some Sydney sealers and/or whalers had called in the recent past.[52] Collecting wild celery for later use in soup, the Russians hurried back on board.

Next day (1 June), Captain-Lieutenant Ivan Zavadovskii and a boat party returned to Ship Cove and forced their way one mile up the creek where the sloops had recently watered. Birds were shot for science and the pot.[53] The wind was high and brought dramatic showers to the cove. Conditions worsened on the 2nd. On 3 June, anchors were weighed and both sloops shifted back to their original, less hemmed-in anchorage; high gusts of wind had grown alarming. Southern winter had arrived. The local Maoris remained ashore and under shelter. Loath to part without contributing a little to the charting of the district, Bellingshausen took a launch into Queen Charlotte Sound. He went some thirteen miles ssw, collecting celery and other greenstuffs, charting carefully, examining the empty huts which, he surmised, the local Maoris used seasonally. Everywhere, it seemed to him, there was abundant food: in such a country, men could hardly starve, nor would the population suffer if it grew. The Russians wondered if the Maoris' endemic warfare had reduced the local group.[54] They saw no more than eighty persons in the Sound, one-fifth the number Cook saw half a century before. Or had the use of British guns from New South Wales accelerated the death rate in the area? The local Maoris were certainly familiar with guns—they feared Russian cannon and did not conceal the fact. And they themselves were well equipped with hardwood spears, clubs, and staves, as well as handsome war canoes (one forty-seven feet in length and almost five feet in the beam).[55] Yet it did not seem to the Russians that their hosts were a warlike group or that they depended upon raiding for their livelihood, as other Maoris unquestionably did. They seemed, in fact, to be a trading people, unbelligerent, with staple food sources (fish, shellfish, ferns, potatoes). Bellingshausen's very presence and behaviour reinforced those agricultural and mercantile propensities more than he could know. *Vostok* and *Mirnyi* left Motuara Island on 4 June but were delayed five days by storms and mounting easterlies. They finally escaped, risking early separation, on the 9th, setting a course for Terawhiti Cape and Rapa Island on the cooler southern fringe of Polynesia's central tract.

For Russians and New Zealanders alike, the real value of the Bellingshausen visit lay in its ethnographical activity. Bellingshausen's was the only one of early European expeditions to the country to do its work among the Maori but of the South Island rather than the North. Given the absence of all other written records and the virtual extinction of traditions that specifically relate to "the Russians' *hapu,*"[56] (who were slaughtered shortly afterwards by the invading Atiawa, allies of the chief Te Rauparaha), this fact makes very significant all the eyewitness accounts of 1820. It is doubly fortunate that five such narratives survive or, more exactly, have been noted in the literature. Like a single beam of light, the Russian pictorial, narrative, and physical evidence illuminates the darkness that would otherwise have swallowed Cook's Ship Cove and "Hippah Island."

The five accounts are, in order of increasing importance from the ethnographic standpoint, Leading Seaman Egor Kiselev's, found in a library

in the provincial backwater of Suzdal' in the early 1930s and first printed
in the travel periodical *Vokrug Sveta* (*Around the World*) in 1941;[57]
Surgeon Galkin's, written at the urging of a southern friend and twice
published in 1822, first in Kazan' then in St. Petersburg;[58] Midshipman
Pavel Novosil'skii's, written thirty years or more after the voyage of
Mirnyi, based on the journal that, like all Russian officers, he had been
duty-bound to keep, and shyly published in the capital in 1853;[59] and,
lastly, those of Simonov and Bellingshausen, which deserve more comment.

RUSSIAN EYEWITNESS ACCOUNTS

The value of a primary account lies in its authenticity as an immediate,
unaltered record of experience. Thus considered, no record of the 1820
visit to Queen Charlotte Sound is more important than the one left by
the expeditionary astronomer, Ivan Mikhailovich Simonov. The journal
("Pamiatnik") that Leading Seaman Kiselev maintained so conscientiously is undeniably as fresh and pungent now as before; but he was
not an educated or especially astute observer of the Maori, about whom
he jotted down only a dozen lines.[60] By contrast, Nikolai Galkin was a
perceptive, highly educated man; but like his comrade Novosil'skii he
was intent on entertaining intellectuals who had an interest in travel literature. Scientific objectivity was good and he respected it, but local colour
also had its place. In short, his "Letters" resulted from a semi-popular
and unofficial manuscript, which derived only indirectly from his 1820
journal. Novosil'skii's journal has not yet come to light, though it was
formally submitted to the Russian Naval Ministry in August 1822 and is
no doubt in Leningrad. From similarities between the order and manner in
which incidents that had occurred in the Pacific were described by Bellingshausen (1831 text) and by Novosil'skii, it appears that the latter's
comments were available to his commander between 1821 and 1824. But,
in the absence of the manuscript itself, it is impossible to say whether or
not his semi-popular account *The South Pole: From the Memoirs of a
Former Naval Officer* was based on notes taken in his youth and perhaps
"improved." It is all the more regrettable, under these circumstances,
that the notebooks Bellingshausen submitted to the Ministry in April 1824
cannot be found today.[61]

   Bellingshausen expected that his journal, which he kept punctiliously
from the first day of his mission to the last, would be required of him
promptly. In fact, however, he had some eighteen months after his return
to Russia to examine all his officers' accounts and to reflect on and
change his own earlier statements. Bellingshausen was an honest man.

The seizure and imprisonment of a subordinate, Lieutenant Torson, for involvement in the anti-autocratic, secret Decembrist movement did not induce him—as it might have at the outset of the sullen reign of Nicholas I—to state that Torson had not performed his duties well.[62] Had he wished to, Bellingshausen could have rearranged events and altered emphases. But there are reasons to believe that the changes he made in the Baltic were essentially stylistic and that he took pains to see that truth was adhered to. There were, in any case, other witnesses to what he wrote; and some, like Lazarev and Zavadovskii, had influence.

On submitting his narrative in 1824, Bellingshausen asked the imperial authorities to finance a first edition of twelve hundred copies. Nothing came of the request and months passed. Then came the uprising of the 14 December 1825 and the arrests of Torson and at least three other naval officers connected with recent South Pacific voyages: Mikhail K. Kiukhel'beker of the *Apollon,* and Dmitrii I. Zavalishin and Fedor P. Vishnevskii, both of the frigate *Kreiser.*[63] Torson's role in the Decembrist insurrection altered Nicholas I's whole attitude towards the Bellingshausen venture and towards the fleet. Another twenty months went by. Bellingshausen sent an open letter to the chairman of the Naval Scientific Committee of the Russian Naval Staff, Rear-Admiral Loggin I. Golenishchev-Kutuzov. Would the government not print six hundred copies of his narrative? Kutuzov sympathized and the request was granted. After more difficulties from officious editors named Chizhov and Nikol'skii, who cut and altered as they pleased for many months, the Bellingshausen narrative appeared in St. Petersburg in 1831. The two volumes were not illustrated but were supplemented by an *Atlas* that included nineteen maps, two views of icebergs, thirteen other views, and thirty drawings by the competent Mikhailov. Both the 1949 (A.I. Andreev) and the 1960 (E.E. Shvede) Soviet editions of *Repeated Explorations . . .* and the English version of the late Frank Debenham and Edward Bullough (Hakluyt Society 1945) rest squarely on the 1831 text. Shvede provides a factually solid introduction to the 1960 Soviet edition. To conclude: the Bellingshausen holograph of 1821–22 cannot be found, but despite the tampering of 1827–28 and Bellingshausen's inability—being on duty on the Danube during the Russo-Turkish struggle—to inspect even the printer's work, it appears that the published text of 1831 correctly mirrors it.[64]

Where Simonov's remarks about *Vostok*'s and *Mirnyi*'s sojourn in New Zealand are concerned, on the other hand, we are spared all discomfort and suspicion. His careful reworking of his manuscript journal of 1819–21 is now held in the Manuscripts Department of Kazan' State University Main Library, Kazan'. The "New Zealand passage" covers five pages (169–74) and is presented below in translation.[65] First, however, let us survey Simonov's persistent and deliberate activity as propagandist for the Russian expedition to Antarctica and Polynesia. This activity included publication of two early and popular accounts of his experiences with *Vostok* and two scientific papers.[66] Both popular accounts were soon reprinted or translated. Thus his personal impressions of the Maori and of New Zealand reached a sizable Swiss, French, and German readership some seven years before Bellingshausen's narrative appeared.

Simonov was extraordinary professor of astronomy and mathematics at Kazan', his alma mater, when he was appointed to *Vostok*. His career had been marked by great precocity and greatly favoured by the friendship of the German-born astronomer who had been his teacher, Joseph-Johann Littrow (1781–1840). He remained in friendly contact both with Littrow and with others who travelled to the infant university from German-speaking regions, and he was fluent in both German and French.[67] In New Zealand he collected artefacts intelligently, paying heed to technique, as shown in half-completed articles. When he returned to St. Petersburg in 1821, he had a store of zoological, botanical, and ethnographic specimens, all packed in boxes, and a set of well-crammed journals that would serve him many years. On the basis of his scientific work in Oceania, he was given a permanent position at Kazan' in 1822. There, on 7 July, he gave a major public lecture on his personal experiences in *Vostok* and on the Bellingshausen expedition in general. It was modestly entitled "A Word on the Successes of the Voyage of the Sloops *Vostok* and *Mirnyi*," and was printed as a pamphlet that same year in Kazan'. To quote from its 450-word New Zealand passage:

> On 29 May we dropped anchor in Queen Charlotte Sound, in the lee of Long and Matuara [Motuara] Islands and facing Ship Cove. No sooner had the natives there seen us than they came out towards the sloop in their little craft. Appreciating that our attitude was a friendly one, they boarded us confidently and supplied us with a good quantity of fish. They bartered their own artefacts, such as woven material, wooden spears, stone chisels, and bone and shell fish-hooks and the like, for our nails, knives, axes, mirrors, and other things of lesser value.
>
> These New Zealanders were of middling height and solid build, with swarthy expressive faces on which we observed various designs. They showed much animation and a fire full of martial spirit shone in their eyes. With us, however, they proved to be well behaved and even quiet, recognizing the superiority of our force and knowing the effectiveness of our armament. We, for our part, were well aware of their treacherous nature and so went ashore and visited their dwelling

places only under armed escort. These were, after all, the same bar-
barians who had perfidiously killed and eaten Marion, the French
captain who had entrusted himself to them, as well as ten of the crew
of Cook's companion, Furneaux, who had merely landed for water.

The New Zealanders stand in greater need of clothing, because of
the moderate climate of their country, than do the natives of New
Holland or of hot climes generally. That being so, they weave material from the so-called New Zealand flax and cover their bodies with
it. Their winter clothing is very coarse in manufacture, with large
filaments, rather like our own heavy coats. A palisade ran round their
village and their huts were roofed with tree leaves or grass, the roofs
being supported from beneath by posts. Of these interior posts, some
were ornamented with carving, though certainly of a crude variety.
The shore by which we stood had a truly majestic aspect. There were
large hills, enveloped by an impenetrable forest and filled with birds,
whose song delighted.[68]

It was understandable that Simonov should wish to draw advantage
from his voyage by speaking publicly to a receptive audience, among
whom there were friends and men of influence within his university. His
"Word" was calculated to appeal to the majority of educated listeners,
being essentially an oral form of travel literature. Already, though, he
was at work on astronomical and physical data collected from *Vostok*,
preparing courses and surveying the resources and equipment of the university. The latter left a lot to be desired. The respect earned by the
twenty-eight-year-old astronomer and publicist is apparent from his being
sent, in June 1823, to purchase physical and astronomical equipment in
Vienna. Simonov left Russia with his colleague Adolph Theodor Kupffer
(1799–1865), and remained abroad for sixteen months. In 1822 he had
initiated or resumed a correspondence with half-a-dozen scientists of
European reputation. These included the astronomers who had been most
closely linked with previous Russian naval expeditions round the globe or
with the ordering of Bellingshausen's enterprise, or both: Johann Caspar
Hörner and Baron Franz Xaver von Zach (1754–1832).[69]

With Zach especially he corresponded heavily in 1822–24. The Aus-
trian savant was widely known in Russian academic circles as the former
head of Seeberg Observatory at Gotha and was personally friendly with
such grandees as Counts Nikolai P. Rumiantsev and A.R. Vorontsov. He
was, besides, the moving force behind two major learned journals of the
day, to which both Simonov and Kupffer had subscribed: *Monatliche
Korrespondenz...* (Gotha 1800–13) and *Correspondence astronomique, géographique, hydrographique* (Genoa 1818–26). Most signifi-

cantly, Zach and Simonov shared common interests in theoretical astronomy and practical geodesy.[70] Shortly after his arrival in Vienna, where he stayed with Littrow, Simonov prepared a German translation, or rather paraphrase, of his "Word." This he sent to Zach, who edited it in the form of letters and printed it in his *Correspondence astronomique* early in 1824. A copy of the issue was presumably sent to Kazan', to which Simonov returned after a lengthy stay in Paris and a briefer but more hectic trip through Italy. We know that he was able and disposed to edit or re-edit Zach's translation of a year earlier, giving his blessing to its publication in *Journal des Voyages, ou Archives géographiques du XIXe siècle* (Paris).[71] While in Paris in 1823–24, Simonov had made numerous acquaintances, with Baron Alexander von Humboldt, Cuvier, Guizot, and other luminaries. He had frequented the Académie des Sciences, and had even been elected, on the basis of his "Word" in German translation, to the (Paris) Geographical Society. His name was thus familiar to the many readers of the *Journal des Voyages* who in 1824 were offered what had now become a "Précis du Voyage de Découvertes, fait... par le capitaine Bellingshausen dans... les mers Australes." The New Zealand passage occupied only one-tenth of its epistle but presented Bellingshausen's visit to New Zealand to a vast audience. Stylistic indicators demonstrate, moreover, that that passage was considerably closer to the manuscript original of 1821 than was the "Word."

It was Simonov's opinion, however, that his manuscript was a source to be exploited, not a work to be presented whole and raw. It might offend; it had been written in a rough-and-ready way; besides, his time and energies were fully occupied with mathematics and, by 1828, administrative duties. He was corresponding member of the conservative Academy of Sciences. His strictly scientific articles had been received with great approval. Then in 1831 Bellingshausen's narrative and *Atlas* appeared. Simonov could see no pressing need to publish a more personal, less comprehensive treatment of the same Pacific/polar expedition.

Over the next ten years, however, he was intermittently reminded of his journal and maintained his interest in seaborne exploration. In 1844 he even published a review of major voyages by European seamen from the sixteenth to the early nineteenth century.[72] Though *rektor* of his university in 1846, he looked at his youthful journal and thought of editing its text; neither energy nor time was now available to him, however, despite his talking to a likely publisher in 1848.[73] At last he started work. The resulting manuscript, MS 4533 at Kazan' State University Main Library, was squarely based on and incorporated notes taken while Simonov was in *Vostok* in 1820. The presentation of material reflects an antecedent ordering by date. Indeed, specific dates can be assigned to given passages.

Misspellings are preserved, such as "Wellnes" and "Belly" for Messrs. Wales and Bayly, who had visited Queen Charlotte Sound with Cook. And simple differences of interpretation or fact between the Simonov account and narratives that had been published long before show that nothing had been done to bring the data in his journal into line with those presented by others.[74] Here is Simonov's account of the 1820 visit to New Zealand, followed, for comparative purposes, by those of Novosil'skii, Galkin, and Kiselev. Because the Bellingshausen text has been long and widely available to English readers in the Hakluyt Society edition (London 1945), it is superfluous to reproduce it here.

IVAN M. SIMONOV'S ACCOUNT

In accordance with the instructions which Captain Bellingshausen had received, we made to pass to the north of New Zealand on our passage to the Society Islands. To do so, the captain wished to steer for Oparo [Rapa] Island, which Captain Vancouver had discovered, straight from New Holland. . . He did not manage to hold so direct a course, however, and for that reason, hopes of getting a favourable wind fading, he decided to pass through Cook Strait. It was his intention to shelter from bad weather for a few days in Queen Charlotte Sound on the north shore of the southern island of New Zealand, that is, the island known as Tavai Posnummu [Te Wai Pounamu].

The shores of New Zealand soon came into view and it was without difficulty that we entered Cook Strait. There, however, we met with an opposing current and strong headwind which obliged our leader to drop anchor quicker than he had intended to, and before he reached the so-called Long and Matuara [Motuara] Islands.

We had scarcely let go anchor before two small canoes filled with natives came out from the shore and approached us. Most of the men were paddling with short paddles, each man for himself and without order. The first canoe having come near our sloop, one individual, probably the senior man among the natives present, stood up and began to address us in a singsong voice. He spoke at length, in a language incomprehensible to us but even so quite pleasant to the ear. We let out our white handkerchiefs in order to make our amicable disposition clear to him, then made signs to him to come right alongside the sloop without fear. Whether or not he understood these gesturings I cannot say, but in all events the natives did, after a while, begin to show more confidence in our intentions. They would not keep their canoes immediately by the sloop, though, and at first only the aforementioned elder would come on board. He shook our hands by way of greeting, and was again about to launch into a lengthy speech when the captain, wanting to cut the address short (since it meant nothing to us and promised to be long), gave him a few presents. These were a small mirror, a small pocket knife, and a few beads. The language of gifts is understood by every nation, and these ones eloquently enough conveyed our friendly attitude. The New Zealand elder was delighted with his presents but evidently wanted something else. With much earnestness, he explained to us that he really wanted *fau* [*whau*], as he termed it; on this occasion, however, we failed to understand him.[75]

Looking up the local word for fish in Captain Cook's *Voyage,* meanwhile, and finding that it was *ika,* we tried it on the elder or chief before us on the deck. He immediately realized that we were in need of fresh fish, turned to the people down in canoes, and shouted *ika! ika!*[76] The natives who were still seated in their craft then repeated after him, several times, *ika! ika!* It was our impression, at this juncture, that their gestures expressed satisfaction that they would be able to satisfy our want without trouble. The captain gave orders that the chief be given a small glass of rum. The chief drank off half of it but did not seem greatly enamoured of our drink and said a few words that we did not understand. Finally, with further gestures to convey his amicability, he went off with the other natives to catch the wanted fish or *ika,* as they called it. These people had no weapons of any sort in their canoes with them—a sure sign of their trust in us.

These were assuredly quite a different people from the New Hollanders. It seemed to us, indeed, that we saw the fire of intellect in their eyes and martial pride in their bearing. Their facial features were not unpleasant. Some individuals even recalled to mind the old Romans depicted in prints, particularly when the New Zealand mantle hung from the shoulders and feathers fluttered on the head. It is true that an undeniable wildness and tattooing combined to spoil their pleasing and regular countenances. Various parts of the body were carefully covered by these tattoos. Still, I was conscious of their relatively tall and very muscular build: they were bony, sturdy, and broad-shouldered, lean in the face. Face and body alike were so swarthy as to be nearly bronzed in hue. Their hair was long and black, straight in some cases, curly in others. They allowed the hair to descend in long locks at the back, but they cut it shorter at the front and either powdered it red or smeared some sort of red colouring substance over it.

Natives of New Zealand certainly need to wear clothing. The part of the country we were in lies in latitude 41°6'S, and there, in the Southern Hemisphere, it can get pretty cold. They have developed a material for the purpose. It is produced from the wide leaves of the plant known as

New Zealand flax (*Phormium tenax*). This yarn can be spun as finely as true flax and is woven into various stuffs, more or less fine or thick as needed. It can look shaggy, like our northern furs.[77] This material goes to make all the New Zealanders' clothing, which, of course, differs in the different seasons of the year. Their clothing consists, first, of a camisole which they wrap round themselves from chest level down to the middle. On top of this they wear another piece of woven material which falls, like a skirt, from the waist to the knee. Camisole and skirt are both held in place by a plaited girdle at the waist. Over all this underclothing goes a cloak, thin or warm depending on the temperature and weather, which is reinforced by a cord at the neck.

Tattooing, or the placing of designs on face and body, is the principal embellishment and affectation of the New Zealand native. The necessary operations are performed from childhood on and commonly produce a fever that lasts for days. As among the natives of New Holland, small openings are later made through the central cartilage of the nose, so that little sticks may be introduced above the upper lip. Larger apertures are made in the ears, through which are passed not earrings proper but bunches of bird's down.

Nature or possibly the lack of inventive genius has deprived the New Zealanders of metals and, by extension, of such significant aids to life in society as derive from the use of iron. That being so, one can only marvel at their clothmaking and shipbuilding skills. We ourselves found them in craft six and a half *sazhen* long [14.8 metres] and nearly two *arshin* wide [1.4 metres], and Captain Cook declares in his work that he measured one canoe nine and three-quarter *sazhen* in length [21.7 metres]. The hulls of these craft were in general scooped out of a single tree trunk. A pair of planks was attached to each of the upper edges of the hull by means of cords, the planks themselves being half an *arshin* [35 cm] broad, and reeds were put in between these and the hull to prevent any leaks. The reeds were covered over by strips of bast about six and a half *vershki* wide [28 cm]. By way of decoration, these canoes had carvings which represented the human face in caricature and, at the stern, a beam some two *arshin* high [1.4 metres]. The carved figures, stern beam, and upper strakes were all coloured red all over.[78]

At 8:00 AM the next morning [29 May], we weighed anchor and tacked against a headwind till midday. The night before, we had been at anchor quite a way from the shore. Finally, after twenty-five tacks, we dropped anchor again in an attractive haven, protected on all sides, between Long, Matuara, and Tavoi Posnummu Islands. Two native canoes followed us all the while, and the natives seated in them were asking to be allowed to come on board. In the circumstances we could not welcome them and instead, by means of gestures, encouraged them to pay us a visit once we had anchored. Very likely they did not understand us. They came after us or the *Mirnyi* for quite some time, but at last went off to the shore.

We dropped anchor and, our work done, sat down to eat. But we were again visited by the New Zealanders, and this time, almost all of them came on board fearlessly. Only one man was left in charge of each canoe. The captain met the chief with all the courtesy of Oceania, embracing him and pressing noses, then, inviting him to take food with us, sat him at table in a place of honour between himself and M.P. Lazarev. The latter was dining with us, together with his officers. Everything on the table before him filled the chief with wonder, and he curiously examined every object. Not till he was sure that we were eating the same food, though, would he eat anything. It was our sweet dishes and biscuits that he consumed with the most evident relish. Wine he did not care for. His people having brought us a fair amount of fish, in the meantime, he again began speaking of *fau* and *toki*. Our captain was doing his very best, by means of word and gesture, to persuade his guest of his own friendly intentions towards the natives of the country. As proof, he finally made the chief a present of a beautifully polished axe. The chief received the gift, which was precious to him, with loud exclamations of *toki! toki!;* and his face was a picture of joy. Now, he exhausted his means of conveying his feeling of gratitude towards the captain, whom he termed his *hoa,* or friend. It was in this way that we learned that *toki* meant axe. Unable to sit still at the table any longer, the chief rushed out to show his precious gift to his fellow-countrymen. We ourselves went after him onto the quarterdeck, dinner being over.

On the quarterdeck, a regular market was being held. On the captain's orders, the commander of our sloop [I. Zavadovskii] exchanged a fair quantity of the nails, small mirrors, silk ribbons and other trifles that we had in store for no less than seven *pood* (250 pounds) of fish, among them cod, mackerel, trout, and flounder. There were other species of fish among them too, which we did not recognize but which turned out to be tasty, on the whole. We obtained this fish and delicious crayfish too at very low cost, considering the very slight cost to us of the objects that the natives took so willingly. Also by barter, the officers acquired New Zealand woven stuffs, finished garments, weapons, domestic articles, fishing tackle, and other things of interest which might be trifling but were even so rare for us as Europeans. And we now discovered that *fau* meant nail.

My own bartering with the New Zealanders will have provided good indications of the value that they placed on our wares even when ignorant of their use. The very well-ground bone needle which I acquired from our chief, for instance, cost me merely a handle broken off a copper candlestick. The handle looked rather like a ring. The needle was of the kind with which these people make cloths. I saw the same fragment again, the very next day. It was serving as an ear ornament for another man, that is, not the man who had had it from me! Another man let me have a bone fish-hook for a tiny piece of red ribbon and jumped for joy. Yet another secretly showed me a nephrite chisel which he had under his cloak. It was obvious that he valued it, since he would not part with it for nails, or a bottle, or even a piece of red braid or a lock, the function of which I tried to explain to him. He let me have it in the end, after I had made numerous unsuccessful propositions, in exchange for a bit of octo-size writing paper: I offered it to him, at the last, in jest! Two of the New Zealanders present on this occasion had half-coats thrown over their shoulders. These had flax sleeves, sewn on by cords. Our seamen got them through barter, one for an ancient handkerchief, the other for a rather threadbare canvas jacket.

Our honoured guests were being entertained with coffee while this haggling proceeded. They liked it very well. The chief even requested a second cup. Finally, the bartering came to an end, and the chief sat his people down on our quarterdeck and proceeded to divide up among them the biscuit that he had obtained from us. To entertain them even further, the captain now had our ship's flautist play the flute while a drummer beat a drum. The New Zealand chief himself wished to try out both instruments. He found that the flute would not obey him; but loud and disconnected booms from the drum, produced by his many blows, quite delighted him.

Wishing to repay us with a similar pleasure, our guests struck up a song. One man would first intone a couplet, then all would join in and shout it with all their might. The melody consisted of perhaps three notes in its entirety—indeed, the singing was mostly a matter of words and cries. However, the New Zealand natives do have music made by wind instruments. It was M.P. Lazarev who acquired from them a pipe made like a flageolet, only much thicker and ornamented with carving. He showed it to me. It had one stop at the end, none on the sides. Such pipes are played like our French horn and have a tone like our hunting horns.[79]

Captain Bellingshausen had a few shots fired as our guests departed, and sent a few rockets up during the evening. In this way, he announced our arrival in Queen Charlotte Sound to natives in the interior of Tavoi Posnummu [Te Wai Pounamu].

The following day [30 May] I busied myself from early morning in seeking a suitable site for astronomical observation. I was at first inclined to make my observations from Hippah Island, on the spot where once stood the field stations of Wellnes [Wales] and Belly [Bayly] of the expedition with Captains Cook and Furneaux. I went round that island. It was clear that I would find it practically impossible to get on top of it with my instruments. When he had ascended the rocky cliff in question, Forster had found it climbable from one angle only and by one very narrow and awkward path. That was forty-seven years previously. We, for our part, managed to climb the islet only with the greatest labour and without any instruments. A small isthmus, which water covers at high tide, connects Hippa and Matuara Islands. The latter is more sloping than the former but is enveloped by dense bush. As our ships were not to remain long in Queen Charlotte Sound, we did not put up a shore observatory. I merely landed every day to make the observations necessary to determine our exact latitude and longitude and, three times daily, checked our chronometers. I found myself a very good spot for these purposes, right on the isthmus. We spotted a number of abandoned huts on the summit of Hippa Island. Perhaps they were the very ones which Forster mentions.

New Zealand natives were often on board *Vostok* and *Mirnyi;* and the commanders of both sloops, as well as all officers, went ashore quite frequently, to shoot birds, collect water, catch fish, or visit natives known and unknown to us. I too, when my occupations on the isthmus between Hippa and Matuara Islands were completed, saw no reason why I should lose such opportunities of getting to know this land and its people rather better. The first time I went ashore at Ship Cove [on 31 May], my ear was charmed by a most delightful blend of sounds: the song of many birds, the gurgling of a stream that was flowing into the Sound. Thick and impenetrable woods covered the hills behind and, illumined by a setting sun, offered the eye a truly magnificent picture of wild nature. Captain Bellingshausen writes that this song of land birds re-echoed with all the beauty of a piano accompanied by flutes; and Captain Cook also writes of the pleasure that these New Zealand birds' singing caused him. It was certainly long since we ourselves had had such a pleasure, nor do I remember having listened to such a harmonious concert of songbirds in any one of the other five parts of this globe. Conditions seemed just like those of a marvelous spring evening. Yet we were here on the last days of May which correspond, in the Southern Hemisphere, to our northern November! The latitude of that part of New Zealand, though, corresponds with that of Rome or Barcelona. Forster, who had been in New Zealand with Cook also towards the end of May in the year 1773, had found greens growing in gardens on Hippa Island which Captain Furneaux had sown on

Plate 1 Iurii Fedorovich Lisianskii (1773-1839), drawn and engraved by Cardine of London (1813)

Plate 2 The *Neva* (ex-*Thames*); drawing by Lisianskii, her commander, of 1805

Plate 3 Otto Evstaf'evich Kotzebue (1788-1846); drawing of 1819 for Kotzebue's
Puteshestvie v Iuzhnyi okean (St. Petersburg 1821)

Plate 4 "Vue de l'Ile de Paques" ("View of Easter Island"), by Ludovik Choris; engraved by Bovet of Paris and published as Planche IX in Choris's *Vues et Paysages des Régions équinoxiales* (Paris 1826)

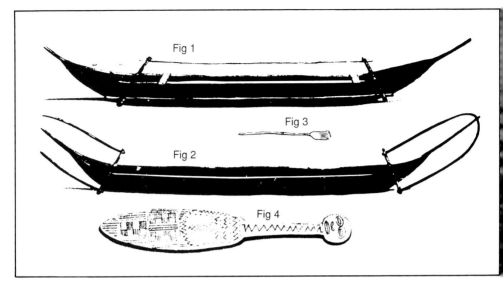

Plate 5 Easter Island craft and paddle, by Choris; lithographed by Langlumé of Paris and printed as Planche X of Choris's *Voyage pittoresque autour du monde* (Paris 1822): figs. 1&2, "Paddling craft"; fig.3, "A Paddle"; fig. 4, "Club from Easter Island"

Plate 6 "Habitans de l'Ile de Paques" ("Natives of Easter Island"), by Choris; also lithographed by Langlumé; Planche XI in *Voyage pittoresque* (1822)

Plate 7 (upper) Ribbed male image (*moai kavakava*) from Easter Island; collected by the Russians in the early 1800s, now No. 736-203 in the Peter the Great Museum of Anthropology and Ethnography, Leningrad; (lower) Grotesque female image (*moai paapaa*), similarly collected, now No. 736-205 in the MAE, Leningrad

Plate 8 Fine specimen of an Easter Island birdman image (*tangata manu*), held at MAE in Leningrad as No. 736-204

Plate 9 Ancient petroglyphs of *tangata manu* on rocks facing Motu Nui, Motuiti, and Moto Kaokao islets, just west of Orongo

Plate 10 Motu Nui, Motuiti, and Motu Kaokao, the islets observed by Lisianskii and Kotzebue on Easter Island's SW tip. The eggs of the sooty tern were sought on Motu Nui and brought back to Orongo by native swimmers.

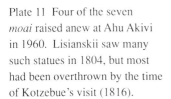

Plate 11 Four of the seven *moai* raised anew at Ahu Akivi in 1960. Lisianskii saw many such statues in 1804, but most had been overthrown by the time of Kotzebue's visit (1816).

Plate 12 The Inventory Book for "the Lisianskii collection" (No. 750) at MAE in Leningrad. The small labels stuck to the pages were attached to those Pacific artefacts, brought back aboard the *Neva* in 1806, which these entries briefly describe.

Plate 13 Captain-Lieutenant Faddei Faddeevich Bellinsgauzen (German: von Bellingshausen); a rough by the artist aboard *Vostok*, Pavel N. Mikhailov, of 1819-20. Now held with Mikhailov's original portfolio in the Drawing Division, State Russian Museum, Leningrad

Plate 14 Mikhail Petrovich Lazarev in full dress uniform; engraving by J. Thomson, circa 1835. Lazarev became Commander-in-Chief on the Black Sea Station.

Plate 15 "Main Settlement of New Zealand South, in Queen Charlotte Sound"; aquarelle with a tincture of white lead by Pavel Nikolaevich Mikhailov, engraved by Ivan P. Fridrits for Bellingshausen's 1831 narrative, *Dvukratnye izyskaniia....* The settlement stood in Little Waikawa Bay and was visited by the Russians in 1820.

Plate 16 "War Dance of the New Zealanders, in Queen Charlotte Sound," by Mikhailov; also engraved and published in St. Petersburg in 1831, this is a composite, incorporating elements of three separate drawings of 1820. The locale is basically Cook's Ship Cove.

Plate 17 Maori war canoe and warriors in Murderers' Bay, New Zealand, 1642; developed from an original drawing and published by N. Witsen in the second (1705) edition of his *Noord en Oost Tartarye*, this drawing gave Russians their first impression of the Maori people.

Plate 18 "A Chief of Southern New Zealand with His Wife," drawn from life by Pavel Nikolaevich Mikhailov. Original in the State Russian Museum, Leningrad

Plate 19 (upper), "Natives of New Zealand," by Mikhailov; unfinished work partly washed with Indian ink; (lower), preliminary roughs by Mikhailov, Queen Charlotte Sound, late May 1820. Note the great economy of space and full use of each sheet in his sketchbook. Originals in the State Russian Museum, Leningrad

Plate 20 Self-portrait by Pavel Nikolaevich Mikhailov, circa 1824. The original hangs in the State Russian Museum, Leningrad.

Plate 21 Maori artefacts collected by the Russians in Queen Charlotte Sound, May-June 1820, now at MAE in Leningrad. (Left), detail of the lower end of a ceremonial bier stay for a dead woman chief, No. 736-120; (right), detail of its upper part. This is ancient Maori carving of very high quality.

Plate 22 Detail of a flat Maori feather-box (*papahou*) lid, carved in the distinctive Wanganui style (SW North Island): MAE No. 736-124 (right), magnified central section of that lid

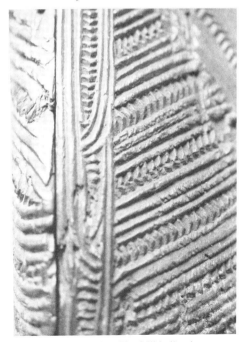

Plate 23 Detail of a *taiaha* (MAE No. 736-115), possibly that depicted by Mikhailov in Plate 18 here; the eyes are mother-of-pearl. (Right), magnified view of a fine *wakahuia* or feather-box, carved in the East Coast (Gisborne) style with stone tools. The Russians acquired three ornamental caskets or feather-boxes in 1820.

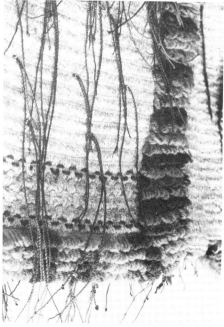

Plate 24 (Top), detail of an unfinished cloak (MAE No. 736-128), 159 cm wide; (left), detail of a *korowai* cloak (MAE No. 736-125), with flax "laces" or tags. Sydney Parkinson had drawn such cloaks during Captain Cook's visit to New Zealand of 1773.

Plate 25 Ivan Mikhailovich Simonov, astronomer and ethnographer aboard *Vostok* in 1819-21, circa 1845

Plate 26 Sketches by Pavel Nikolaevich Mikhailov of 29 June 1820, showing (from top to bottom) Rapa's coastline from N88°E; from S71° E; and a Rapan canoe with seven natives aboard. Note fortifications or hill villages along the coastal hill range.

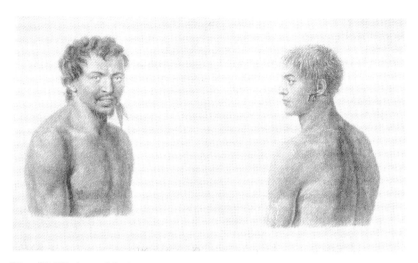

Plate 27 "Natives of the Island of Oparo," drawn by Mikhailov aboard the *Vostok* on 30 June 1820. The Russians considered the 18-year-old at right to be a half-caste.

Plate 28 Rapa's green hills are still covered with overgrown terraces like these, near Morongo Uta, on which Norwegian archaeologists worked with the help of the local people in 1956. The terraces were once the sites of elevated villages.

his previous sojourn there. So they were able, as Forster observes, to regale themselves with European greens even though it was winter there. This was an unexpected pleasure.

As well as *phormium tenax,* that is, the New Zealand "flax" which I mentioned above (which is sent to England to produce a yarn as soft, fine and white as any silk), many very serviceable plants flourish in this country. The pine is noteworthy among large trees, for its leaves can be used as an anti-scorbutic remedy. But palms, breadfruit trees, and fruit-bearing trees are all missing. The natives use the roots of a plant called cabbage palm by Forster as a foodstuff, and also devour one species of fern, termed by them *mamakga*.[80] This is full of a softish substance from which, when the root has been cut off, a sago-like, sticky sap oozes out. European vegetable varieties, including culinary roots and such greenstuffs as were brought to New Zealand by Captains Cook and Furneaux, and by Mr. Forster, all do very well there. The natives have made use of the potato alone as a food, though.

With regard to the larger quadrupeds, early navigators met with only two species in New Zealand: a wood rat and a barkless dog. It was always in human company, as dogs are in our countries. These dogs are in fact very like the sort called sheepdog by Buffon. All the fish and sea creatures of the Eastern and Southern Oceans may be found in waters around New Zealand; and even penguins come there, too, from the Southern Icy Ocean. We ourselves saw a live penguin in Cook Strait. The natives of New Zealand eat them. We also sighted a kind of dove and some small green parrots, remarkably well proportioned, as well as a great number of songbirds. The latter fluttered ahead of us, on the shores of Queen Charlotte Sound. The mineral kingdom is well represented, as is the vegetable. The country is rich in quartz, basalt, and green nephrite, from which the natives fashion domestic tools, and there are also granite, jasper, and different volcanic products. It is the opinion of Forster that iron deposits must surely exist in New Zealand.

We were very hospitably received by the New Zealand natives in their rather unattractive huts. The village nearest Ship Cove stood on both banks of a small stream, both sides of which were edged with stones. These could hardly have been mistaken for a pavement of some sort, though, since they had been laid down without method or plan. The native dwellings were really huts, about twice as high as a man at the central point, much lower at the sides. They were supported inside by carved posts, which were painted red. The carvings were ugly human representations. Reeds formed the walls, and there was quite fine bast matting inside. The huts had two entrances, one at the front and one at the rear. A

species of stone oven stood in the middle of the floor area, fires being lit
both for the warmth and for cooking. More flax matting was laid along
the side walls, and there the inhabitants sat during the daylight hours and
slept at night. The chief, whom we knew from previously, lived in rather
more style, and in a cleaner fashion, than the others. His dwelling was
small, perhaps, but it boasted an antechamber.

Our collection of rarities was considerably enlarged in the course of
this visit to a New Zealand village. By barter, we acquired spears and
javelins, wooden war maces, and other things. The weaponry was often
finished with carvings of fish, or birds, or a man with wide-open mouth
and tongue sticking out, or simply lines and rings.

The natives would not infrequently offer us the entertainment of watching the spectacle that is their wardance, or *heava,* while we were visiting
each other ashore or on the sloops. This dance was expressive of a sort of
wild fury. It was uniformly strange to behold. When dancing, the natives
would generally form a line, stamp their feet in time on one spot, raise
their arms up over the head, and cast furious looks at each other. The
song they then sang was a savage shout, and was rendered while they hor-
ribly distorted their faces. At the conclusion of a couplet, they would suddenly and all together stop, standing on one foot only. Lowering their
heads and left arms, while shaking the right over their heads still, they
would bring the couplet to a finale with a hoarse noise. By this dance,
they express something warlike. It appears that all the New Zealanders
are passionately fond of it, and no sooner does one individual start such a
dance than others are joining him. We took a special liking to one young
native, led him into the wardroom, and fed him with various sweets while
our ship's artist drew his portrait. Once the wild shouts of his countrymen
announced to all that a wardance was starting, though, this young friend
of ours proved quite incapable of sitting still. Excusing himself, he went
up on deck, grabbed a spear or something else from a canoe, and quickly
joined the dancers. His muscles rippled and his eyes flashed. He went
into a frenzy. By the time this dance was over, every participant looked
like a hero rejoicing over the victory just won over his enemies.

We continued to live in harmony with the natives of Tavai Posnummu
until our seven-day stay drew to its close. This, however, was only the result of the fear they entertained for our hand guns and cannon. The natives made it apparent, even on their first visit to *Vostok,* that they very
well knew the effects of our artillery pieces. They pointed to the cannon
and fearfully uttered the word *poo!* Even though they recognized our military superiority, though, we never visited their dwelling places without
arms and an adequate escort.

Stormy gusts of wind in Queen Charlotte Sound, meanwhile, were giving us no peace. The weather had held fair till 2 June and, though there had been occasional cloudiness, the sun had never been long hidden from sight. But the barometer had been sinking, and its predictions were realized early on the morning of the 2nd, when black clouds covered the entire sky and it poured with rain. The winds rose and the sea became quite audible. Its grey waves crashed against the sloop with such force that the single anchor by which we were then held was insufficient. A second anchor was dropped. The whole day was a worrying one, rainy and very tempestuous, lightning flashing and thunder rolling and reverberating in the mountains.

Captain Bellingshausen gave the order to weigh anchor just as soon as I had finished my routine daily observations on 4 June and had returned to the sloop from my shore base. The New Zealanders were aboard *Vostok* for the last time and, by words and signs, their chief expressed his genuine sorrow. He could see that we were making preparations for a prompt departure. His sorrow was genuine, of course, because he was still hoping to exchange trifles for things that he needed. There were even some natives who would readily enough have agreed to come with us to Europe. But the chief kept a careful watch on them and made sure that nobody remained with us at the end. One young native begged us to take him along, promising to work hard on the sloop. Our captain gave his permission, and we gave the youth to understand that the final decision to come or stay rested with him. Our consent delighted him; but the elders were quite aware of his ambition and almost forcibly obliged their enterprising countryman to return to shore with them. He pressed his nose on mine with sad vexation, slowly descending into his relations' canoe. We then weighed anchors, filled our sails, and moved out into Cook Strait. The sizable flotilla of New Zealand craft around us made for the shore.

MIDSHIPMAN PAVEL N. NOVOSIL'SKII'S ACCOUNT

The Simonov narrative is complemented by that of Midshipman Pavel N. Novosil'skii, published anonymously in St. Petersburg in 1853 (*Iuzhnyi polius: iz zapisok byvshago morskago ofitsera*, or *The South Pole: From the Memoirs of a Former Naval Officer*). Novosil'skii judged matters from the deck of *Mirnyi*, not *Vostok;* was a professional Navy man, not a scientist; and had an interest in music and an eye for colour that Simonov lacked. The 1853 text was reprinted, with occasional editorial emendations, in V.N. Sementovskii's collection of primary materials *Russkie otkrytiia v Antarktike v 1819, 1820 i 1821 godakh* (*Russian Discoveries in Antarctica in the Years 1819–21*; Moscow 1951). The "New Zealand passage" therein is on pages 230–37. It does not appear below in its entirety, since certain passages are plainly derivative and were inserted into the *Zapiski,* or rather a redrafting of them, long after Novosil'skii's return to European Russia in 1821.

20 May. We caught up with the *Vostok* by evening. It was a moonlit night. The wind strengthened and lightning flashed from time to time. We were encircled by albatrosses and petrels, our usual companions in the Southern Icy Ocean. They were making for the north, away from the harsh southern winter, while we, driven by a northerly wind, were moving southward to meet them. At four o'clock, Captain Bellingshausen signalled that we should rendezvous in Queen Charlotte Sound. We supposed that the leader of our expedition intended to save time by going through the little-known Cook Strait separating the northern part of New Zealand from the southern, despite the fact that it was stormy thereabouts during the winter.[81]

24 May. Fires gleamed ahead at night, very probably lit by the New Zealanders along the shores that we now followed south. When it grew light, New Zealand stood revealed, with its majestic Mount Egmont. The mountain's summit was lost in clouds, but lower we could see the snow that envelops that giant. Forest and bush could be seen on the shores. Mist lay in the valleys and through the mist smoke forced its way up, indicating the presence of a village.[82]

27 May. We tacked into the Sound itself and were surrounded by high hills. Far off to the north, the southern shore of the north island of New Zealand showed blue. On the western side[83] we observed a fenced-in place, whence two little craft soon came off. There were some twenty men in one of them, fewer in the other. The New Zealanders were sitting in pairs; they were wearing cloaks,[84] had white feathers on their heads, and paddled with little red paddles. One craft went closer to the *Vostok* than to us, and one of the natives in it stood and said something very loudly, waving his arms about. They answered him from *Vostok,* after which both the native craft went alongside her. At 11:00 PM we dropped anchor beside the *Vostok.*

29 May. We weighed anchor in the morning, moving into a little bay that was sheltered from all winds. The western tip of Matuara [Motuara] Island bore N 16°E.

30 May. New Zealanders visited our sloop in the same two craft. They numbered about thirty. Our guests were of middling height. Their faces were ornamented with dark blue patterns, and their clothing consisted of material that covered them from chest to knees. It was fastened at the chest by a basalt pin or a bone. A short cape was thrown over the

shoulders, and left unfastened; it was made of New Zealand flax and resembled the *burka*.[85] Their hair was tied up in a knot on top of the head, and had white feathers stuck through it.

These islanders greeted us by touching noses. The chief and elders were entertained to lunch. They consumed beef with more appetite than anything else, even if it were spoiled beef fat. At the time, the sloop's shrouds[86] were being dried and pulled out and casks were being raised from the hold. The New Zealanders at once undertook to assist our seamen, shouting in time. When a rope they were pulling happened to part, they fell and laughed loudly. Then they began a dance. All stood in a long row, in pairs, hopped from one foot to the other, and chanted loudly:

Hina reko,
Hina reko!
Tovi gide,   Tohi ki
Nei ropo!   Tenei ropu!

This chanting was accompanied by various grimacings: their eyes rolled around frightfully under the forehead, revealing the whites; muscles strained to the limit, the tongue hanging out. They violently stamped their feet, giving themselves up to the most furious movements. This dance of theirs appeared to suggest contempt for an enemy and the triumph of victory.[87]

31 May. Early in the morning, at the invitation of Captain Bellingshausen, we set out for the shore in two cutters mounting falconets.[88] All the officers had guns and pistols with them, and the seamen also carried muskets. We landed at that very place where Cook, during a stay here, had seen how the New Zealanders eat human flesh at a feast.[89] All the inhabitants but one, who was evidently bolder than the rest, scattered at the sight of us. When we showed him kindness and gave him a few gifts, however, the other natives started to gather round. We called on their chief, already an elderly man. He was seated on matting in an open hut. His wife and daughter also showed themselves a little later. The daughter was not unattractive and received the gift of a small hand-mirror from our captain.

From here we set off in the cutters further north, to our previous acquaintances. On approaching their village, we noted a small stream emptying into the sea.[90] To either side of this stream, there extended a palisade higher than a man, which adjoined the woods beyond. On the right side, there was an opening like a wicket, through which we entered the village.

The old chief whom we knew came out to greet us, receiving us in the friendliest fashion, touching noses with us, and leading us toward his house.[91]

We walked along the winding stream, whose banks had been edged with cobblestones. Scattered here and there on either side, without order, were the huts of the islanders, who now followed us in a crowd. We crossed over by a transom or footbridge to the chief's house. Its exterior resembled that of a Russian hut. It contained posts set in three rows. The central posts, which were about one and a half *sazhen* high,[92] ended at the top with crude representations of the human head, decorated red. The outer posts were considerably lower and were joined to the central row by beams, on which rested a roof made of more beams covered with leaves. The house was some three *sazhen* in length, two broad,[93] and had by way of a door an opening two *arshin* across,[94] covered up by a board. A window measuring two feet square had been made at the opposite end of the wall; this was covered by matting when necessary. The little house was divided into two chambers, one large, the other far smaller. In the large chamber, as in our rural huts, wide benches had been set along the walls. On these lay baskets, hollowed out pumpkins to hold water, a smoothly polished basalt slab that looked like a small spade,[95] bones from which to fashion fish-hooks, and other articles. Along the walls, which were covered with fine mats, hung pikes twenty-four feet in length, staffs, the insignia of chiefs, and little idols decorated with a red colouring substance.[96]

To the right of this house, we saw a solitary, thick tree with docked branches, at the top of which a human likeness was already half-carved.[97] The New Zealanders are very adept at carving—there is proof enough of that in the ornamentation on their canoes. And yet, apart from sharp stones and shells, they have no carving implements.[98] The old chief, remembering how well he had been entertained aboard the sloops, wished to repay us as well as he could, so decided to offer Captain Bellingshausen conjugality with a still fairly young, but physically repulsive, New Zealand female. Captain Bellingshausen declined this offer, patting the chief on the shoulder.

On our taking leave of him, the old man detained the captain, ordering his own people to bring out a staff some eight feet long, the top of which was carved into the likeness of a human head with eyes made of shells.[99] The captain at first supposed this staff was meant as a gift for him; but the old man was in fact wishing to sell it. He received two *arshin*[100] of red cloth for it, with which he was very well pleased, showing it to all the other Zealanders.

1 June. Early this morning I went ashore for water in the longboat. The

sun had not yet risen when we stepped ashore: dew lay on the grass and there was a morning mist, but the air, as warm as in a Russian May, was aromatic with flowers that grew in these woods and filled with a wondrous concert of New Zealand nightingales. Even though it was winter here, the trees shone with fresh green leaves. While our men were filling the casks with cold spring water, the spring rising from the hills like the purest crystal, others cast a seine net and caught plenty of fish. The natives did not show themselves to us here, but we were armed, out of a sense of proper caution. Returning to the sloop, we brought, besides the fresh water, enough fish to satisfy our whole company.

2 June. A cruel wind sprang up. We let out much rope and nearly dragged our anchor. Heavy rain was falling meanwhile, and again lightning flashed. Peals of thunder, reverberating from the mountain gorges, produced fearful echoes. Two days later, we were ready to weigh anchor. Once again the New Zealanders came to barter with us, exchanging their woven stuffs, spears, carved boxes, staffs, bludgeons made of green stone, axes, fastenings, and green basalt ornaments for our axes, chisels, gimlets, hand-mirrors, flints, and beads. When they realized that we were indeed departing, they bade us farewell, repeating the words *E! E! E!* One young islander wanted to remain aboard *Vostok* but his companions persuaded him to return to the shore.

The inhabitants of Queen Charlotte Sound are generally of middling height, well built, and strong. The customs of smearing the body with fish oil and ochre and exposing it to all the vicissitudes of the weather render their natural skin tone even darker. The women are plump and not tall. Married women soon lose their freshness but the young girls are sometimes quite pretty: their black eyes are not without expressiveness, and their small teeth gleam like pearls . . .

So significant are the advantages of a noble ancestry among the New Zealanders that it is impossible for those born of commoners to attain the rank of *rangatira;* and these pride themselves greatly on their lineage and chiefly station. On meeting us, they would at once inform us of their station and enquire about ours. The noble savages readily understood our system of naval ranks, promptly comparing those of captain, lieutenant, and midshipman with the corresponding ones in their island . . .

Tattooing is customary amongst them. On other islands this is a decoration, performed only on the outer epiderm; but with the New Zealanders, by contrast, it goes deep and is honoured as a special mark of distinction. Their diet consists of fish, shellfish, fern-roots, *batates,* and potatoes; they will also eat rats and dogs, the only animals found there, and sometimes a shark, which they catch and consider a great delicacy.

The New Zealanders are less clean in their persons than are other South Sea Islanders, and rarely wash or swim. They consider music and dancing pleasant pastimes. Their musical instruments are flutes, but they also have a shell horn, with which they shatter the air for some distance around and summon warriors to battle.[101]

DR. NIKOLAI GALKIN'S ACCOUNT

Nikolai Aleksandrovich Galkin was the second Russian-born and Russian-trained ship's surgeon to reach Oceania from Kronstadt. All the others had been foreigners or Baltic German doctors (Moritz Liband and Karl Mordhorst of *Neva,* Bogdan Brandt of *Diana,* Georg-Anton Schaeffer of *Suvorov,* Johann Eschscholtz of the *Riurik,* and Lorenz Kerner of *Kutuzov*). In his case, as in that of Anton Novitskii of *Kamchatka,* the appointment was an echo of his captain's patriotic, even nationalistic, feelings on the matter of a proper Russian company.

Galkin maintained, and duly surrendered to the Naval Ministry, a careful journal of his voyage in *Mirnyi.* But like Simonov, whose status in the venture was analogous to his, he felt at liberty to write a popular account of his experiences in the Great South Sea. The resulting article appeared in the periodical *Kazanskii vestnik* (*The Kazan' Herald*) in 1822. Galkin had family connections with Kazan', settling there in due course and by the later 1820s serving as director of the city's Main Secondary School or *gimnaziia.* Thus he was able to remain in contact with his former comrade Simonov.

Like Simonov's "Word," Galkin's piece was well received by a patriotic readership with an increasing appetite for travel literature of exotic types. Encouraged by a Little Russian landowner, one Ivanenko, he was soon preparing a set of "personal letters" based on his 1819–21 journal that developed the theme further. Ivanenko sent the "letters," with a covering letter, to the editor of the St. Petersburg journal *Syn otechestva* (*Son of the Fatherland*). All were printed (Volume 82, 1822, pt. 49: 97–115, 157–70), to the pleasure of a far larger audience, under the heading "Pis'ma g. Galkina o plavanii shliupov Vostoka i Mirnago v Tikhom okeane" ("Letters from Mr. Galkin Concerning the Voyage of the Sloops Vostok and Mirnyi in the Pacific Ocean"). The "New Zealand passage," pp. 101–15, is translated here with some omissions. The editor of *Syn otechestva* expected further "letters" from Galkin or Ivanenko, and inserted a note to that effect on p. 170. They were never to be published, however.

Dr. Galkin was a man of "vast knowledge" with "tireless zeal for his work," according to his captain, Mikhail Petrovich Lazarev; and there is no reason to criticize the Soviet historical geographer, Academician Lev S. Berg, for taking that praise at face value (see Berg's *Geschichte der Entdeckungen*, p. 107). Here, however, we see Galkin in a relaxed narrative mood, less anxious to impress than to inform and entertain:

Towards nightfall fires appeared at various places along the shores, reminding us of the brutal inhabitants of this land. Can it be possible, we thought, that the New Zealanders still abandon themselves with enthusiasm to a dreadful vice that is the shame of humanity?... Perhaps, we thought, they are even now roasting creatures like ourselves over those fires, to devour them later. And so we approached the country where Captain Marion and a number of French and English sailors had been eaten by the natives. Having entered Cook Strait finally, and beaten against the winds there, we at last, on 29 May, dropped anchor in Queen Charlotte Sound behind Long and Matuara [Motuara] Islands and opposite Ship Cove. We had completed the passage here from New Holland in twenty-one days. Given a favourable wind, one might do it in a week. But hardly had we anchored before several craft filled with New Zealanders were approaching our sloops... stopping at a distance from us of 5 *sazhen*.[102] A grey-haired, elderly man who had come out in one of them then stood and, in a very loud voice, began to shout an address at us. Now raising his voice, now lowering it, he pronounced certain words most distinctly. It seemed to us that in this lengthy speech he was questioning us, speaking also of himself, and testifying to his strength and valour. At length, ending the address, he awaited our reply. We made signs, inviting all the natives to board us. The old man came up, showing no hesitation, but the others stayed in their craft. It was only when we showed our willingness to rub noses, and when there had been several salutations in their own tongue with allusions to fish (which the old man willingly ordered to be given us) that the New Zealanders would all come on board, one after another, albeit still with timidity. We were obliged to press noses and express our pleasure by pantomime with each one of them.
    These people are of medium stature. In build, they are fairly slender down to the knees, which are thick and, as it were, swollen and so distort the leg's shape. It is perhaps a result of little exercise and much sitting cross-legged. Their face is dark olive in tone, their features are highly expressive, and a fire glows in their dark eyes. Almost all have regular designs pricked out on the face and some have them also on the chest, arms, and legs. These designs are embellished by means of a permanent, dark blue coloration, as a result of which many men have no beard. Their ears are pierced and in some cases the openings are very large, having been

constantly enlarged by the round bones which, together with polished green stones, they wear instead of earrings. Their long, thick black hair falls onto the face in disorder. Some cut it, though, and others, drawing it together, tie it up in a bunch on the crown of the head.

As to their dress, it is pretty simple: they wear a kind of half-caftan with openings for the arms, which they tie at the chest or else fasten with a basalt pin, and secure at the waist with a braid. This clothing is most skilfully woven from the well-known flax plant, then decorated a dark yellow or, around the borders, a black colour. The day of our arrival was a cold one, and for that reason many natives came out wearing, over the caftan, a cape likewise made of flax fibre. It very much resembled the so-called *burka,* which is worn by our mountain peoples.[103] These capes protect them very well against the rain and cold—even such cold as was experienced towards the South Pole by our port and starboard lookouts, who wore the capes as protection.[104] These natives make no use of footwear, though. Many in fact had ulcerated feet and ran about the deck in an attempt to warm them. Some New Zealanders have various sorts of polished basalt, fish bones, pearl shells, or other articles hanging about the chest. One man, wishing to appear in his full glory, decorated himself with feathers of assorted colours, all stuck through his hair, then used a fish oil in place of our pomade, mixing it with red chalk and rouging his cheeks with the resulting compound.[105]

The New Zealanders' craft are narrow. Each is made from several trees. Sometimes two such craft are bound together by stakes, in which case they cannot be capsized by rough seas even though they lack a protective strake (that is, a strip of wood some three inches wide attached by stakes along the length of the hull and parallel to it) such as the New Zealanders themselves and other native peoples use on single craft. Both stern and prow are embellished by crude carvings representing a human or canine head with tongue protruding, the eyes being made of shell. We saw no canoes with sails. In one craft more than ten men may find room, seated one behind the other.[106]

Having more than once seen Europeans before, these New Zealanders were amazed by nothing on our sloops but a few rarities, which they examined with curiosity. Iron objects, of which they knew the worth by experience, attracted them more than anything else. Knowing how miserly they are and how highly they value all property, we thought it necessary at the very outset of our bartering session to follow their example and to show no articles of real significance. In Captain Cook's time, the New Zealanders preferred bottles and shirts to many other items; but now they declined to give even a common fish-hook and line for the former. Nails, on the other hand, delighted them, and to get some each man was immediately offering us shells, fishing tackle, basalt axes, and other things. For a large spike-nail they gave of their best; but so well did they know the price of everything, they forced us to exercise extreme caution in our trading. When it appeared that they had nothing left to barter with, we showed them our knives. They jumped and shouted in their joy, holding out their hands in hopes of receiving them as gifts. Our unwillingness to simply give the knives away revealed their cunning: one after another, the natives now took out, from under their clothing, objects made of green stone and shell of a superior make. Finally they gave us all they had. The chief of these people, who had already visited us, had gone off to the *Vostok,* where the captain gave him an axe as a gift. His joy was extreme. By every conceivable gesture, he gave expression to the idea of the object's utility to him. Pressing noses with everyone, he seemed indifferent to all other articles.

Every day we were here, New Zealanders could come out to the sloops at about 10:00 AM, staying till evening. Having bartered their things for ours, they would eat with us, consuming our rusks, peas, gruel, and sugar with great appetite. But salt-beef did not appeal to them at all, nor were they fond of pork. Rum and wine they could not drink. Sometimes they helped our sailors in their work, and diligent individuals received nails in return. At other times, feeling gay, they would give us the pleasure of seeing and hearing their dances and songs. On these occasions, some fifteen men would stand in a single row and then one, stamping first with his foot, would begin to sing. In the middle of a verse, there would suddenly erupt a general, sharp, wild cry. Arms were now raised aloft, now extended, now lowered.[107] Stamping their feet and twisting the whole body with furious faces, the natives would end this particular song on one knee and with a hellish protracted laugh. Our sailors imitated them excellently and later, towards the South Pole, where daily peril cast the spirits down, they now and then cheered up the whole ship's company by means of such imitations.

On the third day of our visit, we decided to pay a call on our habitual guests and so went off to their villages along the shores facing Matuara Island. The New Zealanders indeed appeared very well disposed towards us, but we took armed seamen with us nevertheless, and all officers carried guns also. Against friends who had eaten English and French sailors and had leapt around us with delight when we showed them our arms and chest, such precautions did not seem excessive.

We had hardly reached the shore before three natives met us and offered us fish-hooks. They evidently did not fear us; but we did notice that several figures had fled into the bush. These were women. Our gentle conduct with the men eventually led the women also to trust us, and one by one they emerged from the woods. Stout and small of stature, they had long black hair that fell untidily over the face, and their lips were pricked and coloured blue. They were smeared with fish oil and yellow colouring substance from head to foot, and what with their soiled clothing, filled with insect life and undone at the breast, they forced the Russian traveller to avert his gaze. Our sailors spat, marvelling that the English could have been anything but totally indifferent to such women. Yet we did not want to make our scorn manifest; so, as a gesture of affection, we hung beads round their necks, put earrings in their ears and, as mementos, slipped a number of rings onto their fingers. After this, we gave each female a little mirror, with which they were well pleased. They again started to touch up their faces. A few had children with them, which they carried on their back, as do our Gypsies.[108] The settlement itself consisted merely of three small, low huts covered with branches and decidedly slovenly inside. But, of course, the New Zealanders only resided here on a temporary basis, when they wanted to catch fish or perhaps in some other circumstances. From this spot, we proceeded to another settlement where some fifty persons lived. There we were met by the old man whom I mentioned above. All were happy at our arrival, and bartering commenced again. The old man, who was hoping to get a second axe, offered us long and extremely sturdy pikes made of a red wood, demonstrating how one thrusts with them; also boxes in which to deposit small articles, all with rather fine carving, considering that it had been done with a stone; and basalt cudgels with which these natives follow each other in war, and basalt hatchets rather like our Polish hatchets;[109] and other things besides. Here all were wealthy and we were able to acquire by barter various rarities that they had not taken out to the sloops, possibly hoping for a still more advantageous trade. The women here were not afraid of us, accepting our gifts but giving nothing in return.

Judging by its layout, this village had been in existence a long time. On the seaward side it was protected by a palisade and behind there was a little stream. To the right, there was a small shed in which fishing nets, tackle, and ropes were kept. Opposite were the first little huts, plastered with clay. The chief's own house was larger than the rest and was made of thick stakes, driven into the ground and interlaced with branches. It was quite solidly finished with unworked flax fibres and well covered with leaves.[110] Inside, the posts supporting the roof were embellished with carving: a human figure, possibly these people's idol, was carved on the post placed in the centre. (We observed no religious rites among the New Zealanders, however.) A little way off from these huts was a fenced-off place where fish was dried. This was all we saw in the village, whose inhabitants comprised, as it were, a single family, each person acting in the friendliest manner towards all the others.

Although in general all New Zealanders have a fiery nature, it did seem to us that in the absence of grievous cause they do not just abandon themselves to a bestial desire to murder their fellows. Throughout our visit, at all events, we observed no vices among them beyond a certain cunning in trade; but then, it would hardly be surprising if the fifty years that had passed since Cook's last stay in the Sound had produced some change in their character. It is true that for an axe they were perfectly willing to sacrifice their wives' chastity (which in fact they value very little); but we could not know whether or not they considered this to *be* a vice. It is possible that their blind religion and coarse habits do not forbid them from making such vile propositions.[111]

Insofar as we could investigate the matter during our short stay there, we found that the shores surrounding Queen Charlotte Sound were covered by nine inches, and in some places up to thirteen inches, of black soil. Under the soil is a stratum of clay, and under this, a variety of yellowish and grey-green rock containing quartz veins. In the hills we discovered granite and slate with iron particles in it; on the shores, we found flint, lava, pumice, and basalt. These last minerals certainly lead one to think that there are volcanoes in New Zealand, but we ourselves saw none . . . [112] Without entering into a description of the plants and trees that are now known to the botanical systems through the work of the Forsters, I will merely mention the cress, grasses, and celery which grow abundantly on the New Zealand coasts and of which most advantageous use can be made by mariners as a remedy for scurvy. Several of the early voyagers left the New Zealanders garden vegetables, which may easily be cultivated there, the soil being excellent in many places; but unfortunately the natives ignored those vegetables and we saw, not far from the settlements, only one kitchen garden of no great size. There we found potatoes. They were not as tasty as our own, but they could indeed be useful to seafarers if the New Zealanders only had more of them.

Captain Cook and others left the natives pigs and sheep as stock, but those animals very likely all perished. We ourselves saw only rats and dogs, the latter resembling the breed called shepherd dogs by Buffon.[113] The natives are very fond of these and keep them with themselves. They gave us a pair in exchange for an axe, though; but the creatures proved unable to adapt to us even after two weeks aboard the sloop. They constantly trembled, hid, refused to eat, and finally died. As to birds, we shot a quantity of handsome gulls which, towards evening, would fly in flocks up to their nests in the ravines on Matuara. They were tasty and we ate

them with relish. Also to be seen in this area were ducks, pigeons, stormy
petrels, falcons, and parrots. The little forest birds had very beautiful
wings and delighted the hearing with their delicate song.[114]

The New Zealanders actually brought us very little fish and our own
fishing was unsuccessful even though we took great pains over it, captains and all other officers participating in it one evening with proper
diligence. Small whales showed themselves in the sound only once. We
saw no large insect whatsoever. The reason, I suppose, was the winter.
While in the sound, we had very good weather until 2 June. On *that* day,
the sky was lost in clouds, rain teemed down, and frightful gusts of wind
obliged us to drop a second anchor, for fear of striking against the rocky
shore of Long Island. Even two anchors scarcely held us... but the
winds subsided the following night and we again had fair weather. During
our five-day stop here, we had managed to effect certain repairs to the
sloops, check the movement of chronometers, and augment our natural
history collection while our indefatigable and talented Academician Mikhailov had increased his collection with portraits of New Zealanders and
many views.

LEADING SEAMAN EGOR' KISELEV'S ACCOUNT

Vostok arrived in New Zealand with a lower deck of 105 men, including
71 trained sailors. Such numbers of armed men sufficed, even without
Mirnyi's supporting force, to convince the Maori of the wisdom of orderly and tranquil barter sessions. Of those 71 sailors, some 20 were
Leading Seamen; and of these, few if any were illiterate. The journal of
Leading Seaman Egor' Kiselev, the only one from *Vostok*'s or *Mirnyi*'s
lower deck known at this point, was found in Suzdal' in the 1930s. It was
printed in the Soviet travel periodical *Vokrug Sveta* (*Around the World*) in
1941 (no. 4: 40–43). Unfortunately, its editor, Iakov Tarnopol'skii, had
the "improving" itch and the resulting text left much to be desired. The
manuscript, headed "Pamiatnik prinadlezhit matrozu 1 stati Egoru
Kiselevu, nakhodivshemusia v dal'nem voiazhe na shliupe 'Vostok' . . .
v 1819, 1820, i 1821 godakh" ("Journal belonging to First Class Seaman
Egor' Kiselev, Who was on a Distant Voyage in the sloop "Vostok" . . .
in the Years 1819–1821"), was reprinted, with far greater textual fidelity, by A.I. Andreev in 1949. Andreev's compilation, which
foreshadowed Sementovskii's in many ways and aroused interest in the
Bellingshausen visit to Antarctica among Soviet readers of a more recent
generation, was entitled *Plavanie shliupov "Vostok" i "Mirnyi" v Antarktiku v 1819, 1820 i 1821 godakh* (*The Voyage of the Sloops "Vostok"
and "Mirnyi" to Antarctica...*). The Kiselev journal, though stylistic-

ally crude, is the work of an intelligent, observant man and suggests the calibre of seamen who arrived in Australasia in the early 1800s with the Russian Fleet's Pacific "special branch."

19 May. High wind and bad pitching, then at eight o'clock in the evening we got such a roller that the ship was pretty near flung over, it went right through and almost flooded us, and that was when we lost the gangway-netting and five swine and a few seamen's sheepskin coats from the starboard side. Water up to the knees on the lower deck, up to sixty inches deep in the hold, the whole crew was scared and didn't know what to do, it was really dark.[115]

26 May. Arrived in the newly discovered Zealand. The savages ate ten of Cook's men here, forty-two years back—he was here a couple of months. High mountains and thick woods, crowds of natives live here and the natives are all covered with drawings: face, arms, legs. They're a crude lot. Wear clothes made out of grass and then decorate their heads with the feathers of different birds and smear themselves with red paint. They've got bone pins in their ears and stuck through the nose, too. They eat mostly fish. Lousy anchorage. We were here nine days. They came out to us three times. We presented one chief with a bronze medal.[116]

4 June. Set course away from Zealand.

6

THE RUSSIAN ETHNOGRAPHIC
RECORD FOR
QUEEN CHARLOTTE SOUND, 1820

GENERAL OBSERVATIONS ON MAORI-RUSSIAN TRADE IN 1820

On returning to St. Petersburg in August 1821, all members of the Bellingshausen-Lazarev Antarctic expedition were obliged to place all artefacts in their possession in the keeping of the Naval Ministry.[1] By 1822 or slightly later, most objects were with that ministry; some were apparently returned to the collectors, so effectively remained in private hands.[2] From the ministry's collection grew the present "1820 Maori" sub-collection (*Fond* 736) in the Peter-the-Great Museum of the N.N. Miklukho-Maklai Institute of Anthropology and Ethnography in Leningrad.[3] It consists of thirty-one separate items. A smaller "Queen Charlotte Sound" assemblage, of eleven items, all collected by Professor Simonov, remains at the Kazan' State University on permanent display. "The collection of today is not large—it originally consisted of 37 objects, in entirety; but it is precious from the scientific standpoint, being one of the earliest such ethnographical collections brought back from Oceania."[4]

For all its shortage of specifically non-naval scientific expertise, the Bellingshausen expedition was in several respects better prepared than Cook's had been to form collections of Pacific artefacts *in situ*. In the first place, Bellingshausen and his officers were highly interested in peoples of the Great South Sea, and deliberately read about them and their way of life, unlike Cook's comrades. In the second place, sufficient time had passed by 1820 for the Rousseauesque approach towards *La nouvelle Cythère* and Nature's children to have lost all favour in St. Petersburg, especially in sober naval circles. In his report Bellingshausen very rightly

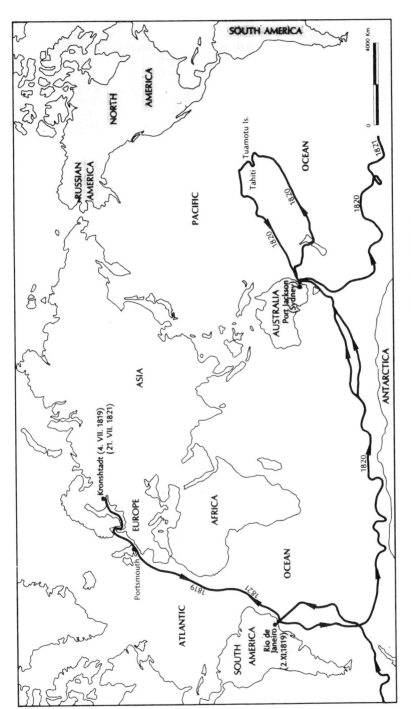

Map 6 Voyage of Bellingshausen and M.P. Lazarev with *Vostok* and *Mirnyi*

represented the official Russian attitude towards all South Sea Islanders
as a benevolent but thoroughly pragmatic one: "His Majesty the Emperor
had it in mind to increase our knowledge of the terrestrial globe, acquaint-
ing savage peoples with Europeans and vice versa."[5] His own approach to
the Polynesians he met in 1820 could not have been less sentimental or
more scientifically enquiring. But there too he was more fortunately
placed than Cook had been: coming late upon the South Seas scene, the
Russians had examples to consider, for example, where the gathering of
"curiosities" or "native products" was concerned.[6] Cook for his part had
taken "Toys, Beeds, and glass Buttons," among other things, in order to
exchange them for provisions and, if any were left over, "curiosities."[7]
In 1804, as I have noted, Kruzenshtern (with Bellingshausen as a youthful midshipman) had let his people barter "trinkets" for the products of
the Nukuhiva Islanders in Taio-hae Bay once the provisioning and watering of ships had been attended to; and both *Nadezhda* and *Neva* had
carried good supplies of trade goods.[8] Those supplies were meagre, however, in comparison with those provided to *Mirnyi* and *Vostok* on their
departure from the Baltic Sea. "In order," writes Bellingshausen, "to induce natives to treat us amicably, and to allow us to obtain from them
through barter fresh provisions and various handmade articles, we had
been supplied at St. Petersburg with such items as were calculated to
please peoples in an almost primitive state of culture."[9] Sixty-two
varieties of trade goods were brought to New Zealand by his sloops. They
included 400 miscellaneous knives, 300 steel flints, 185 bells and
whistles, 125 gimlets, rasps, and the like, 5,000 needles, 1,000 wax
candles, 1,000 mirrors, 120 glasses, 24 kaleidoscopes, and ample rolls of
red flannelette and striped ticking material.[10]

And from the outset Russian barter with the Maoris whom they encountered in Queen Charlotte Sound was orderly. It had been stipulated
that until the needs of both ships' companies were fully satisfied and
ample foodstuffs were on hand and stowed, all trade and commerce
should proceed through special officers. Since the Maori provided fish
and other foodstuffs speedily and willingly and the sweetness and convenience of drinking water at Ship Cove creek was apparent, wider
bartering commenced speedily. It carried on until the Russians left the
sound or, more precisely, moved from Motuara Island anchorage.[11] Both
officers and men traded for Maori artefacts, but did so always in a relatively slow and seemly way. None had the liberty accorded to the French
seamen with Dumont D'Urville six years afterwards, which was as well.
("The sailors, prowling about, discovered some abandoned huts from
which they carried off various objects used by the natives.")[12] It is evident
both from his printed narratives and from the Soviet Queen Charlotte

Sound collections that Simonov played an important role in the collecting process, in the course of which *Vostok*'s and *Mirnyi*'s holds and wardrooms were congested by such articles as cloaks and spears, clubs and basalt ornaments, "domestic artefacts," and handsome specimens of Maori wood carving (feather boxes, ornamented paddles, *tekoteko* figures from the finials of houses). Sadly, objects that are known to have been taken from the sound in 1820 are today not to be found at MAE in Leningrad or in Kazan', having presumably been kept or handed back to their collectors by imperial authority in 1822–24.

Lost somewhere between 1820 and the present were assorted specimens of Maori weaving, spears, one or two well-ground bone needles, and a musical instrument "quite like a flageolet only a good deal thicker," very probably a *putorino* pipe or flute. Conversely, other Maori artefacts that went to St. Petersburg are not mentioned at all in any narrative: mummified heads, for instance (always liable to vanish into secrecy and private drawing rooms as a ghoulish treasure, a source of pleasant horror). Simonov acquired two while in the sound, and Galkin at least one more. One of Simonov's went to Kazan', the other to St. Petersburg's Academy of Sciences; but Galkin's head remained in his possession.[13] Other Maori articles are now in one or other of the Soviet Queen Charlotte Sound collections with precise documentation, yet are not clearly referred to in any text. Among these artefacts are handsome *tekoteko* figures, Simonov's shell necklace, and paddles carved in Taranaki, Gisborne, and Wanganui styles.[14] Something else arrests the eye in connection with the list of Maori artefacts obtained by Bellingshausen's people: a use of plural forms in the Russian narratives, with which the state of the collections do not agree. Greenstone bludgeons, staffs, and spears, for example, are referred to in the plural; but in Leningrad there is a single nephrite *mere* (club), and one lone object (No. 736-113) that might possibly be seen as corresponding to the Russian term *kop'e* (spear). As for staffs, there is, again, but a sole *taiaha* (No. 736-115). Perhaps the Russians viewed the ornamental paddles that they saw as chiefly staffs. There can be little doubt that certain types of Maori artefact reached St. Petersburg in duplicate or triplicate. But it is equally apparent that today we study only part of the original, even richer store that was taken from the sound in 1820.

Such material, in Leningrad especially, is of intrinsic ethnographic value but becomes more valuable when viewed collectively with the material that Captain Cook collected from the very same places (Ship Cove, Cannibal Cove, and "Hippah Island") during the course of three long visits. Thus, the Cook and Bellingshausen-Simonov collections form a precious entity that make possible for us to study the development of culture in the sound over a crucial span of fifty years (1770–1820).[15] It is necessary at this juncture to provide a brief description of the Soviet collections, as a basis for discussing the kinds of evidence they provide. That evidence is fundamentally of trade and inter-island contact and collision after Cook's final departure from Queen Charlotte Sound. The following descriptions are by David R. Simmons of Auckland, made on the basis of materials I provided and/or personal examination in Leningrad.

THE LENINGRAD QUEEN CHARLOTTE SOUND COLLECTION

Clothing

No. 736-125—*Korowai* cape, with natural colour tags, made with double-pair twine 8 mm apart; shaping is provided by five inserts at the shoulders, six at the base. Fringe on three sides. Width 133 cm, depth 100 cm.

No. 736-126—*Korowai* cape very similar to the above, but with double-pair twine 1 cm apart. Width 140 cm, depth 100 cm.

No. 736-128—Part of an *aronui* cloak, unfinished, with black and natural braid, 1.7 cm wide, along the bottom edge. Also along that edge are two weft lines in a strip of *taniko* in alternate black and natural barred-triangle pattern. The warp includes spaced stripes of black and brown, alternately, five times. Length 159 cm, depth 23 cm only.

No. 736-129—Close single-pair twine *kaitaka* cloak, with double *taniko* borders on three sides. The upper hem is finished with an extra black and natural cord. The *taniko* was woven in while the garment was being made, its upper ends being 5 cm above the upper edge of the lower *taniko*. This cloak may once have been decorated with feather quillets, as some weft threads have been stretched. Length 116 cm, depth 106 cm.

No. 736-130—*Kaitaka* feather cloak. A single-pair twine, close canvas weave cloak, with double *taniko* on three sides. The neck edge is painted in brown and natural colour. All the *taniko* has been woven on the same warp threads as the body of the cloak. The cloak is decorated with quillets of *pukeko*, pigeon, and possibly *notornis* feathers, which have been laid on the weaving at 6 to 8 cm apart and spaced in alternate rows, then woven across. In this cloak the natural colour is not golden but a pale cream-white, the fibre being very soft although the weave is like canvas. Length 110 cm, depth 170 cm.

No. 736-131—*Kaitaka* cloak with *taniko* on base. The weft is double-pair twine 1 cm apart with shaping at the shoulder of five inserts and at the bottom of four inserts. The neck band is braided brown and natural. The sides have been finished with a narrow 1-cm band of black, which has been cut off. Length 160 cm, depth 112 cm.

No. 736-132—*Pihepihe* cloak made with double-pair twine 1 cm apart. The top is rolled, the sides tied off, and there is a fringe on three sides. The body of the cloak is decorated with fine rolled strips of flax leaf with scraped and black-dyed sections and some plain fibre tags. Width 153 cm, depth 120 cm.

No. 736-133—*Pihepihe* cloak. Weft double-pair twine 1.2 to 1.5 cm apart. There is shaping at the shoulders of five inserts and at the buttocks of six inserts. There are fine tag fringes on three sides. The body of the cloak is covered with fine rolled flax strips with scraped areas dyed black. Width 154 cm, depth 115 cm.

No. 736-134—Rough cloak made with double-pair twine 1 cm apart. Shaping at the shoulder of six inserts and at the buttocks of nine inserts. The neck band is rolled with a fine tag fringe. The body of the cloak is covered with thick black and natural rolled tags. Length 140 cm, width 116 cm.

No. 736-135—Heavy double cloak woven as one piece with a fringe on the lower edge, made of brown vegetable fibre. Length, top 157 cm, bottom 284 cm; depth 106 cm.

No. 736-136—Rain cloak made with *cordyline* fibre with some *Freycinettia banksii* strands. Single-pair twine weft 3.5 to 4.5 cm apart. One line of shaping at the bottom. The neck band is rolled and the sides plaited off. (*Kahu toi*): Width 135 cm, depth 100 cm.

Weapons

No. 736-115—*Taiaha,* a two-handed club with face and protruding tongue at one end, decorated with two pairs of whorls. Mouth and eyebrow ridges decorated with *pakati* and small spirals. Carving style of Gisborne and made with iron tools. Length 210.5 cm, blade width 8.9 cm, head length 20 cm.

No. 736-116—*Tewhatewha* or two-handed club of axe shape with janus head in south Taranaki style, made with iron tools. There are split hawk feathers attached through the hole in the blade. Length 170 cm, width of head 21.5 cm.

No. 736-117—*Tewhatewha* or two-handed club of axe shape, with a very rounded "blade" weight and barbs on the point. The barbs are grouped up to 19 cm from the point with three on the left, three on the right, two on the left. Length 130.5 cm, blade width 11.2 cm.

No. 736-262—*Mere* of Lake Wakatipu–type greenstone. A flat *mere* with the butt expanded slightly into a dome shape. No defined shoulders. There is a perforation with rolled flax cord looped through with two knots. A South Island style *mere*. Length 37 cm, blade width 8 cm.

Ornaments

No. 736-268—Ear pendant, •*kuru* type. A greenstone ear pendant of "bodkin" shape which could be mistaken for a cloak pin but is much too thick. It has a transverse hole and is slightly curved and pointed. Length 13 cm, diameter 1 cm.

No. 736-269—Adze pendant with curved cutting edge and hole. Length 6.6 cm, width 3.2 cm.

No. 736-265—Adze pendant with asymmetrical outline, bevel and hole. Length 7.1 cm, width 3.8 cm.

Figures

No. 736-118—*Tekoteko,* gable ornament figure, with a ridge for attachment with three holes at the back. A female figure which has a male spiral facial tattoo with a single cheek spiral on each side. In 1844 Shortland, on his journey through Otago, recorded "I afterward met with several other old women of this tribe (Kai Tahu) who had... engraved on their faces many of the marks, which in the North Island I have never seen but on males." In the North Island occasionally male tattoos were put on females, in whole, or in part, to mark a maiden set aside from sex relations of any kind because of unequalled status. Such a female would not appear, as this figurine does, as a *tekoteko,* that is, an ancestress. This would indicate a South Island, specifically Kai Tahu, tribal origin. Length 70 cm, width 12 cm.

No. 736-119—*Tekoteko,* gable apex figure of attenuated body form with an attachment hole through the back and an area cut out of the buttocks. The figure has a long body with thin arms, the left hand on the stomach, the right ending at the wrist on the hip. No sex is shown. It has a partial tattoo with forehead and mouth rays. Length 49.5 cm, width 14 cm.

No. 736-120—A carving of four figures in Gisborne style, made with stone tools. The figures are carved in the round and form a figure 7 with a figure with median crest on the top with feet to the head of the topmost of three figures. The upper figure of the three is a male copulating with a reversed female. There is an attachment point broken off behind the head of the lowest figure. No other attachments are obvious. The purpose of this carving was funerary. Overall length 84 cm, width 10 cm.

Feather boxes

No. 736-121—*Wakahuia,* oval feather box with heads as handles but no bodies. Carved in Gisborne style with metal tools. Length 49 cm, width 11 cm, depth 10 cm.

No. 736-122—*Wakahuia,* oval feather box with heads as handles joined to bodies on the end of the box. The box was carved with metal tools but not completed. The carving style is that of Gisborne or the East Coast of the North Island. Length 53 cm, width 22 cm.

No. 736-123—*Wakahuia,* oval feather box with heads as handles, either end joined onto female bodies on the end of the box. The box was made with stone or soft iron tools and is in the carving style of Gisborne. Length 64 cm, width 26.2 cm, depth 11 cm.

No. 736-124–*Papahou,* flat feather box. This is a rectangular box, with heads as handles at either end, joined onto low-relief bodies on the base. The heads and base were carved with stone tools. The carving style is that of the Wanganui area, also found in the northern South Island. The lid of the box was carved with metal tools. It has two figures on each end with heads on the top of the handles. The figures on the lid have domed foreheads and are carved in the same style as the decoration, that of the Hokianga area of Northland.

The box was originally carved with stone tools. The handles and base carvings were completed at that time. At a later date a carver working in the Hokianga style completed the box with a metal tool, possibly a nail or something used to make a hard edge. The most likely explanation for the disparity in styles is that the box was taken as a souvenir by a northern raider who completed the carving. It later found its way by gift exchange to Queen Charlotte Sound. Length 60 cm, width 18 cm, depth 12.5 cm.

Paddles

No. 736-113—*Hoe.* A flat war canoe paddle with gymnast figure on the handle in Taranaki style. The style of this carving is clearly from the central to southern area of Taranaki, as is the form of the paddle itself. Length 232.5 cm, blade length 108 cm, blade width 12.5 cm.

No. 736-114—A canoe paddle with flat blade painted on one side with *mangopare* (hammerhead shark patterns). The butt of the handle was a round knob but is now broken. At the loom of the blade, a head is carved in Gisborne style with iron tools. Length 178.5 cm, blade width 12.8 cm, blade length 87 cm.

No. 736-168—A paddle with broad dished blade, markedly concave-convex front and back. The blade ends in a blunt hook similar to, though not as large as, those on Mangarevan paddles. On the front of the blade, stretching from the loom of the handle to halfway down, carved figures have been roughly cut with stone tools. The figures are undecorated but the general style can be characterized as Wanganui-Horowhenua, that is, a Cook Strait style. Length 200 cm, blade width 16 cm, blade length 110 cm, length of carving 40 cm.

No. 736-173—A paddle with broad dished blade, markedly concave-convex and ending in a blunt hook. There is a median ridge on the back. On the lower section of the back, stone tool marks show that the final dressing of the blade was from the ridge to the edge. The handle ends in an expanded flat knob. Length 197.5 cm, blade width 15.3 cm, blade length 110 cm.

Adzes

No. 736-263—Asymmetrical nephrite adze. Length 14 cm, width 6.4 cm.

No. 736-264—Nephrite adze. Length 20.3 cm, width 4.7 cm.

No. 736-267—Nephrite chisel of flat cross section. Length 8.4 cm, width 2.4 cm, depth 0.7 cm.

THE COLLECTION AT KAZAN' STATE UNIVERSITY

Clothing

No. 7—*Korowai* cloak of flax of light brown colour; double-pair twine 1.5 to 2 cm apart. Decorated with self-colour tags, 10 to 14 cm apart. Dimensions 136 cm by 80 cm.

No. 8—Specimen of hand weaving, shaped and ornamented with seven dark parallel bands in the warp, 17 to 20 cm apart. Dimensions 136 cm by 114 cm.

No. 9—Unfinished piece of weaving. The commencement of a cloak with striped warp lines grouped in threes and with some single lines 20 to 25 cm apart, dyed a dark brown. Eight lines of double-pair twine weft. Size 136 cm by 6 cm.

No. 10—Unfinished piece of weaving. Five rows of double-pair twine warp with five and six strips of alternate light and dark brown, 26 cm apart. The two ends of this piece are dyed dark brown. One end is thin, the other 3 cm thick. Fringe measuring up to 60 cm. This is a South Island striped cloak in the making, acquired by Simonov as a specimen of the technique. Dimensions 141 cm by 7 cm.

Ornaments

No. 3—Nephrite ornament in the form of a triangle. The edges are rounded, the sides notched. A pendant of Otago type. Length 9.5 cm, width 8.2 cm.

No. 6—Necklace of thirteen univalve shells threaded on vegetable fibre.

Fish-hooks

No. 4—Composite circular fish-hook made of a bent piece of wood 24 cm long. Barbed bone point with serrated outer edge attached by twine.

Twine around snood. Length 15 cm, width 9 cm.

No. 5—Jabbing fish-hook made of a slightly bent piece of wood 10 cm long. Barbed bird-bone point lashed on with twine. One outside barb. The base of the hook has a curved tail which projects past the lashing. Snood wrapping and line still attached. Length 10 cm, width 5.2 cm.

Adzes

No. 1—Rectangular sectioned adze of nephrite sharpened on two sides with cutting scar at side. Length 22 cm, width 5.5 to 2.5 cm.

No. 2—Nephrite adze of almost rectangular cross-section. Length 17 cm, width 5.5 to 2.5 cm.

HANDWOVEN ARTEFACTS COLLECTED BY THE RUSSIANS: OBSERVATIONS

The Soviet collections contain numerous objects that were certainly obtained by gift exchange, trade, or war from areas outside Queen Charlotte Sound. These include the *taiaha,* the carved-figure group (so unhelpfully described at MAE as a "carved phallic group" and specifically identified by Maori informants in 1986),[16] a paddle, and two *wakahuia* (feather boxes), all carved in the Gisborne style from the North Island's East Coast. As a group, these items indicate a fairly close relationship with the East Coast, perhaps by way of Cape Terawhiti and Palliser Bay. By contrast, the *papahou* feather box (No. 736-124), with its odd mixture of carving styles, was quite possibly finished in Wanganui by a Ngapuhi man who had gone south on a musket raid. The handsome box could then have reached the sound by gift exchange.[17] Other items now in Leningrad show a continuation of the Taranaki influence apparent in the woven artefacts from the third Cook voyage, either directly or by way of other regions of the far northern South Island. (The direction of that influence is intimated by an *aronui* cloak with striking *taniko* inserted in the weft, which was collected in 1826 by the French in Tasman Bay.)[18] By contrast with the carved objects in Leningrad, numerous woven articles collected in the sound suggest a South Island technique. Cloaks with chestnut brown and black bands in the warp have never figured in the Northern repertoire.[19] Again, cloaks held at the Hunterian Museum in Glasgow and in Berlin, suggest that single-pair twine weft was a traditional and even normal element of weaving in the sound in the early contact period.[20] It was an aspect of tradition that persisted until 1824, at least in terms of pure technique, despite the changes introduced into the *taniko* under the ever-growing influence of Taranaki style in the later eighteenth century.

The presence of two *korowai* commencements (Nos. 9 and 10) in the Kazan' Collection from the sound is indicative of Simonov's alertness as an ethnologist. Of Bellingshausen's people, he alone appears to have shown an interest in manufacturing technique and therefore realized that an unfinished specimen of weaving often gives more information than a finished one. Taken together, the Kazan' handwoven articles point unmistakably toward a South Island tradition and technique. Like those in Leningrad, they are suggestive of stability of culture in the sound, despite the Taranaki influence and rising tides of musket raiders in the early 1800s. That stability, indeed, is best exemplified by the technology of weaving, which remained the work of female artists.

Cloaks collected on Cook's second voyage had been made with either double-pair spaced twine, single-pair close twine, or with single separated twine, as in rough and heavy garments. Warps included spaced brown lines in double-pair twine cloaks and, where the weaving had been vertically placed, a black-brown braid comprised a solid bottom hem. Braid was also used to start and finish *taniko,* which, mostly simple in design, showed a predominance of black-brown triangles. Dogskin was used as decoration once the garments were complete. As for the cloak from Cook's third voyage with Taranaki-style *taniko* now held in Bern, suffice it to note that it, too, boasts the dogskin strips at bottom corners and braid along the sides that apparently were a feature of the sound. Thus, the cloaks in the Soviet collection not only admirably demonstrate the rising Taranaki influence on *taniko* and style but continue a technology of cloak making that had been evident some forty years before.[21] There are, assuredly, some signs of local change and innovation in these cloaks: for instance, double-pair spaced twine items are well shaped (in the weft), and new ideas are apparent in the double *taniko* beautifully worked between the weft lines at the base. What is significant, however, is a basic technological conservatism, innovation showing mainly in questions of design, fashion, or tone.[22]

The Maori with whom the Russians bartered so effectively for food supplies and artefacts were living in a natural "high volume" trading area. Totaranui was in 1820, as for centuries before, an open gateway to the South, through which passed foodstuffs and obsidian, greenstone and argillite, oils, and ornamental goods. Given the links between Otago and the sound, so convincingly reflected by the presence of the Kai Tahu cloaks in D'Urville's 1826 collection from Admiralty Bay and the pair of

Cook medallions discovered near Dunedin,[23] it would hardly be surprising if a Russian item brought in 1820 were unearthed within Otago, or has come to light already but not been recognized. The Russians' hosts had, after all, some seven years of comparative tranquillity remaining till the onslaught of Puoho's warriors; and must not trade have continued along traditional, albeit changing, patterns? What is plain from Russian evidence is that the Maoris then settled in the sound had not as yet had steady contact with the *pakeha*. As a result, they wore traditional flax garments. There was, first, a "camisole" or piece of cloth wrapped round the body and extending to the lower thigh or knee, held in place by a narrow "girdle." Over this, some wore a kilt that also reached the knee or thigh. This kilt, which doubled as a cape when it was differently worn, was likewise belted. Other individuals preferred a piece of stuff which, from the shoulders, fell directly to the knee or slightly lower and was fastened by a bone or basalt pin. The majority used the indispensable rough rain cape in winter—in the Leningrad collection Nos. 736-132 to 736-134. These were occasionally fastened at the side. Most, though, were fastened at the collarbone so that the stomach was exposed, if not the breasts. Some younger men left cloaks unfastened and, perhaps as evidence of hardiness, eschewed even the camisole. The chiefs and elders wore more clothing than did commoners, also affecting more varieties of ornament.

Although traditionally dressed, however, Maoris whom the Russians met in the vicinity of Motuara Island did know something of the Europeans' clothing practices. They had articles of Maori make but with bizarre features, such as "jersey-like garments" and "half-coats with sleeves of flax sewn on." The Russian terms used to describe these hybrid garments are interesting: *polushubok* having overtones of sheepskin coat, *fufaika* suggesting seamen's sweaters. Both point to the likelihood that sealers and/or whalers in the area had had an influence. Such hybrid items, furthermore, were highly valued, local owners trading them not for a mirror or a nail, but for Russian stuff and clothing (canvas jacket and kerchief). One sees the imitative urge; and yet, significantly, there was no immediate demand for clothes or cloth when *Vostok* and *Mirnyi* arrived. On 28 May, a chief was presented with a length or two of printed Russian cloth and was extremely pleased; but he was equally delighted with his mirror, beads, and knife. Nor did the Russians barter clothing on the 29th during a lengthy trading session. So, at least, the texts suggest. This situation was completely different from that of 1826–27, when the French were simply asked for woollen blankets on arrival in a bay, by men already wearing European blankets.[24] Bellingshausen and his people created a demand for Western garments among Maori but lightly touched by passing sealers. And the market grew abruptly. Within four days of their arrival, Russian officers and seamen had been asked for or had actually traded greatcoats, jackets, handkerchiefs, and shirts. In doing so, they devalued the rolls and bales of cloth they had brought—cloth that was still sufficiently esteemed on 31 May to gain an elegantly carved paddle (No. 736-113 in Leningrad) with a Taranaki-style gymnast figure on the haft. The Maoris, meanwhile, contributed toward a drain of artefacts from their homeland. This fact figures today in the New Zealand government's campaign to have such artefacts returned from European institutions. By being who they were, dressing as they did, and bartering their clothing for local artefacts, the Russians left the Maori of the sound far more disposed than they had previously been to take on European clothing. The effects were felt in 1826, when *Astrolabe* anchored in Tasman Bay.

Was it because the woven artefacts had been produced by craftswomen and artists that the element of technological conservatism was so strong? Probably not; most other artefacts collected by the Russians were conservative in make and manner. It is reasonable to suppose that this reflected local cultural tradition, on the one hand, and the nature of the trading in the sound, on the other. Almost a third of all the articles that Bellingshausen's people brought to Russia were woven objects (Nos. 7 to 10 in Kazan', Nos. 736-125 to 736-136 in Leningrad). It is a commonplace of both economic theory and anthropology that those objects most available for barter are, in all ages and countries, old, redundant, obsolescent, out of style. Surplus could, of course, mean simply that in any rich, secure group; but it could also indicate that cloaks or specific types of cloak, for instance, had shrunk in value for two reasons: they could be replaced with ease by trade or war, or be replaced with "better," European clothing. It would certainly be foolish to dismiss the expanding influence of naval visits and commercial enterprises on Maori trade procedures. Cloaks could easily be made to be traded to other Maori tribes or to the *pakeha* directly, in exchange for nails and hatchets. As the Russians found, the people of Queen Charlotte Sound openly viewed them as a source of *whau, toki,* and related iron goods—and had a fair supply of cloaks to pay for them.

Space is lacking for a detailed commentary on the cloaks taken to Russia from Queen Charlotte Sound in 1821, but brief remarks on certain items are in order. No. 736-125 in the Leningrad collection is Elsdon Best's "tag cloak," a *korowai* of a sort which—thanks to Cook's artist, Sydney Parkinson—we know to have been in use in the so-called "Classical" Maori period (1650–1800).[25] As the eminent Maori ethnologist Sidney M. Mead has observed, it seems not to have been in fashion in the eighteenth century, but gained in popularity in the early nineteenth, thanks in part to the growing availability of wool.[26] The Russians' acquiring such a cape lends weight to the supposition that such garments, with their three-side fringes, were worn in the later Classical period. In dimensions and in weave, the cape is very much like one in the Buck Collection.[27] A lesser density of falling thrums and missing upper fringe, though, suggest "transitional period" *korowai* development and recall Mead's type T6.[28] In No. 736-126, by contrast, warp-thread fringes are obvious, but again the "upper fringe" is missing. Inserts at the shoulders and base provide shaping; but despite the presence of simple wefts, the cape suggests an underlying continuity of regional technique and is of South Island, not Northern, antecedents.

A well-preserved single-pair twine *kaitaka* cloak with wide *taniko* borders, No. 736-129, introduces a major new element into comparison with items from the first two Cook voyages: powerful Taranaki influence. That influence was clearly on the rise in Totaranui in the late 1700s, notwithstanding any predilection for single-pair twine ("canvas weave") on the part of female artists in the sound. It was probably a similar *kaitaka* cloak that caught the eye of George Forster in Queen Charlotte Sound in April 1773.[29] The Russians make no mention, though, of red tones in the borders they admired; and this is noteworthy since the younger Forster's comments on colour use echo Parkinson's of four years earlier.[30] Nor do the Maori encountered by the Russians seem to have used the yellow dye familiar to many tribes and made from *Coprosma* bark. Another *kaitaka* cloak at MAE, No. 736-130, likewise recalls items from Cook's second voyage and appears to have been a popular cloak type in the sound. It is known that such cloaks were often worn by women of rank. One recalls the role played by a "chief's wife" in Little Waikawa Bay in the presentation of a fine piece of material to Bellingshausen.[31] As for 736-131, yet another *kaitaka* cloak, it is a less impressive piece.

The Russians arrived in Queen Charlotte Sound in Southern winter and found their hosts dressed for cold and rainy weather. Accordingly, they acquired a number of rough heavy cloaks and *pihepihe*. Mikhailov drew the "chief's wife" mentioned above in such a cloak. Nos. 736-132 and 736-133, both double-pair twine garments with wefts at least 1 cm apart, are embellished with fine rolled strips of flax leaf, which produce a shaggy effect.[32] Bellingshausen describes the flax strips as "laces," and with reason. Also in Leningrad, finally, is one very capacious rain cloak of *cordyline* fibre with some added *Freycenettia banksii* strands for good measure. Scraped at one end only, the "coarse grass" (as the Russians term it) is attached in successive, kiltlike layers. The presence of this item and of No. 736-135, a very heavy double cloak that had been woven as one piece with particularly close two-strand wefts,[33] underlines the need that Maoris residing in the sound had for effective winter covering. The Russians had a taste of winter storms and driving rains on 5 June and once again on 8 June. On both days, snow and hailstones were mixed in with the rain.

THE RUSSIAN EVIDENCE FOR PERSONAL ORNAMENTATION

The Maori of Totaranui used dress for its aesthetic or decorative aspect. And the Russians fully recognized that certain aspects of the local dress had functions other than the covering of flesh or the denoting of authority, rank, age, or sex. Patterns in woven objects, borders, and the very make of certain garments seemed to Bellingshausen and his people to have a decorative purpose—though they might well have another, more utilitarian advantage. This is clear from the wording and the tenor of the descriptions. For example, it is obvious that Bellingshausen understood the decorative function of the five-inch bone or polished basalt pins, "hung by fine cords lest they be lost," by which some handsome cloaks were fastened at the breast.

Both Bellingshausen and his hosts, however, thought of feathers, *tiki*, clasps, and earrings first and clothing only second where the range of personal embellishment and decoration was concerned. Nor could tattooing be ignored in its aesthetic aspect. Russian evidence of personal ornamentation is of value inasmuch as it bears directly on questions of stability or continuity in local culture and group identity. Collation and comparison of ornaments from Cook's time and from 1820 provide an insight into local cultural history, illuminating the relationship between the people of the sound and other groups to north and south. This insight is sharpened but not much altered by comparing weaponry and carvings from the two periods. To begin, then, with specifics: these varieties of ornament were noted by the Russians Galkin (G), Novosil'skii (N), Simonov (S), or Bellingshausen and Kiselev (B, K):

For the Head
"The hair tied into a bunch at the crown" (B, N)
"A few white feathers stuck through" the topknot (B)
"Decorated with the feathers of various birds" (K)
"Embellished with feathers of various hues" (G)
"Hair powdered red or smeared with red colouring" (S)

"One man ... used fish-oil in place of our pomade" (G)
"Four feathers, light with dark tips, worn in the topknot" (M)
"Numerous leaves attached, almost flat, to a chief's wife's hair" (M)

For the Cheeks
"One man ... used fish oil, mixing it with red chalk and roughing his cheeks with that compound" (G)

For the Ears
"Large openings are made and through them are passed bunches of bird's down" (S)
"Round bones" (G)
"They pass through them pieces of bird's skin with white down on" (B)
"Bone pins" (K)
"Polished green stones" (G)

For the Nose
"Small sticks" (S)
"Bone pins" (K)

For the Neck
"Various clasps and ornaments of green basalt" (B)
"Ugly human images" (B)
"A kind of little knife made of green stone" (B)
"Little bones" (B)
"Fish bones" (G)
"Various sorts of polished basalt" (G)
"Pearl shells and other things" (G)

With regard to body tattooing (*moko*), some men in Queen Charlotte Sound had "regular designs pricked out on the face" (Galkin), these "curved but regular lines" (Bellingshausen) being dark blue. Tattooing was not universal, and seemed "proper to leaders and to older men, rather than to all" (Bellingshausen). Women as a rule had tattooing only on the lips (Galkin). Facial *moko* was evidently produced over an extended period of time, one man of rank having bare skin only in the "ten to twelve o'clock sector" of his face. Some men who were not tattooed had smeared parts of their torso and limbs with "fish oil and ochre," which produced a reddish hue.

Like Cook's people, the Russians were especially attracted by the Maori nephrite ornament, less so by bone or feather items. We must therefore be cautious and not presume that the Maoris' "European" preference led to proportionately fewer bone or feather ornaments and more numerous nephrite articles. In fact, Totaranui must have been depleted of its socially and politically less valuable greenstone objects in the wake of the visits of Cook and Bellingshausen. Yet the Maori of the sound had greenstone objects to barter in 1820, even if they lacked other resources of marketable worth. This greenstone was doubtless from the same South Island source as in earlier times,[34] and had been acquired with trade as well as prestige in view. Five of the six ornaments from the sound that are in Soviet collections now (Nos. 3 and 11 in Kazan', Nos. 736-265, 736-266, and 736-268) are of greenstone. One is a classic Maori *kurukuru* that, like the similar but slightly smaller and more sharply angled pendant, No. 736-266, had originally been a cutting implement; evidently, it too was refashioned into an ornament after the Maori owner's acquisition of a metal tool. By far the most interesting item is No. 736-268 in Leningrad, which the Soviet ethnographers Nikolai A. Butinov and L.G. Rozina erroneously describe, in a 1963 paper, as *kapeu*.[35] In shape and function, the 13-centimetre bright nephrite stick recalls a pendant held at the Peabody Museum in Salem, Massachusetts.[36] And there is ample evidence that in the later eighteenth century some Maoris wore long nephrite pendants from the ears: Sydney Parkinson illustrates a few, giving them about the size attributed to them by the French observer Monneron.[37] The length of No. 736-268, however, suggests that it may have been a cloak-pin or fastener of the sort seen by Bellingshausen and described as five inches in length, with circular cross-section and knifelike appearance.

Comparison of the ornaments seen by the Russians with the recognized list of "Classical Maori Ornamentation" offered by Sidney Mead in 1969, reveals that the Russians' hosts were in nearly all respects ornamented in the manner of half a century earlier. This reminds us that Maori fashion changed but slowly between Tasman's day and Marsden's and apparent innovative tendencies are not always truly that. The 1820 *hapu*, for instance, were using at least two ornaments which, though superficially missing from Mead's list, may be found embedded in it under other names or descriptions. The curving, slender, polished pendant, No. 736-268 has been discussed; the "shell necklace," No. 6 in Kazan', had in all probability been worn round the ankle. One must be especially cautious in claiming that a given ornament or style seen in 1820 indicated local predilections.[38] Still, the ornamentation observed by the Russians did deviate from contemporary styles in, for example, Taranaki or Wanganui. In short, it shows elements of Queen Charlotte Sound style. Furthermore, the 1820 ornaments are distinctly dissimilar as a group from those in the Cook voyage collections. Missing from the Soviet collections, for example, are women's black feather caps, wooden combs with *manaia* carving on the side, dentalium shell necklaces, twisted greenstone pendants for the ear or neck, shark-tooth knives, *hei tiki,* and bunches of discoloured human teeth, all more or less convincingly associated with Cook's first and second voyages. It is by no means certain that the Russians managed to obtain a single *hei tiki.* What is present in the Soviet collections, on the other hand, gains significance when one considers ornaments from Cook's second voyage in the context of their regional provenance; bone toggles from Otago, Terawhiti Cape cloak-pins, Taranaki-style chisel pendants for the ear that are strikingly like Nos. 736-265 and 736-269 in Leningrad. In short, the 1820 collections point to certain links between the Maoris encountered in the sound and both Taranaki and Otago groups. These links were very likely of long standing. No. 736-265, a pendant with deliberately asymmetrical outline, has its counterpart in an irregular ear ornament from the Cook second voyage that though not as indisputably of Kai Tahu origin as No. 3 in Kazan' (Simonov's triangular notched ornament), is almost certainly of South Island antecedents. Taking the second voyage and the 1820 collections of ornaments in their entirety, however, one perceives the latter's greater "Taranaki element." Totaranui contacts with Otago may have dated back for generations, but in 1820 Taranaki influence was stronger in the sound where ornaments and carving were concerned. The 1820 *tewhatewha,* ceremonial carved paddle (No. 736-1130) and above all the double-pair twine cloaks with double *taniko* support the point.

The Russian evidence suggests that wooden combs, tooth necklaces, and *rei puta* pendants were not seen in 1820 or, if seen, were very few indeed. The Russians saw their hosts dressed at their finest, for example, when they landed and were formally received at Little Waikawa Bay. Nor, given the speed with which a portion of a broken Russian candlestick became an earring, is it probable that, if they had them, local people would have hesitated to wear anything that they recognized and prized as an ornament.

A Maori chief is depicted by Mikhailov wearing four feathers on the crown of his head, the fashion having changed since Tasman's day, when one sufficed. Other regional characteristics of personal decoration seem clear: use of fish oil and "red chalk" compound on the face and torso, and the absence of the wooden comb. Nose sticks were seen in 1820. They were not, according to Simonov, inserted through the nasal cartilage in childhood, when the process of facial tattooing sometimes began. The absence of the *rei puta* pendant reflected the fact that whereas sharks were sometimes taken in the sound, beached whales were not. To our knowledge, the Russians collected not one single whalebone article in

1820 in New Zealand. This is interesting in relation to the whalebone *patu* that figure handsomely in the first and second Cook voyage collections.

In summary, the "1820" ornaments are as a group appreciably different from Cook assemblages of ornaments that had, with one or two possible exceptions, been collected in the same locality. There is, indeed, some continuity; but like the 1820 cloak collection at MAE, the 1820 ornaments suggest a growing southwest North Island influence in Totaranui which, however, is perceptible less in technique than in altered local styles. Not technology but *manner* had been modified by influences active in the sound between Cook's third visit and Bellingshausen's arrival. Local culture had survived new, northern influences, but had been modified nevertheless. Imported attitudes or tastes had been absorbed to some extent and in the case of certain items only. This showed a working out of military and political reality about the sound.

THE RUSSIAN EVIDENCE FOR PADDLES AND CANOES

The Russians saw the ordinary working paddle (*hoe*) of the sound in use repeatedly throughout their stay. All agree that it was "short" and "shovel-like." Midshipman Novosil'skii noted that in general the Maori stained it red and used it sitting in their craft, often in pairs, but did not paddle in unison. It seemed to Simonov that each man "paddled for himself, without order." Sixteen men approached the sloops in one canoe, twenty-three in another; but not all paddled. Those who propelled the craft used *hoe* about "five and a half feet long," and could use them for hours at a time: on 29 May, *Vostok* and *Mirnyi* were followed for at least three hours as they tacked off Motuara and Long Islands. It was perhaps then that the Russians saw the Maoris paddling standing upright, to get or maintain greater speed and headway. In general, the paddle seen in 1820 was just as described by Cook and Parkinson: broad at the centre, red, and shovel-like, with the blade set at a slight angle to the handle.

Item 736-173 in Leningrad is such a paddle. Its 15-centimetre broad blade is markedly dished and has a very pronounced median ridge on the back. In this respect, and also in its blunt and hooklike blade end and stone-tool dressing marks, the piece belongs to an ancient family associated with the South Island. In Totaranui, however, almost nothing was straightforward, either culturally or politically, in the early 1800s. Ancient though this paddle is in form, North Island influence is discernible in its style. It is unornamented but was possibly unfinished when Bellingshausen arrived to offer its maker or owner an irresistible price in Russian goods. Leningrad's paddle No. 736-168, on the other hand, has

Wanganui-Horowhenua-style carving on the upper front of the blade (roughly done with stone tools), and is unlike anything in the Cook collections. The British Museum has one similar paddle (No. 1947.Oc4.1), which is depicted in Sarah Stone's watercolours of objects in the Leverian Museum, including objects from Cook's second and third voyages.[39] Another, of the same type and now held by the National Museum of Ireland, is positively attributed to Cook's second or third voyage and is linked with South Island culture. Such paddles, writes H.D. Skinner, "perpetuate East Polynesian features which have been lost in North Island Classic Maori."[40]

The Russians wrought better than they knew in building up a small *hoe* collection from the sound: as the texts make plain, they mistook both No. 736-113 and 736-114 for weapons. The error is pardonable, for some paddles were indeed made—with broad, sharp blades and sturdy hafts—so that they could serve as arms or paddles, as circumstances might dictate. Item 736-113, the flat war canoe paddle with gymnast figure carving on the handle, again in Taranaki style, was in the possession of a chief at Little Waikawa Bay in 1820. The Russians, who referred to it as "an eight-foot-long staff" or "stave," rightly recognized it as a prized and ceremonial object.[41] The open-carved top with tooth pattern is of fine craftsmanship. Such paddles were "rarely seen" even in the 1830s, and it is noteworthy that the chiefly proprietor of 736-113 delayed some time before offering it to Bellingshausen.[42] It was produced at the last moment as his European guests, who had traded many objects of the highest value and utility to him and, for all he knew, possibly had more, were about to leave his village. The chief was willing to give of his best for Russian iron goods, concealing his own best articles till the most telling moment. Items 736-113 and 736-114 were highly valued by the Maori at the time they were acquired by the Russians.

The last paddle in Leningrad from 1820, No. 736-114, brings another factor into play. The stylized head carved at the loom of the blade is in Gisborne, not Taranaki, style. Suffice it to note here that at least four other objects in the Leningrad collection—three feather boxes (736-121, -122, -123) and the beautiful bier stay or carved group (736-120), represent that same regional style of wood carving. It appears that the forebears of the 1820 *hapu* had had dealings with the East Coast people as well as with southwestern North Island. No. 736-114 had probably been used as a paddle in the sound, its efficiency being scarcely reduced by the hammerhead shark pattern painted on the flat blade. It was perhaps a *hoewai* of the sort described by Elsdon Best's informant, Tuta Nihoniho, to be used as a weapon in case of emergency.[43]

In sum, the Russians collected three types of paddle in the sound: flat, with Taranaki carving; flat and painted, with East Coast carving; and dished, with a hook end in Wanganui-Horowhenua style (736-168). This last type was a traditional South Island one. The Russians' hosts had almost constant use for many paddles but willingly traded them.

Bellingshausen and his men saw two small war canoes (*waka taua*) in the area of Little Waikawa Bay and Motuara Island. One they estimated to be forty-seven feet long; another, drawn by the artist Mikhailov, was evidently some thirty-four feet long, judging by the human figure depicted with it. Both Simonov and Bellingshausen, though, imply that there were more such craft in the area. These canoes were hollowed out of single tree trunks but had double top-strakes, each some seven inches across, and stern-pieces that "curved up like a crest to a height of five feet" (Bellingshausen). Figureheads with "snail-patterned open carvings," shell eyes, and protruding wooden tongue, were of the sort seen by Dumont D'Urville in 1826.[44] The caulking was of reed bast, driven in between the strakes and solid hull as Forster had described.[45]

The fishing craft (*waka tete*) that the Russians saw were, by comparison, both short and crudely made. Mikhailov depicts one less than fifteen feet long at the water's edge of the settlement in Little Waikawa Bay, in his beautiful aquarelle *The Main Village in New Zealand South, in Queen Charlotte Sound*. Simonov writes of an unspecified number of craft with "carvings representing the human face in caricature." Double canoes were also to be seen off Motuara Island in 1820. Dr. Galkin is the confident informant: "Sometimes two craft are bound together by stakes, in which case they cannot be capsized in rough seas even though they lack protective strakes." Galkin's phrasing shows that the hulls were lashed together or very nearly so, in which case his double craft, with its coarse carving and modest size ("more than ten men may find room in it"), strongly resembled that observed by George Forster in Dusky Bay in 1774.[46] There was no deck or superstructure. The Russian evidence strongly suggests that, though the double canoe was growing rare even in Cook's time in the North Island, it continued to be numerous in waters further south.[47]

The Maoris of Queen Charlotte Sound fished successfully several times during the Russian visit; on one occasion, they were able to supply Bellingshausen and his people with some 250 pounds of fish, caught with seine or hook-and-line, at little notice. "Many kinds of wooden hooks and fishing lines" were seen in huts along the shore near Matere; baskets and funnel-nets, however, were apparently not used. Simonov collected two or more composite fish-hooks (Nos. 4 and 5 in Kazan'), both made of wood and bird's bone. No. 4 was meant for shark, much resembling item No. 6368 in the Auckland Museum (hook from Waimate, Taranaki) and

E.5513 in the Peabody Museum at Salem.[48] The Kazan' shark hook was clearly made from a specially trained branch.[49] Shark's teeth were much prized as ornaments and tiny knives, and were also used in trade. It is noteworthy, in this connection, that the decorated shark-tooth knife is, like so many other objects in the first and second Cook voyage assemblages, conspicuously absent from the Soviet collections.

The Russian narratives several times call attention to the modest dimensions of paddles and canoes seen in New Zealand. But with what could the Russians have compared them? Presumably, with Australian Aboriginal craft, which they had seen only recently, or with the evidence from British narratives and illustrations of fifty years before. The Australian bark craft were far smaller. The Russians were therefore perhaps thinking of Cook data when they found the canoes of the sound so small. But those craft and paddles were, in reality, only a trifle shorter than the classic mean. The Dominion Museum in Wellington has a *hoe* that is practically identical with No. 736-173. Still, the Russian texts suggest a further point: if the paddle of the sound was rather shorter than its Northern counterpart and more directly linked to the ancient Polynesian form, so too—quite logically—was the canoe that it propelled. The largest *waka taua* seen by the Russians, forty-seven feet long, was by no means large by Maori standards.

OTHER CARVING IN WOOD SEEN BY THE RUSSIANS

Bellingshausen's people saw and were impressed by several types of carved wooden artefact besides the paddle and canoe. These included *tekoteko,* or gable-apex carvings from dwelling houses; *wakahuia,* or feather boxes, for the storage and protection of valuables of small size; weapons such as *tewhatewha* and *taiaha* (two-handed clubs); and the masterpiece of the Soviet 1820 collection, the enigmatic carved group or bier stay. All but one or two of these objects showed carving styles associated with districts remote from the sound where they were collected in 1820.

Both house finials or *tekoteko* carvings in Leningrad show facial tattooing: 736-119 is a neuter figure with partial tattoo, 736-118 a female figure with male facial markings. Travelling through Otago in 1844, Edward Shortland noted that old women of the Kai Tahu tribe had "engraved on their faces, many of the marks which in the North Island I had never seen but on males."[50] The carving style of this piece may be southwest North Island, but such tattooing indicates a South Island origin for the group descended from this ancestress. Both Leningrad *tekoteko* have one leg shorter than the other. House carvings are absent from the well-

documented Cook collections, but the Leningrad *tekoteko* can be compared with two reputed Cook voyage carvings in the Hunterian Museum
in Glasgow (E 328-329).

The group carving, showing three copulating figures with a fourth at an
obtuse angle to them, is of a higher order of Maori craftsmanship and was
long an enigma to its students. It is ancient work, executed with great care
in the Gisborne style, and has a single attachment point, now broken off
behind the head of the lowest figure. According to a Maori informant of
D.R. Simmons (1986), the piece was originally one of a set of carved
supports or stays used to hold firm the corpse of a paramount chief who
was transported by canoe in a bier to her final resting place. The chief is
said to have descended from a union between a Kai Tahu woman and a
Ngatierehere-of-Whakaki man. Having died at Whakaki, near Wairoa,
she was reportedly carried back for burial to the South Island lest the
mana be lost.[51]

As for the feather boxes in the Leningrad collection, they show carving
styles equally remote from Queen Charlotte Sound, and equally intrigu-
ing. Items No. 736-121 to 123 are done in the distinctive Gisborne manner; but the fourth Leningrad box, which is a flat *papahou* with carved
heads for handles, is an altogether different proposition. The underside
was carved with stone tools in the Wanganui style of the southwestern
North Island. So too were the anthropomorphic heads that formed the
handles of the box. The style can be identified with that of a *wakahuia* in
the British Museum (NZ.113), very probably from Cook's first voyage.
The sides and lid of 736-124, however, show Hokianga-style carving—
with metal implements. The piece was perhaps taken as a souvenir by a
Maori raider from the far North who, on one of the musket raids to the
Wanganui area in 1818–19 or to Taranaki in 1810–13, finished it in his
own, northern style.[52] It could then have reached the sound by gift exchange or simple trade—if the raider had not actually settled in the sound.
At all events, the box is a bizarre one and its carving tells a story that is
open to various interpretations.

All is clear, by comparison, where MAE's three wooden weapons are
concerned. Both *tewhatewha,* or axe-shaped two-handed clubs, show
South Taranaki-style carving, whereas the whorled *taiaha* (736-115) was
carved with iron tools in the Gisborne manner.

FOOD, DIET, AND LIFE-STYLE: THE RUSSIAN EVIDENCE

The Maoris encountered by the Russians caught and ate much fish. *Waka
tete* were much in evidence, as were wooden hooks and fishing lines.
Bodies gleamed with fish oil and, to the right in Pavel Mikhailov's

aquarelle *War Dance of New Zealand South, in Queen Charlotte Sound*, we see a large fish-rack on which sizable fish are drying. Late May is winter in New Zealand, when the Maori were dependent on fish and roots for their sustenance.[53] Fishing went on year-round in the sound, but the best season for birding was already over when the Russians came. Long bird-spears were accordingly hung up in the chief's house in Little Waikawa Bay, and the chief was quite prepared to barter some for Russian goods.[54] As for the roots of *Pteris aquilina,* a traditional winter foodstuff, they were kept on the *whata* (platforms) also well depicted by Mikhailov—from seven to fifteen feet off the ground and resting on the docked branches of little trees plus an extra post or two.

As the Russians saw, however, the local people's overall dependence on such foodstuffs had dramatically decreased since Cook's departure. A great deal of the value of their narratives lies in their reporting of that fact. By 1820 the people of Queen Charlotte Sound were no longer without an agricultural base. No longer did they roam in apprehension of attack, prepared for hunger, as they had a century before: they grew potatoes on a regular, seasonal basis in addition to their gourds, which, however, did not flourish half so well.

Bellingshausen saw potato plots and a successful crop on a headland north of modern Te Ahitaore. The Maori had obviously not, as Cook feared they might, left the potatoes planted by himself, Furneaux, Bayly, or Fannen to decay or blossom wild.[55] The potatoes had indeed "spread out considerably, after forty-seven years," observed Bellingshausen, but had done so with the conscious aid of the Maori.[56] Cook's people had sown potatoes in at least four spots in 1773: beside a beach on Long Island, on "Hippah Rock," on the level top and on a lower slope of Motuara Island, and in Ship Cove.[57] The nearest plot to that seen by the Russians had been Fannen's, at the bottom of Ship Cove, a good way off. Self-propagation is assuredly a factor and cannot be totally dismissed here; it may have tended, like the Maori, to "help" the plant towards the headlands, which were far less subject to invasion by the motley undergrowth that quickly covered Bayly's garden,[58] where the Russians saw it prospering in 1820. Nonetheless, the fact remains that cultivation of potatoes had begun some time before and had become a central element of local people's lives. It had, in fact, altered their life-style by introducing a considerable measure of stability, among other things. Baskets had been plaited to contain the vegetables as they were taken to a central storage point. The Russians had been trained to be observant, but they saw no sign of recent troubles or hostilities, no warlike preparations, no defence-works. Cultivation of the headland and a stone-edged stream; a village with a single modest, ditchless palisade; an ample trade in cloaks and greenstone objects—all directly pointed to a relatively settled way of life, based upon trade and agriculture, not on war.

And yet, numbering eighty or perhaps a hundred persons, could the *hapu* be oblivious to warlike prospects in the North? Far Northern tribes had armed themselves with deadly guns since 1800, with the aid of New South Wales trading captains. Few in number, Bellingshausen's hosts had relatives and tribal allies, but essentially they had no choice but to accept the influences or incursions from the North. Their weakness led to their destruction at the hands of Northern warriors in 1827.

ETHNOLOGICAL CONCLUSIONS

Queen Charlotte Sound was a natural gateway between the North and South Islands of New Zealand. It was a nexus for trade in baked argillite, obsidian, greenstone, and perishable food items. As late as 1844, Edward Shortland recorded exchanges of canoes, clothing, and dried kumara for greenstone, mutton birds, and taramea oil between the East Coast and Otago.[59] Such exchanges would have been routed through Queen Charlotte Sound, and links between the sound itself and Otago are evident from written records as well as from artefact collections. One "Kollakh" was in a Kai Tahu party in Queen Charlotte Sound after Bellingshausen's visit. This was Korako, later a Kai Tahu chief at Waikouaiti in Otago.[60] Again, the striped cloaks in the 1820 collection were of Kai Tahu origin, and similar ones were seen by Dumont D'Urville in 1826 at Admiralty Bay. An 1820 dished paddle (736-168) is certainly of South Island type. As for the Leningrad male-tattooed female *tekoteko* figure, it would seem to be possible only from the Kai Tahu, though admittedly we have no information on this practice for other South Island tribes.

One element of the population in Queen Charlotte Sound in 1820, then, can be identified as Kai Tahu, possibly incorporating the earlier Kati Mamoe. (The Kai Tahu hark back to the Rongowhakaata of the Gisborne area, their culture being a variant of the classic North Island Maori.) Specifically Southern aspects of their repertoire could have resulted from Kai Tahu development in the South; but more probably one part of the inventory came from the Kati Mamoe, Waitaha, or other earlier South Island people. In the Soviet collection, as we have seen, two paddles, the carved figure group (736-120), and two *wakahuia* show this relationship with the Gisborne and Hawkes Bay areas. Young Kai Tahu chiefs were traditionally educated among their relatives, the Rongowhakaata, at Turanganui or Gisborne; and the Ngai Tamanuhuri *hapu* of the Rongowhakaata tribe, centred on Muriwai, identify themselves as Ngai Tahu to this day.

The other principal influence discernible in Totaranui artefacts col-lected by the Russians in 1820 is the Wanganui style. It is evident to some extent in all Cook collections as well as in the MAE collection from the sound; but in the later period, the influence is Taranaki and South Tara-naki rather than Wanganui.

The canvas-weave cloaks from the sound are a very distinct cultural form not found in other areas, and stayed in production until the 1840s despite the devastating effects of North Island raids and settlers—and the increasing strength of Northern techniques and decorative features in the sound. The identity of the basic cultural group of Queen Charlotte Sound is well illustrated by the women cloak-weavers, who were continuing their work even though apparently submerged by invading cultural groups. In such a strained situation, tribal names were probably a matter of convenience and in line with prevailing political ties. Warfare against invaders must at times have been unavoidable, but the population of the sound can never have been large enough to sustain a military effort over long periods. The extant material culture, as evidenced by the Soviet and other collections, indicates that although outside influences on Totaranui Maoris were plainly powerful, the Totaranui somehow absorbed them. Foreign elements thus became part of the local culture within a relatively short period. One example of this is the introduction of Taranaki-style *taniko* patterns. The basic and very local technology of cloak making was not submerged; only the decorative elements were affected by a North Is-land import. And this process occurred despite the fact that North Island technology for the production of *kaitaka* cloaks demanded less time yet produced a very handsome garment.

The 1820 collection illustrates the vigour of a local culture that had managed to survive the influx of people from other areas, adopt a new economic base (potato cultivation), but still retain a material culture little changed since 1770. It is a major advantage of the Russian narrative, pic-torial, and physical evidence that one can state unequivocally that Queen Charlotte Sound *had* a strong local culture. This makes it feasible to iden-tify a number of "possible" Cook-period cloaks as being certainly from there. Weapons from 1820 are not as clearly defined, but nonetheless show the same local culture as the cloaks. Other material culture items follow the same pattern, with the local culture re-emerging.

The Russians' Maori hosts would soon be devastated by musket raids conducted by Te Rauparaha of Ngati Toa, some of whose allied fol-lowers, led by Te Ati Awa under Puoho of Taranaki, took over and oc-cupied Queen Charlotte Sound by 1835. (Yet some ten years later, an un-finished canvas-weave cloak identical to Cook pieces collected in the 1770s was being worked on by Mihiorangi of Queen Charlotte Sound. It is now in the Auckland Museum.) Such massive cultural changes and the decimation of the sound people in the early nineteenth century, followed by the Europeanization of remnants and invaders alike, should have spelled an end to the distinctive culture of that place—but they did not. As documentation of the people of Queen Charlotte Sound on the eve of the Te Ati Awa onslaught, the Russian evidence is of the very highest importance.

Four years after Bellingshausen's visit, Captain Duperrey again brought Frenchmen into contact with the Maori of the far North of New Zealand. "The main value of Duperrey's visit," wrote the historian Andrew Sharp, "may be considered to lie in the picture the account of it gives of the impact of European arts, customs and beliefs on the Maori. In the fifty-five years since Cook's first visit to New Zealand, the old Maori culture had undergone vast changes... Diseases were wreaking havoc. The musket was undermining the traditional Maori system of military offence and defence... The primitive food supply was ... modified by the use of pigs... The missionaries were working out their own economic adaptations."[61]

Here, in cameo, is what the Russians had *not* found in 1820 during their visit to the isolated sound. The potato, yes; some knowledge of the use of iron and of Sydney sealers' clothing, yes; knowledge of European guns, most certainly. But this was all, as far as European influences in 1820 went, in the sound. The Bellingshausen visit itself accelerated changing trading expectations in that area. In dress, in decoration, in beliefs and customs, in their skills, the Russians' hosts were still basically living the traditional life-patterns of their people. To the Russians' lasting credit, they perceived this fact and drew the corresponding ethnographic benefit for all, laying the basis for a long-term Russian interest in *Maoritanga* and New Zealand in St. Petersburg.[62]

In recent times the nature of that interest has continued to focus on the natural resources of the country and the fortunes of a people who, potentially, could always rise against their *pakeha* and capitalist "masters." Doctrinally, how could the Party view the *pakeha* if not as stealers of the Maoris' rights and lands? The Maori cause must be defended, of necessity; only the cause must be defined. Thus in the context of New Zealand studies Marxist-Leninist political imperatives are now the ally of the Soviet ethnographer who, while expected to examine ancient Maori life "objectively," is also to present it in a just, anti-colonial perspective.[63] Still, the Bellingshausen expedition's ethnographic work in Oceania is widely recognized in Leningrad today, and Maori studies are encouraged by Academy and University alike.[64]

PAVEL N. MIKHAILOV'S "VOSTOK" PORTFOLIO:
NEW ZEALAND DRAWINGS

Pavel Nikolaevich Mikhailov (1786–1840) was a graduate of the St. Petersburg Academy of Arts and a civilian.[65] Nevertheless, he fell at once within the pale of naval discipline on taking up his duties as official artist with the Bellingshausen-Lazarev Antarctic expedition.[66] His relationship with Bellingshausen proved to be a very good one, with respect and tolerance on either side. The latter wrote a warm letter of recommendation for him at the Southern expedition's end. ("During a two-year campaign, Academician P.N. Mikhailov conducted himself excellently, fulfilling his duties with particular diligence and zeal, and I would willingly take him again in a future command.")[67]

While in New Zealand, Mikhailov worked with a loose-sheet folder, comfortably carried under the arm. Not knowing when he would be able to obtain more paper, or what he might need to draw in coming weeks in Oceania, he used his paper very economically. On some sheets measuring a mere nine by twelve inches, he crammed rough outlines or sketches of half-a-dozen heads or figures besides a few vague landscapes. These sheets are today in the Drawings Division of the State Russian Museum (Gosudarstvennyi Russkii Muzei), on Engineers' Street, Leningrad, under reference R-29001-29308. Few have been published, yet they are ethnographically very significant in their immediacy and as elements from which assorted published illustrations were derived in 1823–24 or later.

In its present form, the "Mikhailov Portfolio" consists of large, light blue cardboard-backing sheets to which original pen sketches, pencilled roughs, and aquarelles of various dimensions have been attached. It is accompanied by a card catalogue and register, from which it emerges that the 1819–21 work has been supplemented by a range of other illustrations made aboard the sloop *Moller* (Captain-Lieutenant Mikhail N. Staniukovich) by Mikhailov. The latter, dating from 1826–29, reflect the *Moller*'s route of 1827 from Chile to Tahiti, Kamchatka, the Northwest Coast, and Oahu, and include a number of fine *paysages* done near Honolulu and individual Hawaiians and Tahitians, many named. Fortunately, the Soviet sheet enumeration is complemented by the original pagination, so that the order of work in 1819–21 can be reconstructed correctly enough. In total, the portfolio contains sixteen little pieces of work dating from *Vostok*'s stay in Totaranui. Six or seven were used by the artist when working up proposed illustrations for Bellingshausen's official account of the expedition. These were lithographs and later published in the *Atlas* accompanying *Dvukratnye izyskaniia*'s *Atlas* (St. Petersburg 1831). The sixteen pieces are shown in Table 1.

TABLE I

Numbering		Title	Subject-Matter/Remarks
29066	66/obv	—	Entrance to Queen Charlotte Sound; Maori adult male at bottom, head and shoulders, right
29067	67	*Entrance to Queen Charlotte Sound, in Southern New Zealand*	View to the sw, Cape Jackson at centre
29077	77	*North Side of the Largest of Queen Charlotte's Island*	In pencil; the word "Vulcan," in English, visible to the right
29201	199	—	Maori male face with heavy tattooing
29202	200	*A Type of New Zealand Native*	
29136	135	*Hut of South New Zealand*	Showing an interior; 10 by 4 cm only; corn coloured thatch
29137	136	—	Two Maori women, the upper carrying a child in a back pouch
29138	137	—	An older Maori man, bearded, facing left, with a cloak which alone has been drawn in detail and coloured; 9 cm by 14 cm
29139	138	—	Rough sketch of a dance, with 8 figures, arms outstretched forward
29140	139	—	Rough sketches of sailors, Maori arms, a cape, human heads
29143	142	—	Preliminary sketches of two heavy raincapes, part of a canoe stern, etc. 9 by 14 cm
29281	279	*The Main Village of South New Zealand*	A semi-finished watercolour, with bright red colouring along a war canoe; stuck to Board 57
29282	280	*A War Dance of South New Zealand*	Attached to Board 58.
29283	281	*A War Dance of South New Zealand*	Far more complete than the above, but upper part only is coloured; much vegetation; hut on right; numerous human figures lightly roughed in
29215	212	—	Maori figures, adult, small
29142	141	*Gestures for a War Dance of the Zealanders*	11 pencil studies of arm and back muscles and dance positions for a *haka;* not used in No. 29282 above

Almost immediately upon his return to Kronstadt in August 1821, Mikhailov surrendered his portfolio to the Naval Ministry, which returned it to him without undue delay. Mikhailov then proceeded with the task, most likely begun earlier, of arranging his drawings by class. He settled on six classes, excluding copies that he had lately made from the *Atlas* of François Péron (which, however, subsequently comprised a little class of their own). The latter nine copies were of Australian Aboriginals and Tasmanians, drawn while *Géographe* and *Naturaliste* were in Australia in 1800, and were of superb workmanship and high colour.

The Queen Charlotte Sound drawings and aquarelles were placed in Class 2 ("Miscellaneous Little Studies Relating to the Voyage," 63 in all), Class 3 ("Small Sketches of Shores of Various Lands or Relating to Them," 61 in all), Class 4 ("Portraits and Figures of the Savages of Various Lands," forty-four in all), and Class 6 ("Views and Customs of Various Lands," thirty-four in all). The addition of drawings from the *Moller* expedition and the removal of items from the 1819–21 collection have led to an adjustment of these subtotals, which now (1986) amount to 286 items. At the same time, Mikhailov was evidently working up those items that he or others thought most appropriate for publication with Bellingshausen's text, with a tincture of white lead. This work occupied him more than a year: the resulting album is now held in the State Historical Museum on Red Square in Moscow. Pages from this album were then (1824) lithographed for the forthcoming *Atlas*. The lithographer was Ivan Pavlovich Fridrits (1803–60), who was completing his studies at the St. Petersburg Academy of Arts under Nikolai I. Utkin. Regrettably, Fridrits was an average craftsman and Mikhailov's original aquarelles lost much in the lithographing process. A comparison of rough sketches in the Leningrad portfolio and of illustrations in the 1831 *Atlas* shows that a number of the sixteen pieces listed above were incorporated in plates.[68] Ever efficient, Mikhailov did not allow much of his 1820 work to go to waste. The fact that his published work of 1831 had been "improved upon," however, makes the ethnographic value of the Leningrad originals even greater.

Unlike Emel'ian Mikhailovich Korneev (1780–1844), the older and professionally more successful artist with *Otkrytie* (Captain Mikhail N. Vasil'ev) on the "Northern prong" of the 1819–21 double polar expedition,[69] Mikhailov has not attracted the attention of Soviet historians of art.[70] To the extent that he is still recalled in Leningrad at all, it is because of honourable mention by the art historian, A.A. Fedorov-Davydov. In preparation for this monumental study of Russian landscape painting of the nineteenth century, published in 1953, Fedorov-Davydov found materials—both in the Archive of the Soviet Academy of Arts and elsewhere—that were then unknown. Some bore upon Mikhailov's career as a student at the St. Petersburg Academy of Arts (1795–1807), illuminating his abilities in portraiture as well as natural scenes.[71] Others, of greater interest perhaps, focused directly on his duties as an artist for the Navy and on the orders and responsibilities of other artists (Stepan Kurliandtsev, Mikhail Tikhanov) who were sent to Polynesia in that period.[72] Fedorov-Davydov viewed Mikhailov as competent but all in all a minor talent. Nonetheless, he made a number of illuminating references to the artist whom Bellingshausen treated as a colleague and whose Australasian work still has much ethnographical importance.

More and more often, in the early 1800s, qualified artists, usually graduates of the Academy of Arts, were sent on expeditions instead of mere journeyman draughtsmen. Thus, whereas still unknown draughtsmen had gone with G.A. Sarychev on his voyage, in 1803 it was proposed to send Academician A. Prichotnikov and "Designate" S. Kurliandtsev on Kruzenshtern's expedition... And in 1819–21, Pavel N. Mikhailov was participating in the voyage round the globe of Bellingshausen and Lazarev. Among his drawings, we find some that are *paysages* of New Holland and, from the standpoint of subject matter, have the very greatest interest ... But the most attractive and even in its way most beautiful aspect of Mikhailov's drawings is a certain "ornamentation" (*uzorchatost'*) about the treatment of vegetation, which is done with great attentiveness and love. It is in this aspect that his drawings stylistically draw near to the engravings in the celebrated *Atlas* of Kruzenshtern's *Voyage*. Artistically, this was undoubtedly the best atlas of the age, even though the dilettantish sketches of the savant Tilesius and probably also of Kurliandtsev formed its basis.[73]

Mikhailov did not fare well in the government's appointment of lithographers to prepare his finished plates for publication in the Bellingshausen *Atlas*. Some plates were taken, as we have seen, by a pupil of Nikolai I. Utkin at the St. Petersburg Academy of Arts, Ivan Pavlovich Fridrits. Others were indifferently worked on by Gonzago and Geitman.

LIEUTENANT KONSTANTIN P. TORSON'S PROJECT AND
REPORT OF 1823

Active though they went as anthropologists, astronomers, and even part-time physicists in 1820, Bellingshausen's officers were first and foremost naval men. The naval aspects of the voyage of *Vostok* and *Mirnyi* were naturally of fundamental interest to them. One such aspect was efficient ship design. Both sloops experienced great storms in southern latitudes: one lengthy gale, as we have seen, largely contributed to their arrival in Queen Charlotte Sound. It was proper that ambitious younger officers should ponder the suitability of Russian sloops that, in the post-Napoleonic period (1816–26), were being sent on complex missions round the world though built originally for a single and perhaps less taxing function. One such officer was Konstantin Petrovich Torson (1793–1851), *Vostok*'s second lieutenant and an incipient Decembrist.[74] The experience of gales in the Tasman Sea had an effect on Torson that emerged when, in St. Petersburg in 1822–23, he was considering inadequate design.

Like other youthful patriots who were to sympathize with anti-autocratic feelings in the Russia of the twenties, even playing active roles in the clandestine Northern or Southern Societies of the Decembrists, Torson recognized that both he and Russia had lost by a scandalous decline of the entire Baltic Fleet since 1810. Since that year, even sailors had been constantly on land manoeuvres, drilling and serving as auxiliary infantry, while port authorities who had responsibility for the abandoned ships reneged on it.[75] Once, équipages of a thousand men or so in eight detachments had belonged and been loyal to specific ships. Since 1812, those old attachments had been loosened or destroyed. It was apparent that the tsar was deeply ignorant about the Navy and, in any case, preoccupied with land strategies. Writing in June 1818 in connection with the *Riurik* expedition, Kruzenshtern observed that while the wars against Napoleon had lasted, the imperial authorities had been unable to despatch a ship on "such an enterprise" as Kotzebue's to the North.[76] But Russia had already been at peace with France for months when work was started on the *Riurik*. The sponsor of the *Riurik* expedition, Count N.P. Rumiantsev, was a very wealthy man, but it was striking that it fell not to the Crown but to an individual to guard the honour of the State in exploration. Kruzenshtern in fact no more than hinted at the pitiful reality of Russia's naval weakness. In the aftermath of the European war, "all ships at Konstadt had been literally rotting, painted up and prettified on one side only—and along that side, during reviews, the Sovereign was invariably led."[77] As for the courtly émigré who was the naval minister, Marquis de Traversay, "his energy was principally directed towards changing or annulling everything achieved by his predecessor."[78] In the postwar years, more than ever, the North Pacific service was distinct from other branches of the Russian naval service. It became even more closely connected with prestige and with expenditures unthinkable to the majority of Admiralty bureaucrats, whose incomes had been swelled by fraud and graft.[79]

Torson had been fortunate to serve (1812–13) aboard the frigate *Amfitrida,* whose commander, Irinarkh Tulub'ev, was in 1821 to take *Apollon* on a voyage to the North Pacific settlements—and die en route to Sydney from Brazil.[80] Nevertheless, his early service had been marred by the shortcomings of Navy ships. While serving in *Vostok,* he made invidious comparisons between her seagoing and other qualities and those of vessels seen at Portsmouth, Teneriffe, and Rio de Janeiro. He saw the links between political and naval competence and, in the quasi-constitutional Brazil of Emperor Dom Pedro, entertained seditious thoughts about his homeland.[81] In the course of an extended and exhausting passage from Port Jackson, Australia, to the fringes of Antarctica, he came to recognize that the entire Russian Fleet needed reform.[82]

Vostok and *Mirnyi* were, in his view, exposed to pointless dangers by the storms and cold conditions they met in 1820. The majority of Russian ships would have suffered even more—or simply sunk. Torson argued that specific standards should be introduced and rigidly enforced for every part of every class of Russian warship. System should be introduced into confusion: it was ludicrous, for instance, that *Mirnyi*, a reconfigured transport and thus a slower sailer, should be holding back her companion around the globe; that masts and rigging should be different from ship to ship within the same class; and that the Naval Ministry should lack the bureaucratic means to draw suggestions for improvements of a practical variety from serving officers and seamen. Torson pondered these and other problems while in Sydney and New Zealand. The results emerged in a report that he submitted to the ministry in 1823, "Observations on the Standards For the Fitting Out of Ships."[83]

Bellingshausen thought highly of Torson. On 23 December 1819, he named a high islet for him off South Georgia in the South Atlantic Ocean. "Torson Island" was renamed "High Island" as a consequence of the lieutenant's fall from grace as a conspirator in the Decembrist revolt, but the name remained, conceivably by error, in the first edition of the Bellingshausen text.[84] His good opinion was shared by Rear-Admiral A.V. Moller, Chief of the Naval Staff in 1821–24. Early in 1822, Torson was sent to St. Petersburg by Moller "to complete certain matters relating to the recent voyage towards the South Pole."[85] These matters included the sorting out of officers' and specialists' reports and journals from the Southern expedition.

Torson returned to the capital that October, this time with more specific orders to "compose the memoir on the Southern Expedition." He did so. The memoir was seized, with Torson's other papers, at the time of his arrest in December 1825. It was afterwards returned to him while he was serving out his term of exile in Siberia and was discovered among his papers at his death.[86] It then unfortunately vanished. Such materials, however, have been surfacing of late in places far removed from Leningrad and Moscow,[87] and Torson's may do so too one day.

It bears repeating that the officers and midshipmen of Bellingshausen's sloops were all obliged to keep regular journals and, moreover, to surrender them to the imperial authorities. Those journals with New Zealand passages from 1820 must have numbered twelve at least, and probably more. Even the use of such materials, however, and their later reappearance in the Bellingshausen narrative, by no means guaranteed that they themselves would become known. Both *Vostok* and *Apollon* had future revolutionaries among their companies (Torson and Mikhail K. Kiukhel'beker); and the *Kreiser* brought Dmitrii Zavalishin to the South Pacific in 1823.[88] This did not dispose the new tsar, Nicolas I, to help such officers as Aleksei P. Lazarev or Karl A. Gillesem to publish their accounts of their experiences in the sloop *Blagonamerennyi*—one of the vessels in the Northern polar enterprise that balanced Bellingshausen's venture in the South.[89] As for *Vostok*'s other lieutenants, Ivan Ignat'ev and Arkadii Leskov, there was no question of supporting *them* at State expense: even the printing of the Bellingshausen text, as we have seen, was doubtful in the grim aftermath of the Decembrist uprising. In sum, numerous records of the 1820 visit to New Zealand by well-educated men were never published. Some at least must be supposed to hold interest for the historian, who may be grateful to those Soviets (Ostrovskii, Lipshits, Kuznetsova, Shur: see Bibliography) who have insisted on that fact in published papers. English-language guides are now available to those who wish to track such records down in Soviet State archives and repositories of manuscript material.[90] From the perspective of New Zealand studies, it is fortunate that Soviet officialdom is deeply conscious of "the problem of Antarctica." All Soviet pretensions to a slice of any cake in the Antarctic resting squarely on the Bellingshausen-Lazarev Antarctic expedition, it is natural that primary materials that bear upon it have been thoroughly examined from all angles.[91] But at least this has resulted in awareness among geographers and scientists of Bellingshausen's presence in New Zealand and the sub-Antarctic islands to its south. That recollection is sustained now by the names of the USSR's permanent research stations on the mainland of Antarctica: Vostok and Mirnyi.[92]

Encouraged by the publication of Professor E.E. Shvede's 1961 edition of Bellingshausen's narrative and by official interest in the preparation of related documents, Mikhail I. Belov, V.V. Kuznetsova, and others at the Arctic and Antarctic Research Institute (AANII) in Leningrad then started work on an edition of the 1819–21 hydrography. The result was a set of fifteen charts, boxed and accompanied by an explanatory and discursive study, *Pervaia russkaia Antarkticheskaia ekspeditisiia 1819–1821 godov i eio otchetnaia navigatsionnaia karta* (*The First Russian Antarctic Expedition of 1819–21 and Its Summary Navigational Map:* Leningrad, "Morskoi Transport" 1963). That work contains no reference to Russian charting in New Zealand, to be sure, because the brief trip of 3 June 1820 thirteen miles into Queen Charlotte Sound did not result in any chart—or at least in any effort Bellingshausen thought proper to mention to his ministry. It does, however, throw suggestive light on certain areas of Soviet research that bear tangentially on New Zealand history. While sorting through files in the Central State Naval Archive of the USSR (TsGAVMF), Kuznetsova's colleague Aleksandr Larionov found the blueprints and other original drawings relating to the building of *Vostok.* Included with these papers were the plans for the 22-foot cutter, 18-foot launch, and other rowing craft in which the Russians made their way between *Vostok, Mirnyi,* and coves along the sound in 1820.[93] Such materials not only bear on Torson's plans but also focus Russian-Maori relations still more sharply. That same year (1962) and in the same archive, Belov examined a report dated 21 March 1823 that had been filed with a mass of "Southern Expedition" papers. It was identified as a report sent to the Chief of Naval Staff, Admiral Moller, by Lieutenant Arkadii S. Leskov, formerly third lieutenant in *Vostok.*[94] It makes brief mention of New Zealand.

Most primary documents relating to or penned by Bellingshausen in the context of the "Southern Expedition" and its outcome are, in fact, at TsGAVMF in Leningrad. That archive is officially still closed to foreign scholars; but its main administration seems increasingly prepared, if foreign visitors have ample time and good credentials, to make documents from earlier collections (*fonds*) available within the premises of adjacent institutions. It was there in 1966 that Kuznetsova found "new documents" relating to the luckless northern branch of Russia's two-poles enterprise, that is, the voyage of the sloops *Otkrytie* and *Blagonamerennyi.* She offered details in 1968.[95] It is improbable that there are no primary documents in TsGAFMR's *fonds* 25, 116, 166, 203, or 367 that bear on the 1820 visit to New Zealand.

For his involvement in the Decembrists' Northern Society and knowledge of plans to murder the tsar, Lieutenant Torson was on 8 July 1826 condemned to hard labour in exile for life. That sentence was mitigated by Nicholas I to twenty years' labour, loss of nobility, and subsequent settlement in a remote outpost; six weeks later, the term was again reduced—to fifteen years.[96] Torson reached the place of banishment, Chita fort, east of Lake Baikal and northeast of Mongolia, in January 1827.[97] There, over the next three years, he played a large part in the life of the "Chitá Academy," whereby the educated exiles sustained each other with informal lecture courses. Torson, like Mikhail K. Kiukhel'beker of the *Apollon,* which had spent some weeks in Australasia, spoke of his voyage round the world and recollections of the Maori.[98] He died in Selenginsk, Siberia, in 1851.

Envoi: Scientific and Political Developments, 1828–32

No other Russian ships called at New Zealand till the frigate *Afrika* (Admiral A.B. Aslanbegov) paused at Auckland in the dying days of 1881.[1] This was unfortunate, for had the colonists *seen* Russian shipping in their ports (as did the Melbourne settlers and Sydneysiders of the post-Crimean period),[2] they would perhaps have moderated their endemic Russophobia.[3] Because the Russians "lurked" unseen, imagination went unchecked, and local hoaxers worked up fears of attack by Russian cruisers to a pitch of outright panic[4] from the early 1870s till 1886.

Although the Russian Admiralty may have had a naval or strategic interest in Australasia in that period (and it is known that if an Anglo-Russian war had broken out over the so-called Afghan Question in the early 1880s, Russian warships would have sailed from Japan to intercept a Melbourne gold-ship, using coal supplied by Anglophobe Americans),[5] the Russian government's awareness of New Zealand in the thirties and the forties was almost non-existent. Any interest shown was in scientific contexts and was immediately linked with the results of the Southern expedition of *Vostok* and *Mirnyi*.

More specifically, this awareness of New Zealand was a consequence of Bellingshausen's narrative and *Atlas* and of Simonov's several published articles (1822–30), most printed in Kazan' by the university of which he was a rising officer.[6] It was inevitable that the Bellingshausen narrative, with its description of a busy Russian visit to New Zealand, should sustain public awareness of that country. Incidentally, however, the publication of some sixteen charts of Southern regions (the South Shetland, South Sandwich, and Georgia Islands, and Macquarie Island,[7] among others, in the *Atlas* did the same thing—in professional and academic circles—in conjunction with the Simonov reports.[8] For while that *Atlas* lacked a chart showing Queen Charlotte Sound in detail, it was the frame in which these reports could best be viewed, and it was also a reminder of the visit to the sound. The emphasis of Simonov's post-expedition papers, whose significance, as M.I. Belov notes, was much increased by the fact that other primary materials were not then being published,[9] is clear from their titles alone: "On Temperature Variation in the Southern and Northern Hemisphere (*Kazanskii vestnik* 1825, pts. 14–15); "Astronomical and Physical Observations of Professor Simonov . . . " (*ZMNP* 1828); "Determining the Geographical Positions of Anchorages of the Sloops 'Vostok' and 'Mirnyi'" (*ZMNP* 1828, pt. 22: 44–68); "Regarding Phenomena of Terrestrial Magnetism" (*Kazanskii vestnik* 1830, pt. 28). These made direct reference to New Zealand in the contexts of geodesy, astronomy, or physics.[10]

Naval and scientific interest in New Zealand and in Southern regions generally, was plainest in the *Proceedings of the Naval Staff's Scientific Committee* (*Zapiski Uchonogo Komiteta Morskago Shtaba*), whose influential first chairman, Admiral Loggin I. Golenishchev-Kutuzov, had translated Cook in his youth and personally helped Bellingshausen overcome the obstacles to the publication of his narrative."[11] This interest stemmed directly from Russian exploration and research. In Part 10 of the *Zapiski* (1833: 187–96) for instance, there appeared a detailed item, "Discoveries in the Southern Icy Ocean," that echoed Bellingshausen's charts and text of two years earlier. It was a piece about the expedition of the brig *Tula* and cutter *Lively* led by Captain John Biscoe (1830–32) to the South Sandwich Islands and Antarctica.[12] That expedition had indeed, as Messrs. Enderby acknowledged, been beset by every species of disaster from disease and storms to shipwreck. On the other hand, it had confirmed the wealth of seals to be had around New Zealand and the Chatham Islands to its east. "The cutter *Lively* had been reunited with *Tula* only in August 1831 and both were forced to put into Port Phillip in New South Wales. Both vessels had then put out to sea again, on 10 October, to hunt marine animals around the shores of New Zealand and then between the Chatham and Bounty Islands. This they pursued until 4 January 1832." The Chatham Islands, those ultimate outposts of the Polynesian people, were referred to more than once again by *Zapiski* in 1834–36. Part 12 (1835), for instance, alludes to a voyage made by Captain Henry Foster, FRS, "to the South Atlantic Ocean in 1828–1830 in His Majesty's Sloop *Chanticleer*... to make observations with the pendulum." "The most crucial spot for such observations in the Southern Hemisphere is, in the view of the Committee of the Royal Society, at Great Britain's Antipodes ... The Chatham or Auckland Islands are the most convenient place, being not far distant from the Antipodes of London itself."

Russians were by now participating in an international effort to determine the positions of the North and South magnetic poles and to conduct effective pendulum experiments at sea. Such work was undertaken in the Southern Hemisphere by Emil Lenz and Ferdinand Petrovich Lütke of *Seniavin* (1826–29), Leontii A. Hagemeister and Dr. Erman of the *Krotkii* (1829–30), and Ivan von Schants of the *Amerika* (1834–36).[13] New Zealand and the islands to its south appeared of course in the *Atlas of the South Sea* (St. P. 1823–26) that was Kruzenshtern's memorial, and in the subsequent appendixes thereto.[14]

The years 1830–31 marked the beginning of a new era of science for the polar seas and for Antarctica. Within a year of the printing of the Bellingshausen narrative and *Atlas,* both the Royal Geographical Society in London and the British Association for the Advancement of Science had been founded—and were dealing with the problem of determining the earth's magnetic fields. Now at peace, Great Britain, Russia, the United States, and other countries placed no bars on the exchange of scientific information, more particularly if it bore upon the art of navigation. Thus, the Russian Admiralty had the data gathered by HMS *Chanticleer*[15] (swinging pendula to fix the force of gravity), while Lenz and Bellingshausen sent material to Johann Karl F. Gauss, the German physicist and theorist of magnetism.[16] As far as Russian interest in any single place or region in the Southern Hemisphere was concerned, all was pleasantly abstract and unpolitical. Alas, the British in New Zealand and in the southern whaling, sealing, and related sea-based industries neither believed that the Russians took a genuinely scientific interest in Australasia and the waters to its south, nor, more significantly, wished to do so. Between November 1830 and September 1831, journals and newspapers in Edinburgh, London, Sydney and (for good measure) Van Diemen's Land published alarmist articles to the effect that if Great Britain did not rapidly annex New Zealand, one or other of "the leading Foreign Powers" would unquestionably do so. Russia was one of those Powers. Information that the Russians had their eyes upon New Zealand as a good "Spot" for a colony, alleged the *Hobart Town Courier* on 26 March 1831, had been provided by a party with connections to the South Seas whaling industry.[17]

It was in fact, as the subscribers of the *Courier* might well have guessed, frustration on the part of those same whaling interests over successive British Cabinets' refusal to annex New Zealand formally that had produced the public warning.[18] Anti-Russian sentiment largely resulted from a wave of indignation at the quashing of the 1830 Polish insurrection, not from anything attempted by the Russians in the East or the Pacific, but this merely modified the phrasing of that warning.[19] It is striking how quickly the "Polish sins" of Russia were applied to a South Pacific setting, both by people in England and by colonists in Hobart Town and Sydney. Local feeling on the matters of New Zealand and the trampled Polish liberties induced the *Sydney Gazette* both to reprint the Hobart caution, with its reference to Russia, and to praise its circumspection.[20]

Did the sounders of these anti-Russian sirens truly fear that the Russians would attempt to found a colony in Australasia and that Russia's flag would fly over New Zealand? Hardly so. Russia was a serviceable bogey—one with naval capabilities, imperial ambitions, and the worst of public images in London and the colonies in 1831.[21] It is significant, nevertheless, that Russian vessels and colonial designs were mentioned at so early a date[22] in the same breath as New Zealand and in the absence of a formal British presence in those seas. The Russian Bear had already assumed its special role: that of a bogey, ever present as an instrument of argument or policy, ever invisible.[23]

Part Three

THE AUSTRAL ISLANDS

The Austral Islands

Tubuai Islands or Austral Islands, volcanic group, S. Pacific, c.330 mi. S. of Society Isls; 21°45'-23°50'S. 147°40'-154°30'W. Consist of 4 isls. (Rimatara, Rurutu, Raivavae, Tubuai) and 1 uninhabited atoll (Maria Island). Tubuai . . . was discovered 1777 by Capt. Cook, annexed 1880 by France. Group is fertile and mountainous; has pandanus, ironwood, coconut trees, livestock. . . Polynesian natives. Tubuai Isls. Administration also governs Rapa (c.325 mi. SE of Tubuai group). (*Columbia Lippincott Gazetteer*, New York 1961: 1956)

The Austral Islands, sometimes called Tubuai. . . consist of five inhabited islands and several rocks lying due southwest and southeast of Tahiti . . . Rapa, the southernmost island, cannot grow some of the more tender plants which can be cultivated in the warmer climates to its north. Modern archaeological expeditions have disclosed that before European "discovery," the islands were heavily populated. Internal wars between 1818 and 1828 killed up to two thirds of the population, and Western diseases reduced it even further. (*Historical Dictionary of Oceania*, ed. R.D. Craig & F.P. King. London 1981: 14)

7

THE BELLINGSHAUSEN CONTACTS, 1820

Lying to the south of the Society Islands, the Tupuai or Austral group is on the cool edge of the southern tropic zone and thus was removed from the shipping routes between Cape Horn or New South Wales and Kamchatka or the Russian Northwest Coast, the normal routes of circumnavigation followed by the Russians. Four of the five high, fertile islands in the group—Rimatara, Rurutu, Tubuai, and Raivavae—form a necklace on the tropic of Capricorn. The fifth, visited briefly by *Vostok* under Bellingshausen and *Mirnyi* under M.P. Lazarev during the southern winter 1820, lies three hundred miles further south. It is Oparo, better known today as Rapa.[1] "This island was discovered by Vancouver, Dec. 22nd 1791, who sailed by it on his way to Tahiti, had some slight intercourse with the natives... Vancouver thought he saw on the tops of the hills fortifications (or pares) which had people in them walking to and fro. For many years very little was known of this island or its inhabitants."[2]

Vancouver's account of the island he believed was called Oparo or perhaps Oparra by its natives[3] was of special interest to Bellingshausen in 1819, when the Naval Ministry was considering the most useful movements of *Vostok* and *Mirnyi* through the tropics.[4] In southern winter there could be no exploration on the fringes of Antarctica, and even summer survey work among the ice floes would make demands on Russian seamen so severe that a physically less taxing summer cruise would be essential. In the first place, it was tantalizing in the context of the brief and wholly inconclusive nature of Vancouver's record. (*Had* the British seen the regional equivalent of the New Zealand *pa* or fort? Had the Oparans and the Maori a common culture?) Secondly, the island could conveniently be inspected on a passage from Port Jackson in Australia, which was the likeliest revictualling point of *Vostok* and *Mirnyi* in March or April 1820 at the close of an initial cruise clockwise from South America to Central Polynesia.[5] And third, other discoveries were possible in the Oparo area. Vancouver had by no means covered it as he made his way from Dusky Sound to the Societies in the teeth of rainy squalls. Bellingshausen's consciousness of Rapa was strengthened by his enforced but ethnographically important sojourn in New Zealand from 27 May to 3 June 1820. Well provisioned for a steady winter cruise across the Tuamotu Archipelago, where he proposed to complement the exploration and hydrography of Kotzebue,[6] Bellingshausen left Port Jackson by a course that would enable him to clear Three Kings Islands at New Zealand's northern tip. He quickly found, however, that winds were fickle and unhelpful in the Tasman Sea early in the southern winter. Day by day *Vostok* and *Mirnyi* struggled north but drifted east towards New Zealand; then both were abruptly hustled eastward by a storm and Bellingshausen found it prudent to repair to Cook's well-mapped Queen Charlotte Sound until the weather improved.[7] Like Vancouver almost thirty years before, the Russians thus found themselves faced with the necessity of making swift but useful passages to the Societies from South Island, New Zealand. Maori *pa* were much in evidence. *Vostok* carried a copy of Vancouver's text and *Atlas*. More than ever, Bellingshausen found it natural to take a look at Rapa.

High, buffeting winds and squalls of rain gave Bellingshausen and his people an uncomfortable, exhausting passage from New Zealand to the Australs. Giant waves drenched the *Vostok* until her carpenters, ingeniously using timber felled at Cook's Ship Cove in Queen Charlotte Sound, built up her sides.[8] Finally, at dawn on 29 June, Rapa was sighted. Sixteen miles off to the northeast, four lofty hills showed black, then grey, then greyish-green as the light improved. Mikhailov immediately sketched them.[9] Close enough though Rapa seemed, however, it was still beyond the ships' reach, and at this point the easterlies grew stronger, making further progress impossible. The Russians' frustration was relieved by the inhabitants of Rapa, Bellingshausen's hosts themselves: "Shortly after midday, craft appeared coming out to us from the shore . . . And we did not have long to wait, for soon they were near. There were 5, 6, or 7 men in each canoe. First they stopped, not coming right up to the sloop, and with much heat and volume they addressed a speech at us."[10]

It was essentially the standard Polynesian welcome that the Russians had already encountered from the Maori *hapu* in the Motuara Island–Ship Cove area a month before. As before, some individuals came cautiously aboard, pressed noses, and accepted Russian goods with open pleasure while the Russians, ever conscious of position and rank, honoured their chief with special treatment—an invitation to the captain's quarters, gifts of printed linen, an axe, and a mirror.[11] It was not long before Russian patience was tested to the limit by the natives' strong propensity for theft: "They... attempted to steal everything their hand fell on. Armed sentinels constantly watched them. One of the islanders who had been in the wardroom managed to get hold of the back of a chair and plunged with it directly into the ocean. As soon as our people spotted this, they aimed at him and he, taking fright, returned the stolen article. These people know the effect of firearms and are terrified of it: when cannon were fired on *Mirnyi,* they all threw themselves overboard."[12]

Bellingshausen's account of the 1820 Rapa visit is complemented by four other published texts, so that the Russian evidence is unusually rich. Besides brief remarks by Midshipman Pavel M. Novosil'skii of *Mirnyi,* dealing largely with an attempted theft on 30 June,[13] and even terser remarks by Leading Seaman Egor' Kiselev (whose journal was found in the ancient town of Suzdal' in the 1930s and first printed in 1941),[14] we have two accounts by *Vostok*'s astronomer, Simonov. One, popular in tone and squarely based on a lecture given at Kazan' University on 7 July 1822, is entitled "A Word on the Successes of the Voyage of the Sloops *Vostok* and *Mirnyi.*"[15] Its "Rapa section" amounts to a single paragraph of two hundred words.[16] The other is, by comparison, an important narrative. Entitled "The sloops *Vostok* and *Mirnyi,* or a Voyage of the Russians in the Southern Icy Ocean and Around the World," and printed with some omissions in 1951, it was Simonov's most serious attempt to leave a description of his personal experiences in *Vostok* as a young scholar seconded to the Navy.[17] Professional success left him too little time to polish and publish it, as he had planned for fifteen years, and "the manuscript broke off with an account of the second passage through Antarctica, of 1821."[18] The holograph remains in the keeping of Kazan' State University. Here are extracts from Simonov's manuscript bearing on Rapa and its people's first encounter with the Russians.[19]

These islanders soon agreed to come aboard, presenting us with sea crabs and some sort of fermented dough. In return we gave them things both rare and useful to them. Taking note of our generosity, they then began to beg for presents: they would part with their crabs only in exchange for something else. And when there remained only a few of the wares they had brought out, they formed pairs and tore a single crayfish in half, each man hoping to exchange his half-crayfish for something!... One islander was wearing a sash made of bark, and he was overjoyed to exchange it for a fish-hook. All, in truth, were accepting any trifles whatever with evident signs of joy; and when I passed a little piece of paper through the ear of one islander, to replace the blade of grass that had been there, they all started to ask

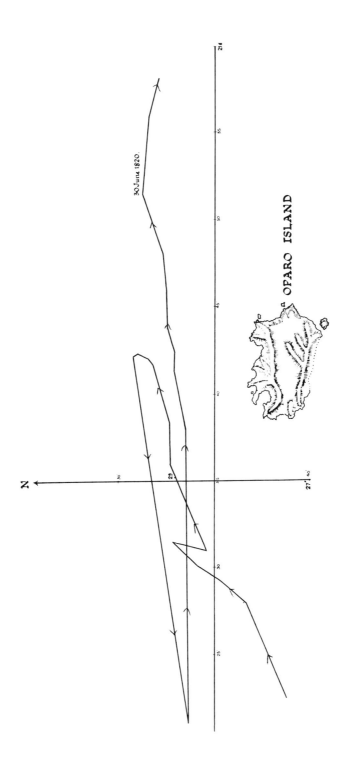

N

30 June 1820.

OPARO ISLAND

27°

Map 7 The movements of *Vostok* and *Mirnyi* past Rapa or Oparo Island, 29-30 June 1820

me for similar decorations. Their chief was given an axe, a bottle, a tumbler, and two bronze medals. Others were given, as gifts or in exchange for crayfish, earrings, rings, and trifles of that sort; but they prized iron above everything else. One of our guests presented the captain with a root like a radish, saying, as he handed it to him, *Ma hippka*. He doubtless wished to say that from such roots they prepared their pickled dough for future use. The natives of the Society Islands prepare a similar dough from breadfruit and call it *Mahi*. This root was cooked there in our presence, and we found it very nutritious and flavourful. But the pickled dough of these islanders was repulsive in its bitter taste and odour, which recalled that of the Tartars' fermented mare's milk or *koumis*. The dough carried out to us from Oparo Island was of two sorts: one was green and seemed old, the other was white and most likely fresh.[20]

As was obvious from their robust physiques and healthy air, these islanders had other food than sourdough and crabs. "Their average height appeared to be 2 *arshin*, 6 *vershki* [5'7''] and the average breadth across the shoulders—more than 10 *vershki* [18'']. In form, the face was not very different from a European's, but the face and body tone were bronze" (Simonov). "The islanders coming out to the sloop were generally of middling build but some were quite tall; in the main, they were well formed and of solid build. Many men were stout. They were quick and agile in their movements" (Bellingshausen). "The Oparans proved to be well-proportioned and of pleasant appearance, with lively black eyes. Apart from the usual girdle, they were naked; the colour of the face and torso was bronze" (Novosil'skii). "No clothes and swimming in the water like fish; they feed themselves on earthbread and are a pretty healthy-looking lot" (Kiselev).[21] Dark brown- or hazel-eyed and curly-haired, they went unshaven but occasionally cut their hair "like Russian peasants," straight all round. The presence of robust old men with grey hair suggested that their diet was adequate. The Rapa Islanders were not tattooed like the Maori. One adolescent had blue eyes and a hooked nose. Light-skinned, he struck the Russians as a half-caste and was well sketched by Mikhailov.[22] Besides their own bark girdles, crabs, and roots, these early visitors brought little out to the *Vostok* but "soaked bast cords round the neck" and "dried gourds, nowhere cut through."[23] The Russians did not understand the latter's use but duly stowed them. Certain islanders seemed almost desperate to get the last possible item from the Russians while they stayed: "making faces and stretching out the hand, they managed to amuse the sailors and so obtain European trifles from them."[24] Bellingshausen and his people were repeatedly invited to repair to the island, where they might succeed in getting hens, fresh fish, or pigs, which they had earlier requested unsuccessfully.[25] But it was judged to be too risky as the wind blew from the east, making *Vostok*'s closer approach impossible.

From a distance of perhaps four miles, Rapa struck Mikhailov and Simonov as being like Teneriffe in miniature. Sharp-peaked hills, bare towards their summits, glowed deep green towards the base; and on the northeast side the Russians saw a waterfall and "fortifications built on hills, with narrow paths leading towards them." In the Russians' view, these indicated that the Rapans—who could well have lived in peace, since they were not troubled by neighbours—were familiar with civil strife and needed strong places of refuge in emergencies.[26] Places bare of forest had a greenish-yellow look, "and on the north shore there were small squares raked up, completely red in colour, most likely from red ochre."[27] Through their telescopes, the Russians saw no huts, or other signs of ordered social life, or even women. What they did see, in the way of craft and clothing, indicated that the islanders were on a culturally lower level than the Maori—"but higher, certainly, than the New Hollanders."[28]

On the first day of the visit, fifteen craft brought eighty natives out to wonder at the sloops' dimensions, to trade, and to steal. On the second day, the numbers rose to twenty-two and 110 or so.[29] Frustrated by the Russian guards and fearful of their weaponry, the natives nonetheless took what they could, and this produced an international crisis on *Mirnyi*. A native on her foredeck managed to pull an iron rod from a ropeway, plunging with it into the sea. Instantaneously, all the other natives leapt for safety, but a solitary old man was too slow and was seized by the Russians and detained as security for the iron rod's return.[30] After a good deal of playacting, the crisis was resolved. Lazarev freed his hostage, even giving him a nail, though he thought it almost certain that the man had been a party to premeditated theft. Like Bellingshausen, he was anxious to avoid unnecessary bloodshed. Leading Seaman Kiselev was not impressed: "On this island," he wrote tartly, "there were quantities of savages, and a thieving people too. They steal a nail as soon as look at it."[31]

Bellingshausen, Simonov, Mikhailov, and Novosil'skii leave a good description of the Rapa canoe of the immediate post-contact period. Such evidence combines with Russian records of canoes at Easter Island, the Tuamotu Archipelago, Hawaii, the Marquesas Islands, the Societies, the Northern Cooks, New Zealand, and Tahiti to comprise a large but hitherto neglected contribution to the study of canoe making and use in Polynesia in the early nineteenth century. These data merit the attention of cultural historians, descendants of Sir Peter Buck and Haddon and Hornell. It is inexcusable that they are totally neglected in contemporary overviews of Polynesian navigation and related arts.[32] Here is Bellingshausen's thumbnail sketch of Rapan craft:

> Probably because the island lacked timber of sufficient width, the canoes were constructed from a number of planks tied together with cords woven from bark fibre. Several were twenty-five feet in length but no broader than one foot, two inches. Along one side of the craft, on booms, lay a beam three and a half inches thick and sharpened at both ends so as to resemble a boat. This served as a balancer. Because of the narrowness of the craft here, stout islanders do not sit in them. Instead, little planks are attached here and there, on which such natives can more comfortably be seated. Mr. Lazarev presented a model of such a craft to the museum of the Admiralty Department. The paddles and bailers were like New Zealand ones, only the hafts had no carving on them whatever.[33]

Landsman though he was, Simonov took note of the structure of the canoes' outriggers. An examination of New Zealand *waka taua* and *waka tete* had sharpened his eye for such detail.[34]

> Such narrow yet rather long craft cannot be very stable in the water and would easily enough tip upside down. It is to prevent such undesirable accidents that beams are tied to one side of the canoe. These are sticks, tied athwart in several places; they hang down over the water surface, and poles of equal length are attached underneath to their ends, vertically. To these, in turn, are attached a quite long horizontal pole. Immersed in the sea at a shallow depth, this does not permit the craft to overturn... On some large craft, we saw double beams protruding on either side and dipping into the sea. The natives also had double craft, which had no need of such beams, since the two hulls, tied together, support each other. It must be observed, however, that in general the Oparans are far behind the New Zealanders in the art of canoe building, as in other arts and crafts. No carved work embellished the Oparans' canoes, nor did any materials cover their bodies.[35]

As a youth in 1804, Bellingshausen had been oppressed by the persistent yelling and commotion of the Nukuhivans, and now, at Rapa, he was distressed by "a wildness and unruliness perceptible in all the facial features, all the movements" of his hosts.[36] Joy was expressed by high-pitched shrieks, and most Rapans had deep and booming voices. So, at least, it seemed after *Vostok*'s decks had swarmed with the islanders for three exhausting hours.

Rapa's geographical position was reckoned independently from *Vostok* and *Mirnyi*. Its latitude was fixed as 27°37'45''S (*Vostok*) or 27°36'40''S (*Mirnyi*); its longitude at 144°14'55''W and 144°25'15''W, respectively. These coordinates agreed within a few minutes with those recorded by Vancouver. Circumnavigating Rapa, Bellingshausen reckoned its circumference as fifteen miles and its greatest length as six. Warning the natives that he intended to go northward, Bellingshausen filled his sails at approximately 3:00 PM on 30 June 1820. All but one of the islanders at once leapt overboard. This man, it seemed, had fallen out with his compatriots and chose to remain aboard *Vostok* and leave his island. For a while, the entreaties and the tears of his countrymen were ineffectual, but finally he too plunged overboard.[37] Under a steady wind and cloudless sky, the Russians pressed northeast, reaching 27°36'S, 143°43'W by dusk.

As he left Rapa, Bellingshausen had his Arrowsmith world map before him. *Vostok* passed through the place where Arrowsmith, following Bass, had marked "Las Quatras Coronadas Island," seen by Quiros on 4 February 1606.[38] No land was spotted. Still remembering the Rapa silhouette, replete with four craggy peaks, and lacking data on the true route of *San Pablo* and *San Pedro* from Callao to the Gilberts, Bellingshausen wrongly posited that Quiros had in fact passed through the Austral group almost two centuries before Vancouver in *Discovery*.[39] "Las Quatras Coronadas" (or "Los Cuatro Coronadas") was actually in the Tuamotu Archipelago, most probably the Actaeons. "La Encarnación," also discussed by Bellingshausen in connection with the Bass-Arrowsmith reckonings, was almost certainly Ducie Island, far away to the northeast.[40] It was not often that the Russian ventured firm, and wrong, opinions on such a matter.

On comparing Vancouver's (1791) and the Russians' (1820) evidence for Rapa, one is struck by the consistency and not by the element of change. In 1820, as in 1791, the natives boarded cautiously, but "made no scruple, even with some force, to take articles of iron."[41] As before, they were curious, strong, largely unarmed; and as before, they had unusually long, narrow canoes (30 in 1791, 23 in 1820). British and Russian evidence of Rapan dress and ornament, behaviour, and canoes tally entirely, suggesting little European contact or influence in the intervening years. Perhaps the Russian ships were visited by slightly fewer craft, among which large double-canoes with room enough for "twenty-five to thirty men'' were less in evidence than earlier.[42] Perhaps those visitors were fewer than the three hundred or so who had examined *Discovery*. But such a difference was easily explained by civil strife, to which the Russian and the British evidence of *pa* (''fortified places resembling redoubts,'' with overhanging palisades and even blockhouses)[43] clearly pointed. Vancouver's men had spotted slings, spears, and clubs in the canoes that met *Discovery*.[44] A period of tension and hostilities would have reduced the time and local inclination to engage in wood carving or other crafts. In ''Chief Korie's'' time the prows of Rapan war canoes (large double craft with high and elevated sterns) had had ''some little ornament.''[45] By 1820 ornamental carving was no longer seen. Oral tradition in the Austral Islands, as recorded by the French historian A.C. Eugène Caillot during the 1920s, lends support to Russian evidence of warfare in the early 1800s.[46] In the Tuamotus, too, the Russian visitors saw signs of tribal clashes.[47] There, however, as at Motuara Island in Queen Charlotte Sound, it was inter-island warfare that caused death and exile. On Rapa, war was locally produced.

Bellingshausen's consciousness of Rapa and of the Australs to its north was reinforced during the course of his revictualling, watering, and instrument-correcting visit to Tahiti from 22 July to 27 July 1820. As he learned from the Reverend Henry Nott, the London Missionary Society had only lately spread its influence from Mo'orea to at least three of the Austral Islands: Tupuai, Rurutu, and Raivavae. The Tupuains' ancestors had moved there from Tahiti, so their tradition claimed. A few brave souls seized the chance to sail in *Daphne* (Captain Folger commanding) to Tahiti with a fresh cargo of Austral sandalwood in 1814. Having already had experience of European wealth and of the Europeans' God as a result of the *Bounty* mutineers' decision to form a settlement on Tupuai a quarter-century before, they hoped to tap the Christian missionaries for European goods and knowledge.[48] Their resolve was rewarded. The natives of Rurutu Island, first sighted by Cook on 14 August 1769, also took passage with the new sandalwood traders to Tahiti and Mo'orea, came in contact with the missionaries' message, and returned in 1816–17.[49] Such men were treated kindly on Tahiti by the missionaries and by King Pomare II and his family. Whereas the former saw them as souls to be saved, however, King Pomare saw political advantages. The Austral Islanders were after all the cousins of the Tahitians, and their islands boasted sandalwood and other salable commodities.

The Reverend Nott glossed over these political and economic considerations when he informed Bellingshausen that the king held sway on Tupuai and Raivavae (High) Islands in 1820. According to Bellingshausen, ''Pomare II added to his rule the island Raivavae, or High, shown in the Arrowsmith chart in Lat. 23°41'S. The occasion for the addition was a rumour which reached him that the inhabitants of Raivavae . . . were anxious to become his subjects. In November 1818 he left on board an American ship to visit the island. The rumour proved correct."[50] Pomare had indeed taken passage in the *Arab* under Captain Lewis, a New England merchantman, but only nine months before *Vostok*'s arrival on the scene and not two years earlier. He had indeed acquired power over Raivavae and adjacent Tupuai, but before the formalities could be concluded, he had been forced to intervene in civil wars then being fought by pagan chiefs who took no interest in his religion. This was difficult at first, as he was often drunk.[51] Determined that the progress of the mission and the king be presented to the Russians in a favourable light, Nott told the truth—but not the whole truth—of the Tupuaian episode. The Russian narrative thus has the secondary but useful function of providing a gauge by which ostensibly objective mission records may be judged.[52]

8

THE RUSSIAN TEXTS

I.M. SIMONOV, 1822 TEXT[1]

After twenty-four days we caught sight of the isolated island of Oparo, whose pointed mountains, craggy below, were covered by thick woods. Its natives did not delay in coming out to us in great numbers in their craft, came aboard the sloop, and brought us sea crayfish[2] and other foods of theirs.

Each man's first step on board was accompanied by wonder. Everything struck these people, who were not tall but were on the other hand unusually strong, completely bronze in skin tone, and quite without clothing. One of them wanted to remain with us. At the start, none of the urgings of his countrymen seemed able to shake him in his intention to sail to Europe; but love of his country finally prevailed: he threw himself into the sea from the height of the sloop, swimming towards the canoes of his comrades, which had already been left behind us some distance. We were forty-eight hours sailing near this island.[3]

I.M. SIMONOV, 1840s TEXT[4]

So, on 28 June, our sails filled by the trade wind bore us swiftly towards Oparo Island, discovered by Vancouver in 1791. At half past five the following morning, I myself spotted that mountainous and craggy island no more than twenty-eight versts off.[5] Oparo resembles Teneriffe in appearance, only it is far smaller. Its mountains rose up, narrow and sharp-ended, bare and rocky below but covered by thick woods towards the summits.[6] At noon, when we were not more than seven versts offshore, the natives spotted us and put out to sea in their craft, calling on us just as we were sitting down to lunch.[7]

These islanders soon agreed to come aboard, presenting us with sea crabs and some sort of fermented dough.[8] In return we gave them things both rare and useful to them. Taking note of our generosity, they then began to beg for presents: they would part with their crabs only in exchange for something else.[9] And when there remained only a few of the wares they had brought out, they formed pairs and tore a single crayfish in half, each man hoping to exchange his half-crayfish for something! They had, in fact, no other interesting or rare articles for us—neither clothing nor weaponry. One islander was wearing a sash made of bark, and he was overjoyed to exchange it for a fish-hook. All, in truth, were accepting any trifles whatever with evident signs of joy; and when I passed a little piece of paper through the ear of one islander, to replace the blade of grass that had been there, they all started to ask me for similar decorations. Their chief was given an axe, a bottle, a tumbler, and two bronze medals. Others were given, as gifts or in exchange for crayfish, earrings, rings, and trifles of that sort; but they prized iron above everything else.[10] One of our guests presented the captain with a root like a radish, saying, as he handed it to him, *Ma hippka*.[11] He doubtless wished to say that from such roots they prepared their pickled dough for future use. The natives of the Society Islands prepare a similar dough from breadfruit and call it *Mahi*. This root was cooked there in our presence, and we found it very nutritious and flavourful.[12] But the pickled dough of these islanders was repulsive in its bitter taste and odour, which recalled that of the Tartars' fermented mare's milk of *koumis*. The dough carried out to us from Oparo Island was of two sorts: one was green and seemed old, the other was white and most likely fresh.

For the most part, the natives of Oparo Island are of medium build, but pretty plump, solid, and wide-shouldered. They must be a powerful people. By my measurements, their average height was 2 *arshin* and 6 *vershki* [5'7''], the average width across the shoulders more than 10 *vershki* [18'']. The shape of their face differed very little from a European's, but the colour of face and body alike was bronze. They have aquiline noses but not long ones, and their lips are ordinary; they have dark brown eyes and black and fairly curly hair, though some have completely straight hair—the hair is cut as our Russian peasants cut it. Their beards are small but quite thick. Our seamen called them "doughboys." We saw amongst them some very aged and some grey-haired men, a sign of longevity.[13]

Wildness and an unbridled nature was noticeable in all their features and all their movements. They expressed their joy with a furious yell. Their voices were deep and thick. They swim with such ease that water seems to be their natural element; but their craft are so narrow that only one man can sit athwart them. On this first day of the visit, twenty-three craft surrounded us, each one containing no less than five men. Such narrow but rather long craft cannot be steady in the water and in fact capsize very easily. It is to avert such undesirable occurrences that outriggers are attached to them, on one side.

These outriggers consist of poles placed across the craft at several places.[14] The poles hang out over the surface of the sea. To their extremities are lashed, vertically, other sticks of equal length; and to the ends of these is attached a long pole, which is parallel to the craft's length and sinks slightly into the water, thus preventing the craft from overturning on the side of the balancer. (This pole, being lighter than water, supports the equipoise of the craft; and its weight makes it impossible for the craft to capsize on the other side.) On large canoes, we observed double outriggers, sinking into the sea on both sides of the craft. And there were also double canoes that had no need of outriggers, since the two hulls were tied together and so supported each other. It must be remarked in general terms, however, that the Oparo natives are far behind the New Zealanders in the art of canoe building as in other arts and crafts: no carving whatever embellished the canoes of Oparo Islanders, nor did any materials cover their bodies. We saw only a few sashes or girdles made from tree bark or grass; other natives had bast twine around the neck.[15] Of all the articles brought out to us from Oparo, the most remarkable was a dried pumpkin which had nowhere been cut through. Captain Bellingshausen acquired it by barter, but we do not know for what purpose it had been intended.[16]

When the natives returned home, they did not give themselves the trouble of descending the ship's ladder, but cast themselves, one at a time, from the deck into the sea, then simply reached their craft by swimming to them.

On the morning of the next day our guests came out from the shore in the same attire, in practically the same numbers, and greeted us with the same ceremony as before, bringing noses together. One of them, who had six fingers on his right hand and red hair, had a thoroughly European appearance. He was about eighteen years old and shook with fear as his portrait was being drawn.[17] In general, all the natives of Oparo Island feared us. Despite this, however, their every step revealed a passion for thievery—though they did not succeed in practicing that art on *us*. In the first place, sentries with loaded guns were watching them as they moved about and, in the second, the threats of shooting and the retention of their elders on board ship obliged them immediately to surrender what they had just stolen.

Having completed a hydrographic survey,[18] the captain told our guests that we should be moving further north. One after another, the islanders cast themselves into the ocean and dispersed in their craft. But they were in a highly agitated state as they took their leave of us, because one of their countrymen had resolved to stay with us on the sloop. Neither persuasions, nor force, nor tears, which I myself saw in the eyes of one native who was attempting to dissuade him, could break his firm resolution to remain. At first, the man had tried to shelter himself from the arguments of his countrymen by simply hiding in the sloop's interior; but our sentries, not understanding his motives and fearing lest he steal something, had not let him onto the lower deck. So then he stood face to face with his own people and announced his intention to remain with us, point-blank. The captain and officers of the sloop had not been persuading him to do this, nor did they now attempt to dissuade him: we did not interfere at all in his argument with his countrymen and, finally, they too left him with us. Their will could not overcome the stubborn desire of their enterprising comrade, who, for his part, long looked back at his vanishing friends. In the end, it transpired that his own will power could not vanquish love of the fatherland, and he threw himself into the sea and set off after his own people towards the shore. They saw him from afar and took him into a canoe. "Even the smoke of the fatherland is pleasant/And sweet to us."[19]

We had not been ashore on Oparo Island and we had seen neither the huts, nor the women, nor the family life of its natives. Even so, one could tell from a single glance at those islanders who had visited us that their domestic culture was on a lower plane than the New Zealanders', but on a higher one no doubt than the New Hollanders'. Oparo Island is about fifteen miles in circumference. Though an unhelpful and feeble wind prevented our approaching it closer than seven and three-quarter versts,[20] we could quite clearly see its pointed heights, a waterfall rushing over cliffs on its northeastern side, and fortifications built on the hills, with narrow paths leading up to them.[21] These fortifications show that, small though the total population of Oparo Island may be, it consists of at least two mutually hostile tribes.[22] They cannot fear external enemies, since their isle is remote from all other South Sea Islands and lies at a distance inaccessible, given the state of the weak paddled flotillas of Oceania of the day. The geographers reckon the island to have fifteen hundred inhabitants.[23] It lies in latitude 27°38′S, longitude 126°35′W.[24]

P.M. NOVOSIL'SKII

At length, on 10 June, we succeeded in leaving that unhappy bay[25] and departing from the shores of New Zealand. We steered a course for Oparo

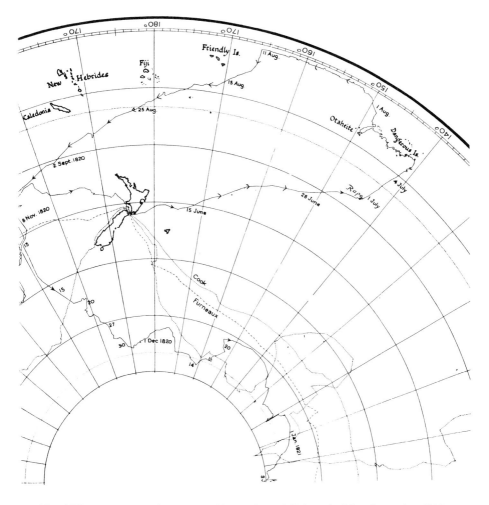

Map 8 The movements of *Vostok* and *Mirnyi* through Polynesia, May-September 1820

Island, situated further south than tropical Polynesia. Changeable and sometimes contrary winds slowed our progress, so that Oparo revealed it-self only at dawn on 29 June. Fifteen craft immediately came out to meet us, each containing five, six, or seven men. We were slightly further off-shore, so these craft went only to the *Vostok*.

On 30 June we moved closer in to the island. The savages did not delay in coming out to us in numerous craft. Coming up on deck, they would greet us by touching noses. These Oparans were slender and of pleasant appearance, with lively black eyes. They were quite naked except for the usual belt, and had bronze facial and body tone. They proved very in-quisitive and would examine every object with great attention, even mea-suring it, as if they did not trust their own eyes. They paced out the length and breadth of the deck. In addition to being curious, however, they were inclined to theft. One islander took from the foredeck an iron sector with the ladder-rope on it,[26] and plunged with it into the water. Instantaneously, all the other islanders followed his example, as if by signal, only one old man not succeeding, because of his advanced years, in casting himself overboard, and so being held. This old man was given to understand that he would not be released until the stolen sector were returned, and we pointed out to him the canoe in which it had been hidden. The old man called the canoe nearer and, having exchanged words with the Oparans seated in it, assured us there was nothing in that craft. Seeing that the old man was not being released from the sloop, the native who had stolen the iron sector, having taken the ladder-rope out [of it], asked: is this the thing they want? Then he rummaged in his canoe and showed us first a broken basket, then a piece of reed. Then, raising his hands, he made signs to the effect that he had nothing else there. But eventually, con-vinced that all his cunning was to no effect and that the captive elder would not be liberated, he was obliged, albeit most unwillingly, to bring the stolen article and surrender it to the sloop. The old man and other is-landers began forthwith to scold the guilty party; but it was easy enough to see that all this was a mere comedy, and that the captured elder was, if not the principal culprit in all this, at least not opposed to the theft. Still, the captain pretended he did not suspect the old man of anything and, on letting him go, gave him a nail. The islanders brought us taro root, which was like potato in flavour.

Oparo Island is six miles long and three and a half wide. It is mountain-ous, the lower slopes and inclines of mountains being covered with forest. A waterfall descends from the top of one mountain to the sea,[27] and fortifications of some sort were visible on others. It was apparent that the islanders, having no external foes, waged war among themselves. The large craft on which the Oparans came out to us were up to twenty-five feet long, but only a foot broad.[28] For stability in agitated seas, they had been fitted with outriggers consisting of beams sharpened at both ends; these beams lay in the water parallel to the keel of the canoe, being joined to the latter by transverse poles.

F.F. BELLINGSHAUSEN[29]

At 6:00 AM on 29 June, just as day broke, we sighted Oparo Island sixteen miles off, N 88°E. It looked rather high and seemed to have four separate mountains or peaks.[30] But the wind now shifted to the eastward and no longer assisted us in our approach to the island. I still hoped to reach it by beating to windward, but the natives themselves forestalled us: we saw their canoes coming off from the shore before 1:00 PM and I gave orders for the main topsails to be furled.[31] We had not long to wait, for the canoes, each manned by five, six, or seven men, approached us with some speed. They stopped first a little way off from the sloop, one of them delivering a passionate speech in a loud voice.[32] I showed them a few objects and made signs that they should approach, and they at once resolved to come on board. I greeted the most important among them by touching noses and gave them a few gifts. Some time later a very tall, well-built, thick-set man came aboard. Both his appearance and the respect shown him by all the other natives declared him to be the chief; and so he introduced himself to us.[33] I invited him to come into the cabin, which at first he was unwilling to do, but after a while he did enter it— and was delighted by all he saw. I now presented him with an axe, a mirror, and a few *arshin*s of printed linen.[34]

The Oparo Islanders showed a great tendency toward theft, doing their best to seize anything within reach. Our sentries, who had loaded guns, were obliged to keep a keen watch on them. One of the islanders, finding himself in the wardroom, managed to steal the back of a chair and vanished into the water with it. As soon as we had spotted this, we levelled a gun at him. The man was very frightened and returned the stolen object at once. It was obvious that the effect of firearms was familiar to these people and inspired them with dread. When the *Mirnyi* fired her guns, they all plunged from the deck. But they had brought nothing with them but shellfish, small taro roots, and some hard, stale dough that was wrapped in leaves ready for use. We bartered a few pails and water-scoops for these; and the natives immediately made use of the scoops to bail water out of their canoes. Having spent some time on board, our guests returned to shore: they had come out in fifteen craft. Mr. Lazarev was further offshore than we were, so the islanders did not pay him a visit. At 1:30 PM, when they had all left, we spread more canvas, altering course to westward, towards night, so as to draw near the island again next morning.

30 June. There was a very light southerly wind and a slight swell. Stars lit up the sky. We were unable, however, to get nearer than four and a half miles to the island during this day, the wind having fallen off. The natives again boarded us at about 8:00 AM as we lay directly off a bay.[35] The previous day I had asked them to bring out fish, swine, and hens, by pointing to those we still had aboard, but they had not fulfilled my wishes and now carried out only a small quantity of shellfish and taro. The islanders were astounded by the size of the sloop and by all the articles in her, which were new to them. One man measured the length of the upper deck by the span of his arms, lying down on the deck several times and stretching his arms out to their fullest extent. Then he measured the breadth of the quarterdeck. Our guests made no use of the companion ladder on leaving ship, simply plunging into the sea and then climbing onto their canoes. I presented them with assorted trifles, earrings, mirrors, knives, tinderboxes, and the like; every man received something.[36] This day, as many as twenty craft came out alongside us, and as our two ships were lying close to each other, the natives who had just received presents from me hastened off to Mr. Lazarev for the same purpose. And having been given a few articles by him, they then hurried back to *Vostok,* holding out their hands and indicating, by signs, that they had been given nothing at all! They remained aboard more than an hour, but then suddenly dived into the water, one after another. Only one individual stayed behind, and he begged to be permitted to remain with us, which I was willing for him to do. He stood on the gangway, watching his countrymen . . .

Oparo or Rapa Island was discovered by Captain Vancouver in the year 1791, on his voyage from Dusky Bay in the south of New Zealand to the Society Islands. He named it "Oparo" because the natives were constantly using the word.[37] Captain Vancouver did not find a suitable anchorage anywhere and we ourselves, because of the light and contrary winds, could not approach it closer than four and a half miles. But we did examine the island, which appears to be made up of ridges of steep and fairly high mountains, lying in an east-west direction. Low-lying areas and the feet of these mountains were wood-covered, bare parts being yellowish-red in colour. On the northern side, we observed small patches of light red, which were most likely red ochre.[38] A waterfall plunged over cliffs into the ocean on the northeastern shore; and on the northwestern side there is what appears to be a navigable bay.

Oparo Island is about 6 miles long along the parallel and some 3½ miles broad, with a 15-mile circumference. On the tops of some mountains stood structures that seemed to be forts, accessible only by small paths. We fixed the position of this island by observations, as follows: latitude 27°37'45''S, longitude 144°14'55''W (compass variation 5°21'E), from *Vostok;* latitude 27°36'40''S, longitude 144°25'15''W (compass variation 6°24'E), from *Mirnyi.* On 22 December 1791, Captain Vancouver had fixed the position in latitude 27°36'S, longitude 144°01'32''W, his variation reading being 5°40'E.

The islanders who boarded our sloops were mostly of middling height, but a few were quite tall. Almost all were powerfully built and many were stout. They were agile and quick in all their movements, with curly hair and bright black eyes. They did not shave their beard and their face and body were dark red in tone. Their features were agreeable and not disfigured by tattooing, as is the case with many South Sea Islanders. One of the Oparans, who was about seventeen or eighteen years old and slimly built, had light reddish hair, blue eyes, a rather aquiline nose, and the fair skin of Northern Europeans. One could hardly doubt that he was the offspring of an Oparo woman and some European visitor. Mr. Mikhailov made a very good sketch of this islander, and of some others too.[39] Wanting to receive gifts from us, these natives made various grimaces and stretched out their hands. This made the seamen laugh and give the natives some trifles of European manufacture. The islanders were constantly inviting us ashore, but it was risky to venture ashore from such a distance and a light headwind made it impossible for us to move closer in.

Since there are no other islands in the area, it would seem that the natives here, enjoying a fine climate and lacking none of the necessities of life, might well live in unbroken peace. However, fortified places on the summits of mountains, within which huts were visible, led us to conclude that these people were in fact divided into factions, had had reasons for breaking off friendly relations among themselves, and had thus been obliged to find refuge and protection in these forts.[40] We did not manage to examine any examples of their handiwork beyond the canoes in which they came out to visit us. These craft were made of planks bound together by ropes of the twisted fibres of tree bark, most likely because timber of sufficient thickness was lacking on the island.[41] Some of these canoes are as long as twenty-five feet, but they have a breadth of a mere fourteen inches. On one side they carry a beam about three and a half inches wide, which tapers at both extremities just like a little craft and enables the canoe itself to maintain its balance.[42] Such is the narrowness of the craft that it is impossible for the plump islanders even to sit down in them, so they attach boards across the hull at several places and sit on those in comfort. Mr. Lazarev obtained a model of one of these canoes for the Imperial Admiralty Department's museum.[43] The paddles and water-scoops used by these people much resemble those of the New Zealanders, except that the scoops are fitted with handles but lack carving.[44] The scoops of Oparo are more like those used by Europeans for bailing the water out of rowboats. We observed a few small white birds with forked tails.

As it was not worthwhile waiting for a fair wind to call at a little islet off the north shore of Oparo or to run into the bay situated on its north-western side[45] (where it looked as if there might be a good anchorage), I continued—once the natives had departed—on an easterly course. Holding that course until dusk, we reached latitude 27°36'30''S, longitude 143°43'W. The fine weather continued throughout this day, with a cloudless sky and a clear horizon. Had there existed any islands equal in elevation to Oparo Island, to the east or in any other direction, we would have sighted them at a distance of forty miles; but despite a good lookout at the topgallant masthead, nothing was seen.[46]

LEADING SEAMAN EGOR' KISELEV

29 June. Arrived at Oparo Island. On this island there are a great number[47] of savages and they are a thieving people: every man on the look out for a nail to steal. Twenty-two craft came out to us; no clothing, and they swim in the water just like fish. These people feed themselves with ground bread, and a healthy lot they are.[48]

9

REFLECTIONS ON
THE ETHNOGRAPHIC EVIDENCE

The Russian pictorial and narrative records of 1820 throw a useful light on the development of Rapan coasting craft (single-canoes) and point out the certainty of local warfare in that period. Among the drawings made by Pavel Mikhailov as the *Vostok* approached the island on 29 June was one of a single *kami'a* canoe. Numbered 23 in his original portfolio, it is reproduced here (Plate 20). It perfectly complements Simonov's word picture of such craft.

Mikhailov's illustration shows how very little the craft had changed at Rapa since Vancouver first observed them in 1791: still plank-built (for want of larger standing timber), still unusually narrow by contemporary Polynesian standards, they were evidently fitted with the upcurved stern and long projecting head that had so long characterized single-canoes in the Society and Marquesas Islands. From Mikhailov's drawing, it is also clear that, as James Hornell expresses it in his essential study of canoes in Oceania, such vessels "were constructed of short planks, sewn together with the local *nape*, here braided of hackled *kiekie*."[1] Information on the ancient Rapan craft being exiguous, Mikhailov's and Simonov's joint picture has the value of substantiating archaeology: "From the evidence afforded by old canoe planks found buried and in caves," observes Hornell further, "it is proved that the old canoes were largely if not entirely plank-built, being . . . about 1 foot wide. From one set of planks found in a taro patch at Akanaae, a local canoe-builder estimated that the hull length when put together must have been 40 feet."[2]

Rapan single canoes seen by the Russians differed in no essential way from those seen by Cook at Tubuai in 1777.[3] Nor, according to the Reverend William Ellis, who compared Tubuaian with Rapan craft, had changes occurred in the years immediately following Bellingshausen's brief call.[4] In this century, Rapa's plant-built craft were replaced by dugouts made from the introduced *tira* tree (*Melia azadirachia*). Yet more recently, these have given way to French-style boats, at least in Ahurei Bay and its vicinity.

Mikhailov's coastal sketches being marked with compass bearings, it is possible to identify, at least approximately, the location of physical features shown. His drawing of fortified places or *pa* has above it, in pencil, "29 June 1820," and below it "SE71°," that is S 71°E. From Bellingshausen's data on *Vostok*'s movements of that day, we infer that the *pa* stood on headlands near Tupuaki, Akananue, or possibly even Angaira'o Bay.

The Russians seem to have been offered taro prepared in an ancient manner: long stored uncooked in underground pits, then baked. Taro thus kept in underground pits was in former days a useful reserve for times of siege, such as the early 1800s were. The hardness of such taro was not lost in the baking.[5] The resulting foodstuff had a purplish hue.

Mikhailov's evidence for Rapan single-hulled canoes (*kami'a*) and for the brooding hilltop forts along the north shores of the island was of genuine historical significance and ethnographic value. Yet because it was not published with the Bellingshausen narrative in 1831, it played no role in the particularly sluggish growth of European knowledge of the Austral Island culture. A full century elapsed after the Russians' and the Reverend William Ellis's departures from the scene before a competent ethnologist named Stokes arrived on Rapa to investigate its social anthropology. Nor even in the early 1950s had a single archaeologist set foot there, to dig among the "blockhouses" and *pa* that George Vancouver and his officers believed that they had glimpsed so long before. Thus, the Norwegian expedition led by Thor Heyerdahl, which came to Rapa in the southern spring of 1956, came to an ethnological *tabula rasa* in the wake of the *Kon-Tiki*'s major triumph.[6] (Heyerdahl believed that drift voyages had taken place from Rapanui, better known as Easter Island, to its distant, speck-like namesake, Rapa-iti. And, in search of ethnological and other kinds of data to substantiate a theory of Polynesian migrants' spread with which few recognized authorities agreed, he had his colleagues dig at one "deserted city," Morongo Uta.) Heyerdahl had this to say, in *Aku-Aku* (1958), on the subject of Morongo Uta *pa*:

> But who had built this lofty dream castle, and its counterparts on all the other hill-tops? And what purpose had these buildings really served? No living soul on the island could tell us. When Captain Vancouver discovered this remote speck of land in 1791, he thought he

saw people running about on top of one of them. But he never went ashore to examine it ... After Ellis came Moerenhout. He praised Rapa Iti's strange mountain scenery, with its peaks that resembled towers, castles, and fortified Indian villages. But he too failed to go up and take a closer look ... No archaeologist had yet set foot on the island. When we stood looking over hill and valley, we knew we were in virgin country ... No one knew what we might find.[7]

What the Norwegians found was not a fort but an entire mountain village once inhabited by hundreds. For, ignoring rich and fertile valley floors, Rapa Islanders of other times had built their homes and found security on jagged precipices.[8] So they lived for generations in a state of constant vigilance and inter-tribal conflict. So the Russians found them still, in 1820.

Russian science has a deep sense of tradition. Topics, problems, and locales in which the Russians took an interest in other times are, not infrequently, reverted to by their compatriots, We see this in the long-term, special interest that Soviets have taken (and are taking) in the planet Venus. Lomonosov, after all, discovered Venus's several "rings," more than two centuries ago. We see it also in the way that certain point in Oceania – the Ratak Chain of Micronesia's Eastern Carolines, Oahu, Nukuhiva in the Washington-Marquesas Group – attracted Russian ships and captains, not in dozens certainly, but both persistently and potently throughout the nineteenth century. It is not therefore surprising that the Soviet authorities should, at the time of writing, 1988, be making plans to send a research ship to Rapa on her way south to Antarctica. The two permanent Soviet land stations on the fringes of that continent are called, in Bellingshausen's memory and for the more important purpose of reminding other nations of the relative antiquity of Russians' presence there, Vostok and Mirnyi. Once again, we see the working of the Russian principle: persist, endure, succeed.

Notes

ABBREVIATIONS

ANSSSR   Akademiia Nauk Soiuza Sovetskikh Sotsialisticheskikh Respublik (Academy of Sciences of the USSR)

AGO   Arkhiv Vsesoiuznogo Geograficheskogo Obshchestva SSSR (Archive of the All-Union Geographical Society, Leningrad)

BAN   Biblioteka Akademii Nauk (Library of the Academy of Sciences of the USSR, Leningrad)

BCHQ   *British Columbia Historical Quarterly*

DNB   *Dictionary of National Biography* (London, 1885–1912)

DNZ   *Dictionary of New Zealand Biography*, ed. G. Scholefield (Wellington 1940)

ES   *Entsiklopedicheskii slovar'*, ed. Andreevskii (St. P.)

HRA   *Historical Records of Australia, Series I* (Sydney 1921)

HRNSW   *Historical Records of New South Wales*

IVGO   *Izvestiia Vsesoiuznogo Geograficheskogo Obshchestva* (Proceedings of the All-Union Geographical Society)

JPS   *Journal of the Polynesian Society* (Wellington)

JRAHS   *Journal of the Royal Australian Historical Society* (Sydney)

L.   Leningrad

M.   Moscow

NZSJ   *New Zealand Slavonic Journal* (Wellington)

MM   *Mariner's Mirror*

MAE   Muzei Antropologii i Etnografii (Museum of Anthropology and Ethnography, Academy of Sciences, Leningrad)

LOAAN   Leningradskoe Otdelenie Arkhiva Akademii Nauk (Leningrad Division of the Archive of the Academy of Sciences)

OMS   *Obshchii Morskoi Spisok* (General Navy List, St. P. 1885–1907)

PSZRI   *Polnoe Sobranie Zakonov Rossiiskoi Imperii* (Complete Collection of the Laws of the Russian Empire, 1830–1916)

PRO   Public Record Office, London

PHR   *Pacific Historical Review*

RBS   *Russkii Biograficheskii Slovar'*, ed. Polovtsov, Modzalevskii (Russian Biographical Dictionary: St. P., 1896–1918)

razr.   *Razriad* (category)

ROGPB	Rukopisnyi Otdel Gosudarstvennoi Publichnoi Biblioteki (Manuscripts Division, State Public Library, Leningrad)
SEER	*Slavonic and East European Review* (London)
SMAE	*Sbornik Muzeia Antropologii i Etnografii* (Collection of the Museum of Anthropology and Ethnography)
SPB	*Sorevnovatel' Prosveshcheniia i Blagodeianiia* (Emulator of Enlightenment and Beneficence)
St. P.	St. Petersburg
TIIE	*Trudy Instituta Istorii Estestvoznaniia* (*Proceedings of the Institute for the History of Natural Science*)
TNZI	*Transactions of the New Zealand Institute* (Wellington, NZ)
TsGADA	Tsentral'nyi Gosudarstvennyi Arkhiv Drevnikh Aktov (Central State Archive of Ancient Acts, Moscow)
TsGALI	Tsentral'nyi Gosudarstvennyi Arkhiv Literatury i Iskusstva (Central State Archive of Literature and Art)
TsGIAE	Tsentral'nyi Gosudarstvennyi Istoricheskii Arkhiv Estonskoi SSR (Central State Historical Archive of the Estonian Republic, Tartu)
TsGIAL	Tsentral'nyi Gosudarstvennyi Istoricheskii Arkhiv v Leningrade (Central State Historical Archive in Leningrad)
TsGAVM	Tsentral'nyi Gosudarstvennyi Arkhiv Voenno-Morskogo Flota SSSR (Central State Naval Archive of the USSR)
TsVMM	Tsentral'nyi Voenno-Morskoi Muzei (Central Naval Museum, Old Stock Exchange, Leningrad)
ZAD	*Zapiski Admiralteiskago Departamenta* (Proceedings of the Admiralty Department)
ZMNP	*Zapiski Ministerstva Narodnogo Prosveshcheniia* (Proceedings of the Ministry of Education)
ZGDMM	*Zapiski Gidrograficheskogo Departamenta Morskogo Ministerstva* (Proceedings of the Hydrographic Department of the Naval Ministry
ZUKMS	*Zapiski Uchenogo Komiteta Morskago Shtaba* (*Proceedings of the Scientific Committee of the Naval Staff*)

CHAPTER ONE: PREPARATIONS FOR A VOYAGE

1 For surveys and original materials, see A.I. Andreev, *Russkie otkrytiia v Tikhom okeane i Severnoi Amerike v XVIII–XIX vekakh* (M.-L. 1944); S.B. Okun', *The Russian-American Company*, trans. C. Ginsburg (Cambridge, MA 1952); G.R. Barratt, *Russia in Pacific Waters, 1715–1825: A Survey of the Origins of Russia's Naval Presence in the North and South Pacific* (Vancouver 1981.)

2 Details in V.N. Berkh, *Khronologicheskaia istoriia otkrytiia Aleutskikh ostrovov* (St. P. 1823), pp. 70–72. See also S.R. Tompkins and M.L. Moorehead, "Russia's Approach to America: From Spanish Sources, 1761–75," *BCHQ*, 13 (1949): 235ff.

3 These matters are covered by G. Williams, *The British Search for the Northwest Passage in the Eighteenth Century* (London 1962), pp. 169–84, and W.L. Cook, *Flood Tide of Empire: Spain and the Pacific Northwest, 1543–1819* (London & New Haven 1973), ch. 4.

4 Cook, *Flood Tide of Empire*, pp. 69–84; Tompkins and Moorehead, "Russia's Approach," pp. 248–50).

5 See J.C. Beaglehole, ed., *The Journals of Captain James Cook: The Voyage of the "Resolution" and "Discovery," 1776–1780* (Cambridge 1967), 3:649–66, 1240; also appendix to vol. 4: "Cook and the Russians," contributed by Ia.M. Svet.

6 Beaglehole, *The Journals*, 3:lxxxix; G.R. Barratt, "The Russian Navy and New Holland," *JRAHS*, 64 (1979): 220–22; T. Armstrong, "Cook's Reputation in Russia," in R. Fisher and H. Johnston, eds., *Captain James Cook and His Times* (Vancouver 1979), pp. 128ff.

7 Beaglehole, *The Journals*, 3:714.

8 Ibid., pt. 2, pp. 1473–75; also F.W. Howay, *A List of Trading Vessels in the Maritime Fur Trade, 1785–1825*, ed. R.A. Pierce (Kingston, Ont. 1973), pp. 3–5.

9 S.D. Watrous, ed., *John Ledyard's Journey through Russia and Siberia, 1787–88* (Madison, WI 1966), 10.

10 Beaglehole, *The Journals*, 3:714.

11 Ibid., p. 1474; Martin Sauer, *An Account of a Geographical and Astronomical Expedition . . .* (London 1802), 1:5–12.

12 C. Vinicombe Penrose, *A Memoir of James Trevenen, 1760–1790*, ed. R.C. Anderson and C. Lloyd (London 1959), pp. 87–89.

13 Ibid., p. 90; also Barratt, "Russian Navy and New Holland," pp. 223–24.

14 Okun', *Russian-American Company*, pp. 16–17.

15 Details in Howay, *List of Trading Vessels*, pp. 3–5.

16 Cited in Barratt, *Russia in Pacific Waters*.

17 Vinicombe Penrose, *Memoir*, p. 96.

18 I.F. Kruzenshtern, *Puteshestvie vokrug sveta v 1803, 4, 5, i 1806 godakh na korabliakh Nadezhde i Neve* (St. P. 1809–12), pt. 1, pp. 345–58; K. Voenskii, "Russkoe posol'stvo v Iaponiiu v nachale XIX veka," *Russkaia starina*, 96 (St. P. 1895).

19 A.P. Sokolov, "Prigotovlenie krugosvetnoi ekspeditsii 1787 goda pod nachal'stvom Mulovskago," *ZGDMM*, 6 (1851): 168–87; L.I. Golenishchev-Kutuzov, *Predpriiatiia Imperatritsy Ekateriny II dlia puteshestviia vokrug sveta v 1786 godu* (St. P. 1840), pp. 12ff.; Cook, *Flood Tide of Empire*, pp. 115–16.

20 TsGAVMF, *fond* 172, *delo* 367, pp. 1–13. Also Okun', *Russian-American Company*, pp. 16–20.

21 TsGAVMF, *fond* 172, *delo* 367, pp. 320–22.

22 Andreev, *Russkie otkrytiia*, pp. 85ff.

23 Sokolov, "Prigotovlenie," pp. 173–78; *PSZRI*, 22: doc. 16530.

24 See M.S. Anderson, *Britain's Discovery of Russia, 1553–1815* (London 1958), ch. 2; also his article, "Great Britain and the Growth of the Russian Navy in the Eighteenth Century," *MM*, 42 (1956): no. 1, pp. 132–36.

25 *OMS*, 4: 406–8; also A.G. Cross, *By the Banks of the Thames: Russians in Eighteenth-Century Britain* (Newtonville, MA 1980), pp. 159–60.

26 TsGADA, *fond* Gosarkhiva, *razr.* 10, op. 3, *delo* 16, pp. 132–33.

27 Okun', *Russian-American Company,* p. 17; J.R. Gibson, *Feeding the Russian Fur Trade: Provisionment of the Okhotsk Seaboard . . . 1639–1856* (Madison, WI 1969), chs. 9–10.

28 Cross, *By the Banks of the Thames,* pp. 156–61; also his article, "Samuel Greig, Catherine the Great's Scottish Admiral," *MM,* 60 (1974): no. 3, pp. 251–66. R.C. Anderson's list of "British and American Officers in the Russian Navy," *MM,* 33 (1947) is flawed and incomplete but suggestive by its very length.

29 Okun', *Russian-American Company,* p. 14; Barratt, "Russian Navy and New Holland," p. 228.

30 On Golenishchev-Kutuzov's versions of Cook, see V.I. Sopikov, *Opyt Rossiiskoi bibliografii,* ed. Rogozhin (St. P. 1813; reprint by Holland House, London 1962), nos. 9206–8; also G.N. Gennadi, *Spravochnyi slovar' o russkikh pisateliakh i spisok russkikh knig s 1725 po 1825 god* (Berlin 1876–80), 1: 232–33.

31 See M.I. Belov, "Shestaia chast' sveta otkryta russkimi moriakami," *IVGO,* 90 (1962): 107–8; Armstrong, "Cook's Reputation in Russia," p. 125; Otto von Kotzebue, *A New Voyage Round the World in the Years 1823, 1824, 1825 and 1826* (London 1830), 2: 173. For relatively early criticism of Cook with regard to his treatment of native peoples, see M.I. Ratmanov, "Vyderzhki iz dnevnika krugosvetnogo puteshestviia na korable Nadezhda," *Iakhta* (St. P. 1876): nos. 16, 18.

32 A.J. von Kruzenshtern, *Voyage Round the World . . . ,* trans. R.B. Hoppner (London 1813), 1:190, 216; 2:203, 222; Otto von Kotzebue, *Voyage to the South Sea and to Beering's Strait . . .* (London 1821), 1:6. See also my study, *Bellingshausen: A Visit to New Zealand, 1820* (Palmerston North, NZ 1979), pp. 1–9, 13.

33 Kruzenshtern, *Puteshestvie,* 1: 16–19; V.V. Nevskii, *Pervoe puteshestvie Rossiian vokrug sveta* (L. 1951), pp. 25–27; *OMS,* 4 (1890): 163–67.

34 PRO Adm./1/498, cap. 370 (Murray to Stephen, 16 August 1794: re sailing of HMS *Thetis* for the North American station, etc.); F.F. Veselago, *Admiral Ivan Fedorovich Kruzenshtern* (St. P. 1869), pp. 7ff.; Barratt, *Russia in Pacific Waters,* pp. 107–10. On Lisianskii's sea actions, see E.L. Shteinberg, *Zhizneopisanie russkogo moreplavatelia Iuriia Lisianskogo* (L. 1950), pp. 74–76, 88–90, and I.F. Lisianskii, *Voyage Round the World . . .* (London 1814), pp. xvii–xviii.

35 *Materialy dlia istorii russkogo flota* (St. P. 1886), 11:40–43; V.A. Bilbasov, ed., *Arkhiv grafov Mordvinovykh* (St. P. 1902), 3:337–39.

36 Lisianskii's MSS journals of this period are held by TsVMM ("Zhurnal leitenanta Iuriia Lisianskago s 1793 po 1800 god," no. 9170/1938) and by TsGALI ("Zapiski leitenanta Iuriia Fedorovicha Lisianskago, vedennye im vo vremia sluzhby ego volonterom . . . ," *fond* 18-ogo veka, no. 5196, pp. 1–175). For Lisianskii's journey of 1795 through the United States (Boston, Washington, Philadelphia, etc.), see N.N. Bolkhovitinov, *Rossiia i SShA: stanovlenie otnoshenii, 1765–1815* (M. 1980), pp. 196–203.

37 Shteinberg, *Zhizneopisanie,* pp. 77–78; Nevskii, *Pervoe puteshestvie,* p. 33.

38 TsGALI, *fond* 18-ogo veka, no. 5196, pp. 41–42 (letter of January 1795).

39 Shteinberg, *Zhizneopisanie,* p. 79; Barratt, *Russia in Pacific Waters,* pp. 109–10.

40 J. Ralfe, *Naval Biography* (London 1828), 3:212 and 4: 98–99; W. James, *A Naval History of Great Britain from the Declaration of War by France . . .* (London 1822–26), 1:495; Lisianskii, *Voyage,* p. xviii. Kruzenshtern was almost captured by a French frigate

off the Irish coast, as he relates in an unpublished paper headed "O ekspeditsii frantsuzov v Irlandiiu v 1796 godu," held at AGO (Leningrad): *razr.* 119, *delo* 361.

41 Shteinberg, *Zhizneopisanie*, pp. 99–100; S. Ryden, *The Banks Collection: An Episode in Eighteenth-Century Anglo-Swedish Relations* (Stockholm 1965), pp. 67–68 (naval expeditions and the infancy of ethnography).

42 PRO Adm.1/1516, cap. 404 (Boyles to Nepean, 16 March 1797: re the sailing of HMS *Raisonnable* for Cape Colony with the Russians, etc.); *Vneshniaia politika Rossii XIX i nachala XX veka* (M. 1961–70), 2:297–98; L. Dermigny, *La Chine et l'Occident: Le commerce à Canton au XVIIIe siècle* (Paris 1964), 3:1240–42.

43 Kruzenshtern, *Puteshestvie*, 1:13. The vessel of 100 tons was *Caroline* (ex-*Dragon*, Captain Lay). Details in Howay, *List of Trading Vessels*, pp. 33–35.

44 Barratt, *Russia in Pacific Waters*, p. 111.

45 N.I. Turgenev, *Rossiia i russkie*, 3d ed. (M. 1915), pp. 90–92; Nevskii, *Pervoe puteshestvie*, pp. 35–37.

46 Kruzenshtern, *Puteshestvie*, 1:17; Bilbasov, *Arkhiv grafov Mordvinovykh*, 3:312.

47 Nevskii, *Pervoe puteshestvie*, p. 35; F.I. Shemelin, "Istoricheskoe izvestie o pervom puteshestvii Rossiian krugom sveta," *Russkii invalid* (St. P. 1823): no. 23.

48 Voenskii, "Russkoe posol'stvo," pp. 125–28.

49 Nevskii, *Pervoe puteshestvie*, p. 37; P. Tikhmenev, *Historical Review of the Formation of the Russian-American Company*, trans. D. Krenov (Seattle 1939–40), 1:121–23 (Company-Navy arrangements); V.G. Sirotkin, "Dokumenty o politike Rossii na Dal'nem Vostoke v nachale XIX veka," *Istoricheskie zapiski* (M. 1962): 87–88.

50 Kruzenshtern, *Puteshestvie*, 1: 2–3; Barratt, *Russia in Pacific Waters*, p. 115.

51 Further on this question, see Bibliography, Archival Material 1(b).

52 Nevskii, *Pervoe puteshestvie*, 57 n.

53 Voenskii, "Russkoe posol'stvo," p. 126; S. Novakovskii, *Iaponiia i Rossiia* (Tokyo 1918), pp. 77–79.

54 Notably Captain Vasilii M. Golovnin of the Russian Navy: see Barratt, *Russia in Pacific Waters*, p. 197.

55 Voenskii, "Russkoe posol'stvo," pp. 128ff.; G.A. Lensen, *The Russian Push toward Japan: Russo-Japanese Relations, 1697–1875* (Princeton 1959), pp. 126–27; Ratmanov, "Vyderzhki iz dnevnika," no. 22, p. 30.

56 Barratt, *Russia in Pacific Waters*, pp. 114–15; Nevskii, *Pervoe puteshestvie*, 54 n.

57 Barratt, *Russia in Pacific Waters*, p. 116.

58 Novakovskii, *Iaponiia i Rossiia*, pp. 74–77; Lensen, *The Russian Push*, pp. 144–45.

59 Kruzenshtern, *Puteshestvie*, 1:8.

60 Ibid., p. 2.

61 F.F. Veselago, *Kratkaia istoriia russkogo flota* (M. 1939), pp. 178–90. For further details of the officers who visited Hawaii in 1804, see N.A. Ivashintsev, *Russian Round-the-World Voyages from 1803 to 1849*, trans. G.R. Barratt (Kingston, Ont. 1980), pp. 112–13, and W. Lenz, ed., *Deutsch-Baltisches Biographisches Lexikon, 1710–1960* (Köln-Wien 1970): on V.N. BErkh (Berg), the Kotzebues, et al.

62 Kruzenshtern, *Puteshestvie*, 1:2–3.

63 Nevskii, *Pervoe puteshestvie*, pp. 57–59, 269–70.

64 Kruzenshtern, *Puteshestvie*, 1:13.

65 TsGIAL, *fond* 15, op. 1, *delo* 1, fols. 5ff.

66 Ibid., fols. 7–8.

67 B.N. Komissarov, *Grigorii Ivanovich Langsdorf* (L. 1975), pp. 15–16; Nevskii, *Pervoe puteshestvie*, p. 57; H. Plischke, *Johann Friedrich Blumenbachs Einfluss auf die Entdeckungsreisenden seiner Zeit* (Göttingen 1937), pp. 61–64.

68 TsGADA, *fond* 183, *delo* 89: "Ob otpravlenii iz Sankt-Peterburga morem na Vostochnyi okean . . . Rezanova." The South Pacific writings of other graduates of that Institution, e.g., Aleksei Rossiiskii's 1814 sketch of New South Wales ("Zhurnal shturmana Alekseia Rossiiskago . . . ," printed in *SPB* [1820]: no. 11, pp. 125–46; no. 12, pp. 246–56), make these exclusions seem regrettable, even despite Hörner's competence.

69 Nevskii, *Pervue puteshestvie*, pp. 269–70.

70 See Armstrong, "Cook's Reputation in Russia," pp. 121–25.

71 Kruzenshtern, *Voyage*, 1:190, 216; 2:203, 222.

72 Cook's orders with regard to science are to be found in Beaglehole, *The Journals*, 1:cclxxiii. They were unchanged for the second and third Pacific voyages. The Cook artefacts now in Leningrad are described in detail in L.G. Rozina, "Kollektsiia Dzhemsa Kuka v sobraniiakh Muzeia Antropologii i Etnografii," *SMAE*, 23 (1966). More recently, they have been discussed by Adrienne Kaeppler in several published papers.

73 M.V. Severgin, "Instruktsiia dlia puteshestviia okolo sveta . . . ," *Severnyi vestnik* (St. P. 1804): nos. 2–3. Zoological instructions were written in 1803 by Academician A.F. Sevastianov.

74 TsGIAL, *fond* 15, op. 1, *delo* 1, fol. 159.

75 Kruzenshtern, *Puteshestvie*, 1:5; LOAAN, *razr.* 4, op. 1, *delo* 800a (the appointment of Tilesius von Tilenau, his terms of service); *Vestnik Evropy* (St. P. 1803): 167–71 (contemporaneous reactions to the expeditionary aims, etc.).

76 Selective list in Nevskii, *Pervoe puteshestvie*, pp. 269–71.

77 N.P. Rezanov, "Pervoe puteshestvie Rossiian vokrug sveta, opisannoe N. Riazanovym . . . ," *Otechestvennye zapiski*, 12 (St. P. 1822): 211; Kruzenshtern, *Puteshestvie*, 1:35.

78 Komissarov, *Grigorii Ivanovich Langsdorf*, pp. 8–15.

79 Ibid., p. 19 (Banks's gifts to Langsdorf, etc.); Plischke, *Johann Friedrich Blumenbachs Einfluss*, ch. 1.

80 TsGAIE, *fond* 1414, op. 3, *delo* 3 (E.E. Levenshtern's account); A.S. Sgibnev, "Rezanov i Kruzenshtern," *Drevniaia i novaia Rossiia*, 1 (1877): no. 4; Voenskii, "Russkoe posol'stvo," pp. 127ff.

81 Lisianskii, *Puteshestvie*, 1:91–93; Kruzenshtern, *Puteshestvie*, 1:113.

82 G.H. Langsdorf, "Vypiska iz pis'ma k Akademiku Kraftu o Kamchatke," *Tekhnologicheskii Zhurnal*, 3 (St. P. 1805): pt. 2, pp. 156–57.

83 Lisianskii, *Puteshestvie*, 1:67; V.M. Golovnin, *Sochineniia* (St. P. 1864), 1:144; Iu. Shokal'skii, "Stoletie so vremeni otpravleniia russkoi antarkticheskoi ekspeditsii," *IVGO*, 60 (L. 1928): 183.

84 Nevskii, *Pervoe puteshestvie*, p. 98.

85 Lisianskii, *Puteshestvie*, 1:78–80.

86 Lisianskii, *Voyage*, pp. 49–50; Langsdorf, *Voyages and Travels*, 1:84; Korobitsyn, "Journal," pp. 148–49.

87 Lisianskii, *Voyage*, p. 50; on Lisianskii, see Shteinberg, *Zhizneopisanie*, chs. 1–3;

Nevskii, *Pervoe puteshestvie*, pp. 32–33; Barratt, *The Russian Discovery of Hawaii, 1804: The Ethnographic Records* (Honolulu 1987), pt. 2.

88 E. Marchand, *Voyage autour du monde* (Paris 1798–1800), p. 1; J. Machowski, *Island of Secrets*, trans. M. Michael (London 1975), pp. 57–58.

89 See Langsdorf, *Voyages and Travels*, 1: 85 n (his knowledge of "a work very little known," *Twee Jaarige Reyse* . . . , etc.); A. Sharp, ed., *The Journal of Jacob Roggeveen* (Oxford 1970), pp. 14–19; A. Métraux, *Easter Island*, trans. M. Bullock (London 1957), pp. 39–40; B.G. Corney, ed., *Voyage of Don Felipe Gonzalez to Easter Island in 1770–71*, (Cambridge 1908), p. 100. L. Wafer, *A New Voyage and Description of the Isthmus of Panama* (London 1699), pp. 214–15; W. Dampier, *A New Voyage Round the World*, 2d ed. (London 1697), 1:352.

90 Métraux, *Easter Island*, p. 29.

91 Kotzebue, *Voyage into the South Sea and Beering's Strait* (London 1821) 1:133–34.

92 Métraux, *Easter Island*, p. 39.

93 Sharp, *Journal of Jacob Roggeveen*, p. 95 (10 April 1722).

94 Ibid., pp. 96, 103.

95 Ibid., p. 102.

96 Ibid., p. 98; see also Corney, *Voyage*, pp. 100–2; and T. Heyerdahl and E.N. Ferdon, eds., *Archaeology of Easter Island*, vol. 1 of *Reports of the Norwegian Archaeological Expedition to Easter Island and the East Pacific* (New Mexico 1961).

97 Here and below I base my comments on Métraux's *The Ethnology of Easter Island*, (Honolulu 1940) and Scoresby Routledge's *The Mystery of Easter Island* (London 1919), with reference also the W.J. Thomson, *Te Pito te Henua; or Easter Island*, U.S. National Museum Annual Report, 1889, pt. 2; and J. Geiseler, *Die Oster-Insel* (Berlin 1883).

98 Corney, *Voyage*, pp. 104ff.

99 Beaglehole, *The Journals*, 1:122–24.

100 J.F. de G. La Pérouse, *Voyage autour du monde* (Paris 1797), 1: chs. 3–4.

101 Métraux, *Easter Island*, pp. 46–60.

102 Ibid., pp. 149–70; Kotzebue, *Voyage*, 1:139–40; Thomson, *Te Pito te Henua*, pp. 512ff. (260 *ahu* platforms, etc.).

103 N.N. Miklukho-Maklai, "Ostrova Rapa-nui, Pitkairn, i Mangareva," *Izvestiia Imperatorskago Russkago Geograficheskago Obshchestva*, 8 (St. P. 1873): 42–55; "Sur les Kohau-rongo-rongo de Rapa-Nui," *Izvestiia Imperatorskago Russkago Geograficheskago Obshchestva* (1892: French text).

104 Lisianskii, *Voyage*, p. 51; Korobitsyn, "Journal," p. 148; Nevskii, *Pervoe puteshestvie*, pp. 104–5.

105 Métraux, *Easter Island*, p. 61.

106 Korobitsyn, "Journal," p. 150.

107 Métraux, *Easter Island*, p. 130; also W. Wolff, *Island of Death* (New York 1973), passim, on the bird-man cult and bird symbolism.

108 Wolff, *Island*, pp. 8–9; Métraux, *Easter Island*, p. 40.

109 Wolff, *Island*, pp. 49–52 pl. 15; Routledge, *Mystery of Easter Island*, pp. 235–70 and "The Bird Cult of Easter Island," *Folklore*, 28 (London 1917): 354–55.

110 *SMAE*, 18:317ff.

111 Lisianskii, *Voyage*, p. 52.

112 Métraux, *Easter Island*, p. 152.

113 Anders Sparrman, *A Voyage Round the World with Captain James Cook* (London 1944), pp. 122–23; Beaglehole, *The Journals*, 2:344.

114 Métraux, *Easter Island*, p. 162.

115 Sharp, *Journal of Jacob Roggeveen*, pp. 98–99; Métraux, *Easter Island*, pp. 151–52; Beaglehole, *The Journals*, 2:344–45; Lisianskii, *Voyage*, p. 59.

116 Lisianskii, *Voyage*, p. 53; *Neva*'s movements are indicated on the map of Easter Island published in *Sobranie kart i risunkov* (1812).

117 Métraux, *Easter Island*, pp. 83–84.

118 Lisianskii, *Voyage*, p. 53.

119 Ibid., p. 52.

120 Métraux, *Easter Island*, p. 131; also Thomson, *Te Pito te Henua*, pp. 478–83 (the stone houses' functions).

121 Lisianskii, *Voyage*, p. 53.

122 See n. 114 and Métraux, *Easter Island*, pp. 40–42.

123 Lisianskii, *Voyage*, p. 54; Machowski, *Island of Secrets*, pp. 59–60.

124 Lisianskii, *Voyage*, pp. 54–55.

125 Métraux, *Easter Island*, pp. 70–71; Sharp, *Journal of Jacob Roggeveen*, pp. 101–2 & n. 2; Wolff, *Island*, p. 22.

126 See pl. 2.

127 Details in my *Russian Discovery of Hawaii*, pt. 2.

128 Archive ref.: AGO, *razr.* 99, op. 1, *delo* 141; see A.I. Andreev, intro. to *Russkie otkrytiia v Tikhom okeane i Severnoi Amerike v XVIII–XIX vekakh* (M. 1944). Trans. Carl Ginsburg as *Russian Discoveries in the Pacific and in North America in the Eighteenth and Nineteenth Centuries* (Ann Arbor: ACLS 1952). Korobitsyn's "Journal" is cited from this source.

129 Korobitsyn, "Journal," p. 150.

130 Lisianskii, *Voyage*, p. 57.

131 Ibid., p. 58; see also Sharp, *Journal of Jacob Roggeveen*, pp. 93, 104, and Heyerdahl and Ferdon, *Reports of the Norwegian Expedition*, 1:534–35 (ancient use of reed floats).

132 Lisianskii, *Voyage*, p. 58.

133 Korobitsyn, "Journal," p. 150.

134 Beaglehole, *The Journals*, 2:352; Routledge, *Mystery of Easter Island*, pp. 280–81; Wolff, *Island*, pp. 29–30. Soviet ethnology has dealt repeatedly with the question of "the Long-eared Men," e.g., in N.A. Butinov's "Korotkoukhie i dlinnoukhie na ostrove Paskhi," *Sovetskaia etnografiia*, 1 (M. 1960): 72–82 and A.M. Kondratov's "Kto zhe oni, 'dlinnoukhie'?" *Znanie-Sila* (M. 1966): bk. 2, pp. 18–22. Like the mystery of the Easter Island sacred script tablets (*rongo-rongo*), the matter was considered by Miklukho-Maklai, whose influence continues to be felt in the emphasis of Soviet ethnology and anthropology.

135 See Kotzebue, *Voyage*, 3:226.

136 Korobitsyn, "Journal," p. 150; Métraux, *Ethnology*, pp. 237–48.

137 Lisianskii, *Voyage*, p. 59.

138 Ibid., p. 58.

139 See p. 31.

140 Métraux, *Easter Island*, p. 79.

141 Korobitsyn, "Journal," p. 151; compare Beaglehole, *The Journals*, 2: 351.

142 Lisianskii, *Voyage*, p. 58.

143 Métraux, *Easter Island*, p. 63.

144 Lisianskii, *Voyage*, p. 56.

145 Sharp, *Journal of Jacob Roggeveen*, pp. 95–96.

146 Korobitsyn, "Journal," p. 151.

147 Métraux, *Easter Island*, pp. 74–75, and *Ethnology*, pp. 210–11; Sharp, *Journal of Jacob Roggeveen*, pp. 100–1; Routledge, *Mystery of Easter Island*, pp. 140–41.

148 Métraux, *Easter Island*, p. 75; Korobitsyn, "Journal," p. 151.

149 Sharp, *Journal of Jacob Roggeveen*, p. 101, n. 1.

150 Lisianskii, *Voyage*, p. 58; see also Wolff, *Island*, p. 22.

151 Lisianskii, *Voyage*, p. 59.

152 C.F. Behrens, *Histoire de l'expédition de trois vaisseaux, envoyés par la Compagnie des Indes Occidentales* ... (The Hague 1739), 1:134; Corney, *Voyage*, p. 97; Métraux, *Easter Island*, p. 41. Lisianskii's expectations rested in part on G. Forster's *Voyage Round the World* (London 1777), vol. 1 of which contained a lengthy section on Easter Island (pp. 551–602). Further on sexual relations with Russian and other visitors, see I.K. Fedorova, "Areoi na ostrove Paskhi," *Sovetskaia etnografiia* (M. 1966): no. 4, pp. 66–82.

153 Kotzebue, *Voyage*, 1:140.

154 Métraux, *Easter Island*, p. 42.

155 Lisianskii, *Voyage*, p. 57; La Pérouse, *Voyage autour du monde*, 2: 102; Métraux, *Easter Island*, pp. 65–66.

156 Lisianskii, *Voyage* pp. 56–57; compare Sharp, *Journal of Jacob Roggeveen*, pp. 97, 99–100 (*umu* cooking).

157 Lisianskii, *Voyage*, pp. 59–60.

158 F.M. Keesing, *The South Seas in the Modern World* (New York 1941), p. 306; Wolff, *Island*, p. 19; Métraux, *Easter Island*, pp. 63–64 (depopulation).

159 Barratt, *Russia in Pacific Waters*, pp. 138–40.

160 *Russkii invalid* (St. P. 1839): no. 31; Nevskii, *Pervoe puteshestvie*, p. 427.

161 Shteinberg, *Zhizneopisanie*, p. 209.

162 Piatidesiatiletie Rumiantsovskago Muzeia v Moskve, *1862–1912: Istoricheskii ocherk* (M. 1912), pp. 164–66; *Sbornik materialov dlia istorii Rumiantsovskago Muzeia* (M. 1882), bk. 1, pp. 108–17.

163 F. Russov, "Beiträge zur Geschichte der etnographischen und antropologischen Sammlungen ... ," *Sbornik Imperatorskogo Muzeia Antropologii i Etnografii* (St. P. 1900): 1; Barratt, *Bellingshausen*, pp. 130–31.

164 See N.A. Butinov and L.G. Rozina, "Nekotorye cherty samobytnoi kul'tury Maori," *SMAE*, 21 (L. 1963): 84–85.

164 Barratt, *Bellingshausen*, p. 106 (Maori artefacts in Russia, etc.).

166 See pp. 3–4.

167 Lisianskii, *Voyage*, p. 59.

168 *ZGDMM* (St. P. 1850): pt. 8, p. 144. Reprinted and annotated by A.P. Sókolov in his edition of *Russkaia morskaia biblioteka: period chetvertyi* (St. P. 1883), pp. 137–38.

169 P. Bartenev, ed., *Arkhiv kniazia Vorontsova* (M. 1870–95), 19:114–15 (letter of P.V. Chichagov to A.R. Vorontsov).
170 TsVMM, no. 9170–22zh (1938): "Ukaz ob otstavke Iu.F. Lisianskago"; see also *Ob-shchii morskoi spisok*, 4: 174 and the anonymous essay "Iu.F. Lisianskii," in *Morskoi sbornik* (St. P. 1894): no. 1.
171 *ZGDMM*, (1850): pt. 8, pp. 444–45.
172 See my *Russia in Pacific Waters*, ch. 9.
173 *Morskoi sbornik* (1894): no. 1; TsVMM, no. 9170–3 (1938): rough drafts of Lisianskii's letters to relatives and others, 1803–32; also Nevskii, *Pervoe puteshestvie*, pp. 192–94.
174 V.G. Belinskii, *Sobranie sochinenii v 3 tomakh*, ed. Golovenchenko (M. 1948), 3: 112.
175 *ZGDMM*, (1850): pt. 8 p.444.
176 Shteinberg, *Zhizneopisanie*, ch. 6.
177 This slander on Roggeveen was current throughout Europe: see Sharp, *Journal of Jacob Roggeveen*, pp. 91–97.
178 Langsdorf, *Voyages and Travels*, p. 84 (and 85 on 12-foot giants).
179 Ibid., p. 86.
180 I.K. Gorner, "O nekotorykh dostoprimechatel'nykh svoistvakh morskoi vody," *Tekhnologicheskii zhurnal*, 5 (St. P. 1820): pt. 3; Nevskii, *Pervoe puteshestvie*, p. 108.
181 Kotzebue's account of his voyage, *Puteshestvie v Iuzhnyi okean i v Beringov proliv . . . v 1815, 1816, 1817 i 1818 godakh na korable Riurike*, 3 pts. (St. P. 1821), appeared in English that same year. On the voyage, see Kotzebue, *Novoe puteshestvie*, pp. 5–8; Barratt, *Russia in Pacific Waters*, pp. 180–84; H.R. Friis, ed., *The Pacific Basin: A History of its Geographical Exploration* (New York 1967), pp. 191–92; Ivashintsev, *Russian Round-the-World Voyages*, pp. 23–31.
182 Mahr, *The Visit of the "Rurik" to San Francisco in 1816* (Stanford 1932) pp. 11–22; G. Menza, *Adelbert von Chamissos "Reise um die Welt mit der Romanzoffischen Entdeckungs-Expedition in den Jahren 1815–1818"* (Frankfurt am Main 1979); X. Brun, *Adelbert de Chamisso de Boncourt* (Lyon 1896), pp. 139–45, 211–18. Eschscholtz, on whom see Lenz, *Deutsch-Baltisches Biographisches Lexikon*, pp. 199–200, was the subject of a biography in 1975: T.A. Lukina, *Iogann Fridrikh Eshchol'ts* (Moscow).
183 Mahr, *Visit*, pp. 18–19.
184 TsGIAE (Tartu), *fond* 1414, op. 3, *delo* 42.
185 Mahr, *Visit*, p. 21.
186 Details in Brun, *Adelbert de Chamisso*, pp. 212ff.
187 Menza, *Adelbert von Chamissos*, pp. 52–55.
188 Chamisso, *Werke*, ed. Bartels (Leipzig 1836), 3:18. On Shishmarev, see Aleksei P. Lazarev, *Zapiski o plavanii voennogo shliupa Blagonamerennogo v Beringov proliv . . .* (M. 1950), pp. 29–30.
189 Further on the ethnography of *Riurik*, see my *Russian View of Honolulu, 1809–1826* (Ottawa 1988).
190 Kotzebue, *Voyage*, 1:133–36.
191 Chamisso, *Werke*, 1:115.
192 See Nevskii, *Pervoe puteshestvie*, p. 105, n.i.
193 Kotzebue, *Voyage*, 3:224–25 (Chamisso's "Remarks and Opinions": "Waihu, or Easter Island—Sala y Gomez").
194 Métraux, *Easter Island*, pp. 64–65.
195 Kotzebue, *Voyage*, 1:136–37.
196 Métraux, *Easter Island*, p. 71.
197 Kotzebue, *Voyage*, 3:225; Chamisso, *Werke*, 1:115–16.
198 Kotzebue, *Voyage*, p. 137. Henceforth the Kotzebue and Chamisso texts are complemented by that of Choris's *Vues et paysages des régions equinoxiales recueillis dans un Voyage autour du monde* (Paris 1826), pp. 17–18 (accompanying Plate ix, *Vue de l'Ile de Pâques*).
199 Kotzebue, *Voyage*, 1:137–38.
200 Ibid., 3:225.

201 Métraux, *Easter Island*, p. 70 and pl. 11; Wolff, *Island*, pl. 4.
202 Kotzebue, *Voyage*, 1:138.
203 Ibid., 3:225; Métraux, *Easter Island*, pp. 42–43.
204 Métraux, *Easter Island*, pp. 67–69, 71.
205 Kotzebue, *Voyage*, 3:225.
206 Ibid., 1:139; compare F.W. Beechey, *Narrative of a Voyage to the Pacific and Bering's Strait, in the Years 1825–26–27–28* (London 1831), 1:32ff.
207 Kotzebue, *Voyage*, 1:140; also Beaglehole, *The Journals*, 2:350–51.
208 Beechey, *Narrative of a Voyage*, 1:32; also Métraux, *Easter Island*, pp. 43–45; Barratt, *Bellingshausen*, pp. 144–47 (Maori *haka* described); Wolff, *Island*, p. 23 (dance to weaken an enemy).
209 Kotzebue, *Voyage*, 3:226.
210 Erroneously included with Hawaiian objects in Lisianskii's 1812 *Sobranie kart i risunkov* . . . , pl. 2a (see my *Russian Discovery of Hawaii*, pt. 4, b-c), and omitted from the list of Marquesan artefacts in Rozina, "Kollektsiia MAE po Markizskim ostrovam," *SMAE*, 21 (L. 1963): 110–19. Another specimen shown in Wolff, *Island*, pl. 6a.
211 Métraux, *Easter Island*, pp. 79–80.
212 Sharp, *Journal of Jacob Roggeveen*, p. 96.
213 Kotzebue, *Voyage*, 1:140; Sharp, *Journal of Jacob Roggeveen*, p. 97; Métraux, *Ethnology*, pp. 236ff.; Thomson, *Te Pito te Henua*, pp. 462–64.
214 Kotzebue, *Voyage*, 1:141.
215 Ibid., and 3:227.
216 Choris, *Vues et paysages des régions équinoxiales*, pls. 10–11.
217 See intro. to Choris's *Voyage pittoresque autour du monde* (Paris 1822); associated papers in TsGIAE, *fond* 1414, op. 3, *delo* 42. On Easter Island, *Vues et paysages*, pp. 17–18.
218 Kotzebue, *Voyage*, 1:319ff. On weaponry not seen in 1804 or 1816, Forster, *Voyage Round the World*, p. 476.
219 Kotzebue, *Voyage*, 1:352–53; R.A. Pierce, ed., *Russia's Hawaiian Adventure, 1815–1817* (Berkeley 1965), passim; F.W. Bradley, *The American Frontier in Hawaii*, pp. 38, 54.
220 Kotzebue, *Voyage*, 1:143.
221 Choris, *Vues et paysages*, p. 18.
222 See Machowski, *Island of Secrets*, pp. 63–64; V. Gartvig, *Chelovek i priroda na ostrovakh Velikogo okeana* (M. 1877), p. 79; Nevskii, *Pervoe puteshestvie*, p. 111.
223 Outline by M.E. Wheeler, "Empires in Conflict and Cooperation: The Bostonians and the Russian-American Company," *PHR*, 40 (1971): 419–41.
224 George Vancouver, *Voyage* (London 1801: 2nd ed.), 5:134. R.J. Cleveland, *In the Forecastle, or, Voyages and Commercial Enterprises of the Sons of New England* (New York 1855), pp. 104–5; F. Howay, *A List of Trading Vessels*, pp. 38–39.
225 R.G. Ward, ed., *American Activities in the Central Pacific, 1790–1870*, 8 vol. (Ridgewood, NJ 1966–67), 3:534–35; 7:173; also 2:230–31 (re visits to Easter Island, 1806–22;) L.T. and P.L. Ritter, eds. and trans., *The European Discovery of Kosrae Island* (Stanford 1981), p. 1 n; Barratt, *Kosrae, 1827: Russian Ethnographic Records* (Saipan 1988).
226 Métraux, *Easter Island*, p. 42.

CHAPTER TWO: THE RUSSIAN TEXTS

Georg Heinrich Langsdorf

1 Compare Lisianskii, *Voyage*, pp. 49–50; Korobitsyn, "Journal," p. 149; Kruzenshtern, *Voyage*, 1:100.
2 Kruzenshtern, *Voyage*, 1:83, 103.
3 Ibid., 1:9; Nevskii, *Pervoe puteshestvie*, p. 56.
4 La Pérouse, *Voyage Round the World*, 1:323, 329.

5 I.e., maize.

6 Kruzenshtern, *Voyage*, 1:102–3.

7 Langsdorf had access aboard *Neva* both to George (Johann Georg Adam) Forster's *Voyage Round the World, in His Britannic Majesty's Sloop Resolution* . . . (London 1777) and to Johann Reinhold Forster's *Reise um die Welt während den Jahren 1772 bis 1775* . . . (Berlin 1778–80). For comparative purposes, however, we may best collate the Russian texts describing the 1804 visit to Easter Island with the elder Forster's journal, edited by Michael E. Hoare: *The Resolution Journal of Johann Reinhold Forster, 1772–1775* (London 1982), 3: 460–77. La Pérouse's recent *Voyage* (Paris 1798) had been translated into Russian by Loggin Ivanovich Golenishchev-Kutuzov and had appeared in St. Petersburg as *Puteshestvie La Peruza v Iuzhnom i Severnom Tikhom Okeane* eighteen months before Langsdorf's departure thence.

8 Langsdorf here appended a footnote: "The island was discovered by Roggewein, who made a landing there on 6 April 1722. The passage that follows here is taken from a Dutch work with the title *Twee Jaarige Reyse rond om de Wereld*, &c., te Dordrecht, by Joannes van Braam, 1728. It is a very little known work." As Boris N. Komissarov notes in *Grigorii Ivanovich Langsdorf* (L. 1975), p. 52, Langsdorf wrote his narrative in 1808–10 on the basis of his *Nadezhda* journals but with reference to many published works, including those of the Forsters, Cook, and La Pérouse, and *Tweejaarige Reyze rondom de Wereld, ter nader ontdekkinge der onbekende zuydlanden, met drie schepen* . . . (1728; 3d ed., Dordrecht 1764; 4th ed., Amsterdam 1774). In St. Petersburg, he had access to such works also as Jean Pierre Bérenger's *Collection de tous les Voyages faits autour du monde* (Paris 1798), vol. 5, and Alexander Dalrymple's *Historical Collection* (London 1771), vol. 2, containing lengthy extracts from *Carl Friedrich Behrens Reise durch die Süd-Länder und um die Welt* (Frankfurt and Leipzig 1737; 2d German and French translation 1739). The text suggests, however, that Langsdorf had looked at *Tweejaarige Reyze* before reaching the South Pacific early in 1804. In this case his preliminary reading echoed that of Captain Cook and the Forsters where Easter Island was concerned: see Beaglehole, *The Journals*, 2:338 n.2) and Forster, *Resolution Journal*, p. 468.

9 I.e., the Netherlands.

10 Lisianskii (1814 text) judged some men seen at Hanga-roa in 1804 to be six feet tall.

11 Kruzenshtern, *Voyage*, 1:104ff.

Nikolai I. Korobitsyn

12 24 March, New Style.

13 Compare Lisianskii, *Voyage*, pp. 49–50. Kruzenshtern made less serious efforts to remain in company on 24–25 March, judging by his own *Voyage*, 1:100.

14 *Neva* was following *Resolution*'s track of 9–11 March 1774 rather than that of *Boussole* and *Astrolabe* of April 1786 (see Forster, *Resolution Journal*, fig. 22), suggesting that Lisianskii had Cook's chart open before him. Lisianskii was a lifelong admirer of Cook, a "truly great man" (Lisianskii, *Voyage*, p. 109), even though, as Terence Armstrong points out in his paper "Cook's Reputation in Russia," p. 3, "he was perhaps not quite as prepared as Kruzenshtern to accept Cook's determinations of position, expressing some puzzlement about Cook's coördinates for Easter Island and some real doubt about his estimate of the island's population."

15 *Neva* maintained a rate of 5 knots on this day, despite the fickleness of the wind and the apparent imminence of squalls. So much is clear from the log kept by Navigator Danilo Kalinin, who drowned in the wreck of *Neva* in 1813. The log is now held at TsVMM in Leningrad, under reference 9170-8 (1938). She thus moved from a point some "35 Italian miles" sse of Poike at 10:00 AM (or 11:00 AM, according to Lisianskii) to a position just off the island's eastern tip by 5:00 PM. She was, accordingly, no more than ten or twelve miles out when her cannon were fired, one after the other. Given the wind direction, this gunfire was almost certainly audible to the Easter Islanders.

16 Lisianskii's chart of Easter Island, headed "Roggeveen or Easter Island, Described by the

Ship *Neva* in the Year 1804" and reproduced by N.V. Dumitrashko in his 1947 Soviet edition of Lisianskii's *Puteshestvie vokrug sveta* (St. P. 1812), p. 77, shows the ship's movements of 17 April, not the day of her arrival.

17 Korobitsyn means garments other than girdles over the sexual parts, and here echoes La Pérouse: see *Voyage*, 1:324–25 and 2:333 (observations by Rollin). J.R. Forster likewise refers to the islanders as "naked," before proceeding to describe their cloth: Forster, *Resolution Journal*, pp. 464–65.

18 Lisianskii, *Voyage* pp. 54–55.

19 The French had similarly been shouted at by some five hundred natives at Hanga-roa on 10 April 1786: see La Pérouse, *Voyage*, 1:318. Povalishin was a little north of the spot where the French had landed, and still further north of the place, off Punta Roa, where *Resolution* had anchored on 14 March 1774: see Beaglehole, *The Journals*, 2:339 and G. Forster, *Voyage Round the World*, 1:560–61.

20 The islanders had shown more confidence in dealing with European visitors in 1786: La Pérouse, *Voyage*, 1:315.

21 *Musa sapientum* L., also used in barter in 1774 and 1786.

22 *Convolvulus batatas*, according to the elder Forster (*Voyage Round the World*, p. 467); now *Ipomoea batatas*.

23 Lisianskii provides further details: see below, p. 57.

24 Povalishin (or, as Polish scholarship prefers in nationalist vein, Powaliszyn) evidently submitted a written report to Lisianskii, who incorporated data from it in his essay "A Description of Easter Island" (*Opisanie Ostrova Sv. Paskhi*); that, in turn, was incorporated in the fourth chapter of his *Puteshestvie* (1812).

25 Compare La Pérouse, *Voyage*, 2:333 and Forster, *Resolution Journal*, pp. 466, 475. The redness resulted from application of turmeric-based colouring substance, not the sun's heat.

26 See Beaglehole, *The Journals*, 2:35; also Forster, *Resolution Journal*, pp. 466 and 475, and La Pérouse, *Voyage*, 2:333. Cook does not, in fact, claim that the ear lobes reached down to the shoulders, speaking merely of "enormous holes."

27 This local bark cloth was made of *Broussonetia papyrifera*, the paper mulberry. Larger pieces were known as *kahu*.

28 Untrue: the Easter Islanders had cloaks measuring five feet by four feet (see Beaglehole, *The Journals*, 2:351), sometimes dyed a bright yellow (Forster, *Resolution Journal*, pp. 466–67). La Pérouse had seen some in 1786 (*Voyage*, 1:318 and 2:334), and Povalishin spotted a number in 1804, despite this remark by Korobitsyn (Lisianskii, *Voyage*, p. 58).

29 Beaglehole, *The Journals*, 2:352, 823 (Wales's journal); Forster, *Resolution Journal*, p. 471; La Pérouse, *Voyage*, 1:323–24.

30 This would seem to have been borrowed and adapted from La Pérouse, *Voyage*, 1:324, etc., accessible to Korobitsyn in the 1801 Golenishchev-Kutuzov version.

31 Lisianskii concurs: *Voyage*, p. 52. Cook and his people are, by comparison, very sour in their remarks about the island's appearance (see Beaglehole, *The Journals*, 2:343, 349; 2:822–23). Yet *Resolution* had come up from latitude 71°10'S, on the harsh rim of Antarctica, whereas *Neva* was last from Staten Land in the south of South America.

32 Both Cook and La Pérouse had noted plantain under native cultivation (Beaglehole, *The Journals*, 2:344-45, 349), and the French noted "banana trees planted in lines" (La Pérouse, *Voyage*, 1:328). Though Forster was as struck by banana trees as Korobitsyn was to be (Forster, *Resolution Journal*, p. 467), Richard Pickersgill of *Resolution* failed to make a single mention of that fruit when reporting to Cook at the conclusion of his inland tour of 16 March 1774.

33 *Ahu* platforms, formerly used as burial vaults and evidently corresponding to the *marae* of other parts of Polynesia: see Métraux, *Ethnology*, pp. 284, 290; Peter Buck, *Vikings of the Sunrise* (New York 1938), p. 234.

34 *Pukao*, formalized topknots. Compare Beaglehole, *The Journals*, 2:344–45, 823–24; Forster, *Resolution Journal*, pp. 468–69 and fig. 26; La Pérouse, *Voyage*, 1:321–22; and Lisianskii, *Voyage*, p. 56.

35 The Russians saw no sign of descendants of the livestock left on Easter Island by La Pérouse (*Voyage*, 1:329). The livestock had not, however, included cattle.
36 Lisianskii's chart gives the more precise readings for Hanga-roa Bay of lat. 27°09′23″S, long. 109°25′20″W. Both these readings are within a minute of modern reckoning, and *Neva*'s instruments (on which see Kruzenshtern, *Voyage*, 1:7–9) gave a latitudinal reading 4′ more accurate than Wales had finally achieved in 1774 (Beaglehole, *The Journals*, 2:350, n.2).

Archpriest Gedeon

37 *Neva* had left Santa Catarina Island, Brazil, on 4 February, seventy-two days earlier: Gedeon's dating is Old Style and slightly inaccurate.
38 The text of Gedeon's journal, now kept at TsGIAL under reference *fond* 796, op. 90, *delo* 273 (pp. 33–34 on Easter Island), does not suggest that this comment was added later, as one might think.
39 Two miles.
40 Of the Russians, Gedeon alone refers specifically to potato (*kartofelia*) as well as sweet potato (*sladkogo kartofelia*).
41 La Pérouse, *Voyage*, 2:319ff.

Iurii F. Lisianskii, 1812 Text

42 To the WNW: see Lisianskii's chart of Easter Island.
43 The "first rock" was Motu-nui, centre of the bird-man cult: Métraux, *Easter Island*, pp. 130–39. The shores lost in gloom (literally, "thick darkness") were Orongo cliffs.
44 Compare Beaglehole, *The Journals*, 2:336 (white terns and grey noddies seen from *Resolution*, identification, etc.).
45 Like Cook in 1774, Lisianskii failed to notice Motu-iti, sheltering behind Motu-nui and southwest of Motu-kaukau, in the thickening dusk as well as daylight.
46 Danilo Kalinin; see fig. 27 in S. Englert, *La Tierra de Hotu Mat'ua* (Padre las Casas, Chile 1948), p. 141.
47 Literally, "alleys," possibly the arrangement called by Cook and Pickersgill "Plantain Walks": Beaglehole, *The Journals*, 2:344; also La Pérouse, *Voyage*, 1:328 ("planted in lines").
48 Beaglehole, *The Journals*, 2:356 (Easter Island *umu*, or earth ovens).
49 Lisianskii apparently meant "southeastern shore": *Neva* was moving WNW to NW and modern-day Cape Cummings was out of sight by 9:00 AM. One monument group almost equidistant from Cape Roggeveen and South Cape was at Acahanga: see Englert, *La Tierra*, archaeological sites maps, nos. 203–8. The blackness suggests *ahu* of basalt.
50 Lisianskii amended this in his English version to "mound," which was certainly more correct.
51 In Hanga-roa Bay.
52 1:321–22 and 2:350–52; *Cartes*, no. 11.
53 Presumably Lisianskii means between Hanga Tetenga and Vaihu on the SE coast.
54 See Métraux, *Ethnology*, pls. 2–3 (*tupa* watchtower, *tapu* pillar, and other rock structures).
55 The Russians hopelessly underestimate the total number of figures: see Englert, *La Tierra*, "Isla de Pascua" chart.
56 This was in the area of Hotu-iti, where Captain Geiseler noted the ruins of a sizable village in 1883 (Geiseler, *Die Oster-Insel*, p. 40). Métraux (*Ethnology*, p. 14) mistakenly identifies the area as Vinapu. See also Corney, *Voyage*, p. 90; Forster, *Voyage Round the World*, 1:557–59; and La Pérouse, *Voyage*, 2:332, on sugarcane plantations.
57 These were inland-facing statues, *moai*, on *ahus*, with hats of red vesicular tuff (*hau hitirau moai*) that boasted white stone ornaments or wedges: see J. Roggeveen, *Extracts from the Official Log of Mynheer J. Roggeveen, 1721–1722* (London 1908, p. 16);

Corney, *Voyage*, p. 93; Routledge, *Mystery of Easter Island*, p. 199.

58 *Sterna lunata, manutara,* grey-backed tern; the "tropical" bird, *Phaeton* sp., *tavake*) had been seen here by Cook (see Beaglehole, *The Journals*, 2:336) and other voyagers. It is probable that Lisianskii also saw grey noddies. Like *Resolution* and *Astrolabe, Neva* came at the wrong season to witness the swarming of sooty terns around Motu-nui and the nearby ocean outcrops: Métraux, *Ethnology*, pp. 331–41.

59 I.e., westward north of La Pérouse Bay (Te Pito Kura) and past Anakena to Hanga-o-Teo.

60 This confirms Roggeveen, *Extracts*, p. 19 and Corney, *Voyage*, p. 102; but in 1866–72 there were relatively large groups of islanders living at Anakena and La Pérouse Bay: F.E. Eyraud, "Lettre du Père F. Eugène Eyraud au T.R.P. supérieur général," *Annales de l'Association de la Propagation de la Foi*, 38 (Lyon 1866): 53; P. Loti, "Expédition der Fregatte 'La Flore' nach der Osterinsel, 1872," *Globus*, 23 (Braunschweig 1873): no. 5, p. 65.

61 Lisianskii shared Roggeveen's misgivings about anchoring in Te Pito Kura (Roggeveen, *Extracts*, pp. 10–12), and had no way of knowing that Felipe Gonzalez y Haedo had successfully anchored off Hanga-o-honu in 1770, landing on Ovahe beach. It was along that stretch of the coast, though, that he put *Neva*'s boat off for an hour or two.

62 Lisianskii's interest in these had been aroused five months before, off the Cape Verde Islands, by *Nadezhda*'s naturalist Georg Heinrich Langsdorf: see Kruzenshtern, *Voyage*, 1:55–56. Easter Island lacks a coral reef, red or otherwise.

63 The islanders thus had ample notice of the ship's approach.

64 In Russian, *naboiki.*

65 In fact, much use is made of Povalishin's observations also.

66 The "hillock" was Katiki (Pu Akatiki); the "hill," Maunga Pui or Puki, with Rano Raraku and Raburea below its silhouette.

67 Hanga-nui and Hanga Maihiku off the SE coast; Hanga-roa; and La Pérouse Bay, east of Anakena.

68 110 metres.

69 278 metres.

70 740 metres.

71 42 metres. *Neva* echoes *Resolution*'s manoeuvres of 1774: see Beaglehole, *The Journals*, 2:338–39, and Forster, *Resolution Journal*, pp. 465–66.

72 La Pérouse, *Voyage*, 1:317.

73 See La Pérouse's *Atlas* (Paris 1797) for a large-scale map of Hanga-roa Bay and village drawn by M. Bernize of *Boussole*. As Métraux notes (*Ethnology*, p. 129), Lisianskii's description confirms that representation of the village site.

74 The "spots" were caused by application of white and red colouring substances, with unoxidized tuff and volcanic earth bases: J.L. Palmer, "Visit to Easter Island, or Rapa Nui, in 1868," *Royal Geographical Society Journal*, 40 (1870): 178; Métraux, *Ethnology*, p. 294; Beaglehole, *The Journals*, 2:344–45.

75 Cook, *Voyage*, 1:289, 284.

76 On Antigua in January 1795: TsGALI, *fond* 18 veka, no. 5196: "Zapiski leitenanta Iuriia Fedorovicha Lisianskago, vedennye im vo vremia sluzhby ego Volonterom ... ," pp. 40–41.

77 La Pérouse, *Voyage*, 1:325, 334. See Métraux, *Ethnology*, pp. 11–12 for a discussion of water sources, which justifies the Russians' skepticism.

78 *Neva* carried a copy of Forster's *Observations Made During a Voyage Round the World* (London 1778): hence Lisianskii's lieutenant's familiarity with the word "*Heeo*, which signifies Friend": see Forster, *Resolution Journal*, p. 471. In a paper of 1977, however, the Danish student of Pacific ethnolinguistics W.W. Schumacher gave convincing arguments in favour of interpreting that word not as "friend" (based on *hoa*) but as "pull" or "grasp" (based on *hio* and with reference to sugar cane branches): see W.W. Schumacher, 1976 "On the Linguistic Aspect of Thor Heyerdahl's Theory: The So-Called Non-Polynesian Number Names from Easter Island," *Anthropos*, 71 (1976): 806–47.

79 Local attitudes towards ironware and iron implements had changed dramatically since

1774: Beaglehole, *The Journals*, 2:354, and Forster, *Resolution Journal*, p. 476.
80 Perhaps under European influence: Métraux, *Ethnology*, p. 219.
81 La Pérouse, *Voyage*, 1:327; Haddon and Hornell, *Canoes of Polynesia*, 1:97ff.; Métraux, *Ethnology*, pp. 204–7. The "clumps of reed" were *pora*, bulrush mat rafts or conical bundles, seen in use by Du Petit-Thouars (*Voyage autour du monde sur la frigate La Vénus, 1836–1839* (Paris 1841), 2:228 and Dumont D'Urville (*Voyage*, 3:387) in the later 1830s.
82 These were not *maro* but single strips of tapa, not sewn together yet.
83 Compare Forster, *Resolution Journal*, p. 475; Beaglehole, *The Journals*, 2: 351–52.
84 *Pukao*: Métraux, *Ethnology*, pp. 300–2, for details.
85 The bag was similar to that type in which food had been offered to Cook's people (see Forster, *Voyage Round the World*, 1:590): it is well represented in the major collections, though not in Leningrad. It was of dried banana strips or bulrush: see Buck, *Ethnology of Tongareva*, pp. 134–35, for probable technique. The mat was a *pora* raft or swimming float: see Du Petit-Thouars, *Voyage*, 2:231, and Palmer, "Visit to Easter Island," p. 172 (resemblance to a sedge elephant tusk or wheat sheaf).
86 The "lace" or cord was of *hau* (*Triumfetta semitriloba*), and the "rushes" were reeds (*Scirpus riparius*) from the lakes Rano-kao or Rano-aroi. Métraux, *Ethnology*, p. 212, reports that small baskets of the kind acquired by Povalishin were known as *kete-rauhiri*.
87 Modern fix: 27°08′06′′S, 109°25′54′′W. Lisianskii's readings compare very favourably, in point of accuracy, with those of his British contemporaries; but then he had British instruments.
88 Discussion in Métraux, *Ethnology*, pp. 20–21.
89 See Kruzenshtern, *Voyage*, 1:8 (compasses by Troughton of London, etc.).

Iurii F. Lisianskii, 1814 Text

90 This was 17 April, the shore being the Poike Peninsula.
91 The 230-foot high rock, Motu-Kaukau. The elder Forster had likewise been struck by its height and appearance: see Forster, *Resolution Journal*, p. 463, and pl. 27 in Englert, *La Tierra*. The Russians were, of course, half expecting to see the 450-ton sloop *Nadezhda* off Easter Island, which was the appointed rendezvous before Port Anna-Maria, or Taiohae Bay, on Nukuhiva in the Marquesas. Lisianskii was, in view of that expectation, disinclined to embark upon shore investigations of the thorough sort that he undertook both on Nukuhiva a month later and on Hawaii's Kona Coast (Kealakekua-Kaawaloa).
92 See n. 49 above. It must be observed that basaltic statues did stand along the south coast in small numbers, and that others, of a dark soft rock, stood on an *ahu* by Ana-o-keke, on the Poike headland. What Lisianskii thought "very pleasant" had struck J.R. Forster as "rather bleak" and "parched up" (*Resolution Journal*, p. 463), while Lieutenant Charles Clerke, like Cook, found it positively "barren" (Beaglehole, *The Journals*, 2:758, 349.
93 Round the seacliffs of Rano Kao, between Vaiatare and Orongo, the strata being hard vesicular basalt interspersed with tuff: see Métraux, *Ethnology*, pp. 290–91.
94 Deliberate action is implied; the point is pursued by Beechey in his *Narrative of a Voyage to the Pacific and Bering's Strait, in the Years 1825–26–27–28* (London, 1831), 1:45–56. The *moai* seen by the Russians may be supposed to have rested upon *ahus* no. 6, 7, or 8 by Englert's enumeration of 1974; nos. 6 and 8 (unnamed *ahu* and *Ahu* Pea) are the strongest candidates, given the archaeological data and *Neva's* course due east. The Russians were looking a shade to the north of *Ahu* Tautira, large blocks from which were used to build the stone jetty or mole at Hanga-roa in 1932.
95 Lisianskii's interest in La Pérouse's fate had been boosted by Loggin Ivanovich Golenishchev-Kutuzov's introduction to his 1800 Russian rendering of the 1797 *Voyage*: see V. Sopikov, *Opyt Rossiiskoi bibliografii* (St.P. 1813), nos. 9206–08, etc., and Gennadi, *Spravochnyi slovar'*, 1:232, etc., on the Kutuzov translations of Cook and La Pérouse.
96 See n.2. As the Russian text insists, Lisianskii had from the very outset turned away from

the idea of investigation ashore; his sailing instructions required him to do the hydrographic and meteorological work that he duly performed off Easter Island on 16–21 April 1804: TsGIAL, *fond* 853 (Buldakova, M.M.), no. 74 ("Zhurnal prikazov kapitana Kruzenshterna komande sudov"); M.V. Severgin, "Instruktsiia dlia puteshestvii . . . v otnoshenii k teorii zemli," *Severnyi vestnik*, (St. P. 1804): nos. 2–3. Nevskii, *Pervoe puteshestvie*, pp. 39–43, 56.

97 *Neva* was, like La Pérouse's ships, in good repair and carrying a cheerful company when she arrived at Easter Island. La Pérouse's remarks on the results of that circumstance bear on the Russian accounts of the place: *Voyage*, 1:319.

98 *Ahu* Vinapu (?), which had at one time boasted seven *moai*: Englert, *La Tierra*, archaeological chart no. 242. This group stood sixty feet above sea level and was among the largest seen by Lisianskii in 1804. Since some *ahu* had had a dozen or more statues (Métraux, *Ethnology*, pp. 293, 296) and since few images suffered significantly from weathering despite the softness of tuff, this would seem to indicate that *moai* had already been destroyed by human hands in large numbers. *Neva* coasted past *Ahu* Akahanga four miles ENE of Vinapu, within an hour or so of passing the latter, but sighted no more than two or three figures there; yet *Ahu* Akahanga had once boasted 12 or 13 statues, 8 with hats (Métraux, *Ethnology*, p. 293; Englert, *La Tierra*, p. 271).

99 This was Hanga-nui, the "monuments" most probably including the *Ahu* Tongariki, one of the three largest on the island (145 square metres, 15 statues). The last vestiges were destroyed in 1960.

100 Roggeveen's baskets containing white stones (or *moai*)? Many visitors saw such white stones (Roggeveen, *Extracts*, p. 16; Corney, *Voyage*, p. 93; Du Petit-Thouars, *Voyage*, 2:225).

101 Great shoals were common off Easter Island in spring and had surrounded *Resolution* in 1774: Forster, *Resolution Journal*, p. 460. *Neva* carried no artist capable of painting them, but *Nadezhda* had the German naturalist Wilhelm Gottlieb Tilesius von Tilenau (1769–1857), whose excellent representations of Pacific fish and other fauna—in the 1803–6 diary now held at LOAAN in Leningrad: *razr.* 4, vol. 1, no. 800a—reflected his interest in icthyology.

102 See Englert, *La Tierra*, p. 260, and Métraux, *Ethnology*, p. 298.

103 Probably an error, but see Beechey, *Narrative*, 1:42.

104 Pieces of broken cask hoop from Kronstadt.

105 See n. 2 above.

106 The usual barter produce: Beaglehole, *The Journals*, 2: 339, 342, 349; Forster, *Resolution Journal*, p. 467; La Pérouse, *Voyage*, 1:328, 333; Kotzebue, *Voyage*, 1:138. The Russians saw no taro.

107 The *Neva*'s chart is reproduced here.

108 Curious: Cook, Forster, and La Pérouse report on Easter Island fowl, and the French left assorted animals there in April 1786. Rats were also eaten, as Cook recognized.

109 Compare Corney, *Voyage*, p. 123; Bernizet in La Pérouse, *Voyage*, 2:349–50; Forster, *Voyage Round the World*, 1:570. The elder Forster's drawing of a thatched house with central conical door (reproduced in *Resolution Journal*, fig. 25) is well complemented by Russian data of 1804 and 1816.

110 I.e., *moai* were visible on all the island's coasts.

111 *Voyage*, 2:350–52; *Cartes*, figs. 8–10.

112 Beaglehole, *The Journals*, 2:356; Métraux, *Ethnology*, pp. 161–63.

113 But not recent ones.

114 La Pérouse, *Voyage*, 1:325. Lisianskii had been rereading this passage, but the wandering albatross (*Diomedea exulans*) was in any case on his mind because two months previously, on 14 February, he had barely escaped serious injury or even death from the explosion of a gun with which he had been shooting them for the galley. The British had, in the later eighteenth century, killed albatrosses by safer methods: Beaglehole, *The Journals*, 2:41 n.3, 315 n.2.

115 This must have been a virtuoso attempt at mime by Povalishin, since neither Cook

(through Pickersgill) nor Forster had included the necessary words or grammatical structures in their Easter Island word lists (Beaglehole, *The Journals*, 2:360; Forster, *Observations*, p. 284/obv.; Forster, *Resolution Journal*, p. 464, n.4).

116 The Russians failed to recognize the natives' pleasure at getting any wood, even in small pieces.

117 So must dozens of the islanders who met *Neva*.

118 These were *pora:* see Métraux, *Ethnology*, p. 210.

119 It proved nothing of the sort, and in 1816 the Russians saw craft basically identical with those La Pérouse had seen: Kotzebue, *Voyage*, 1:136–37; Métraux, *Ethnology*, pp. 204–5 (craft drawn by Choris).

120 Short commoner's *kahu,* tied over right shoulder or in front of the neck, seen again by Kotzebue in 1816 (*Voyage of Discovery*, 1:140) and fully described by Pierre Loti (*Expedition*, p. 66) and Geiseler (*Die Oster-Insel*, p. 29); chiefs and women wore longer cloaks of tapa, to judge by Russian evidence.

121 This phrase suggests that Lisianskii had been consulting Georg Forster's *Voyage Round the World* as well as the elder Forster's *Observations*, and reminds us how well Lisianskii could read and speak English.

122 A correct supposition: see Beechey, *Narrative*, 1:52; Thomson, *Te Pito te Henua*, p. 463; Eyraud, "Lettre," p. 67 (survival of ear-mutilation among women).

123 See n.2. These *moai* had vanished by 1816: Kotzebue, *Voyage*, 1:139–40.

124 Techniques described by Métraux, *Ethnology*, pp. 208–12.

125 April 1804.

126 Actually, Cook's *Voyage*, 1:288, gave the latitude (presumably of the Hanga-roa anchorage), as 27°5′30′′S. He had probably gotten this from his astronomer, William Wales, whose reckonings were certainly better than those of other men aboard *Resolution* (see Beaglehole, *The Journals*, 2:350, 828). Lisianskii's figures being for the island's centre, his reckoning and Cook's were less at variance than he then supposed: but see Armstrong, "Cook's Reputation," p. 3.

127 Cook, *Voyage*, 1:289.

128 Beechey concurred: *Narrative*, 1:51.

129 See Kruzenshtern, *Voyage*, 1:8 (azimuth compasses by Edward Troughton of London, etc.); Nevskii, *Pervoe puteshestvie*, pp. 38–40 (Russian marine astronomy).

Adelbert von Chamisso

130 Compare Cook, *Voyage*, 1:294; Beechey, *Narrative*, 1:41. Chamisso's phrase is *in gradlinigte Felder.*

131 Métraux, *Ethnology*, pp. 153–58, on cultivated plants.

132 Chamisso had been rereading Cook's *Voyage* or a translation thereof, and so linked the island's stoniness with shortages of timber and water: see Beaglehole, *The Journals*, 2:344–45, etc.

133 Machowski (*Island of Secrets*, p. 12) asserts boldly that the statues in question had "been overthrown during civil strife" since 1804. Lisianskii, *Voyage*, p. 59.

134 The trade goods are unspecified..

135 By small shot from a gun, Kotzebue notes.

136 I.e., other Polynesians; see La Pérouse, *Voyage*, 1:327–29.

137 From muskets. On the accuracy of stone hurling, see Beechey, *Narrative*, 1:49 and Métraux, *Ethnology*, p. 165.

138 In German, *zierlichen Fischernetze. Hoa* meaning "friend."

139 *Riurik's* artist, Ludovik Choris, was unacquainted with "the bathing places of Europe," but had travelled through the Caucasus by 1813: see L. Choris, *Vues et paysages des régions équinoxiales* (Paris 1826), p. v; Barratt, *Russian View of Honolulu*, pt. 4.

140 The blue tone resulted from application of *kere,* prepared from charred *ti* leaves mixed with *Solanum nigrum* juice: Geiseler, *Die Oster-Insel*, p. 51. Choris sketched a fully tatooed Easter Islander: *Vues et paysages*, pl. 10; Métraux, *Ethnology*, pp. 241, 247 for commentary.

141 Paper mulberry (*mahute*) was evidently doing better on the island than Cook and Forster had led Chamisso to expect: Beaglehole, *The Journals*, 2:347, 349; Forster, *Resolution Journal*, pp. 465, 475. Cloaks (*kahu*) were dyed yellow with turmeric.

142 The flat shell was *repu reva;* it was worn suspended from a human-hair or vegetable-fibre cord: Roggeveen, *Extracts*, p. 22; Geiseler, *Die Oster-Insel*, p. 49.

143 This was a classical Easter Island style: Roggeveen, *Extracts*, p. 15; it was disappearing throughout the nineteenth century: Beechey, *Narrative*, 1:52; Thomson, *Te Pito te Henua*, p. 463.

144 This train of thought had been encouraged by J.R. Forster, see Métraux, *Ethnology*, pp. 24–25. Chamisso was ignorant of the alleged division of the Easter Islanders into the "Long-ears" and "Short-ears" (Métraux, *Ethnology*, pp. 71–74).

145 See Forster, *Voyage Round the World* 1:564; Corney, *Voyage*, p. 122; Eyraud, "Lettre," 38:56. The red dye was *kiea,* pulverized mineralized tuff from the western slope of Poike Peninsula.

146 Chamisso had read the literature on this vexed subject: Cook, *Voyage*, 1:289; Forster, *Voyage Round the World*, 1:577; J.R. Forster, *Observations*, p. 423.

147 Indigenous long-legged fowls: Cook, *Voyage*, 1:288; La Pérouse, *Voyage*, 1:328.

148 Kotzebue, *Voyage*, 1:141–42, 352. The Russians met Captain Alexander Adams of the *Kahumanna* (ex-*Forester* of London; Kotzebue, *Voyage*, 1:324) at Honolulu in late November 1816, and on 13 December Adams related what he knew of a violent visit to Easter Island, supposedly in 1805, by the New England brig *Nancy*, of New London. Further details in the Kotzebue text and notes.

Johann Friedrich von Eschscholtz

149 Text from the "General Observations" (*Allgemeine Bemerkungen zur Reisebeschreibung*) appended to vol. 3 of Kotzebue's *Reise um die Welt* (Weimar 1821) and issued with the separate flyleaf title *Bemerkungen und Ansichten auf einer Entdeckungs-Reise . . . von dem Naturforscher der Expedition, Adelbert von Chamisso* (Weimar), pp. 185–86. Although published anonymously, unlike the following zoological papers, "General Observations" may be identified as Eschscholtz's on the basis of a remark that at Teneriffe the author and Chamisso had "made a three-day trip" (p. 184).

150 This was Kotzebue's "uninjured pedestal" at Hanga-roa. Eschscholtz has *Fussgestell* (German).

151 Probably *moai* made of volcanic tuff from Rano-raraku crater, not of basalt: distance and poor light made colour identification tricky, but see Métraux, *Ethnology*, p. 291.

152 Chamisso saw several: Kotzebue, *Voyage*, 3:226.

153 See Choris's *Vue de l'Ile de Pâques*. The lapilli in the island's ashes are exclusively volcanic, with no traces of metamorphic rock. Surprisingly, the Russians seem not to have collected small lava samples at Hanga-roa for the mineralogical cabinets of St. Petersburg or Dorpat (modern Tartu): see Kotzebue, *Voyage*, 3:346–52.

154 These were *puraki* dots, running alongside facial parallel lines, and were noted by most visitors: Forster, *Voyage Round the World*, 1:564; Palmer, "Visit to Easter Island," p. 171; Geiseler, *Die Oster-Insel*, p. 53. Eschscholtz had the doctor's power of observation under pressure.

155 Discussion pp. 78–79.

156 In German, *Schenkel bis zum knie ganz dicht schwartz punctirt*, what the Easter Islanders termed *humi i te vae:* Thomson, *Te Pito te Henua*, p. 467 and fig. 36, and Alphonse Pinart, "Voyage à l'Ile de Pâques," *Le Tour du Monde*, 36 (Paris 1878): 238–39. Choris depicts different leg tattooing.

157 *Riurik* reached Tongareva (Penrhyn) Island in the Northern Cooks on 30 April 1816, and an amicable exchange ensued: Kotzebue, *Voyage*, 1:162–65 and 3:217–19. Eschscholtz probably heard *hoa!* (friend!), transcribed by Chamisso, as *Hoë!* Lieutenant Povalishin's *tio*, or *teeo* in the 1814 edition of Lisianskii's *Voyage* (p. 57), merely confuses the issue, which has been studied by W.W. Schumacher on the basis of not only published material from Cook's second voyage (G. Forster's *Voyage Round the World*, 1:556–58 and J.R.

Forster's *Observations*, pp. 283–84) but also the latter's unpublished MS on the vocabulary of the Polynesian languages spoken in the South Pacific and on Easter Island especially (Staatsbibliothek Preussischer Kulturbesitz, Berlin: MS 62). It is clear, however, that unlike *tio*, neither *Hoë* nor *Hoio* could easily have been mangled forms of W. Churchill's *hio* (grasp): the very context of the Hanga-roa encounter of 1816 argues against it. On the other hand, it must be kept in mind that the Easter Island word for iron, *ohio* (W. Churchill, *Easter Island: The Rapanui Speech* . . . [Washington 1912] p. 288), *could* possibly have been recorded by Eschscholtz, a non-linguist, as *hoio*, or distorted by the printers in 1821.

Ludovik Choris, 1822 Text

158 As French was Choris's third language, this text was read and lightly edited for him by the journalist and traveller Jean-Baptiste-Benoit Eyriès (1767–1846): see Choris, *Voyage pittoresque autour du monde*, (Paris 1822), p. iv. Eyriès, a major contributor to the *Annales des Voyages* (Paris), in 1826 arranged Choris's election to the Société de la Géographie, of which he was a founding member. It was through Chamisso, however, that Choris had in 1820–21 made the acquaintance of Baron Georges Léopold Cuvier, the zoologist and palaeontologist, and Karl Sigismund Kunth, the Berlin botanist, both of whom annotated the *Voyage pittoresque*.

159 Enigmatic: Kotzebue suggests that *Riurik* approached the island from east and south.

160 In the plural, *pourvues de balanciers;* Kotzebue, *Voyage*, 1:137.

161 Lieutenant Gleb Semenovich Shishmarev used small shot ineffectually. See Métraux, *Ethnology*, pp. 144–47, for a discussion of theft on Easter Island in its cultural context.

162 Choris depicts such rectangular fields or planted areas in *Vue de l'Ile de Pâques*: Cook had noted them (*Voyage*, 1:294), as would Beechey (*Narrative*, 1:41).

163 By *nuds* ("naked"), Choris appears to have meant merely wearing a bunch of grass suspended from a string round the waist (*mauku* uta): see *Habitans de l'Ile de Pâques*. The "mantles" were dyed or undyed *kahu*.

164 Kotzebue says 17 men and Choris draws 19.

165 Notably large knives and adzes.

166 To judge by Choris's *Vue de l'Ile de Pâques*, this was a *tupa* (turtle watchtower: Métraux, *Ethnology*, pp. 189–90 and pl. 2b) or at least a structure raised by the same technique. Since the European visitors of 1774 and 1786 do not record this, just north of Hanga-roa, it presumably had been built recently. The tower near which Cook's people had spotted a subterranean room (behind the more recent *ahu* Okahu) evidently stood on another site: see Cook, *Voyage*, 1:570. It is significant, however, that both Cook's and La Pérouse's people noted the proximity of such an underground chamber and watchtower: see La Pérouse, *Voyage*, 2:255. Bernizet, who alone entered an underground chamber, found it full of prized possessions and provisions; fear of being robbed would certainly explain the islanders' unwillingness to have the Russians, who were well armed, land at that spot.

167 These were *tapu* pillars (*pipi hereko*), the top stone of which was painted white, placed to indicate an interdiction often but not invariably associated with the placement of human remains on or by an *ahu*: see Cook, *Voyage*, 1:296; Du Petit-Thouars, *Voyage*, 2:225; Geiseler, *Die Oster-Insel*, p. 28; Routledge, *Mystery of Easter Island*, p. 232.

168 The long-handled club (*ua*) was both weapon and parade staff for chiefs, and hence an insignia of dignity: Thomson, *Te Pito te Henua*, p. 475; Geiseler, *Die Oster-Insel*, p. 34.

Ludovik Choris, 1826 Text

169 In French, *des clôtures en ligne droite*, suggesting loose stone walls. See A. Delano, *A Narrative of Voyages and Travels in the Northern and Southern Hemispheres* (Boston 1817), p. 356; Cook, *Voyage*, 1:294; Beechey, *Narrative*, 1:42 for complementary impressions.

170 On Easter Island's poor flora, see Forster, *Resolution Journal*, pp. 467, 475.
171 Quite untrue: Métraux, *Ethnology*, pp. 15–18.
172 The Russians saw yams at Hanga-roa.
173 See Beechey, *Narrative*, 1:46–50 for a very similar sequence of events in 1825, and Métraux, *Ethnology*, pp. 236–37, on dyes.
174 This incident and Russian distortions of it is discussed on pp. 46–47.

Otto von Kotzebue

175 I.e., rounded Motu-nui in the *Resolution*'s track of 13 March 1774: Beaglehole, *The Journals*, 2:337–38.
176 Probably untrue; but see Cook, *Voyage*, 1:292 and Forster, *Resolution Journal*, pp. 463–64.
177 Chamisso reports that each had three paddlers, but Choris agreed with his captain and seized this opportunity to draw both canoes and a paddle: *Voyage pittoresque*, pl. x, fig. 3, and Métraux, *Ethnology*, pp. 208–9.
178 Both Roggeveen (*Extracts*, p. 19) and Forster junior had seen canoes about ten feet long, and the Russian evidence supports the French (La Pérouse, *Voyage*, 1:76) in pointing to an increasing wood shortage.
179 Discussion in Métraux, *Ethnology*, pp. 204–5.
180 This sequence of events was traditional: see Roggeveen, *Extracts*, pp. 11ff.; Beaglehole, *The Journals*, 2:345; Métraux, *Ethnology*, pp. 144–467.
181 Punta Roa.
182 See Beechey, *Narrative*, 1:43–44 for similar events in 1825.
183 Ibid., p. 48, and Métraux, *Ethnology*, pp. 236–37. According to Hippolyte Roussel ("Ile de Pâques," *Annales des Sacres Coeurs* [Paris 1926]: 423), the application of black dye, or *ngarahu*, was a normal warlike preparation.
184 More specifically, with Marquesans of Nukuhiva.
185 At least one had been designed—by Fincham of London—to withstand high surf and breakers: Kotzebue, *Voyage of Discovery*, 1:17–18. Choris depicts it heading for Hanga-roa shoreline in *Vue de l'Ile de Pâques*, with 12 men aboard.
186 See p. 96.
187 La Pérouse, *Voyage*, 1:90.
188 Ibid., p. 76 and Cook, *Voyage*, 1:288; also Corney, *Voyage*, p. 122 (economic value of indigenous fowls, etc.).
189 This was the *tupa* of *ahu* Akapu, seen by the British in 1774 (Forster, *Voyage Round the World*, 1:570) and accurately described for the French by Bernizet (La Pérouse, *Voyage*, 2:254). The interior chamber measured 24 feet by 6 feet.
190 Kamehameha I had acquired the *Forester*, a French-built privateer captured by the British and then purchased by John Jacob Astor (1763–1848), the New York capitalist and fur trader, in April 1816. Adams's former captain in *Forester*, William J. Pigott, who had had frequent dealings with the Russians at Sitka and Petropavlovsk-in-Kamchatka in 1814–15, had sailed to Hawaii with Richard Ebbets (1789–1824), who concluded the actual sale. He was, in fact, on his way overland to St. Petersburg to collect monies allegedly owed him: see K.W. Porter, "The Cruise of the Forester," *Washington Historical Quarterly*, 23 (1932): 261–85, and R.A. Pierce, *Russia's Hawaiian Adventure, 1815–1817* (Berkeley 1965), pp. 13, 19, 159 n. Kotzebue, *Voyage of Discovery*, 1:324–25 and 352, for Kotzebue's encounters with the ship and her master in late November 1816.
191 *The Columbian Centinel* of Boston reported on 9 November 1805 that a Captain Crocker had taken the *Nancy* of Boston from Europe to Canton via the Eastern Caroline Islands in 1804–5, incidentally discovering "Strong's Island," which is now called Kusaie: see Findlay, *Directory of the North Pacific Ocean*, 3d ed. (London 1886), p. 975, and R.G. Ward, ed., *American Activities in the Central Pacific, 1790–1870* (Ridgewood, NJ 1967), 3:534–35. It is entirely possible that, as Adams said, Crocker had spent part of

1805 at Mas Afuera Island, due west of Valparaiso, Chile, hunting seals for the Canton market; and had sailed thence to Easter Island to seize workers and slaves. From the outset, however, some Russians supposed that Adams himself had commanded *Nancy;* that he wished to hide his guilt behind a veil of anonymity; and that the whole story was cloudy. It became more so as an unfortunate result of (a) a typographical slip at St. Petersburg in the printing of the Kotzebue *Puteshestvie,* rightly noted and deplored by Chamisso (*Werke,* Bd. 1:117 n), and (b) the inability of Chamisso and Choris, because of time and distance pressures that same year, to check the facts and emend the printer's error (see Choris, *Voyage pittoresque,* p. 18). Recent writers have compounded the problem by confusing Crocker and Adams and by suggesting yet other dates for the *Nancy* raid (e.g., Machowski, *Island of Secrets,* p. 63). The item in the *Columbian Centinel's* "Nautical and Shipping Memoranda" of 9 November 1805 was reprinted in the *Boston Gazette* and the *Salem Gazette* on 11–12 November, but, not surprisingly, Crocker had nothing to say about murder and outrage in the later stage of his voyage.

192 Captain Nathan Winship (1787–1820) left Boston with *Albatross* in July 1809, reaching Honolulu via Easter Island in early February 1810. He had served as chief mate under his older brother Jonathan (1780–1847) in the 280-ton trader *O'Cain* in 1805–8, making contact with the Russians at Sitka. Adams had known the Winships in that period, i.e., ten years before he became master of the *Kahumana.* Nor was his the only other New England vessel to visit Easter Island in 1806–9: see Delano, *Narrative,* pp. 355–58.

193 Pitcairn was eventually visited by the Russians in February 1833, when Lieutenant Fedor Bodisko, who had landed on Tahiti from the *Ladoga* in 1823, went ashore with a party of seamen and three Pitcairn natives from the naval transport *Amerika* (Captain V.S. Khromchenko): TsGIAE, *fond* 2057, op. i, *delo* 381 (Kiril T. Khlebnikov diary); Andrei P. Lazarev, *Plavanie vokrug sveta na shliupe "Ladoga" v 1822–1825 godakh* (St. P. 1832), 4; Ivashintsev, *Russian Round-the-World Voyages,* pp. 71, 112. Khromchenko had been Kotzebue's mate in 1815–18 and was mindful, as commander of his own ship in 1831–33, of Kotzebue's failure to visit Pitcairn Island, so well described by Beechey in his *Narrative.* That work had appeared four months before *Amerika* left Kronstadt on 26 August 1831 for Oceania, by way of Portsmouth roads. Bodisko landed at Bounty Bay on 12 February 1833, returning with ample foodstuffs. The visit is ignored by Soviet Pacific scholarship (e.g., K.V. Malakhovskii, N.P. Nikolaev, eds., *Okeaniia: spravochnik* [M. 1982], pp. 335–37; K.V. Malakhovskii, *Istoriia kolonializma v Okeanii* [M. 1979], pp. 74–75).

CHAPTER THREE: THE SCIENTIFIC LEGACY

1 3:00 AM to 7:00 PM: Kotzebue, *Voyage,* 1:136, 141.

2 *Sobranie kart i risunkov* . . . , pls. 1–2. Discussion in my study, *The Russian Discovery of Hawaii,* pt. 4, d–e.

3 Lukina, *Iogan Fridrikh Esholts,* passim; Otto von Kotzebue, *Novoe puteshestvie,* ed. D.D. Tumarkin (Moscow 1981), p. 317; Barratt, *Russian View of Honolulu,* chs. 2–3; for surveys of Choris's artistic career, see Bantysh-Kamenskii, *Slovar' dostoprimech. liudei russkoi zemli* 5 (M. 1836); *Moskovskie vedomosti* (1828): nos. 57, 71; *RBS,* 21: 413–14.

4 *Moskovskii telegraf* (1826): no. 22, pp. 336–41; *RBS,* 23:460–62.

5 TsGADA, *fond* 183, *delo* 89 (enclosed with "Ob otpravlenii . . . kamergera Rezanova . . . ," in the B.N. Bosnin Collection). On Sevast'ianov, see *RBS,* 18:266–68 and *St-Peterburgskie Vedomosti* (1825): no. 81, pp. 957–59.

6 "Instruktsiia dlia puteshestviia okolo sveta po chasti mineralogii . . . ," *Severnyi vestnik* (St. P. 1804): nos. 2–3.

7 Biographical sketch by E. Escher, *Hörner's Leben und Wirken* (Zurich 1834); also Berthelot, ed., *La Grande Encyclopédie,* 20:280 and Nevskii, *Pervoe puteshestvie,* pp. 269–70.

8 Kotzebue, *Voyage,* 1:41–83.

9 Ibid., 1:41.
10 See Chamisso, *Werke*, 1:115.
11 Barratt, *Bellingshausen*, pp. 6–8.
12 Ibid., pp. 4–6.
13 Kotzebue, *Voyage*, 1:1–15.
14 Ivashintsev, *Russian Round-the-World Voyages*, p. 24.
15 Kotzebue, *Voyage*, 1:90–91, 94; Chamisso, *Werke*, 3:18–19; Mahr, "Visit of the 'Rurik'," pp. 12ff.; on Morten Wormskiöld, see Carl Christensen, *Den danske Botaniks Historie* (Copenhagen 1924–26), 1:242–45; 2:163.
16 Kotzebue, *Voyage*, 1:10–11.
17 Winship had had dealings with Chief Manager Baranov at Sitka on the Russian Northwest Coast as chief mate of the *O'Cain* in 1806–7. He left Boston with the 165-ton *Albatross* in July 1809, apparently calling at Easter Island en route to Honolulu, in January 1810: see Pierce, *Russia's Hawaiian Adventure*, pp. 229, 245, etc.
18 *DNB*. 10:1300–1.
19 See Beaglehole, *The Journals*, 2:338.
20 *Carl Friedrich Behrens Reise durch die Süd-Länder und um die Welt* ... (Frankfurt & Leipzig 1737; 2d ed. 1739); a French version, *Histoire de l'Expédition de trois vaisseaux ... aux Terres Australes en MDCCXXI* (Paris 1739), was preferred by Alexander Dalrymple, Jean Bérenger, and other eighteenth-century compilers, and also by Cook. Georg H. Langsdorf, on the other hand, put greater confidence in the work entitled *Tweejaarige Reyze rondom de Wereld* ... (Dordrecht 1728), apparently published by Joannes van Braam on the basis of Jacob Roggeveen's text (see Langsdorf, *Voyages and Travels*, 1:85); despite Cook's doubts about that book's reliability, Langsdorf made the right judgment.
21 Alexander Dalrymple, comp., *A Historical Collection of the Several Voyages and Discoveries Made in the South Pacific Ocean* (London 1770–71). Kruzenshtern was familiar with the work in 1804.
22 Beaglehole, *The Journals*, 2:351 and n.2.
23 Forster, *Resolution Journal*, p. 475.
24 See somatological and related data adduced by H.L. Shapiro in Métraux, *Ethnology*, p. 28.
25 Ibid., p. 21.
26 Forster, *Resolution Journal*, p. 475.
27 See Routledge, *Mystery of Easter Island*, pp. 280ff.; Métraux, *Ethnology*, pp. 73–74.
28 Roggeveen, *Extracts*, p. 15; see also P. Loti, *Reflets sur la sombre route* (Paris n.d.), p. 258.
29 Corney, *Voyage*, p. 96.
30 La Pérouse, *Voyage*, 1:323.
31 Roggeveen, *Extracts*, pp. 9–10; Corney, *Voyage*, p. 121; Delano, *Narrative*, p. 356; Beechey, *Narrative*, 1:41–42.
32 Forster, *Voyage Round the World*, 1:571; Thomson, *Te Pito te Henua*, p. 456; Métraux, *Ethnology*, p. 156.
33 Technique described by Te Rangi Hiroa and given in extract by Métraux, *Ethnology*, pp. 211–12.
34 Behrens, *Histoire de l'Expédition*, 1:130.
35 Forster, *Voyage Round the World*, 1:589–90; Forster, *Resolution Journal*, p. 472.
36 Corney, *Voyage*, p. 123; Cook, *Voyage*, 1:288.
37 Cook, *Voyage*, 1:288; La Pérouse, *Voyage*, 1:328; see also Geiseler, *Die Oster-Insel*, p. 37 (later proliferation of fowl).
38 Summary in Métraux, *Ethnology*, pp. 172–74.
39 Cook, *Voyage*, 1:289; Forster, *Observations*, p. 423.
40 Summary in Métraux, *Ethnology*, p. 20.
41 Kotzebue, *Voyage*, 3:227.
42 Choris, *Voyage pittoresque*, p. 12.

43 Roggeveen, _Extracts_, p. 11; Forster, _Voyage Round the World_, 1:577; Cook, _Voyage_, 1:289.

44 See Cook, _Voyage_, 1:291; Du Petit-Thouars, _Voyage_, pl. 44; and Loti, _Expedition_, pp. 66–68.

45 Métraux, _Ethnology_, fig. 30.

46 H. Lavachéry, _L'Ile de Pâques_ (Paris 1935), p. 256.

47 Beechey, _Narrative_, 1:53.

48 Palmer, "A Visit to Easter Island," p. 171; also A. Pinart, "Voyage à l'Ile de Pâques," _Le Tour du monde_, 36 (1878): p. 239 on triangular patches, etc..

49 Du Petit-Thouars, _Voyage . . . Atlas_, pl. 44.

50 Beechey, _Narrative_, 1:53; W.J. Thomson, _Te Pito te Henua or Easter Island_ (Washington D.C. 1889): p. 467; Loti, _Expedition_, p. 68. The neck tattoo of Choris's subject might equally be said to correspond to Beechey's "curved lines of a dark Berlin blue colour."

51 Discussion of Choris's drawings from Hawaii and Oahu in K.P. Emory, _Hawaiian Tattoing_, Bishop Museum Occasional Papers No. 17, vol. 18 (Honolulu 1946); see also Peter H. Buck, _Arts and Crafts of Hawaii_, Bishop Museum Spec. Publ. 45 (Honolulu 1957), pp. 554–55, and Jean Charlot, _Choris and Kamehameha_ (Honolulu 1956).

52 _Vue de l'Ile de Pâques_, pl. ix in _Voyage pittoresque_, was lithographed under the direction of Alexis Nicolas Noël whose family had a financial interest in the work, by E. (?) Bovet: see Bénézit, ed., _Dictionnaire critique et documentaire des peintres_ (Paris 1948–55), 2:86, and U. Thieme, ed., _Allgemeines Lexikon der Bildenden Künstler_, 36 vol. (Leipzig 1907–47), 6:527; 25:498. The two Easter Island (compound) plates of _Vues et paysages_ (1826), x and xi, were the work of the more prolific Parisian lithographer Langlumé: Thieme, _Allg. Lexikon_, 22:351.

53 Thomson, _Te Pito te Henua_, fig. 4.

54 Roggeveen, _Extracts_, p. 17; see also Delano, _Narrative_, p. 356.

55 Cook, _Voyage_, 1:290.

56 Forster, _Voyage_, 1:564; Eyraud, "Lettre," 38:56.

57 Corney, _Voyage_, p. 122 (source of chalk-white tuff); Geiseler, _Die Oster-Insel_, p. 15 (source of yellow pigment on Rano-kao).

58 Beechey, _Narrative_, 1:52; Eyraud, "Lettre," 38:67.

59 Métraux, _Ethnology_, pp. 228–29.

60 Geiseler, _Die Oster-Insel_, p. 35.

61 Chamisso's term, _Kopfputze aus schwartzen federn_, suggests a diadem: for a discussion, see Métraux, _Ethnology_, pp. 220–24. MAE in Leningrad has a shell ornament of more recent provenance: details in Butinov and Rozina, "Kollektsiia s ostrova Pashki," _SMAE_, 18: pp. 316–17 (_repu reva_, no. 402–201b).

62 See Métraux, _Ethnology_, pp. 230–33.

63 Beaglehole, _The Journals_, 2:347.

64 Ibid., p. 349; also Forster, _Resolution Journal_, p. 467.

65 La Pérouse, _Voyage_, pl. 11; Loti, _Expedition_, p. 66; Gaspard Zumbohm, "Lettres du Père . . . sur la mission de l'Ile de Pâques," _Annales de la Congrégation des Sacrés-Coeurs de Jésus et de Marie_, 5 (1879–80): 664.

66 Cook, _Voyage_, 1:291; also Beaglehole, _The Journals_, 2:352.

67 Choris, _Voyage pittoresque_, p. 17; compare Forster, _Resolution Journal_, p. 471 ("never to a height above 2, 3, or 4 feet"), and Beaglehole, _The Journals_, 2:347.

68 Eyraud, "Lettres," 38:68, on vanity versus practical need as the chief motive for this passion for clothing; also Thomson, _Te Pito te Henua_, p. 467ff. It is significant that MAE in Leningrad does not hold a single Easter Island garment or tapa specimen. The islanders did not readily part with such cloth or clothing as they had.

69 See my _Russia in Pacific Waters_, pp. 113ff.

70 Instructions of 29 May 1803: cited by Nevskii, _Pervoe puteshestvie_, p. 37.

71 On this aspect of Cook's influence in Russia, see my _Russians at Port Jackson_, pp. 5–6.

72 TsGALI, _fond_ 18 veka, _delo_ 5196, pp. 40–41, 86–87; TsVMM, no. 9170/1938 ("Zhurnal leitenanta Iuriia Lisianskago s 1793 po 1800 . . ."); see also _Morskoi sbornik_

(St. P. 1894): no. 1 ("Neofitsial'nyi otdel"), p. 20, and E.L. Shteinberg, *Zhizneopisanie*, p. 209.
73 L.G. Rozina, "Kollektsiia Muzeia Antropologii i Etnografii po Markizskim ostrovam," *SMAE*, 21 (L 1963): 110; also my *Russian Discovery of Hawaii*, pt. 2a.
74 N.I. Korobitsyn, "Zapiski," given in A.I. Andreev, ed., *Russkie otkrytiia v Tikhom okeane i Severnoi Amerike v XVIII–XIX vv.* (M.-L. 1944), p. 168 and n.
75 Shteinberg, *Zhizneopisanie*, p. 160; Lisianskii, *Voyage*, pp. 64–67.
76 Shteinberg, *Zhizneopisanie*, p. 166.
77 Lisianskii, *Voyage*, p. 102.
78 See my *Bellingshausen*, pt. 3.
79 LOAAN, *fond* 2, op. 1 (1827), no. 3, p. 13 (Pacific artefacts to the Admiralty Department Museum); *fond* 142, op. 1 (1719–1827), no. 108, p. 1 (other artefacts from *Neva* for the Academy of Sciences); Shteinberg, *Zhizneopisanie*, p. 209; T.V. Staniukovich, *Etnograficheskaia nauka i muzei* (L. 1978), p. 62.
80 *Piatidesiatiletie Rumiantsovskago Muzeia v Moskve, 1862–1912: istoricheskii ocherk* (M. 1912), p. 164. For data on Polynesian artefacts from the early Russian voyages that remained on public display in Moscow intermittently throughout the later nineteenth century, see *Sbornik materialov dlia istorii Rumiantsovskago Muzeia*, bk. 1 (M. 1882), pp. 108–17. That paper is preceded by another (pp. 90–107) touching on Count Rumiantsev's encouragement of natural history and ethnography by naval officers, among others.
81 T.V. Staniukovich, "Muzei etnograficheskogo i istoricheskogo profilia v period Velikoi Otechestvennoi Voiny," *Sovetskaia Etnografiia* (1975): no. 5, pp. 64–66, and personal comments to the writer of 21 May 1985.
82 Materials on this in the archive of the Academy of Sciences in Leningrad include, besides those mentioned in n. 79 above, an inventory of 1807 in Lisianskii's own hand ("Katalog Iskusstvennym Veshcham i Odezhde raznykh Narodov" or "Catalogue of Artificial Objects and Clothing of Various . . . Peoples": *fond* 142, op. 1, no. 108; a list based on this inventory, drawn up at the *Kunstkammer* also in 1807, headed "Spisok Veshchei, Podarennykh Iu. Lisianskim v Kunstkammeru Imp. Akademii Nauk v 1806 godu" ("A List of Articles Donated to the *Kunstkammer* of the Imperial Academy of Sciences by Iu. Lisianskii in 1806"): *fond* 1, op. 2 (1807), no. 20; and the Acquisitions Book of the Peter the Great Museum at MAE for the period 1719–1836 (Arkhiv MAE: Zhurnal Postuplenii za 1719 po 1836 god), pp. 44–46.
83 Article in *Russkii invalid* (St. P. 1839): no. 31.
84 LOAAN, *fond* 2, op. 1 (1827), no. 3, p. 13.
85 See F. Russov, "Beiträge zur Geschichte der etnographischen und antropologischen Sammlungen der Kaiserlichen Akademie der Wissenschaften zu St Petersburg," *SMAE*, 1 (St. P. 1900); and n. 79.
86 *ZGDMM*, pt. 8 (St. P. 1845), pp. 444–45; this material was reprinted and annotated by A.P. Sokolov in a second edition of *Russkaia morskaia biblioteka: period chetvertyi* (St. P. 1883), pp. 137–38. Drafts of letters to various persons from Lisianskii written up to 1832, held at TsVMM (no. 9170-3/1938), reflect a continuing interest in Pacific expeditions as well as social connections with members of the imperial family. A fully satisfactory biography of Lisianskii has yet to appear.
87 See n. 80.
88 Iu.M. Likhtenberg, "Gavaiskie kollektsii v Sobraniiakh Muzeia Antropologii i Etnografii," *SMAE*, 19 (L. 1960): 169.
89 Kotzebue, *Voyage*, 1:311.
90 *Linnaea: ein Journal für die Botanik*, 1 (Berlin 1826): 388–89. The plant was *Umbellifer*. *Apium graveolens* L.: further details in "Botany" section. Chamisso exaggerates the brevity of his time ashore on Easter Island (Kotzebue, *Voyage*, 3:225) when speaking of "a moment."
91 Beechey, *Narrative*, 1:44.
92 MAE, Otdel Avstralii i Okeanii: Opis', kollektsiia no. 736, p. 1 (registration of artefacts by L.G. Rozina, 1964–65). I thank Nikolai A. Butinov and Tamara K. Shafranovskaia

for free access to this inventory in 1985. See also *SMAE*, 19:169, 21:85, and 39:16, for Soviet contentions that the articles in collection 736 were moved to the *Kunstkammer* in 1830, 1828, and 1826! In reality, most artefacts were transferred in 1827–28: LOAAN, *fond* 1, op. 2 (1827), no. 462; *fond* 2, op. 1 (1827), no. 3, pp. 12ff. (transfer of material acquired in Oceania by *Vostok* and *Mirnyi* in 1820–21, etc.).

93 T.K. Shafranovskaia and A.I. Azarov, "Katalog kollektsii otdela Avstralii i Okeanii MAE," *SMAE*, 39 (1984): 16. Collection 736 today contains 326 items.

94 TsVMM developed from this museum, which was always distinct from the Kronstadt Maritime Museum (see *ES*, 20:117). After 1828, the forerunner of TsVMM continued to transfer ethnographica to the Academy of Sciences or other institutions; very few are among the present 32,000 storage units there.

95 See n. 92 above and *SMAE*. 21:85.

96 Ibid.; see also L.G. Rozina, "Kollektsiia MAE po Markizskim ostrovam," *SMAE*, 21:110.

97 E.g., in *Cook Voyage Artifacts in Leningrad, Berne, and Florence Museums*, Bernice P. Bishop Special Publication 66 (Honolulu 1978).

98 Examination of artefacts by the writer, May 1985. On obsidian tools, J.L. Palmer, "A Visit to Easter Island," pp. 171–72, and Métraux, *Ethnology*, pp. 272–81.

99 Rozina, "Kollektsiia MAE po Markizskim ostrovam," pp. 112, 114. See also my *Russian Discovery of Hawaii*, pt. 4e, for a discussion of similarly identifiable 1804 Hawaiian objects taken aboard *Neva*.

100 E.g., 750–12, 113, and 16, represented in *Sobranie kart i risunkov* (St. P. 1812), pl. 1, as W, U, E.

101 LOAAN, *fond* 142, op. 1 (1719–1827), no. 108: "Katalog Iskustvennym Veshcham i Odezhde."

102 The Petri inventory was itself supplemented in 1964 by another by Rozina, but remains in the Peter-the-Great Museum file ("Opis': Kollektsiia No. 750"). It is headed "Inventarnyi Spisok Kollektsii Muzeia . . . imeni Imperatora Petra Velikogo: No. 750." The handwriting on the labels in question was kindly identified as Lisianskii's by A.I. Andreev on the basis of Lisianskii's service journal of 1793–1800 ("Zhurnal leitenanta Iuriia Lisianskogo s 1793 goda po 1800 god"), held at TsVMM under reference MS 41821/1. For a recent discussion of the surviving original Lisianskii diaries and their relationship to each other, see N.I. Bolkhovitinov, *Stanovlenie otnoshenii, 1765–1815: Rossiia i SShA* (M. 1980), pp. 199–203 and notes.

103 Thick paper, 1″ by 1½″, no watermark.

104 Labels occasionally indicate that enumeration changed twice: modern 750-10, for instance, was evidently no. 27 in the early 1800s, no. 28 at another time: a clerk's slip might explain it.

105 N.N. Miklukho-Maklai, "Ostrova Rapa-Nui, Pitkairn, i Mangareva," *Sobranie sochinenii*, 1 (L. 1950): 50–51; 5 (1954): 339–400, 411–13; also *Journal of the Royal Anthropological Institute* 5 (London 1896): 114. On Sviatlovskii's collecting and career, see L. G. Rozina's paper in *SMAE*, 30 (1974): 127–39. See *SMAE*, 18 (1958): 306–8, for the growth of the Russian collection of Easter Island artefacts.

106 *SMAE*, 18:308–14 and figs. 1–2; Métraux, *Ethnology*, pp. 250ff.

107 Routledge, *Mystery of Easter Island*, pp. 257–63 and "The Bird Cult of Easter Island," pp. 337–81; Thomson, *Te Pito te Henua*, pp. 482ff.; Beaglehole, *The Journals* 2:336–38.

108 S. Chauvet, *L'Ile de Pâques et ses mystères* (Paris 1936), fig. 112; see also Friedrich Schulze-Maizier's *Die Oster-insel* (Leipzig n.d.), p. 121, on this carved image.

109 Métraux, *Ethnology*, p. 251 for further data; description of 736–204 in Butinov and Rozina, "Kollektsiia s Ostrova Paskhi," p. 308.

110 *SMAE*, 18:314.

111 Métraux, *Ethnology*, pp. 254–55.

112 Ibid., pp. 42–45.

113 Maurice Desmedt, "Les funérailles et l'exposition des morts à Mangareva," in *Bulletin*

de la Société des Américanistes de Belgique (Bruxelles 1931), pp. 134–36; Routledge, *Mystery of Easter Island*, pp. 269–70.

114 Teuira Henry, *Ancient Tahiti*, Bishop Museum Bulletin 48 (Honolulu 1928), p. 203; Elsdon Best, *The Maori* (Wellington, 1924), 1:281, 2:60; E. Shortland, *Traditions and Superstitions of the New Zealanders* (London 1854), p. 63.

115 Métraux, *Ethnology*, p. 249.

116 Thomson, *Te Pito te Henua*, p. 449.

117 Beaglehole, *The Journals*, 2:352.

118 La Pérouse, *Voyage*, 2:256; see also Delano, *Narrative*, p. 356 and Beechey, *Narrative*, 1:55.

119 La Pérouse, *Voyage*, 2:256–57.

120 Forster, *Voyage Round the World*, 1:570–71.

121 Cook, *Voyage*, 1:570, and Métraux, *Ethnology*, pp. 193–94.

122 See also above, ch. 2, n. 166.

123 Cook, *Voyage*, 1:296; La Pérouse, *Voyage*, 1:70; also Du Petit-Thouars, *Voyage*, 2:225 and Routledge, *Mystery of Easter Island*, p. 232.

124 Palmer, "Visit to Easter Island," p. 174; Geiseler, *Die Oster-Insel*, p. 28; Métraux, *Ethnology*, pp. 327–28.

125 See James Hornell's comments in Haddon and Hornell, *Canoes of Oceania*, pp. 103ff.; also R.B. Dixon, *The Building of Cultures* (New York 1928), pp. 75–76, and Métraux, *Ethnology*, pp. 204–5.

126 Corney, *Voyage*, p. 121; LaPérouse, *Voyage*, 1:76.

127 Haddon and Hornell, *Canoes of Oceania*, p. 98.

128 Kotzebue, *Voyage*, 1:137; Métraux, *Ethnology*, p. 205.

129 Haddon and Hornell, *Canoes of Oceania*, p. 62. Kotzebue himself passed by Takapoto in March 1824 (see Sharp, *Discovery of the Pacific Islands*, pp. 206–7), but saw no more of Tuamotuan canoes and navigation than Bellingshausen had in July 1820: Bellingshausen, *Voyage* 1:228–33.

130 Churchill, *Easter Island*, pp. 49–63.

131 Métraux, *Ethnology*, p. 205.

132 See Dumont-D'Urville, *Voyage au Pôle sud* (1841), 3:387, and Du Petit-Thouars, *Voyage*, 2:231, on swimming, with or without *pora* supports, far from shore.

133 Forster, *Voyage Round the World*, 1:590.

134 See Métraux, *Ethnology*, pp. 211–12.

135 See n. 132 and Palmer, "A Visit to Easter Island," p. 172.

136 Thomson, *Te Pito te Henua*, p. 475; also Cook, *Voyage*, 1:291 and Forster, *Voyage Round the World*, 1:536.

137 See Métraux, *Ethnology*, fig. 6.

138 *Schorn's Kunst-Blatt* (Stuttgart) (1821):88, 224; Bénézit, *Dictionnaire critique*, 2:86, 3:228, etc.; E. Béllier-Auvray, *Dictionnaire général* (Paris 1885), vol. 2; Barratt, *Russian View of Honolulu*, pt. 5.

139 H.W. Singer, ed., *Künstler-Lexikon* (Frankfurt-am-Main 1920), 1:256; Ul. Thieme, ed., *Allgemeines Lexikon der Bildenden Künstler* (Leipzig 1907–47), 6:527, 13:435–37.

140 Thieme, *All. Lexikon der Bildenden Künstler*, 25:498. Bénézit, *Dictionnaire critique*, vol. 3.

141 The attribution (bottom right) of several of Choris's 1826 illustrations, e.g., of Easter Island, "Romanzoff Island," and Penrhyn (Tongareva), is to "de Bové dirigée par Noël ainé et Cie." Despite the fact that *Vue de l'Ile de Pâques* (pl. ix) demonstrates the stippling technique of engraving in dots associated with Eduard Bovet (see Bénézit, *Dictionnaire critique*, 2:86), it seems certain that it was the work of Auguste-André Bovet, the most accomplished student of David Detalla (1761–1836) and an inveterate traveller himself.

142 See E. and J. Goncourt, *L'Art du XVIIIe siècle* (Paris 1882), 2:453–56; J. Guiffrey, *L'Oeuvre de P.P. Prud'hon* (Paris 1924); *La Gazette des Beaux-Arts*, 4 (1859): p 113; 10(1861): 246.

143 The published literature on Langlumé (and Choris's other French lithographers: see Thieme, *All. Lexikon der Bildenden Künstler*, 22: 351) has yet to be collated with relevant archival material, e.g., Choris's letters to I.F. Kruzenshtern from Paris of 1821–22, held at TsGIAE (Tartu), *fond* 1414, op. 3, *delo* 42 (microfilm copy at Elmer E. Rasmuson Library of the University of Alaska at Fairbanks: Shur Collection, reel 118). Pacific ethnography and ethnohistory, among other sciences, will benefit considerably from a thorough study of Choris's illustrative record and its fate in 1820–26.

144 His major works were *Übersicht der zoologischen Ausbeute* (Weimar 1830), also printed as an appendix to Kotzebue's *Neue Reise um die Welt* of that year, and *Zoologischer Atlas* (Berlin 1829–31), also accompanying Kotzebue's *Voyage* in *Predpriiatie* (1823–26). Further details in T.A. Lukina, *Iogan Fridrikh Eshsholts* (Leningrad 1980). On Wormskiöld, see *Dansk Naturhistorisk Forening Videnskabelige Meddelelser* (Copenhagen 1889), pp. 253–81, and Carl Christensen, *Den danske Botaniks Historie* (Copenhagen 1924–26), 1:242–46.

145 See my *Russian Exploration in the Mariana Islands, 1816–1828*, Micronesian Archaeological Survey Report 17 (Saipan 1984), pp. 55–56, and Lukina, *Eshsholts*, pp. 24–25.

146 See G. Menza, *Adelbert von Chamissos "Reise"*, and E. du Bois Reymond, *Adelbert von Chamisso als Naturforscher* (Leipzig 1889), chs. 3–4.

147 P. Engelstoft. ed., *Dansk Biografisk Leksikon* (Copenhagen 1944), 26:301.

148 Kotzebue, *Puteshestvie*, (St. P. 1821): intro. The references are to Karl Asmund Rudolphi (1771–1832) and Martin Heinrich Lichtenstein (1780–1857), professors respectively of anatomy and natural history in Berlin. Karl-Friedrich Ledebour (1765–1812), Director of the Botanic Garden at Dorpat, 1811–36.

149 Kotzebue, *Voyage*, 1:94, 184.

150 *Dansk Biogr. Leksikon*, 10 (1936): 599–603.

151 1816, pp. 750–53; 1817, pp. 235–38; 1818, pp. 349–51, 735–36.

152 Hornemann evidently saw the journal (*Dagbog*): see *Dansk Literatur-Tidende* (1817): 238.

153 *Chamissos Werke* (Leipzig 1836): Bd. 1(*Reise um die Welt . . .* :Erster Theil, Tagebuch), pp. 115—19 (Easter Islalnd section).

154 See Menza, *Adelbert von Chamissos "Reise"*, pp. 70ff.

155 Kotzebue, *Voyage*, 1:138; Ivashintsev, *Russian Round-the-World Voyages*, p. 138.

156 Zakharin was unwell: Kotzebue, *Voyage*, 1:90, 111, 184; Mahr, *The Visit of the "Rurik"*, p. 12.

157 Kotzebue, *Voyage*, 1:131–36 and 3:327.

158 See ch. 2, nn. 7, 8, 14, 78, 132, and 146, on Russian willingness to be prepared for Easter Island encounters.

159 *Linnaea*, 1:388–89 6 (1831): p 86.

160 Chamisso, *Werke*, 1:347; Barratt, *Russian View of Honolulu*, ch. 10 (Chamisso's botanizing on Hawaii and Oahu, etc.).

161 *Grande Dictionnaire Universel* (Larousse), 15:1341–42.

162 *Linnaea*, 1:8.

163 Ibid., p. 388.

164 *De plantis*, p. 67, n. 36; see also Beaglehole, *The Journals*, 2:cliii n.2.

165 See H.A. Gleason, *Illustrated Flora of the Northeastern United States . . .* (New York 1952), 2:621.

166 *Linnaea*, 6:76–82 ("Labiatae").

167 Georg. F. Kaulfuss, *Enumeratio filicum quas in Itinere circa terram legit Adalbertus de Chamisso* (Lipsiae 1824), for those brought back aboard *Riurik*.

168 *Linnaea*, 6:83ff. Lessing groups *Centaurea* under the heading *Synanthereae* rather than *Compositae*, for historical reasons.

169 See his *Reise durch Norwegen . . .* (Berlin 1831).

170 *Linnaea*, 6:86, no. 5.

171 The "1815–18 Chamisso" herbarium at BIAN in Leningrad holds no Easter Island

specimens; but see my *Russian View of Honolulu*, ch. 10, on the 25 extant specimens from Hawaii or Oahu that remain at the V.L. Komarov Institute of Botany (Higher Plants Division) in Leningrad.

172 Nevskii, *Pervoe puteshestvie*, pp. 35–38.

173 Kruzenshtern, *Voyage*, 1:102.

174 Barratt, *Russia in Pacific Waters*, pp. 113–15.

175 *Protokol Konferentsii Akademii Nauk ot 13 aprelia 1803 goda* (St. P. 1803); also F.F. Veselago, *Admiral Ivan Fedorovich Kruzenshtern* (St. P. 1869), chs. 2–3; A. Sgibnev, "Rezanov i Kruzenshtern," *Drevniaia i Novaia Rossiia*, 1 (St. P. 1877): no. 4; K. Voenskii, "Posol'stvo Rezanova v Iaponiiu v 1803–1805 godakh," *Morskoi sbornik* (April 1919), pp. 29–64.

176 Lionel Wafer, *A New Voyage* ... , ed. L.E. Joyce (London 1934), see pp. 125–26; W. Dampier, *A Collection of Voyages* (London 1729), 1:352.

177 See *Russkaia starina* (St. P. 1895), bk, 7, pp. 127ff.; I.F. Kruzenshtern, *Sobranie sochinenii, sluzhashchikh razborom* (St. P. 1823), pt. 1, pp. 111–12; *Hamburgische Neue Zeitung* (1802): no. 137; *Vestnik Evropy* (St. P. 1802): no. 5, p. 146.

178 Kruzenshtern, *Voyage*, 1:102–3; Barratt, *Russia in Pacific Waters*, p. 122.

179 Nevskii, *Pervoe puteshestvie*, p. 102.

180 "Otkrytiia Tasmana, s prilozheniem sochineniia o polozhenii Ontong-Iavy," *Tekhnologicheskii Zhurnal*, 3 (St. P. 1806): pt. 3, pp. 134–85.

181 *Tekhnologicheskii Zhurnal*, 2 (1805): pt. 2.

182 TsGIAL, *fond* 15, op. 1, *delo* 1, fols. 24ff.; Kruzenshtern, *Voyage*, 1:9.

183 B.A. Vorontsov-Vel'iaminov, *Ocherki istorii astronomii v Rossii* (M. 1956).

184 Printed in *Severnyi vestnik* (St. P. 1804): nos. 2–3.

185 See Nevskii, *Pervoe puteshestvie*, pp. 247–48.

186 P. Inokhodtsev, "Prodolzhenie kratkikh vypisok ... ," in *Tekhnologicheskii Zhurnal*, 2 (1805): pt. 3, pp. 133–38, etc.

187 Kruzenshtern, *Puteshestvie*, 3:228–60, 413–48.

188 F.P. Litke (Lütke), "Soobshchenie o smerti admirala I.F. Kruzenshterna," *Zapiski Russkogo Geograficheskogo Obshchestva* (St. P. 1847), bk 2, pp. 13–20; *St-Peterburgische Zeitung* (1839): nos. 28, 30, 32–37.

189 G.A. Sarychev, *Pravila, prinadlezhashchie k morskoi geodezii, ... kak opisyvat' moria, berega, ostrova* (St. P. 1804); P. Ia. Gamaleia, *Vyshniaia teoriia morskago isskustva*, 4 pts. (St. P. 1801–4). For a useful survey of these developments, see A.I. Alekseev, "Russkaia morskaia gidrograficheskaia nauka v XIX-nachale XX vekov," *Trudy Instituta Istorii Estestvoznaniia i Tekhniki*, 42 (L. 1962): bk. 3, pp. 86–89.

190 Notably, Arrowsmith's world map of 1794 and map of the South Pacific Ocean of 1798: see Nevskii, *Pervoe puteshestvie*, p. 250.

191 Veselago, *Admiral Ivan Fedorovich Kruzenshtern*, pp. 11–12. As Chamisso noted in 1820 (Kotzebue, *Voyage*, 3:95–96), Kruzenshtern had made excellent use of the Pacific work of Don José Espinosa y Tello (1763–1815): Berthelot, *La Grande Encyclopédie*, 16:367.

192 *Tekhnologicheskii Zhurnal*, 2 (1805): pt. 2 ("O sushchestvovanii Devisovoi zemli ... ," etc.); Kotzebue, *Voyage*, 1:133.

193 Lisianskii, *Voyage*, pp. 50–51; E. Marchand, *Voyage autour du monde* (Paris 1798–1800).

194 Lisianskii, *Voyage*, p. 50.

195 Kotzebue, *Voyage*, 3:96.

196 Ibid., 1:134; Chamisso, *Werke*, 1:115.

197 A. von Chamisso, *Bemerkungen und Ansichten auf einer Entdeckungs-Reise* (Weimar 1821), p. 142.

198 Kotzebue, *Voyage*, 1:136.

199 Veselago, *Admiral Ivan Fedorovich Kruzenshtern*, p. 12; also Nevskii, *Pervoe puteshestvie*, pp. 251–54.

200 Lisianskii, *Voyage*, facing p. 61.

201 Kotzebue, *Voyage*, 2:294. Kruzenshtern was aware of a report in the *Courier* of Norwich, Connecticut, dated 13 April 1803 ("Marine Intelligence"), detailing a sighting by James Gwyn of the merchantman *Wareham* the previous year. The "small island or heap of rocks . . . about three quarters of a mile in circumference" reportedly lay in lat. 26°26', long. 100°30'W. Modern coordinates are lat. 26°27'S, long. 105°28'W: Findlay, *Directory of the North Pacific*, 3d ed. (London 1886), pp. 514–15.

202 See n. 191 and Nevskii, *Pervoe puteshestvie*, p. 250, n.3.

203 Kruzenshtern, "Otkrytiia Tasmana," pp. 136ff. (Spanish errors en route from South America to Tahiti, etc.)

204 Kruzenshtern, *Beyträge zur Hydrographie der grössern Ozeane* (Leipzig 1819); Kotzebue, *Voyage*, 3:95–96, 224.

CHAPTER FOUR: EARLIER RUSSIAN KNOWLEDGE OF NEW ZEALAND

1 M.D. Khmyrev, "Svedeniia o Vasilii Kiprianove, bibliotekare Moskovskoi Grazhdanskoi Tipografii pri Petre I," *Russkii arkhiv*, 9 (1865): 1299; also *Polnoe Sobranie Zakonov Rossiiskoi Imperii*, 6 (St. P. 1830–1916): doc. 3682.

2 On the "discovery" of Tasman, see A. Sharp, *The Voyages of Abel Janszoon Tasman* (Oxford 1968), pp. 341–46; on Russo-Dutch links before 1696 and the role of Andrei Vinius, see N. Ustrialov, *Istoriia tsarstvovaniia Petra Velikogo* (St. P. 1858), 2:125–28, and *Pis'ma i bumagi Imperatora Petra Velikogo*, 1 (St. P. 1887–1917 and Leningrad 1922–52): docs. 71ff.

3 I.I. Golikov, *Deianiia Petra Velikago, mudrogo preobrazitelia Rossii*, 2d ed. (M. 1837), 1:120–23; I. Scheltema, *Peter de Groote, Keizer van Rusland in Holland en te Zaandam in 1697 en 1717* (Amsterdam 1814), 1:131–34; I. Scheltema, *Rusland en te Nederlanden beschouwd in derzel ver wederkeerige Betrekkingen* (Amsterdam 1817–19), 1:181–86; M.M. Bogoslovskii, *Petr I: materialy dlia biografii* (M. 1941), 2:146–18, etc.; E.H. McCormick, *Tasman and New Zealand: A Bibliographical Study*, Alexander Turnbull Library Bulletin 14 (Wellington 1959), pp. 13–18.

4 McCormick, *Tasman and New Zealand*, p. 54; Sharp, *The Voyages of Tasman*, p. 345.

5 As "Een kort Verhael uyt het Journael van den Kommanduer Abel Janszoon Tasman," pp. 56–64 of part 2 of *Eenige Oefeningen*.

6 For Witsen's life and career, see G.D. Schotel, ed., *Van der Aas Biographisch Woordenboek* (Haarlem 1877), 20:354–59.

7 BAN (Library of the Academy of Sciences, in Leningrad) holds a copy of this edition: pp. 217–23, on canoes in Oceania and the East Indies; pl. 38 for illustrations thereof.

8 Essay by W.R. Veder in P.C. Molhuysen, ed., *Nieuw Nederlandsch Biographisch Woordenboek* (Leyden 1918), 4:1473–79; see also J.F. Gebhard, *Het leven van Mr. Nicolaas Corneliusz. Witsen* (Utrecht 1881–82), chs. 2–4.

9 Ian Grey, *Peter the Great* (London 1960), p. 108; Bogoslovskii, *Petr I*, 2:146 (Witsen as agent for the building of the ship *Sviatoe Prorochestvo* for Russia, etc.).

10 Details in McCormick, *Tasman and New Zealand,* pp. 17, 57–58.

11 Molhuysen, *Nieuw Nederlandsch Woordenboek*, 4:1476–77; Scheltema, *Rusland en de Nederlanden*, 1:181–86.

12 I thank Professor Boris Petrovich Polevoi, of the N.N. Miklukho-Maklai Institute of Anthropology and Ethnography, Leningrad, for drawing my attention to Peter's acknowledgment.

13 Pp. 217–18. I standardize tense usage; the original mixes past and present tenses.

14 *Noord en Oost Tartarye*, p. 173. Paddles are termed *pargays*, in echo of the French.

15 Sharp, *The Voyages of Tasman*, pp. 42 (Haalbos-Montanus account of 1671), pp. 121–23, 276–77.

16 McCormick, *Tasman and New Zealand*, pp. 17–18. On Gilseman, see J.E. Heeres, "Abel Janszoon Tasman: His Life and Labours," in *Abel Janszoon Tasman's Journal* (Amsterdam 1898), p. 107, and Sharp, *The Voyages of Tasman*, pp. 29, 38, etc.

17 Copies of both first (1692) and second (1705) editions were sent to Peter. Sharp reproduces Gilseman's original drawing (p. 130).
18 *Noord en Oost Tartarye*, p. 176.
19 *Pamiatniki diplomaticheskikh snoshenii Drevnei Rossii s Derzhavami inostrannymi* (St. P. 1867), 8:915; Scheltema, *Peter de Groote*, 1:131–34.
20 *Pamiatniki*, 8:916; A. Venevitinov, *Russkie v Gollandii: velikoe posol'stvo 1697–1698 godov* (M. 1897), pp. 220–21.
21 Bogoslovskii, *Petr I*, 2:148, n.3.
22 R.P. Meyjes, ed., *De Reizen van Abel Janszoon Tasman en Franchoys Jacobszoon Visscher in 1642–3 en 1644* (The Hague 1919), pp. 264–68.
23 Heeres, *Abel Janszoon Tasman's Journal*, pp. 77–78. The best early reproduction of the floor was in D. Danckerts, *Afbeelding van 't Stadt hus van Amsterdam* (Amsterdam 1661); see also, on the celebrated floor hemispheres, J. Burney, *Chronological History of the Discoveries in the South Sea* (London 1803–17), 3:182, and McCormick, *Tasman and New Zealand*, p. 11.
24 Meyjes, *De Reizen*, pp. xcix, 264–66; F.C. Wieder, ed., *Monumenta Cartographica* (The Hague 1929), vol. 3, pl. 51.
25 Burney, *Chronological History*, 3:181; McCormick, *Tasman and New Zealand*, pp. 11, 52: D.M. Lebedev, *Geografiia v Rossii petrovskogo vremeni* (M.-L. 1950), passim.
26 See N.V. Zdobnov, *Istoriia russkoi bibliografii do nachala XX veka* (M. 1951), pp. 37–38, on books printed at Amsterdam in Russian (1699–1706) by Tessing and Kopievskii. On Cruys, see *Van der Aa's Biog. Woordenboek*, 3:903–7.
27 Wieder, *Monumenta Cartographica*, vol. 3, pl. 51.
28 Apparently in connection with the work of the geographer Ivan Kirillovich Kirilov (1669–1737), compiler of the General Map of the Russian Empire (1734), whose duties included collecting.
29 See M. Destombes, *Cartes Hollandaises* (Saigon 1941), pp. 10ff.
30 R.H. Major, *Early Voyages to Terra Australis* (London 1869), p. xcvi (an atlas for Charles II, etc.).
31 McCormick, *Tasman and New Zealand*, pp. 12–13.
32 Sharp, *The Voyages of Tasman*, p. 345.
33 Rare Books Room, BAN. The relevant pages are 56–64.
34 McCormick, *Tasman and New Zealand*, pp. 18–20, 58, on Coreal.
35 Johann-Daniel Schumacher, *Palaty Sanktpeterburgskoi Akademii Nauk biblioteki i Kunstkamery*, 2d ed. (St. P. 1744), p.2.
36 McCormick, *Tasman and New Zealand*, p. 17.
37 Ibid., p. 59.
38 I.e., in *An Account of Several Late Voyages and Discoveries*, pp. 134–36.
39 Berthelot, *Grande Encyclopédie*, 8:293.
40 C. Bricker and R.V. Tooley, *Landmarks of Mapmaking* (Amsterdam 1968), p. 260.
41 Duc de Saint-Simon, *Mémoires*, ed. Boislisle (Paris 1920), 31:374–88 (Peter at the Académie, etc.); Lebedev, *Geografiia*, p. 111.

42 F.A. Golder, *Bering's Voyages* (New York 1922), 1:29–30, 311.
43 Lebedev, *Geografiia*, pp. 254–56 (J.-N. Delisle's role in Russia); Barratt, *Russia in Pacific Waters*, chs. 3–4; G. Williams, *The British Search for the Northwest Passage in the Eighteenth Century* (London 1962): index under Delisle, Müller.
44 Lebedev, *Geografiia*, pp. 133–35; E.V. Tarle, *Chesmenskii boi i pervaia russkaia ekspeditsiia v Arkhipelag* (M. 1945); M.S. Anderson, "Great Britain and the Russian Fleet, 1769–70," *SEER* 21 (London 1952): 148–64.
45 So did Mikhail V. Lomonosov: see V.F. Gnucheva, "Lomonosov i Geograficheskii Departament Akademii Nauk," in *Lomonosov: sbornik statei i materialov* (M.-L. 1940), pp. 122–40. On the Russian Admiralty agent in London in the 1750s, see Anderson, "British and American Officers," p. 26 (Tate the elder); V. Aleksandrenko, *Russkie diplomaticheskie agenty v Londone v XVIII veke* (Warsaw 1897); on Nagaev, *Obshchii*

morskoi spisok (St. P. 1885), 1:268–71, and *RBS*, 11:7–10.

46 P. Pekarskii, *Nauka i literatura v Rossii pri Petre Velikom* (St. P. 1862), 1:555–57; Zbodnov, *Istoriia Russkoi bibliografii*, pp. 42–43; *RBS*, 23:534–36, for a biographical sketch of Schumacher.

47 See n. 35.

48 *Bibliothecae Imperialis Petropolitanae, Partes I–IV*, and controversial *Rossiiskie pechatnye knigi, nakhodiaschchiesia v Imperatorskoi Biblioteke*, (the so-called *Kamernyi katalog:* for overview of opinions on authorship, see Zdobnov, *Istoriia*, pp. 495–96).

49 The *Knizhnaia Palata's* offerings were announced in *Verzeichniss allerhand Lateinischer, Französischer . . . neuen Bücher, welche in Buchladen bey der Academie der Wissenschaften zu bekommen sind*, 6 issues (St. P., 1728–34), in the newsgazette *Sankt-Peterburgskie Védomosti* in the same period, and subsequently in more specialized listings, e.g., *Catalogue des livres français qui se vendent à l'Académie des Sciences . . .* (1737–50). These featured, among others, Melchisdech Thévenot's *Relations de Divers Voyages Curieux* (Paris 1696) and Francois Coréal's *Voyages aux Indes Occidentales* (Amsterdam 1722, 1738).

50 Zdobnov, *Istoriia* pp. 78–79.

51 Bibliographical data in McCormick, *Tasman and New Zealand*, pp. 60–63.

52 Pp. 29–72 ("Novye do geografii kasaiushchiesia otkrytiia . . . ," together with Banks's letter to the Paris Académie des Sciences).

53 This reappeared in *Sobranie sochinenii vybrannykh iz mesiatsoslovov* (St. P. 1789), 3:260–99. The map was headed "Polushar iuzhnoi chasti Sveta . . . i put' aglinskikh moreplavatelei." The Zubkov family took a keen interest in seaborne exploration, Semen Zubkov in 1804 publishing a survey of discoveries made in Oceania and referring to "the Fifth Part of the Terrestrial Globe" as *Polinesiia:* see *Svodnyi katalog russkoi knigi grazhdanskoi pechati XVIII veka, 1725–1800* (M. 1963–67), no. 8105, anad V. Sopikov, *Opyt rossiiskoi bibliografii . . .* , 5 pts. (St. P. 1813–21; reprint by Holland House, London 1962), no. 9205.

54 Bilbasov, *Arkhiv grafov Mordvinovykh*, 1:189–90; M.S. Anderson, "Great Britain and the Growth of the Russian Navy," *MM*, 42 (1956): no. 1, pp. 132–46. *By the Banks of the Thames*, Cross, "Samuel Greig," pp. 251–65; Barratt, *Russia in Pacific Waters*, pp. 70–71, 89–91.

55 Cross, "Samuel Greig," pp. 251–65; Barratt, *Russia in Pacific Waters*, pp. 70–71, 89–91.

56 Barratt, *Russia in Pacific Waters*, pp. 76–78.

57 Beaglehole, *The Journals*, 3:649–66, 1240.

58 Ibid., vol. 4, appendix ("Cook and the Russians," contributed by Ia.M. Svet); also 3: lxxxix; Barratt, *The Russian Discovery of Hawaii*, ch. 1.

59 Barratt, "The Russian Navy and New Holland," *JRAHS*, 64 (1979): no. 4, pp. 220–22; Armstrong, "Cook's Reputation," pp. 128ff.; J.R. Gibson, *Imperial Russia in Frontier America* (New York 1976), pp. 3–15.

60 See n. 58 and my *Russia in Pacific Waters*, p. 75.

61 Beaglehole, *The Journals*, 3: 1554 (Harris to Earl of Sandwich, 18 January 1780, re copies of British charts, etc.).

62 Such items appeared in *The London Magazine* (July and December 1780) and A.F. Busching's *Wöchentliche Nachrichten von neuen Land-Charten . . .* (Berlin 1779–80).

63 See Beaglehole, *The Journals*, 3:ccv–ccvii, and M.K. Beddie's essential Bibliography of Captain James Cook, 2d ed. (Sydney 1970).

64 Zimmermann's *Poslednee puteshestvie okolo sveta Kapitana Kuka* appeared in St. P. in 1786: Sopikov, *Opyt rossiiskoi bibliografii*, no. 4862 (9204 for 1792 ed.), and C.M. Hotimsky, "Bibliography of Captain James Cook in Russian—1772–1810," *Biblionews and Australian Notes and Queries*, 5 (1971): no. 2, pp. 10–11.

65 G. Gennadi, *Spravochnyi slovar'* (Berlin 1876–80), 1:232.

66 Sopikov, *Opyt rossiiskoi*, no. 9206; Beddie, *Bibliography* no. 1235.

67 Ch. 3: 133–60; ch. 4: 161–212; ch. 5: 213–27; ch. 6: 228–35; ch. 8: 254–83; ch. 9: 284–90.

68 Hotimsky, "Bibliography," p. 7; Beddie, *Bibliography* nos. 1223 and 1235; *Svodnyi katalog russkoi knigi*, 3344; F. Veselago, *Ocherki istorii morskago kadetskago korpusa* (St. P. 1852); *Voennaia Entsiklopediia* (1912), 8:354–55.
69 Hotimsky, "Bibliography," p. 8.
70 See M. Hoare, *The Tactless Philosopher: Johann Reinhold Forster* (Melbourne 1976); also, on the Forsters' Russian connections, A.I. Herzen, *Polnoe sobranie sochinenii i pisem*, ed. Lemke (Petrograd 1919), 3:305–8; Iu.A. Moshkovskaia, *Georg Forster—nemetskii prosvetitel' i revoliutsioner XVIII veka* (M. 1961).
71 F.Ia. Priima, "Georg Forster, perevodchik Lomonosova," *Doklady i Soobshcheniia Filolog. Instituta* (L. 1951), bk. 3.
72 *Puteshestvie v iuzhnoi polovine zemnago shara*, pt. 1, pp. 176, 263–64. J.R. Forster, (*Resolution Journal*, 2:248–49) and Cook (Beaglehole, *The Journals*, 2:116) place these events on 7 April. Suard's text echoes Georg Forster's *Voyage*, 1:137–38 (and 1:210–13, for the 29 May exchanges, also described—without mention of sexual dealings—in Beaglehole, *The Journals*, 2:168). To the extent that Golenishchev-Kutuzov offered Russians the emphasis on British seamen's "amorous transactions" found in Georg Forster's *Voyage*, William Wales (see *Remarks*, p. 54) was justified in attacking the younger Forster as one very ready to show the British in a bad light abroad.
73 Larousse, *Grand Dictionnaire Universel*, 6:397 and 14:1164.
74 Sopikov, *Opyt rossiiskoi*, no. 4862. This was based on La Harpe's edition of Prévost D'Exiles (Beddie, *Bibliography*, no. 10), from which maps and engravings (by J.N. Bellin and C.N. Cochin) was also copied in Moscow.
75 *Sobranie liubopytnykh i sootvetsvenno iunosheskomu vozrastu sochinennykh puteshestvii*, 4 pts. (pt. 4 has 548 pp.); based on Beddie, *Bibliography*, no. 722.
76 Beddie, *Bibliography*, no. 657 (*Geschichte der See-Reisen und Entdeckungen*).
77 See n. 68.
78 Barratt, *Bellingshausen*, pp. 31, 41, 63.
79 J. Goodliffe, "The Image of New Zealand in Russia," *NZSJ*, Old Series (Wellington 1973): no. 12, pp. 142–52, and "New Zealand through Russian Eyes: The Image Improves," *NZSJ* (1979): no. 2, p. 51 and n.
80 J.R. Gibson, *Imperial Russia*, p. 75.
81 Barratt, *Russia in Pacific Waters*, chs. 6–7; Nevskii, *Pervoe puteshestvie*, pp. 247–50.
82 Kruzenshtern, *Voyage*, 1:9; Nevskii, *Pervoe puteshestvie*, pp. 37–38.
83 Veselago, *Admiral Ivan Fedorovich Kruzenshtern*, pp. 11ff.; Nevskii, *Pervoe puteshestvie*, pp. 250–54.
84 "Otkrytiia Tasmana, s prilozheniem sochineniia o polozhenii Ongtong-Iavy ... " (1806): pt. 3, pp. 134–85.
85 "Prodolzhenie ob otkrytiiakh Tasmana" (1806): pt. 4, pp. 110–57.
86 See Sharp, *The Voyages of Tasman*, pp. 117–26, etc.
87 "Prodolzhenie ob otkrytiiakh," pp. 112–14.
88 Heeres, "Abel Janszoon Tasman," p. 112, n.8; Meyjes, *De Reizen van Abel Janszoon Tasman*, pp. lxviii-lxix.
89 Sharp, *The Voyages of Tasman*, p. 132.
90 Kruzenshtern, "Prodolzhenie ob otkrytiiakh," p. 115–16. See also Beaglehole, *The Journals*, 2:142 and nn. 3–4 (Cook recognizes Golden Bay) and 2:156 (reckoning Mount Egmont's position).
91 Sharp, *The Voyages of Tasman*, pp. 122–23.
92 Kruzenshtern, "Prodolzhenie," pp. 183–84.
93 N.A. Galkin, "Pis'ma o plavanii shliupov 'Vostoka' i 'Mirnago' v Tikhom okeane," *Syn otechestva* (St. P. 1822): no. 49, p. 101; Bellingshausen, *Voyage*, 1:211; Beaglehole, *The Journals*,2:lxix, 656 nn. Kruzenshtern knew of John Rowe's murder by the Maori (17 December 1773) from Cook's *Voyage* of 1784, Cook having looked into the Grass Cove massacre in February 1777, and had aboard *Nadezhda* a copy of Crozet's *Nouveau Voyage à la Mer du Sud, commencé sous les Ordres de M. de Marion ...* (Paris 1783). Hence, Kruzenshtern was familiar both with the Maori attack on N.-T. Marion-Dufresne (8 June 1772) and with the outline of J.-F.-M. de Surville's New Zealand visit of 1769. For Soviet

summaries of the earliest English and French visits to New Zealand and dealings with the Maori, see Ia.M. Svet, *Istoriia otkrytiia i issledovaniia Avstralii i Okeanii* (M. 1966), pp. 165–67, 191–92, etc., and L.P. Savel'eva, "Ranii etap angliiskogo proniknoveniia v Novuiu Zelandiiu," in K.V. Malakhovskii, ed., *Proshloe i nastoiashchee Avstralii i Okeanii* (M. 1979), pp. 9–21. The latter collection of essays also contains a treatment by V.P. Oltarzhevskii (pp. 3–8) of New Zealand in Soviet historiography.

94 Lisianskii, *Voyage*, p. 316; Nevskii, *Pervoe puteshestvie*, pp. 190, 247.
95 Gos. Arkhiv Permskoi Oblasti, *fond* 445 (K.T. Khlebnikova), op. 1, *delo* 43, pp. 3–5; *RBS,* 4:97–98; A.S. Berezhnoi, "Krugosvetnyi moreplavatel' L.A. Gagemeister," *Izvestiia Akademii Nauk Latviiskogo SSR* (Riga 1984): no. 8, pp. 48–59; *Dorpater Jahrbücher* (1835), Bd. 4, no. 2, p. 181; Barratt, *Russia in Pacific Waters*, pp. 141–42, 154 nn.
96 V.M. Golovnin, *Puteshestvie na shliupe "Diana" iz Kronshtadta v Kamchatku* (M. 1961).
97 Ivashintsev, *Russian Round-the-World Voyages*, p. 15.
98 TsGAVMF, *fond* 7, op. 1, *delo* 2, pp. 255ff.
99 Golovnin, *Puteshestvie na shliupe "Diana,"* pp. iii–vi; TsGAVMF, *fond* 7, op. 1, *delo* 2 ("Zapisnaia knizhka"), pp. 240–43.
100 Barratt, *Russia in Pacific Waters*, pp. 89–91, 98.
101 TsGAVMF, *fond* 7, op. 1, *delo* 2, pp. 3–4.
102 Golovnin, *Puteshestvie*, pp. 7–8; P. Mel'nitskii, *Admiral Rikord i ego sovremenniki* (St. P. 1856); L.I. Rikord, *Admiral Petr Ivanovich Rikord: biograficheskii ocherk* (St. P. 1875); W. Laird Clowes, *History of the Royal Navy*, (London 1899–1904), 4:395, 408–12; Ivashintsev, *Russian Round-the-World Voyages*, p. 137.
103 Golovnin, *Puteshestvie*, pp. 55–58.
104 Ibid., pp. 132–34; Ivashintsev, *Russian Round-the-World Voyages*, pp. 16–18.
105 Golovnin, *Puteshestvie*, pp. 144–49.
106 G.H. Scholefield, ed., *Dictionary of New Zealand Biography* (Wellington 1940), 2:144–45; R.A. Sherrin, in *Brett's Historical Series: The Early History of New Zealand* (Auckland 1890), p. 130; *HRA:* 1:322, 3:631, 5:658–60; J.L. Nicholas, *Narrative of a Voyage to New Zealand* (London 1817), 2:369.
107 Surveys in G.W. Rusden, *History of New Zealand* (London 1883), 1:93ff.; E.J. Tapp, *Early New Zealand* (Melbourne 1958), pp. 7–20.
108 *HRA;* 5:658–60 and 8:92; R. McNab, *From Tasman to Marsden* (Dunedin 1914), pp. 154–57; *DNZ,* 2:145.
109 J. Savage, *Some Account of New Zealand* ... (London 1807), pp.108–10; P. Dillon, *Narrative and Successful Result of a Voyage in the South Seas* ... (London 1829), 1:201.
110 *DNZ,* 2:261–62.
111 Golovnin, *Puteshestvie*, pp. 140–42; *HRA,* 5:658–60; *HRNSW,* 5:642 and 6:81.
112 Summary in J. Binney, *The Legacy of Guilt* (Auckland 1968), pp. 16–17; see also *HRA,* 7:291–92 and *Hobart Town Gazette*, 8 August 1818 (the massacre).
113 R. McNab, ed., *Historical Records of New Zealand* (Wellington 1908–14), pp. 298–99.
114 Golovnin, *Puteshestvie*, p. 142 n. Internal textual evidence indicates that Matara was at Cape Town between August and October 1808. See *Sydney Gazette*, 1 September 1810, for official response to the *Boyd* massacre.
115 Galkin, "Pis'ma o plavanii shliupov," p. 101; V. Sementovskii, *Russkie otkrytiia v Antarktike*, pp. 124–25.
116 Further on these matters, see my *The Russians and Australia* (Vancouver 1988), ch. 6.
117 *RBS,* 7:149–51; M.A. Tikotin, *P.A. Zagorskii i pervaia russkaia anatomicheskaia shkola* (M. 1950).
118 W.S. Vucinich, *Science in Russian Culture, to 1860*, passim.
119 Larousse, *Grand Dictionnaire Universel*, 15:162.
120 See *Annales du Museum d'Histoire Naturelle*, IX cahier (Paris 1803), pp. 228–36, with reference to a paper on *Phormium tenax* by La Billardière "lu à l'Institut en Nivose, An II."

121 P.A. Zagorskii, "Vypiska iz zamechanii g. Tuenia o lene Novoi Zelandii," *Tekhnologicheskii Zhurnal*, 7 (St. P. 1810): pt. 1, pp. 105–20.
122 *Sorevnovatel' prosveshcheniia* (St. P. 1820): no 11, pp. 125–46; no. 12, pp. 246–56; Samarov, *Russkie flotovodtsy*, 1:11–60; Ivashintsev, *Russian Round-the-World Voyages*, pp. 20–23.
123 Samarov, *Russkie flotovodtsy*, 1:62–64.
124 *HRA*, 8:588–89.
125 Mitchell Library: Lachlan Macquarie Journals: CY A771:215–17; *OMS*, 3; *RBS*, 3:489–90; and *Kronshtadtskii vestnik* (1879): nos. 123–24, on Macquarie's principal host at Kronstadt, Captain-Lieutenant Ivan P. Bunin (1773–1846).
126 For the ethnographic aspect of their Sydney visit, see my *Russians at Port Jackson*, pp. 7–8, 23–26.
127 S. Ia. Unkovskii, "Istinnye zapiski moei zhizni," given in Samarov, *Russkie flotovodtsy*, 1:24.
128 *HRA*, 7:561; Nicholas, *Narrative of a Voyage*, 1:3ff.; McNab, *From Tasman to Marsden*, pp. 169–72.
129 J.R. Elder, *Marsden's Lieutenants* (Dunedin 1934), p. 44; *Proceedings of the Church Missionary Society from 1815 to 1840*, 5:552; Tapp, *Early New Zealand*, pp. 29–31; *DNZ*, 2:262.
130 Samarov, *Russkie flotovodtsy*, 1:24; Binney, *Legacy of Guilt*, pp. 23–25.
131 R.A. Sherrin in *Brett's Historical Series: Early History of New Zealand* (1890), pp. 141–42; J.R. Elder, ed., *The Letters and Journals of Samuel Marsden, 1765–1838* (Dunedin 1932), p. 79.
132 *DNZ*, 2:262; *Registers of the C.M.S., from 1816 to 1840*, 1816, pp. 260–62; Tapp, *Early New Zealand*, pp. 31–32.

CHAPTER FIVE: THE RUSSIANS IN NEW ZEALAND

1 Kotzebue, *Voyage*, vol. 1, ch. 7.
2 B.M. Gough, ed., *To the Pacific and Arctic with Beechey* (Cambridge 1973), p. 4; see also G. Williams, *The British Search for the Northwest Passage in the Eighteenth Century* (London 1962), pp. 271–72.
3 Cited by L.P. Kirwan in *The White Road* (London 1960), p. 77.
4 Kotzebue, *Voyage*, 1:29–30; A.S. Day, *The Admiralty Hydrographic Service, 1795–1919* (London 1967), pp. 27–29.
5 See E.E. Shvede's introduction to *F.F. Bellinsgauzen: Dvukratnye izyskaniia v iuzhnom ledevitom okeane* (M. 1960), pp. 8ff.
6 Veselago, *Kratkaia istoriia russkogo flota*, pp. 246–47; Barratt, *Russia in Pacific Waters*, pp. 176–79.
7 TsGAVMF, *fond* 25, op. 1, *delo* 114; *fond* 315, *delo* 476, pp. 11–14.
8 Beddie, *Bibliography*, no. 1223; Sopikov, *Opyt rossiiskoi*, no. 9206.
9 New Style (Gregorian calendar).
10 A.P. Lazarev, *Zapiski o plavanii voennogo shliupa Blagonamerennogo v Beringov proliv ...* (M. 1950), pp. 5–6, 21–30; K. Gillesem, "Puteshestvie," *Otechestvennye zapiski*, 66 (St. P. 1849): sec. 8; Kuznetsova, "Novye dokumenty," pp. 237–45.
11 See my *Russia in Pacific Waters*, pp. 200–2.
12 Veselago, *Admiral Ivan Fedorovich Kruzenshtern*, p. 3; Vinicombe Penrose, *A Memoir of James Trevenen*, pp. 89ff.; Watrous, *John Ledyard; Gentleman's Magazine*, 55 (1785): pt. 2, pp. 570–71.
13 See E.S. Dodge, "The Cook Ethnological Collections" in R. Duff, ed., *No Sort of Iron: The Culture of Cook's Polynesians* (Auckland 1969).
14 For Cook's instructions, see Beaglehole, *The Journals*, 1:cclxxiii.
15 See H.J. Braunholtz, "Ethnography since Sloane," in *Sir Hans Sloane and Ethnography* (London 1970); A.C. Begg and N.C. Begg, *James Cook and New Zealand* (Wellington 1969).

16 Bellinsgauzen, *Dvukratnye izyskaniia* (1960), pp. 69, 77.
17 TsGAVMF, *fond* 25, op. 1, *delo* 114, pp. 6–21; Veselago, *Kratkaia istoriia*, pp. 290–91.
18 Bellinsgauzen, *Dvukratnye izyskaniia*, p. 83; *Allgem. Deutsche Biographie*, 17:401–2, 21:470.
19 Bellinsgauzen, *Dvukratnye izyskaniia*, p. 49; P. Novosil'skii, *Iuzhnyi polius: iz zapisok byvshago morskago ofitsera* (St. P. 1853) p. 6. Mertens sailed to Oceania in 1826 as naturalist in Seniavin (Captain F.P. Lütke), working mostly in Micronesia: see F.P. Litke, *Puteshestvie vokrug sveta* ... , 2d ed. (M. 1948), passim.
20 TsGAVMF, *fond* 25, op. 1, *delo* 114, pp. 20–21.
21 On Ratmanov, *Morskoi sbornik*, 15 (1855): no. 3, pp. 331-55 and *RBS*, 15:496–97; on Torson, A.B. Sheshin, *Dekabrist Konstantin Petrovich Torson* (Ulan-Ude 1980), esp. pp. 32–37; crew lists in Ivashintsev, *Russian Round-the-World Voyages*, pp. 139–40.
22 E.W. Hunter Christie, *The Antarctic Problem* (London 1951), p. 109; see also Iu.M. Shokal'skii, "Stoletie so vremeni otpravlenii russkoi antarkticheskoi ekspeditsii ... ," *IVGO*, vol. 60 (L. 1928), pp. 37ff; and F. Nordman, "Po povodu predlozheniia postavit' v Kronshtadte pamiatnik," *Kronshtadtskii vestnik* 28 April 1868, no. 48.
23 Sementovskii, *Russkie otkrytiia v Antarktike*, p. 21–22, 192; TsGAVMF, DMM, 1819, *delo* 660, pt. 2, pp. 92–97.
24 *Syn otechestva* (St. P. 1822): no. 49, pp. 100–15; Novosil'skii, *Iuzhnyi polius*, pp. 3–4; Ivashintsev, *Russian Round-the-World Voyages*, p. 140.
25 Sementovskii, *Russkie otkrytiia v Antarktike*, p. 285.
26 I.N. Aleksandrov, "Professor I.M. Simonov ... ," in *Uchennye Zapiski Kazanskogo Pedagogich. Instituta* (Kazan' 1950), bk. 9; N.I. Vorob'ev et al., "Etnograficheskie nabliudeniia I.M. Simonova na ostrovakh tikhogo okeana," *IVGO*, 81 (1949): bk. 5, pp. 497–504; Shokal'skii, "Stoletie," pp. 56ff.
27 *Moskvitianin* (1855): no. 2, pp. 163–74; *RBS*, 18:488–90.
28 V.R. Kabo and N.M. Bondarev, "Okeaniiskaia kollektsiia I.M. Simonova," *SMAE*, 30 (L. 1974): 101–11.
29 *ZMNP* (1855): no. 4, pp. 32–40.
30 See n. 25 and *Shestoi kontinent, ili kratkoe obozrenie plavanii k iugu ot Kuka do Rossa* (St. P. 1854), introduction.
31 Bellinsgauzen, *Dvukratnye izyskaniia*, pp. 67–68.
32 Ibid., p. 77 (Third Set, Instructions from Admiralty Dept., Sec. 12).
33 Ibid., p. 5.
34 Ibid., pp. 66–67.
35 Ibid., pp. 12–15; Novosil'skii, *Iuzhnyi polius*, pp. 2–3; Lazarev, *Zapiski*, pp. 3–7, etc.; Ivashintsev, *Russian Round-the-World Voyages*, p. 42; Ryden, *The Banks Collection*, pp. 67–68.
36 Novosil'skii, *Iuzhnyi polius*, p. 5; Bellinsgauzen, *Dvukratnye izyskaniia*, pp. 87–88; Sementovskii, *Russkie otkrytiia v Antarktike*, pp. 32–34; Kotzebue, *Voyage*, 1:16; Golovnin, *Puteshestvie vokrug sveta na voennom shliupe "Kamchatka" v 1817, 1818, i 1819 godakh* (M. 1965), p. 30.
37 Bellinsgauzen, *Dvukratnye izyskaniia*, pp. 113–17; Sementovskii, *Russkie otkrytiia v Antarktike*, pp. 79–91.
38 Hunter Christie, *The Antarctic Problem*, pp. 100–1.
39 Barratt, *Russians at Port Jackson*, passim; V. Fitzhardinge, "Russian Ships in Australian Waters, 1807–1835," *JRAHS*, 51 (1965): no. 2, pp. 119ff.
40 Bellingshausen, *Voyage*, 1:183–87; Novosil'skii, *Iuzhnyi polius*, pp. 38–39; Sementovskii, *Russkie otkrytiia v Antarktike*, pp. 37–38.
41 A. Sharp, *The Discovery of the Pacific Islands* (Oxford 1960), pp. 198–99.
42 Bellinsgauzen, *Dvukratnye izyskaniia*, pp. 222–23.
43 Ibid., p. 227.
44 Further on this encounter, see my *Bellingshausen*, pp. 73–78, 96–97 (canoes, attitudes, etc.).

45 Beaglehole, *The Journals*, 2:143, 737–38. The *heica* (for fish) of Cook's "Catalogue of Words" had become *giyka* in Russian guise, but was promptly understood. The passage here used (Bellingshausen, *Voyage*, 1:200–2) has parallels with many of the period, e.g., Dumont D'Urville's *Voyage pittoresque*, 2:350.

46 Bellingshausen, *Voyage*, Vol. 1, pl. 21; Barratt, *Russians at Port Jackson*, pp. 13–14 (on Mikhailov); on Maori music and chanting, as recorded by the Russians, see my *Bellingshausen*, pp. 91–96; on sealers from New South Wales in the South Island before 1820, see R. McNab, *Murihiku and the Southern Islands* (Invercargill, NZ 1907), passim; McNab, *From Tasman to Marsden*, pp. 110ff; McLintock, *History of Otago*, pp. 60–61; Tapp, *Early New Zealand*, pp. 13–19.

47 Bellinsgauzen, *Dvukratnye izyskaniia*, p. 77 (sec. 15).

48 See Beaglehole, *The Journals*, 1:236, and M. Trotter in G.R. Barratt, ed., *Queen Charlotte Sound, New Zealand* (Ottawa 1987), pt. 5.

49 Bellinsgauzen, *Dvukratnye izyskaniia*, p. 231.

50 A *kaitaka* cloak, very likely No. 736–129 in the Leningrad Maori collection: see my *Bellingshausen*, pp. 116–17 pl. 24.

51 No. 736–113 in Leningrad: ibid., p. 107, pl. 1.

52 See my *Bellingshausen*, pp. 120–21 (clothing); Beaglehole, *The Journals*, 2:247; D.R. Simmons, "Cyclical Aspects of Early Maori Agriculture," *Records of the Auckland Institute and Museum*, 12 (1975): 89–90; Begg and Begg, *James Cook and New Zealand*, p. 115; E. Best, *Maori Agriculture*, Dominion Museum Bulletin No. 9 (Wellington 1925), pp. 148–49 (potato cultivation).

53 Bellinsgauzen, *Dvukratnye izyskaniia*, pp. 234–35; Sementovskii, *Russkie otkrytiia v Antarktike*, pp. 132, 234; C. Cockayne, *The Vegetation of New Zealand* (Leipzig 1928), pp. 155–56.

54 On this question, see A.P. Vayda, *Maori Warfare* (Wellington 1960).

55 Bellinsgauzen, *Dvukratnye izyskaniia*, p. 237; E. Best, *The Maori Canoe*, Dominion Museum Bulletin No. 7 (Wellington 1925), pp. 110ff.; Haddon and Hornell, *Canoes of Oceania*, pp. 195ff.

56 On this, see S. O'Regan, "Traditional Records," in Barratt, *Queen Charlotte Sound, New Zealand*.

57 Ia. Tarnopol'skii, ed., "Pamiatnik prinadlezhit matrozu pervoi stat'i Egoru Kiselevu," *Vokrug sveta* (1941): no. 4, pp. 40–43. The text was reproduced with greater fidelity by A.I. Andreev in *Plavanie shliupov "Vostok" i "Mirnyi" v Antarktiku v 1819, 1820 i 1821 godakh* (M. 1949).

58 "Pis'ma g. Galkina o plavanii shliupov Vostoka i Mirnago v Tikhom okeane," *Syn otechestva*, 82 (St. P. 1822): pt. 49, pp. 100–15.

59 Novosil'skii, *Iuzhnyi polius*.

60 See my *Russians at Port Jackson*, p. 17 and Sementovskii, *Russkie otkrytiia v Antarktike*, pp. 183, 301.

61 L.S. Berg, *Geschichte der russischen geographischen Entdeckungen*, trans. R. Ulbricht (Leipzig 1954), p. 107.

62 Further on this, Sheshin, *Dekabrist*, pp. 32–33; M.M. Pokrovskii, ed., *Vosstánie dekabristov: materialy po istorii vosstaniia dekabristov: dela verkhovnogo ugolovnogo suda* (M.-L. 1925–71), 14:201ff.

63 V.M. Pasetskii, *Geograficheskie issledovaniia dekabristov* (M. 1977), pp. 34–52, 70–81 and nn.

64 TsGAVMF, *fond* 162, op. 1, *delo* 20, pp. 40–41 (Apollon A. Nikol'skii, Golenishchev-Kutuzov, and the Bellingshausen MS).

65 I thank Dr. A.S. Gur'ianov, Director of the Kazan' University Main Library, for showing me this MS and a copy thereof.

66 RBS, 18:490–91.

67 *Sovremennik* 52 (1855): 159–62; *ES*, 33:56; 34: 836 (Kupffer and Littrow); Vucinich, *Science in Russian Culture*, pp. 133ff; Aleksandrov, "Professor I.M. Simonov," pp. 55ff.

68 *Slovo o uspekhakh plavaniia shliupov "Vostok" i "Mirnyi" okolo sveta, i osobenno v iuzhnom ledovitom okeane, v 1819, 1820 i 1821 godakh* (Kazan' 1822), pp. 8–9. Simonov had read of Marion du Fresne's death (April 1772), actually in revenge for Maori deaths at the hands of Surville's men (December 1769), in Crozet's *Nouveau Voyage à la Mer du Sud* (Paris 1783) and Kruzenshtern's 1806 study of Tasman's movements around New Zealand.

69 *ZMNP* (April 1855): 32–40; *RBS*, 18:489–90; Kotzebue, *Voyage*, 1:41–83; Larousse, *Grand Dictionnaire Universel*, 15:1444.

70 Simonov's preparatory reading for "Determination of the Geographical Positions of the Anchorages of the Sloops *Vostok* and *Mirnyi*," *ZMNP*, 22 (1828): 44–68 had included Zach's *L'Attraction des montagnes et ses effets sur le fils à plomb* (Avignon 1814).

71 69 cahier, July 1824, pp. 5–26. The subsequent "Précis du Voyage de Découvertes" was itself translated back into Russian and appeared in *Severnyi arkhiv*, 7 (St. P. 1827) as "Izvestie o puteshestvii kapitana Bellinsgauzena v 1819, 1820 i 1821 godakh."

72 "Kratkii istoricheskii vzgliad na puteshestviia znamenitneishikh moreplavatelei," *ZMNP*, 42 (1844): 92–115.

73 N.P. Barsukov, *Zhizn' i trudy M.P. Pogodina* (M. 1896), 10:389.

74 E.g., Galkin in 1822, Bellingshausen in 1831.

75 In Maori, *whau* (iron). Simonov heard the initial consonant as labiodental and "hard."

76 *Vostok* carried copies of the Cook-King *Voyage* (London 1784), Loggin Golenishchev-Kutuzov's Russian version thereof, George Forster's *Voyage* (London 1777), and—of course—the Cook *Voyages* describing the first and second visits to New Zealand. These and other works were bought from booksellers in London in August 1819: Novosil'skii, *Iuzhnyi polius*, pp. 5–6; Bellingsgauzen, *Dvukratnye izyskaniia*, p. 88. Beaglehole, *The Journals*, 1:286–87 and n., on Maori words collected by *Endeavour* in January–March 1770 and available to the Russians. (*Ika* = Cook's *Heica*, the introductory particle having been incorporated into the noun).

77 In rough rain capes (*pake*): P. Buck (Te Rangi Hiroa), *The Coming of the Maori* (Wellington 1949), pp. 160–61. Simonov's "skirt" is the kilt, tied with a dressed fibre belt (pp. 175–76). On his "red colouring substance," body oil mixed with such ochre (*horu*), etc., see Elsdon Best, *The Maori As He Was* (Wellington 1952), pp. 222, 233.

78 These were seagoing canoes (*waka tete*), mostly used for fishing or coastal skirting, with gunwale strakes (*rauawa*), upright stern piece (*taurapa*), and bow piece (*tauihu*) with grotesque carved head: classic craft of the Maori. Buck, *Coming*, pp. 203–4; E. Best, *The Maori Canoe* (Wellington 1925), passim; Haddon and Hornell, *Canoes of Oceania*, pp. 195ff.

79 This *putorino*, actually nearer to the alto bugle-flute than the European flageolet (see J.C. Andersen, *Maori Music with Its Polynesian Background* [Wellington 1934] p. 273), is missing from the modern Soviet collections. Bellingshausen records hearing a "fife-like" wind instrument, certainly a Maori flute (Buck, *Coming*, pp. 262–67), and Novosil'skii writes of the Triton shell trumpet (*pu tatara*), though it is improbable that he himself heard one blown. The Maori liking for drums—*Vostok* carried a flautist and a drummer: Bellinsgauzen, *Dvukratnye izyskaniia*, p. 63—had already been noted by Cook (Beaglehole, *The Journals*, 2:118), so did not surprise the Russians. No bull-roarers, *pahu* gongs, or calabash whistles were noted in the sound in 1820.

80 *Mamaku*, or tree-fern, produced an edible pith much used as food in the South Island. Simonov's "cabbage palm" is *ti*, or *Cordyline*. The two foodstuffs were sometimes cooked together in earth ovens: see Best, *Maori Agriculture*, pp. 141–42.

81 Cook Strait was not "little-known" in 1820, having featured in Purdy's *The Oriental Navigator* (London 1816); but Russians had had little use for such mariner's aids to the Pacific yet.

82 On the Taranaki coast or Kapiti Island.

83 I.e., the western side of Queen Charlotte Sound south of Waihi Point, not off *Mirnyi*'s port bow. I omit comments on Mt. Egmont.

84 In Russian, *v epanchakh, ili burkakh,* suggesting Circassian thick felt cloaks, the rough side being turned outward.

85 A common rain cape, of a type collected and presently at MAE in Leningrad (Nos. 736–132 to –133).

86 Sets of rope leading from the masthead, serving to relieve the lateral strain; part of the sloop's standing rigging.

87 Simonov describes a song or chant performed seated on *Vostok*'s quarterdeck on 29 May—probably a *ruri,* or topical song. This, by contrast, is a *haka;* and, though performed in response to an unforeseen incident involving ropes, it was a part of the *hapu*'s repertoire. I discuss it elsewhere: see my *Bellingshausen,* pp. 94–95, 144–47.

88 In Italian, *falconetto.* Light cannon or bow-chasers.

89 Incorrect: Cook had seen positive proof of cannibalism on 17 January 1770, not in Ship Cove, where the Russians now landed, but in "Cannibal Cove" to its northeast: see Beaglehole, *The Journals,* 1:236–37.

90 In Little Waikawa Bay.

91 Mikhailov drew the chief (pl. 18), whose *whare whakairo,* or carved house, used as a sub-tribal community gathering point, forms the centre of modern Historic and Archaeological site No. S16/125. The site was partially excavated in 1978 and 1982 by Michael M. Trotter of Canterbury Museum, Christchurch: see Barratt, *Queen Charlotte Sound,* ch. 6.

92 3.3 metres.

93 6.4 by 4.3 metres.

94 56 inches. The door "board" was a sliding wooden slab; the roof "leaves" were layers of *raupo;* the "central posts" (*pou tahuhu*) were ridgeposts, evidently with unusually placed carvings at the top, not by the base. Russian evidence shows that this carved house was also functionally a *whare puni:* the chief's immediate family slept in it. Buck (*Coming,* p. 122) indicates that the thatch may have been of *toetoe* leaves.

95 A *patu onewa, hue taha* (water containers: Buck, *Coming,* p. 91), plaited flax baskets (pp. 154–55).

96 The "pikes" were bird-spears (*here*), probably of *tawa* wood; the "little idols" were carved heads or stylized humanoid figures (Buck, *Coming,* pp. 96, 312); "insignia" were *taiaha.*

97 A cenotaph *tiki;* see my *Bellingshausen,* pp. 84–90 (structures seen by the Russians).

98 Untrue—and objects collected by the Russians included some that had been carved with iron tools, e.g., Nos. 736–115, –116, –121, and –122.

99 A flat war canoe paddle with Taranaki-style gymnast figure, No. 736–113 at MAE; not a *ko* (digging tool), as suggested by Butinov and Rozina, but a ceremonial and chiefly *hoe.*

100 56 inches of red baize.

101 Here and earlier, Novosil'skii introduces secondary material from Cook, the Forsters, and other writers, which I omit: further on this padding, see my *Bellingshausen,* pp. 22, 139–43.

102 10.5 metres.

103 Circassian tribesmen of the Caucasus. Mikhailov drew one man with elegant facial tattooing (pl. 19), on the value of which see E. Best, *The Maori* (Wellington 1924), p. 238 and Buck, *Coming,* pp. 322–25. Galkin's Ukrainian friend, Ivanenko, added a note to the observation that the Maori were often beardless in the Galkin MS sent to *Syn otechestva* in 1822: "I have seen at Mr. Galkin's the dried head of a New Zealander, the skin, hair, and tattoo on which are all perfectly preserved—a unique curiosity." To this the editor of *Syn otechestva* himself added: "There are two such heads in the Admiralty Department Museum in St. Petersburg." See Best, *The Maori,* pp. 222–29 on *putiki* topknots, ear pendants; Buck, *Coming,* pp. 284–87 on hair, cloak-pins.

104 Items like Nos. 736–132 to 134 at MAE.

105 Evidently, *waka tete* were sometimes lashed together, with simple cross-booms, for particular service.

106 See Best, *The Maori* (1924), pp. 222, 233 (red ochre, oils, etc.).

107 Beaglehole, *The Journals,* 1:173, 182, 184 (Cook's early bartering in New Zealand); E.

Best, *Games and Pastimes of the Maori* (Wellington 1925), pp. 46ff. (posture dances).
108 Bellingshausen, acutely conscious of Cook's seamen's "amours" with Maori girls in 1773, quoted Georg Forster on the topic (*Dvukratnye izyskaniia*, p. 233). Mikhailov drew a young Maori mother with a child strapped to her back (pl. 19).
109 The thrusting "pikes" were hardwood *huata* spears, the boxes *waka huia*, the "basalt cudgels" *mere* or *patu*, and the Polish "hatchets" *tewha-tewha*, or long clubs with a flat edge, such as Nos. 736–116 and –117 at MAE.
110 Buck, *Coming*, pp. 121–22.
111 Galkin was right, albeit prejudiced.
112 A brief discussion of New Zealand geology is omitted.
113 The Maori *kuri*: Buck, *Coming*, p. 64; E. Best, *The Maori* (1924), fig. 40. Bellingshausen, who took a pair aboard *Vostok* (*Voyage*, 1:215), was also familiar with the *Histoire Naturelle* (Paris 1785–91) of Georges Louis, Comte de Buffon (1707–88); and with his "Chien de berger."
114 Buck, *Coming*, pp. 93–102, on birds eaten.
115 Bellinsgauzen, *Dvukratnye izyskaniia*, p. 222, and Novosil'skii in Sementovskii, *Russkie otkrytiia v Antarktike*, p. 231, paint less dramatic pictures from a higher vantage point.
116 Bellinsgauzen, *Dvukratnye izyskaniia*, p. 65 (commemorative medals from St. Petersburg Mint and their purposes).

CHAPTER SIX: THE RUSSIAN ETHNOGRAPHIC RECORD FOR
QUEEN CHARLOTTE SOUND, 1820

1 Bellinsgauzen, *Dvukratnye izyskaniia*, pp. 77–78.
2 Further on this, see Lazarev, *Zapiski*, p. 154; Barratt, *Russians at Port Jackson*, pp. 82–83.
3 LOAAN, *fond* 1, op. 2 (1827), no. 462; *fond* 2, op. 1 (1827), no. 3 (ethnographica from *Vostok* and *Mirnyi* sent to the *Kunstkammer*); N.A. Butinov and L.G. Rozina, "Nekotorye cherty samobytnoi kul'tury Maori," *SMAE*, 21 (1963): 78ff.
4 V.R. Kabo and N.M. Bondarev, "Okeaniiskaia kollektsiia I.M. Simonova," *SMAE*, 30 (1974): 103. See also N.I. Vorob'ev et al., "Etnograficheskie nabliudeniia I.M. Simonova na ostrovakh Tikhogo okeana," *IVGO*, 81 (1949): bk. 5, pp. 497–504.
5 Bellinsgauzen, *Dvukratnye izyskaniia*, p. 65.
6 Beaglehole, *The Journals*, 1:520–21.
7 See H.J. Braunholtz, "Ethnography Since Sloane" in *Sir Hans Sloane and Ethnography* (London 1970) and E. Miller, *That Noble Cabinet* (London 1973), on the fate of the "curiosities."
8 TsGIAL, *fond* 853 (M.M. Buldakova), *delo* 1, no. 74; L.G. Rozina, "Kollektsiia Muzeia Antropologii i Etnografii po Markizskim ostrovam," *SMAE*, 21 (1963): 110–19; Ryden, *The Banks Collection*, pp. 67–68.
9 Bellinsgauzen, *Dvukratnye izyskaniia*, p. 66; Beaglehole, *The Journals*, 1:cclxxxiii.
10 Bellinsgauzen, *Dvukratnye izyskaniia*, pp. 66–67.
11 Ibid., pp. 227–36.
12 O. Wright, ed. and trans., *New Zealand, 1826–1827: From the French of Dumont D'Urville* (Wellington 1950), p. 73.
13 *Syn otechestva* (1822): no. 49, p. 103 n; Kabo and Bondarev, "Okeaniiskaa kollektsiia Simonova," p. 103, n. 7; Butinov and Rozina, "Nekotorye cherty," pp. 108–9.
14 I am indebted to David R. Simmons, former Ethnologist of the Auckland Museum, for carving style identifications.
15 Further on this, see Barratt, *Queen Charlotte Sound*, ch. 1.
16 Butinov and Rozina, "Nekotorye cherty," p. 97.
17 See S. Percy Smith, *Maori Wars of the Nineteenth Century*, 2d ed. (Christchurch 1910), p. 61 (Murupaenga's raid of 1810).
18 Musée de l'Hôpital de la Marine, Rochefort, France.
19 D.R. Simmons, "The Lake Hauroko Burial and the Evolution of Maori Clothing," *Re-*

cords of the Otago Museum of Anthropology, 5 (Dunedin 1968): 9–10.

20 Berlin No. vi.490; Hunterian Museum No. e422; see, on this, S.M. Mead, *Traditional Maori Clothing* (Wellington 1969), pp. 48–52; also A.L. Kaeppler, *Artificial Curiosities: Being an Exposition of Native Manufactures Collected on the Three Pacific Voyages of Captain James Cook, RN*, Bishop Museum Special Publication 65 (Honolulu 1978), fig. 324 (Vienna cloak No. 25 with triangle *taniko*).

21 See Ryden, *The Banks Collection*, on the "Banks cloak" held at the Stockholm Museum (1848.1.63); and Kaeppler, *Cook Voyage Artifacts*, on the Bern cloak (third voyage). The Stockholm cape may be allied with No. D14.84 at Cambridge University and piece found in "Dr. Pope's Box" at Oxford, now in the Pitt Rivers Museum there.

22 Further on this, Mead, *Traditional Maori Clothing*, passim.

23 H.D. Skinner, "Murdering Beach Collecting and Excavating: The First Phase, 1850–1950," *JPS*, 68 (1959): 221; H.D. Skinner and D.R. Simmons, *The Maori Hei Tiki* (Dunedin 1966), p. 20; D.R. Simmons, "Little Papanui and Otago Prehistory," *Records of the Otago Museum of Anthropology*, 4 (1967): 55.

24 Wright, *New Zealand, 1826–1827*, p. 129.

25 Mead, *Traditional Maori Clothing*, pp. 58, 135.

26 P. Buck, *The Evolution of Maori Clothing* (Wellington 1926), p. 302 and pl. 20.

27 Mead, *Traditional Maori Clothing*, fig. 37b.

28 See H. Ling Roth, *The Maori Mantle* (Halifax 1923), p. 9.

29 Ibid., pp. 8–9 and n. 27.

30 S. Parkinson, *A Journal of a Voyage to the South Seas* (London 1784), p. 95.

31 Bellinsgauzen, *Dvukratnye izyskaniia*, pp. 231–32.

32 Buck, *Evolution of Maori Clothing*, pl. 19.

33 Further on this type, see my *Bellingshausen*, p. 118.

34 E. Best, *The Stone Implements of the Maori*, Dominion Museum Bulletin No. 4 (Wellington 1912), pp. 214–15.

35 Butinov and Rozina, "Nekotorye cherty," p. 102; see also E.S. Dodge, *The New Zealand Maori Collection in the Peabody Museum of Salem* (Salem, MA 1941), p. 16 (related pendant, No. 30).

36 A 6.3-cm-long alleged *kurukuru*.

37 R. McNab, *Historical Records*, 2:283.

38 Feather use in topknots seems to do so: compare McNab, *Historical Records*, 2:22, Parkinson, *Journal of a Voyage*, pls. 14–16, and Mikhailov's *Chief of Southern New Zealand* (feathers ranging from one to four).

39 R.W. Force and M. Force, *The Art and Artefacts of the Eighteenth Century* (Honolulu 1968), fig. 128; also A.L. Kaeppler, "Tracing the History of Hawaiian Cook Voyage Artefacts in the Museum of Mankind," in T.C. Mitchell, ed., *Captain Cook and the South Pacific* (London 1979), pp. 174–75, on Sarah Stone.

40 H.D. Skinner, *Comparatively Speaking* (Dunedin 1974), p. 133.

41 Bellinsgauzen, *Dvukratnye izyskaniia*, p. 233; Best, *The Maori Canoe*, p. 158 and fig. 120.

42 Sementovskii, *Russkie otkrytiia*, pp. 233–34.

43 Best, *The Maori Canoe*, p. 158ff.

44 Ibid., fig. 59, upper.

45 Haddon and Hornell, *Canoes of Oceania*, p. 202.

46 Forster, *Voyage Round the World*, 1:132.

47 Haddon and Hornell, *Canoes of Oceania*, p. 195.

48 Dodge, *The New Zealand Maori Collection*, pl. 13; E.W. Gudger, "Wooden Hooks...," *Anthropological Papers of the American Museum of Natural History*, 28 (1927): pt. 3, p. 235.

49 Kabo and Bondarev, "Okeaniiskaia kollektsiia I.M. Simonova," pp. 107ff.

50 E. Shortland, *The Southern Districts of New Zealand: A Journal* (London 1851), p. 18.

51 D.R. Simmons to author, January 1986.

52 See n. 17.

53 D.R. Simmons, "Cyclical Aspects of Early Maori Agriculture," *Records of the Auckland Institute and Museum*, 12 (1975): 85, 89.

54 Galkin, "Pis'ma o plavanii," p. 110; Sementovskii, *Russkie otkrytiia v Antarktike*, p. 233.

55 Beaglehole, *The Journals*, 2: 287.

56 Bellinsgauzen, *Dvukratnye izyskaniia*, p. 239; Best, *Maori Agriculture*, p. 149.

57 Beaglehole, *The Journals, 2:167, 287, 741.*

58 *Begg and Begg, James Cook and New Zealand*, p. 115.

59 Auckland Museum: Edward Shortland MSS: "Middle Island Journal."

60 Simmons, "Little Papanui and Otago Prehistory," p. 55.

61 A. Sharp, *Duperrey's Visit to New Zealand in 1824* (Wellington 1971), p. 23. See also T.L. Buick, *Old Marlborough* (Palmerston North, NZ 1900), pp. 182–83 (value of the 1820 evidence).

62 See Butinov and Rozina, "Nekotorye cherty," p. 85; L.G. Rozina, "V.V. Sviatlovskii—sobiratel' kollektsii iz Okeanii," *SMAE* 30 (1974): 127–39 (ethnographic legacy); *Morskoi sbornik*, 51 (St. P. 1861): no. 2, pp. 248–50; 66 (1863): no. 5, pp. 26–29; 71 (1865): no. 4, pp. 171–73 (naval interest in New Zealand fed by British).

63 For "correct" Soviet views of New Zealand history of the early 1800s, see K.V. Malakhovskii, *Bor'ba imperialisticheskikh derzhav za Tikhookeanskie ostrova* (M. 1966), pp. 39–42, etc; his *Istoriia kolonializma v Okeanii* (M. 1979), pp. 120–21; and Malakhovskii and V.P. Nikolaev, eds., *Nezavisimye gosudarstva Okeanii* (M. 1984), pp. 24ff.

64 Rudolf F. Its is both professor of ethnography at LGU and Director of the Peter-the-Great Museum of Anthropology and Ethnography of the adjacent Academy of Sciences of the USSR. Nikolai A. Butinov remains at the latter's "Australia and Oceania Division" as *konsultant*. Inventories and other printed and manuscript materials of that Division relating to New Zealand material culture are presently (1988) in the care of Tamara K. Shafranovskaia.

65 Biographical data in my *The Russians and Australia*, ch. 4.

66 Bellinsgauzen, *Dvukratnye izyskaniia*, pp. 77–78.

67 Gosudarstvennyi Russkii Muzei, Leningrad—R9750: "Attestat," dated 15 August 1821, Kronstadt; in P.N. Mikhailov folder.

68 Notably, *War Dance of New Zealand South, in Queen Charlotte Sound, The Main Village of New Zealand South*, and *A Chief of Southern New Zealand with His Wife*. Auckland Institute and Museum Library's Photographic Collection holds prints of Mikhailov's original sketches Nos. 137 (Du436.61.Q3), 142, 65, 141, 136, 28, 279, 138, 280, and 199.

69 S.N. Kondakov, ed., *Iubileinyi spravochnik Imperatorskoi Akademii Khudozhestv* (St. P. 1914), pt. 2; P.N. Petrov, *Sbornik materialov dlia istorii Imp. St-Peterburgskoi Akademii Khudozhestv za sto let eio sushchestvovaniia* (St. P. 1864), 1:346, 390, 416–16.

70 See N. Goncharova in *Iskusstvo*, 35 (1972), 6:62–63.

71 A.A. Fedorov-Davydov, *Russkii peizazh XVIII-nachala XIX veka* (M. 1953), p. 324 (Arkh. Akad. Khud. (1819), op. 20, *delo* 28, etc.).

72 Fedorov-Davydov, *Russkii peizazh*, pp. 219–20.

73 Ibid., pp. 220, 227.

74 For a biographical study, see Sheshin, *Dekabrist Torson*; service record, etc. in M.V. Nechkina, ed., *Vosstanie dekabristov: materialy . . .* , (L. 1976), 14:195–213.

75 V.M. Golovnin, "O sostoianii Russkogo Flota v 1824 godu," in *Sochineniia Michmana Morekhodova* (St. P. 1861), pp. 1–2; Veselago, *Kratkaia istoriia*, pp. 263–264; Sheshin, *Dekabrist Torson*, pp. 42–44.

76 Kotzebue, *Voyage*, 1:7.

77 Mikhail A. Bestuzhev, cited in my *Voices in Exile: The Decembrist Memoirs* (Montreal 1974), pp. 42–43.

78 Veselago, *Kratkaia istoriia*, pp. 290–91.

79 See A.L. Shapiro, *Admiral D.N. Seniavin* (M. 1958), pp. 297–302.

80 S.P. Khrushchev, "Plavanie shliupa *Apollona* v 1821–1824 godakh," *ZAD*, 10 (St. P. 1826): 200–20; Sheshin, *Dekabrist Torson*, pp. 13–14.

81 Nechkina, *Vosstanie dekabristov: materialy*, 14:201, 211.

82 TsGAVMF, *fond* 212, op. 1, *delo* 479, pp. 23–26, 34–41; *delo* 1252, pp. 1–2.

83 TsGAVMF, *fond* 161, op. 1, *delo* 14.

84 Bellinsgauzen, *Dvukratnye izyskaniia*, pp. 135, 139 n. 97.

85 TsGAOR, *fond* 109, op. 5, *delo* 61, pt. 69, pp. 27–35.

86 A.B. Sheshin, *Dekabrist K.P. Torson* (Ulan-Ude 1980), ch. 8.

87 See Kuznetsova, "Novye dokumenty," pp. 237–39; Lazarev, *Zapiski*, pp. 6–12; Barratt, *Russians at Port Jackson*, p. 17; L.A. Shur, "Dnevniki i zapiski russkikh puteshestvennikov kak istochnik po istorii i etnografii stran Tikhogo okeana," in *Avstraliia i Okeaniia* (M. 1970), pp. 201–12.

88 D.I. Zavalishin, "Krugosvetnoe plavanie fregata 'Kreiser' v 1822–1825 godakh, pod komandoiu Mikhaila Petrovicha Lazareva," *Drevniaia i novaia Rossiia* (St. P. 1877), nos. 6, 7, 10, 11; Barratt, "Russian Warships in Van Diemen's Land," *SEER*, 53 (London 1975): no. 133, pp. 566–78; ROGPB, *fond* 449, *karton* 2, *delo* 19, pp. 1–2 (M.K. Kiukhel'beker journal extract, Brazil, February 1822;) TsGAVMF, *fond* 166, op. 1, *delo* 666, pp. 314–15 (Zavalishin and Fedor G. Vishnevskii appointed to *Kreiser*).

89 Lazarev, *Zapiski*, pp. 6ff.

90 Further on these matters, see my paper, "Russian Naval Sources for the History of Colonial Australia to 1825," *JRAHS*, 67 (1981): pt. 2, pp. 159–75.

91 See, for instance, A.F. Treshnikov's *Istoriia otkrytiia i issledovaniia Antarktiki* (M. 1963), pp. 19–32; L.S. Berg, "Bellinsgauzen i Pal'mer," *IVGO*, 83 (1951); V.L. Lebedev, "Geograficheskie nabliudeniia v Antarktike ... ," in *Antarktika: doklady komissii 1960 goda* (M. 1961).

92 The bases of an ongoing research programme that began in 1955 (see M.M. Somov, ed., *Sovetskaia Antarkticheskaia Ekspeditsiia: pervaia kontinental'naia ekspeditsiia, 1955–1957* [L. 1959]) and is now being sustained by a 25th expedition. Eighty volumes of scientific results have been published by the Arctic and Antarctic Research Institute in Leningrad.

93 TsGAVMF, *fond* 327, op. 1, nos. 2904–7, 4766, 5052, etc: see Larionov, "Korabli ... ," in Belov, *Pervaia russkaia*, pp. 129–34.

94 TsGAVMF, *fond* 116, op. 1, *delo* 2596, pp. 1–4.

95 V.V. Kuznetsova, "Novye dokumenty o russkoi ekspeditsii k severnomu poliusu," *IVGO* (1968): no. 3, pp. 237–45.

96 Nechkina, *Vosstanie dekabristov: materialy*, 14:204–7; S.A. Artem'ev, "Sledstvie i sud nad dekabristami," *Voprosy istorii* (1970): no. 3, pp. 115–17.

97 A.E. Rozen, *Zapiski dekabrista* (St. P. 1907), pp. 143–45; N.V. Basargin, *Zapiski* (Petrograd 1917), pp. 88–93; N.I. Lorer, *Zapiski dekabrista* (M. 1931), pp. 125–35.

98 Rozen, *Zapiski*, pp. 155–56; Lorer, *Zapiski*, pp. 137–38; D.I. Zavalishin, *Zapiski dekabrista* (St. P. 1906), pp. 263–65; Sheshin, *Dekabrist Torson*, p. 116.

ENVOI

1 Details in my paper, "The Visit of the Russian Cruiser *Afrika* to Auckland, 1881," *NZSJ* (1978): no. 1.

2 G.I. Butakov, reports in *Morskoi sbornik*, 57 (St. P. 1862): no. 2, pp. 65–66; 58 (1862): no. 3, pp. 178–82; D. MacCallum, "The Alleged Russian Plans for the Invasion of Australia, 1864," *JRAHS*, 44 (1959): pt. 5: 301–22; Fitzhardinge, "Russian Naval Visitors," pt. 2.

3 See my study, *Russophobia in New Zealand, 1838–1908* (Palmerston North, NZ 1981), passim.

4 Ibid., pp. 48–53 (David Luckie and the 1873 "Kaskowiski Scare").

5 New Zealand National Archives: Confidential Despatches & Memoranda, c/16/7: F.D. Bell to Prime Minister, NZ, 2 December 1884: Memorandum by Major-General E.H. Steward, RE on a "projected attack upon the Australian settlements ... in 1878."

6 Aleksandrov, "Professor I.M. Simonov"; *Moskvitianin* (1855): no. 2, pp. 163–74; *ZMNP* (April 1855): pp. 32–40; *Sovremennik* (1855): no. 33.
7 Details in M.I. Belov, ed., *Pervaia russkaia Antarkticheskaia ekspeditsiia 1819–1821 godov, i eio otchotnaia navigatsionnaia karta* (L. 1963), pp. 11–19, 152 (Macquarie). Bellingshausen's account of his 17–19 November 1820 visit to Macquarie Island (*Dvukratnye izyskaniia*, pp. 371–77), where Mikhailov made quick drawings of animals and sub-Antarctic birds, was brought to the notice of New Zealand readers by Robert McNab, who placed long extracts in his *Murihiku* (Dunedin 1907).
8 *RBS*, 18:489–90; Belov, *Pervaia russkaia*, p. 8.
9 See my *Russians at Port Jackson*, pp. 94–95, and Belov, *Pervaia russkaia*, pp. 8ff.
10 Simonov's more popular accounts of the Queen Charlotte Sound visit had been offered slightly earlier, in *Kazanskii vestnik* (1822): pts. 4–5; *Journal des Voyages* (Paris 1824): no. 69, pp. 12–14; *Severnyi arkhiv*, 7 (St. P. 1827); etc. His southern science has yet to receive a definitive treatment, but see I.P. Shpitsberg's essay on his astronomical methods in M.I. Belov, *Pervaia russkaia*, pp. 121–27.
11 See Bellinsgauzen, *Dvukratnye izyskaniia*, pp. 5–7 and Belov, *Pervaia russkaia*, p. 12, n.1.
12 Survey in R. Owen, *The Antarctic Ocean* (London 1941), pp. 74–79; Hunter Christie, *The Antarctic Problem*, pp. 117–20.
13 Ivashintsev, *Russian Round-the-World Voyages*, pp. 98, 105, 113–16; Hunter Christie, *The Antarctic Problem*, pp. 127–29 (Captain Henry Foster's work).
14 Kruzenshtern, *Dopolneniia k izdannym v 1826 i 1827 godakh ob'iasneniiam* . . . , sec. 7.
15 *ZUKMS*, 12 (1835): 179ff.; Hunter Christie, *The Antarctic Problem*, pp. 127–29.
16 Belov, *Pervaia russkaia*, p. 18, n. 3; Hunter Christie, *The Antarctic Problem*, pp. 129–30.
17 See R. McNab, *Historical Records of New Zealand*, 1:663–66, 707–8.
18 A.H. McLintock, *Crown Colony Government in New Zealand* (Wellington 1958), pp. 12–17.
19 *Sydney Gazette*, 24 September 1831; L. Paszkowski, *Polacy w Australii i Oceanii, 1790–1840* (London 1962), pp. 5–12.
20 *Sydney Gazette*, 21 April 1831; see also Great Britain, *Parliamentary Papers*, 1838/680, p. 11 (evidence of J.L. Nicholas), and J. Gleason, *The Genesis of Russophobia in Great Britain* (Cambridge MA 1950), pp. 113–20.
21 Gleason, *Genesis*, chs. 2–3.
22 See, in this connection, PRO C.O.209/4 ("Prospectus of the Scots New Zealand Land Company . . . ", and Great Britain, *Parliamentary Papers*, 1840/33, p. 607 (Matthew and Motte testify).
23 See n.3 above.

CHAPTER SEVEN: THE BELLINGSHAUSEN CONTACTS, 1820

1 Sharp, *Discovery of the Pacific Islands*, pp. 168–69.
2 C.W. Newbury, *The History of the Tahitian Mission, 1799–1830; by John Davies* (Cambridge 1961) p. 279.
3 George Vancouver, *A Voyage of Discovery* (London 1798), 1:74–76.
4 Shvede, *Bellinsgauzen*, pp. 64ff.
5 "Donesenie kapitana 2 ranga Bellingauzena iz Porta Zhaksona o svoem plavanii," *ZAD*, 5 (St. P. 1823); V.L. Lebedev, "Geograficheskie nabliudeniia v Antarktike . . . ," *Antarktika: doklady kommissii, 1960 god* (M. 1961); Iu.M. Shokal'skii, "Stoletie so vremeni otpravleniia russkoi antarkticheskoi ekspeditsii . . . ," *IVGO*, 60 (M. 1928): 195–97.
6 See Ivashintsev, *Russian-Round-the-World Voyages*, pp. 25–26.
7 Barratt, *Bellingshausen*, pp. 27–28.
8 Shvede, *Bellinsgauzen*, p. 243 (shipwright Stoke's shortcomings); see also, on the Russians' voyage up from New Zealand, Nikolai A. Galkin, "Pis'ma o plavanii shliupov

Vostoka i *Mirnago* v Tikhom okeane," *Syn otechestva*, 82 (St. P. 1822): pt. 49, pp. 157–70. Galkin was *Mirnyi*'s surgeon. His perspective was therefore different from those of Simonov and Mikhailov, who sailed in *Vostok*.

9 Reproduced in the Shvede edition of Bellingshausen's 1831 text.

10 Shvede, *Bellinsgauzen*, p. 244.

11 Four accounts of these events are conveniently found together in Sementovskii, *Russkie otkrytiia*, pp. 39, 134–37, 183, 238–39. They are, respectively, by Simonov, Simonov again, Leading Seaman Egor' Kiselev, and P.M. Novosil'skii. Textual histories in Barratt, *Bellingshausen*, pp. 18–24.

12 Shvede, *Bellinsgauzen*, p. 244.

13 First published as *Iuzhnyi polius: iz zapisok byvshego morskago ofitsera* (St. P. 1853).

14 *Vokrug sveta* (M. 1941): no. 4, pp. 40–43: introduction by Ia. Tarnopol'skii, editor of Kiselev's "Pamiatnik."

15 On the Maori and Rapan artefacts brought to Kazan' by Simonov, see V.R. Kabo and N.M. Bondarev, "Okeaniiskaia kollektsiia I.M. Simonova," *SMAE*, 30 (1974): 101–11; on Kazan' University as the alma mater of Simonov and N.I. Lobachevskii, see Vucinich, *Science in Russian Culture*, pp. 219–20, 317–20.

16 Sementovskii, *Russkie otkrytiia*, p. 39. Text also printed and lightly annotated by A.I. Andreev, ed., *Plavanie shliupov "Vostok" i "Mirnyi" v Antarktiku v 1819, 1820 i 1821 godakh* (M. 1949).

17 Barratt, *Bellingshausen*, pp. 19–21.

18 Kabo and Bondarev, "Okeaniiskaia kollektsiia," p. 102.

19 Kazan' State University Library: *otdel rukopisei*, MS 4533, sec. 5.

20 Reproduced in Sementovskii, *Russkie otkrytiia*, pp. 134–35.

21 Ibid., pp. 183, 238.

22 Shvede, *Bellinsgauzen*, p. 401/obv.

23 Sementovskii, *Russkie otkrytiia*, p. 136.

24 Shvede, *Bellinsgauzen*, p. 247; for *Vostok*'s trade and barter goods, see my *Bellingshausen*, pp. 102–3; on Rapan material culture, J. Maireau, "Notes sur Rapa," *Journal de la Société des Etudes Océaniennes*, 5 (Papeete 1936): 561–67; retrospective by Buck, "A Visit to Rapa Island," pp. 71–81. See also nn. 33 and 45 below.

25 Shvede, *Bellinsgauzen*, p. 245; compare Vancouver, *Voyage*, 1:75.

26 Shvede, *Bellinsgauzen*, p. 247; Sementovskii, *Russkie otkrytiia*, p. 137 (Simonov's hypothesis re "at least two warring tribes").

27 Shvede, *Bellinsgauzen*, p. 246. Russian evidence of this sort complements A.C. Eugène Caillot's *Histoire de l'Ile Oparo ou Rapa* (Paris 1932); for material culture sources, see n. 24 above.

28 Shvede, *Bellinsgauzen*, p. 246.

29 Sementovskii, *Russkie otkrytiia*, p. 183.

30 Ibid., pp. 238–39.

31 Ibid., p. 183; see also Caillot, *Les Polynésiens orientaux au contact de la civilisation* (Paris 1909), chs. 4–6.

32 Haddon and Hornell, *Canoes of Oceania*.

33 Shvede, *Bellinsgauzen*, pp. 247–48; see also, on Rapa craft, R.T. Aitken, *The Ethnology of Tubuai*, (Honolulu, Bernice P. Bishop Museum 1930), and Maireau, "Notes sur Rapa," pp. 564ff.

34 Barratt, *Bellingshausen*, pp. 96–100.

35 Sementovskii, *Russkie otkrytiia*, p. 136.

36 Ibid., and p. 239.

37 Ibid., pp. 39, 137.

38 Sharp, *Discovery of the Pacific Islands*, pp. 57–58; Nevskii, *Pervoe puteshestvie*, p. 250, n. 2 (Kruzenshtern and Arrowsmith); Kruzenstern, *Atlas de l'Océan Pacifique: hémisphère australe* (St. P. 1824)—Russian familiarity with George Bass's chart of 1799–1800 showing the track of *Nautilus* (Captain Bishop).

39 Shvede, *Bellinsgauzen*, p. 248.

40 Sharp, *Discovery of the Pacific Islands*, p. 58; A.G. Findlay, *Directory for the Navigation of the Pacific Ocean* (London 1851), 2:799; Sementovskii, *Russkie otkrytiia*, p. 140.
41 Vancouver, *Voyage*, 1:75.
42 Ibid., 1:77. Data on Rapa craft in Haddon and Hornell, *Canoes of Oceania*, and in Aitken, *Ethnology of Tubuai*. On their modern descendants, D.S. Marshall, *Ra'ivavae: An Expedition* (Garden City, NY 1961).
43 Vancouver, *Voyage*, 1:77; Sementovskii, *Russkie otkrytiia*, p. 137.
44 Vancouver, *Voyage*, 1:75. In 1820, the Rapans came out unarmed.
45 Ibid., 1:76. On the very utilitarian tapa seen by the Russians, see Kabo and Bondarev, "Okeaniiskaia kollektsiia," pp. 101ff. and E.S. Dodge, "Austral Islands Tapa," *Journal of the Polynesian Society*, 50 (1941): 107–13.
46 Caillot, *Histoire de l'Ile Oparo*, passim.
47 See Bellingshausen, *Voyage*, 2:256.
48 Newbury, *History of the Tahitian Mission*, pp. 273–84.
49 Ibid., p. 282; also G.R. Barratt, *Russian Exploration in the Mariana Islands, 1816–1828* (Saipan, 1984), p. 47 (Russian encounter with Folger at Guam, March 1828).
50 Bellingshausen, *Voyage*, 2:285.
51 Newbury, *History of the Tahitian Mission*, pp. 273, 277.
52 Ibid., pp. xlviii–xlix (L.M.S. histories, complementary accounts); L.A. Shur, "Dnevniki i zapiski russkikh puteshestvennikov kak istochnik po istorii ... ," in *Avstraliia i Okeaniia* (M. 1970), pp. 201–12; Lipshits, "Etnograficheskie issledovaniia," pp. 320ff.; G. Dening, "Ethnohistory in Polynesia: The Value of Ethno-Historical Evidence," *Journal of Pacific History*, 1 (1966): 22–25.

CHAPTER EIGHT: THE RUSSIAN TEXTS

1 *Slovo o uspekhakh plavaniia shliupov "Vostok" i "Mirnyi" okolo sveta* ... (Kazan' 1822), pp. 9–10. This booklet was based on a public lecture at Kazan' University of 7 July 1822: details in Sementovskii, *Russkie otkrytiia*, p. 289, and Barratt, *Bellingshausen*, pp. 18–19.
2 In Russian, *morskikh rakov.* These were red-eyed crayfish.
3 A generous estimate: Bellingshausen records that Oparo was in sight for some 40 hours, from 6:00 AM on 29 June till nightfall on the 30th.
4 MS "Shliupy Vostok i Mirnyi, ili Plavanie Rossiian v Iuzhnom Ledovitom Okeane i okolo Sveta," Kazan' State University Main Library, no. 4533, pt. 4. I thank Dr. A.S. Gur'ianov of that institution for making the manuscript available to me.
5 The first of Mikhailov's three sketches of Rapa was made from about this distance, the SW coast, between Ma'i'i Bay and Anarua Bay, at SW 27° from *Vostok*.
6 Compare Vancouver, *Voyage*, 1:76–77.
7 Bellingshausen's chart, reproduced by Debenham in 1945 (see Bellingshausen, *Voyage*, 1:224), indicates that these craft put out from the west coast and not from Ha'urei Bay, where the main population centres now lie.
8 *Popoi*, made by smashing boiled taro corms with a rock, was indeed a dough or thick paste but not necessarily fermented; see F.A. Hanson, *Rapan Lifeways: Society and History on a Polynesian Island* (Boston 1970), pp. 11, 73–76.
9 This echoed events of 22 December 1791: Vancouver, *Voyage*, 1:75.
10 Ellis, *Polynesian Researches* (1829), 1:42–45, and Caillot, *Histoire de l'Ile l'Oparo*, pp. 72–73.
11 Enigmatic: *ma'a* is certainly "food" (see Hanson, *Rapan Lifeways*, pp. 62ff.), but *hippka*—or, to transliterate more precisely, *gippka*—may be interpreted in various ways. I tentatively suggest *he apura*, on the basis of Aitken, "Ethnology," p. 17.
12 See Debenham, *Voyage of Captain Bellingshausen*, 2: 268 and pl. 27.
13 All this accords well with Vancouver (*Voyage*, 1:77–78); the remark about "very aged" men shows that Simonov had read his Vancouver. See also Hanson, *Rapan Lifeways*, pp. 26–27.

14 Depicted by Mikhailov (see Plate 20). The Russians saw Rapan *vaka* (single-outrigger canoes)and *taurua* (double canoes) of the same types seen by Vancouver, i.e., essentially Tubuaian, sail-less, of planks sewn together with *nape:* Haddon and Hornell, *Canoes of Oceania*, pp. 147–48; Cook and King, *Voyage*, 2:7; Ellis, *Polynesian Researches*, 1:54.

15 As an ornament, not to hold a "mat" or cloak: *Vostok* and *Mirnyi* were visiting in summer, unlike *Discovery*. The "sashes" were made of *ora'a*, or paper-mulberry cloth. Cook and King, *Voyage*, 2:7.

16 Storing and transporting water.

17 It is rather poorly reproduced in Sementovskii, *Russkie otkrytiia*, p. 135 (right-hand fig.).

18 Actually, a running survey from Ma'i'i Bay, on Rapa's sw, clockwise round to the northern cape of Akatanui Bay, in the ENE. Bellingshausen's chart omits the deeply indented Ha'urei Bay on Rapa's east side, despite the fact that Tauturou Islet was visible off its SE extremity. Pariati Bay's size is exaggerated and that of Akatamiro Bay is underestimated by the Russians.

19 A.S. Griboedov, *Woe From Wit* (1824), act 1, line 7 offers the same phrase (taken from Gavriil Derzhavin's *Arfa* (1798).

20 Above Angaira'o Bay.

21 Vancouver's "block houses": *Voyage*, 1:77; studied by J.F.G. Stokes of the Bernice P. Bishop Museum, whose unpublished MS, "Ethnology of Rapa Island" (1930), remains on file there in 5 volumes. Mikhailov drew several that stood near Anarua Bay: see pl. 15 here. See also W. Mulloy, "The Fortified Village of Morongo Uta," in T. Heyerdahl and E.N. Ferdon, eds., *Miscellaneous Papers*, vol. 2 of *Reports of the Norwegian Archaeological Expedition to Easter Island and the East Pacific*, Monographs of the School of American Research and the Kon Tiki Museum, no. 24, pt. 2 (1965), pp. 22ff., complementing Stokes, "Ethnology of Rapa," pp. 366–68.

22 Warfare was endemic in later pre-contact times: discussions in Caillot, *Histoire de l'Ile Oparo*, pp. 38–42, 64–68 and Hanson, *Rapan Lifeways*, pp. 16–18.

23 Vancouver, *Voyage*, 1:77.

24 A misprint: Bellingshausen gives an approximately correct fix of latitude 27°37′45″S for Rapa's centre, but his longitude estimate of 144°14′55″ is improved upon only by Lazarev.

25 I.e., Queen Charlotte Sound: Bellingshausen, *Voyage*, 1:216–17. Midshipman Novosil'skii's account, published as *Iuzhnyi polius* (St. P. 1853), appears in extract in Sementovskii, *Russkie otkrytiia*, pp. 191–283 (238–39 on Rapa). Further details in my *Bellingshausen*, pp. 15, 22–23.

26 This is obscure, but presumably means an iron stanchion plus coiled ladder-rope.

27 This was in summer: see Hanson, *Rapan Lifeways*, p. 5 (winter cataracts).

28 See n. 14 above.

29 *Dvukratnye izyskaniia*, (St. P. 1831), ch. 4.

30 *Vostok* was due west of Hiri Bay, the "four peaks," which led Bellingshausen to reflect unprofitably on Las Quadro Coronadas Islands of Quiros (*Voyage*, 1:225), being actually the jagged basaltic remains of the rim of a large extinct volcano.

31 *Vostok* paused NW of Rapa, Pariati Bay being the nearest point from which canoes could have left.

32 The Maori reception in Queen Charlotte Sound had been similar: Bellingshausen, *Voyage*, 1:200.

33 This was the *ariki* of a ramage or descent group, presumably in possession of a ridge fort commanding the Pariati or an adjacent valley: see Caillot, *Histoire de l'Ile Oparo*, pp. 63–66 and Stokes, "Ethnology of Rapa," pp. 658–60, 707–24. The Russian phrasing, together with the hurried circumstances of this encounter of 29 June, suggest that the chief was not the Ngaitapana "king" who, Stokes believed, had already gained hegemony by then: see Hanson, *Rapan Lifeways*, pp. 25–26 and n. 7.

34 Compare Vancouver, *Voyage*, 1:75.

35 Pariati Bay. Simonov writes that 23 canoes had put out the previous day; thus, his reckoning and Bellingshausen's ("as many as 20 craft" for 30 June) coincide. Clearly, the Rus-

sians were met by a maximum of 150 natives, a mere half of the numbers estimated to have surrounded *Discovery* in 1791 (Vancouver, *Voyage*, 1:77). This also suggests that Rapa's most important ramage had no dealings with Russians.

36 See Bellingshausen, *Voyage*, 1:12–13 for details of trade goods taken to Rapa.
37 Vancouver, *Voyage*, 1:75–76.
38 In fact, these were patches of decomposed bare lava.
39 Bellingshausen, *Voyage*, vol. 1, pl. 21.
40 Discussion in Buck, *Vikings of the Sunrise*, pp. 176–77. See also n. 21 here, on *maunga pare.*
41 *Hau* bark cordage was used throughout the Austral Islands: Aitken, "Ethnology of Tubuai," pp. 78–79. Vancouver, *Voyage*, 1: 77 on lack of large trees, etc.
42 The "beam" was *ama,* the booms were *iato:* Aitken, "Ethnology," pp. 68–71; Haddon and Hornell, *Canoes of Oceania,* pp. 147–48; also Cook and King, *Voyage*, 2:7 and Ellis, *Polynesian Researches*, 1:54.
43 It could not be located in 1985 at MAE in Leningrad.
44 Obscure: many Maori bailers (*ta wai*) had handles: Haddon and Hornell, *Canoes of Oceania,* p. 216.
45 Angaira'o Bay, not Ha'urei.
46 See Debenham, *Voyage of Captain Bellingshausen,* 1:225, for commentary on the *Vostok's* nearness to Maratiri Islands.
47 Russian: *premnozhestvo.* Kiselev implicitly compares the Rapan numbers with the total *hapu* of 80 persons in Queen Charlotte Sound. In 1791, Vancouver reckoned that at least 300 had been round the *Discovery:* Vancouver, *Voyage*, 1:77.
48 More echoes of Vancouver, here: ibid., 1:75 (seizing of iron, etc.) "Ground bread" or "earth bread" (*zemlianym khlebom*) are other names for yams.

CHAPTER NINE: REFLECTIONS ON THE ETHNOGRAPHIC EVIDENCE

1 Haddon and Hornell, *Canoes of Oceania,* p. 147.
2 Ibid., p. 148.
3 Cook and King, *Voyage*, 2:7.
4 Ellis, *Polynesian Researches*, 1:54.
5 I am indebted for this information to Professor Allan Hanson of the University of Kansas, who conducted field work on Rapa in 1964.
6 The results of archaeology on Rapa appeared in T. Heyerdahl and E.N. Ferdon, eds., *Reports of the Norwegian Archaeological Expedition to Easter Island ... : Volume 3,* Monographs of the School of American Research and the Museum of New Mexico, No. 24 (New Mexico 1961).
7 Heyerdahl, *Aku-Aku,* p. 241.
8 Ibid., pp. 252–55.

Bibliography

SELECT ARCHIVAL MATERIAL

Archival Material

1. *Central State Archives of the USSR*
(a) Tsentral'nyi Gosudarstvennyi Istoricheskii Arkhiv (TsGIAL)

fond 853 (M.M. Buldakova), *delo* 74 ("Zhurnal prikazov kapitana Kruzenshterna komande sudov 'Nadezhda' i 'Neva'—Kruzenshtern: instructions to his people in Oceania, re procedures, hygiene, barter with Polynesians, etc.).
fond 15, op. 1, *delo* 1, pp. 149ff. ("Instruktsiia Glavnago Pravleniia Rossiisko-Amerikanskoi Kompanii... 29 maia 1803 god"—(Company Main Office directive to Kruzenshtern, routes to be followed).
fond 796, op. 90 (1809), *delo* 273 ("Donesenie ieromonakha Aleksandro-Nevskoi Lavry Gedeona... o plavanii na korable 'Neva' v 1803–1806 godakh"—Archpriest Gedeon's report on his voyage, with comments on the visit to Easter Island of 21 April 1804).
fond 796, op. 84 (1803), *delo* 408, pp. 1–3 ("Po Predlozhennomu pis'mu ... o vozlozhenii v Amerikanskie Zavedeniia ieromonakha Gedeona"—Service record and biographical details of Gedeon, whose diary entries on Easter Island remain unpublished).

(b) Tsentral'nyi Gosudarstvennyi Arkhiv Voenno-Morskogo Flota SSSR (TsGAVMF)

fond 14 (I.F. Kruzenshterna), op. 1, *dela* 12–13 (Kruzenshtern: early service, promotions, interests); *delo* 200, p. 71 (letters inward: F.F. Bellingshausen to Kruzenshtern, circa 1843, re his extracting data on longitudinal readings from "old ships' journals" for the German physicist Gauss); *delo* 149 ("Zhurnal Leitenanta M.I. Ratmanova"—Ratmanov's *Nadezhda* journal, 1803–6: a later variant is at the ORGPB—see below); *delo* 898 (*Neva* leaving Brazil, preparations for the passage round Cape Horn). This *fond* contains 529 items, many bearing on Polynesia.
fond 166, op. 1, *delo* 2596, pp. 1–3 (report from Lieutenant Arkadii, Leskov, ex-*Vostok*, to A.V. Moller, Chief of Naval Staff, 21 March 1823: Russian achievements in the far South, prospects, etc.); *delo* 2698, pp. 1–2 (report to A.V. Moller from

L.I. Golenishchev-Kutuzov, Head of Naval Scientific Committee, 17 March 1825: accounting of all materials presented to the Admiralty Department up to October 1824 by Bellingshausen, including 59 notebooks and 19 charts).

fond 212, op. 9, *delo* 477 and 479 (official response to *Vostok*'s successful voyage: annual pension for K.P. Torson of 1,440 roubles); delo 479, p. 34 (A.V. Moller suggests that Admiralty send Torson to St. Petersburg to "complete matters with regard to the Voyage toward the South Pole"); op. 1, *delo* 1252 (Torson's orders of 30 October 1822 to prepare an official account of *Vostok*'s and *Mirnyi*'s voyage. On the subsequent fate of this work, see A.B. Sheshin, "Dekabrist-moreplavatel'," *IVGO*, (1976): bk. 1, pp. 68–69).

fond 215, op. 1, *delo* 762 ("O postupivskikh v Muzeum redkostiakh ot kapitanov Povalishina i Lisianskago"—"On the Rarities Received by the Museum from Captains Povalishin anad Lisianskii": Polynesian artefacts submitted to the Admiralty Department's Museum, collected by *Neva* in 1804–5).

fond 327, op. 1, nos. 2904–7 ("Skhematicheskii plan oruzhiinoi paluby"—"Schematic Plan of the Gun-Deck"—dated Kronstadt, 3 October 1819: *Vostok*'s deck and arrangements on sailing); nos. 4766, 5052, 5076 (drawings of her rowing-boats: 22-foot, 8-oared cutter; 18-foot, 4-oared yawl); no. 2932 (theoretical plan of *Mirnyi* by master shipwright Amosov).

fond 25, op. 1, *delo* 114, pp. 1–21 ("Zapiski ob . . . ekspeditisii"—I.F. Kruzenshtern's memorandum of 31 March 1819 on the forthcoming *Vostok-Mirnyi* venture: recommending officers; need "to investigate countries around the South Pole").

fond 166, op. 1, *delo* 660, pt. 1, pp.492–93 (books taken aboard those sloops to Oceania, supplied by Academy of Sciences or other government agencies).

fond 315, *delo* 476, pp. 6–10 ("Kratkoe Obozrenie plana predpolagaemoi ekspeditsii"—Otto von Kotzebue's memorandum on the Bellingshausen venture, stressing exploration in southern latitudes, complementary cruising); *delo* 476, pp. 11–14 (Admiral Gavriil A. Sarychev's memorandum, hydrographic objects, etc.).

fond DMM (1819), *delo* 660, pt. 1, pp. 364–65 (Bellingshausen and M.P. Lazarev both decline to take an Orthodox priest aboard on the Pacific-Antarctic venture); pt. 2, pp. 92–97 (full list of *Vostok*'s and *Mirnyi*'s officers and men, salaries and other benefits).

2. *Other Manuscript Repositories in Leningrad*

(c) Leningradskoe Otdelenie Nauk Arkhiva Akademii (LOAAN)

fond 1, op. 2 (1802), *delo* 345 (Academician V.M Severgin's and Professor A.F. Sevast'ianov's instructions for *Nadezhda* and *Neva*, 1803: physics, geology, zoology in the Pacific).

fond 1, op. 2 (1807), *delo* 20 (ethnographica from Polynesia submitted to the Academy's *Kunstkammer* by Lisianskii, 1806–7).

fond 1, op. 2 (1827), *delo* 462 and *fond* 2, op. 1 (1827), no. 3, p. 12 (ethnographica from Polynesia gathered by Bellingshausen, Lazarev, and their people in 1820 and likewise sent to the *Kunstkammer:* clothing and weaponry from New Zealand and Tahiti; other Polynesian objects to be transferred from the Admiralty Department Museum, administrative procedures, duplicates, etc.).

fond 142, op. 1 (1719–1827), no. 108, pp. 1–2 ("Katalog iskustvennym veshcham i odezhde raznykh . . . narodov"—Lisianskii's original list of artefacts brought from Oceania and North America by *Neva* in 1806).

razr. 4, op. 1, *delo* 800a (travel journal of W.G. Tilesius von Tilenau, kept aboard *Nadezhda* in 1804).

(d) *Tsentral'nyi Voenno-Morskoi Muzei* (TsVMM)

No. 41820/2 ("Vakhtennyi zhurnal leitenanta Iuriia Fedorovicha Lisianskago . . . "—journal kept by Lisianskii in 1797–1800 in HMS *Raisonnable, Sceptre,* and *Loyalist.* This journal contains long extracts from observations made by Admiral Sir Erasmus Gower, 1742–1814, who had been master's mate in HMS *Dolphin* and lieutenant in HMS *Swallow,* both in mid-Pacific in 1764–69).

No. 41821 "Zhurnal Leitenanta Iuriia Lisianskago s 1793 po 1800 god"—Lisianskii's diary as a Russian Volunteer abroad: p. 60 on his intention to sail from Bombay to Sydney in April 1799 to assist Captain Matthew Flinders and undertake hydrography in Australasia).

No. 9170–8 (1938) ("Zhurnal korablia 'Neva', 1803–1806"—log of the *Neva* kept by navigator Danilo Kalinin, with data on Easter Island).

No. 9170–3 (1938) ("Chernoviki pisem Lisianskago k raznym litsam s 1803 po 1832 god"—originals of letters to various persons, the effects of the voyage on his life and career).

(e) Arkhiv Geograficheskogo Obshchestva SSSR (AGO)

razr. 99, op. 1, no. 141 ("Zhurnal . . . prikazchika Nikolaia Ivanovicha Korobitsyna"—holograph of Korobitsyn's journal kept aboard *Neva:* Easter Island visit).

(f) Saltykov-Shchedrin Public Library: Manuscripts Department (ORGPB)

fond 1000, op. 2, no. 1146 ("Zhurnal M.I. Ratmanova"); 1947/88 (Iu.E. Bronshtein's 1939–40 introduction to a proposed Soviet edition of the 1803–6 journal of Lieutenant Makar Ivanovich Ratmanov of *Nadezhda*). There are several extant variants of that journal: one is at the Département des Manuscrits, Bibliothèque Nationale, Paris: Slav, NN. 103(1), 104.

F.IV.59 ("Zhurnal Rossiisko-Amerikanskoi Kompanii . . . prikazchik Fedora Ivanovicha Shemelina"—Shemelin's MS journal, covering *Nadezhda*'s failure to make Easter Island, the stay at Taio-hae Bay, Nukuhiva, etc.).

fond 791 (Sobranie A.A. Titova), no. 2272, fols. 37–38 ("Pis'mo F. Romberga k druziam": Lieutenant Romberg on the 1803–4 voyage out from Kronstadt to Kamchatka).

3. Archives in the Estonian SSR: Tartu and Tallin

(g) Tsentral'nyi Gosudarstvennyi Istoricheskii Arkhiv Estonskoi SSR (TsGIAE)

fond 14, *delo* 224, pp. 40–60 (correspondence, to Kruzenshtern from N.S. Mordvinov and Lisianskii, 1802, re purchase of ships for a Pacific expedition, official support for it, etc.).

fond 1414, op. 3, *dela* 3–4 (Lieutenant Emelian E. Levenshtern's *Nadezhda* diary: very candid data on Nukuhivans and Hawaiians of ethnographic value; comments on trade and bartering); *delo* 5 (Levenshtern's official journal, 1803–6).

fond 2057, op. 1, *delo* 235–350, pp. 77–79 (F.P. Wrangel's praise of Kruzenshtern's *Atlas*, its importance for South Pacific navigation of all nations).

(h) Eesti NSV Riikliik Ajaloomuuseum (Estonian State Museum of History, Tallin)

fond 225, op. 1, *delo* 20 (typewritten copy of Levenshtern's diary of 1803–6: p. 122 on *Nadezhda* and Easter Island. The museum's archive holds many papers relating to families of Russian Baltic-German naval officers who visited the South Pacific in 1804–26, and to their early life: Bellingshausen, Levenshtern, Kotzebue, Berg, Wrangel. Complementary materials and illustrations in the archive and library of the nearby Academy of Sciences of the Estonian SSR (Tallin Division: *Teaduste Akadeemia Teaduslik Raamatukogu*).

4. Archives Outside the USSR

(i) Public Record Office, London

Adm. 1 (in-letters and despatches): Peter Puget, "Log of the proceedings of His Majesty's Armed Tender *Chatham*" (1793). Adm. 1/498, cap. 370 (Geo. Murray to Stephen, 17 May 1794, re HMS *Thetis* sailing for North Atlantic station; TsGAVMF, *fond* 14, *delo* 227, pp. 49–52 holds two letters to Kruzenshtern from Admiral Murray's brother, who commanded *Thetis,* in which the youthful Kruzenshtern visited the West Indies).

(j) The Hocken Library, Dunedin, New Zealand

E. Shortland MSS, no. 22: "Middle Island Journal, 1843–44: General Report on the Tribes South of Kaikoura ... , etc."

Biographical and Bibliographical Aids

Allgemeine Deutsche Biographie. Leipzig 1888–91.
Allgemeines Lexikon der Bildenden Künstler von der Antike bis zur Gegenwart. Ed. U. Thieme and F. Becker. 36 vols. Leipzig 1907–47.

Australian Dictionary of Biography. Ed. D. Pike. 3 vols. Melbourne 1788–1850, 1966–67.

Australian Encyclopaedia. 10 vols. Sydney 1958.

Biographisch Woordenboek der Nederlanden door A.J. Van der Aa. Ed. G.D. Schotel. 21 vols. Haarlem 1852–78.

Bogatkina, N.S., comp. "Literatura ob ekspeditsii Bellinsgauzena-Lazareva." In E.E. Shvede, ed., *F.F. Bellinsgauzen: Dvukratnye izyskaniia v iuzhnom ledovitom okeane.* M. 1960.

Chentsov, N.M. *Vosstanie dekabristov: bibliografiia.* M. 1929.

Dansk Biografisk Leksikon. Ed. P. Englestoft. København 1933–44.

Dictionary of National Biography. Ed. L. Stephen and S. Lee. London 1885–1912.

Dictionary of New Zealand Biography. Ed. G. Scholefield, 2 vols. Wellington 1940.

Entsiklopedicheskii slovar'. Ed. I. Andreevskii and K. Arsen'ev. St. P. 1890—1904.

Entsiklopediia voennykh i morskikh nauk. St. P. 1893.

Genealogisches Handbuch des deutschen Adels. Glucksburg 1951–58.

Grand Dictionnaire Universel du XIXe siècle. Ed. P. Larousse. 15 vols. Paris 1866–84.

Grande Encyclopédie inventaire raisonnée des Sciences, des Lettres, et des Arts. Ed. Berthelot. 31 vols. Paris.

Great Soviet Encyclopaedia. Ed. A.M. Prokhorov. 31 vols. New York and London 1970–79. Translation of *Bol'shaia Sovetskaia Entsiklopediia*, 3d. ed.

Horecky, P.L. *Russia and the Soviet Union: A Bibliographical Guide to Western Language Publications.* Chicago 1965.

Hotimsky, C.M. "Bibliography of Captain James Cook in Russian." *Biblionews and Australian Notes and Queries,* 5 (1971): no. 2, pp. 3–12.

Ivashintsev, N.A. "Russkie krugosvetnye puteshestviia." *ZGDMM,* 7 (1849): 1–116; 8 (1850): 1–190. Expanded and printed in book form in 1872.

Lenz, W., ed. *Deutsch-Baltisches Biographisches Lexikon, 1710–1960.* Köln-Wien 1970.

Mesiatsoslov s nastavleniami na 1769–1786 god. St. P. Akademii Nauk 1786.

Obshchii morskoi spisok. 14 vols. St. P. 1885–1907.

Russkii biograficheskii slovar'. Ed. A.A. Polovtsov and B. Modzalevskii. 25 vols. St. P. 1896–1918.

Smirdin, A. *Rospis' rossiiskim knigam dlia chteniia.* St. P. 1828.

Sopikov, V. *Opyt rossiiskoi bibliografii, ili polnyi slovar' sochinenii i perevodov...* 5 pts. St. P. 1813–21. Reprinted and enlarged, St. P. 1904–6; fascimile ed. London 1962.

Svodnyi katalog russkoi knigi grazhdanskoi pechati XVIII veka: 1725–1800. 5 vols. M. 1963–67.

Veselago, F.F. *Materialy dlia istorii russkogo flota.* St. P. 1880–1904.

European Maritime Activities in Southern Polynesia up to 1825: Select Reference Works and Document Collections

Beaglehole, J.C. *Early Exploration in the Pacific.* London 1934.

Boxer, C.R. *The Dutch Seaborne Empire, 1600–1800*. New York 1965.

Brodie, W. *Remarks on the Past and Present State of New Zealand*. London 1845.

Busby, J. *Authentic Information Relative to New South Wales and New Zealand*. London 1832.

Deschanel, P. *Les intérets français dans l'Océan Pacifique*. Paris 1888.

Diccionario maritimo Espagnol. Madrid 1864.

Dumont D'Urville, J. *Histoire universelle des Voyages*. Paris 1860.

Faivre, J.P. *L'Expansion française dans le Pacifique, 1800–1842*. Paris 1960.

Harris, J. *Navigantium atque itinerantium bibliotheca; Or, A Complete Collection of Voyages and Travels*. London 1744–48.

Historical Records of Australia: Series I. 26 vols. Sydney 1914.

Historical Records of New South Wales, 1762–1811. 7 vols. Sydney 1893–1901.

Historical Records of New Zealand South Prior to 1840. Ed. R. Carrick. Dunedin 1903.

James, W. *Naval History of Great Britain from the Declaration of War by France*. 5 vols. London 1822–26.

Jore, L. *L'Océan Pacifique au temps de la Restauration et de la monarchie de juillet, 1815–1848*. Paris 1959.

McNab, R. *Old Whaling Days*. Christchurch 1913.

Mitchell, D.W. *A History of Russian and Soviet Seapower*. London 1974.

Morison, S.E. *The Maritime History of Massachusetts, 1783–1860*. Boston 1941.

Nouvelles Annales de Voyage. Paris 1826.

Nozikov, N. *Russkie krugosvetnye moreplavaniia*. 1941.

Paulding, H. *The Journal of a Cruise in the United States Schooner Dolphin*. New York 1831.

Ralfe, J. *Naval Biography*. 5 vols. London 1828.

Registers of the Church Missionary Society, from 1816 to 1840. London 1844.

Magidovich, I.P. *Ocherki po istorii geograficheskikh otkrytii*. M. 1957.

Sharp. A. *The Discovery of the Pacific Islands*. Oxford 1960.

Svet, Ia.M., ed. *Tret'e plavanie kapitana Dzhemsa Kuka: plavanie v Tikhom okeane, 1776–1780 godakh*. M. 1971.

Veselago, F.F. *Ocherk russkoi morskoi istorii*. St. P. 1875.

Wakefield, E.J. *The British Colonization of New Zealand*. London 1837.

Zubov, N.N. *Otechestvennye moreplavateli—issledovateli morei i okeanov*. M. 1954.

Primary Printed Material

Akademiia Nauk. *Protokoly zasedanii konferentsii St-Peterburgskoi Akademii Nauk s 1725 po 1803 god*. vol. 4 St. P. 1911.

Andreev, A.I., ed. *Plavanie shliupov "Vostok" i "Mirnyi" v Antarktiku v 1819, 1820, i 1821 godakh*. M. 1949. Contains extracts from writings of Egor' Kiselev, Mikhail P. Lazarev, and Ivan M. Simonov on the *Vostok-Mirnyi* expedition, 1819–21.

———*Russkie otkrytiia v Tikhom okeane i Severnoi Amerike v XVIII–XIX vekakh*. M.-L. 1944.

Bartenev, P., ed. *Arkhiv kniazia Vorontsova*. M. 1870–95.

Basargin, N.V. *Zapiski.* Petrograd 1917.

Beaglehole, J.C., ed. *The Journals of Captain James Cook: The Voyage of the "Endeavour," 1768–1771.* Cambridge 1955; *The Voyage of Resolution and Adventure, 1772–1775.* Cambridge 1961; *The Voyage of "Resolution" and "Discovery," 1776–1780.* 2 vols. Cambridge 1967.

Beechey, F.W. *Narrative of a Voyage to the Pacific and Bering's Strait, in the Years 1825–26–27–28.* London 1831. Ed. B.M. Gough as *To the Pacific and Arctic with Beechey.* Cambridge 1973.

Behrens, C.F. *Histoire de l'Expédition de trois Vaisseaux, envoyés par la Compagnie des Indes Occidentales.* 2 vols. La Haye 1739.

Bell, E. "The Log of the *Chatham.*" *Honolulu Mercury* (1929): no. 4.

Bellinsgauzen, F.F. "Donesenie kapitana 2 ranga Bellinsgauzena iz Porta Zhaksona o svoem plavanii." *ZAD,* 5 (1823).

————*Dvukratnye izyskaniia v Iuzhnom ledovitom okeane i plavanie vokrug sveta v prodolzhenie 1819, 1820, i 1821 godov.* St. P. 1831. *Atlas* published separately, 1831. 2d ed. introduced by A.I. Andreev, M. 1949; 3d ed., introduced and annotated by E.E. Shvede, M. 1960. Large parts of the 1831 text were presented in English by Frank Debenham, ed., as *The Voyage of Captain Bellingshausen to the Antarctic Seas, 1819–1821.* 2 vols. Cambridge 1945.

Belov, M.I., ed. *Pervaia russkaia antarkticheskaia ekspeditsiia 1819–1821 godov i eio otchetnaia navigatsionnaia karta.* L. 1963. Booklet to accompany the Soviet edition of the Bellingshausen-Lazarev expedition's southern charts of 1819–21.

Belinskii, V.G. *Sobranie sochinenii v 3 tomakh.* Ed. Golovenchenko. M. 1948.

Bérenger, J.P. *Collection de tous les Voyages faits autour du monde.* 5 vols. Paris 1789.

Berkh, V.N. *Khronologicheskaia istoriia otkrytiia Aleutskikh ostrovov.* St. P. 1823.

Bidwill, J.C. *Rambles in New Zealand.* London 1841.

Bilbasov, V.A., ed. *Arkhiv grafov Mordvinovykh.* St. P. 1902.

Bogoslovskii, M.M., ed. *Petr I: materialy dlia biografii.* 3 vols. M. 1941.

Braam, J. van, ed. *Twee Jaarige Reyse rond om de Wereld.* Dordrecht 1728.

Brosses, C. de. *Histoire des Navigations aux Terres Australes...* Paris 1756.

Buffon, G.L. de. *Histoire naturelle.* Paris 1785–91.

Burney J. *Chronological History of the Discoveries in the South Sea.* 6 vols. London 1803–17.

Busching, A.F., ed. *Wöchentliche Nachrichten von neuen Land-Charten.* Berlin 1779–80.

Butakov, G.I. "Doneseniia." *Morskoi sbornik,* 57 (1862): no. 2, pp. 65–66; 58 (1862): no. 3, pp. 178–82.

Chamisso, A. von. *Bemerkungen und Ansichten auf einer Entdeckungs-Reise unternommen in den Jahren 1815–1818... von dem Naturforscher der Expedition, Adelbert von Chamisso.* Weimar 1821. Vol. 3 of Otto von Kotzebue's *Reise um die Welt* (1821), published in German and Russian.

————"Reise um die Welt ... Erster Theil: Tagebuch." In *Werke.* Bd. 1. Leipzig 1836.

————*Reise um die Welt mit der Romanzoffischen Entdeckungs-Expedition in den Jahren 1815–1818.* In *Werke.* 4 vols. Berlin 1864.

Choris, L. *Voyage pittorésque autour du monde.* Paris 1822.

———*Vues et paysages des régions équinoxiales.* Paris 1826.

Cleveland, R.J. *In the Forecastle, or, Voyages and Commercial Enterprises of the Sons of New England.* New York 1855.

Cook, James. *A Voyage towards the South Pole and Round the World . . .* London 1777.

———and J. King. *A Voyage to the North Pacific . . . in the Years 1776, 1777, 1778, 1779 and 1780.* London 1784.

Coréal, F. *Voyages aux Indes Occidentales.* Amsterdam 1722; new ed. 1738.

Corney, B.G., ed. *The Voyage of Don Felipe Gonzalez to Easter Island in 1770–71.* Cambridge 1908.

Crozet, J. *Nouveau Voyage à la Mer du Sud.* Paris 1783. Partially trans. H. Ling Roth as *Voyage to Tasmania and New Zealand.* London 1891.

Dalrymple, A. *Historical Collection . . .* 2 vols. London 1771.

Dampier, W. *A New Voyage Round the World.* London 1697.

Davies, John. "Extracts from the Journal of a Visit to the Islands of Rapa (or Oparo), Raivavai, and Tupuai." *Quarterly Chronicle of Transactions of the London Missionary Society,* 3 (1827): 323–61.

Delano, Amasa. *A Narrative of Voyages and Travels in the Northern and Southern Hemispheres.* Boston 1817.

Dillon, P. *The Narrative and Successful Result of a Voyage in the South Seas.* London 1829.

Dumont D'Urville, J.S.C. *Voyage au Pôle sud et dans l'Océanie.* 10 vols. Paris 1841.

Du Petit-Thouars, A. *Voyage autour du monde sur la fregate "La Vénus," 1836–1839.* 4 vols. Paris 1841.

Ellis, W. *Polynesian Researches.* London 1829; 2d ed., 1840.

Eschscholtz, J.F. von. *Zoologischer Atlas.* Berlin 1829–31.

Eyraud, F.E. "Lettre du Père F. Eugène Eyraud au T.R.P. supérieur général," *Annales de l'Association de la Propagation de la Foi,* 38 (1866): 44–71; 39 (1867): 250–59.

Findlay, A.G. *Directory of the North Pacific Ocean for Navigation.* London 1851; 3d ed., 1886.

Forster, G. *A Voyage Round the World in His Britannic Majesty's Sloop "Resolution" . . . in 1772, 1773, 1774 and 1775.* 2 vols. London 1777.

———*Florae insularum australium prodromus.* Göttingen 1786.

Forster, J.R. *Observations Made During a Voyage Round the World.* London 1778.

———*Reise um die Welt wahrend den Jahren 1772 bis 1775.* Berlin 1778–80.

———*The Resolution Journal of Johann Reinhold Forster, 1772–1775.* Ed. M.E. Hoare. London 1982.

Galkin, N.A. "Pis'ma g. Galkina o plavanii shliupov 'Vostok' i 'Mirnyi' v tikhom okeane," *Syn otechestva* (1822): no. 49, pp. 100–15.

Gamaleia, P.Ia. *Vyshniaia teoriia morskago isskustva.* 4 vols. St. P. 1801–4.

Golenishchev-Kutuzov, L.I. *Predpriiatiia Imperatritsy Ekateriny II dlia puteshestviia vokrug sveta v 1786 godu.* St. P. 1840.

Golikov, I.I. *Deianiia Petra Velikago, mudrogo preobrazitelia Rossii.* 2d ed. M. 1837.

Golovnin, V.M. *Sochineniia.* St. P. 1864.

————*Puteshestvie na shliupe "Diana" iz Kronshtadta v Kamchatku v 1807–1811 godakh.* M. 1961.

————*Puteshestvie vokrug sveta na voennom shliupe "Kamchatka" v 1817, 1818, i 1819 godakh.* M. 1965.

Gorner (Hörner), J.C. "O nekotorykh dostoprimechatel'nykh svoistvakh morskoi vody." *Tekhnologicheskii Zhurnal*, 5 (1820): pt. 3.

Hamilton, A. "Notes on Old Flax Mats Found in Otago." *Transactions of the New Zealand Institute*, 25 (1892): 486–88.

Heeres, J.E., ed. *Abel Tasman's Journal.* Amsterdam 1898.

Herzen, A.I. *Polnoe sobranie sochinenii i pisem.* Ed. Lemke. Petrograd 1919.

Inokhodtsev, P. "Prodolzhenie kratkikh vypisok." *Tekhnologicheskii Zhurnal*, 2 (1805): pt. 3.

Kalendar' ili mesiatsoslov geograficheskoi na 1768–1776 god. St. P. 1768–76.

Kaulfuss, G.F. *Enumeratio filicum quas in itinere circa terram legit Adalbertus de Chamisso.* Lipsiae 1824.

Khrushchev, S.P. "Plavanie shliupa *Apollona* v 1821–1824 godakh." *ZAD*, 10 (1826): 220–20.

Kiselev, Egor'. "Pamiatnik prinadlezhit matrozu pervoi stati Egoru Kiselevu, nakhodiv-shemusia v dal'nem voiazhe na shliupe 'Vostok' v 1819–21 godakh." *Vokrug sveta* (1940): no. 4, pp. 40–43. See also Sementovskii below.

Korobitsyn N.I. "Zapiski." In A.I. Andreev, ed., *Russkie otkrytiia v Tikhom okeane i Severnoi Amerike v XVIII–XIX vekakh.* M. 1944.

Kotzebue, O. von. *Puteshestvie v iuzhnyi okean i v Beringov proliv v 1815–1817 godakh.* 3 vols. St. P. 1821. German edition published (Weimar 1821) as *Reise um die Welt.* Hannibal Lloyd's English translation of German text given as *A Voyage of Discovery into the South Sea and Beering's Straits, Undertaken in the Years 1815–1818.* London 1821. Vol. 3 is Chamisso's "Observations and Remarks."

Krusenstern, A.J. von. *A Voyage Round the World... in the Years 1803 to 1806.* Trans. R.B. Hoppner. London 1813.

Kruzenshtern, I.F. "Otkrytiia Tasmana, s prilozheniem sochineniia o polozhenii Ontong-Iavy." *Tekhnologicheskii Zhurnal*, 3 (1806): pt. 3, pp. 134–85.

————*Puteshestvie vokrug sveta v 1803, 4, 5, i 1806 godakh, na korabliakh Nadezhde i Neve.* 3 pts. St. P. 1809–12.

————*Atlas k puteshestviiu vokrug sveta kapitana Kruzenshterna.* St. P. 1813.

————*Beyträge zur Hydrographie der grössern Ozeane.* Leipzig 1819.

————*Sobranie sochinenii, sluzhashchikh razborom...* St. P. 1823.

————*Atlas Iuzhnogo moria.* 2 pts. St. P. 1823–26.

————*Dopolnenie k izdannym v 1826 godakh ob'iasneniiam, posluzhivshikh dlia sostav-leniia Atlasa Iuzhnogo moria.* St. P. 1836.

————"O sokhranenii zdorov'ia matrosov na korabliakh." *ZUKMS*, 14 (1838).

Langsdorf, G.H. *Bemerkungen auf einer Reise um die Welt in den Jahren 1803–1807.* 2 vols. Frankfurt am Main 1813. Translated as *Voyages and Travels in Various Parts of the World...* 2 vols. London 1813–14.

————"Vypiska iz pis'ma k Akademiku Kraftu o Kamchatke." *Tekhnologicheskii Zhurnal*, 3 (1805): pt. 2 pp. 156–57.

La Pérouse, J.F. de G. *Voyage . . . autour du monde*. Paris 1797. English trans., London 1798.

Lazarev, Aleksei P. *Zapiski o plavanii voennogo shliupa Blagonamerennogo v Beringov proliv i vokrug sveta dlia otkrytii v 1819–1821 godakh*. M. 1950.

————*Plavanie vokrug sveta na shliupe "Ladoga" v 1822–1825 godakh*. St. P. 1832.

Lisianskii, Iu. F. *Puteshestvie vokrug sveta v 1803, 1804, 1805 i 1806 godakh, na korable "Neva," pod nachal' stvom Iuriia Lisianskago*. St. P. 1812. Translated by the author as *Urey Lisiansky: A Voyage Round the World in the Years 1803, 4, 5 & 6*. London 1814. 2d Russian ed., M. 1947.

————*Sobranie kart i risunkov, prinadlezhashchikh k puteshestviiu flota kapitana . . . Lisianskago na korable "Neva."* St. P. 1812.

Litke (Lütke), F.P. *Puteshestvie vokrug sveta na voennom shliupe "Seniavin" v 1826–1829 godakh*. St. P. 1835. French translation as *Voyage autour du monde*. Paris 1835. 2d Russian ed., M. 1938.

————"Soobshchenie o smerti admirala I.F. Kruzenshterna." *Zapiski Russkogo Geograficheskogo Obshchestva* (1847): bk. 2, pp. 13–20.

Marchand, E. *Voyage autour du monde*. Paris 1798–1800.

Marsden, Samuel. *Letters and Journals of Samuel Marsden, 1765–1838*. Ed. J.R. Elder. Dunedin, NZ 1932.

McNab, R., ed. *Historical Records of New Zealand*. 2 vols. Wellington 1908–14.

Meyjes, R.P., ed. *De Reisen van Abel Janszoon Tasman en Franchoys Jacobszoon Visscher in 1642–3 en 1644*. The Hague 1919.

Miklukho-Maklai, N.N. "Ostrova Rapa-nui, Pitkairn, i Mangareva." *Izvestiia Imp. Russkogo Geograficheskogo Obsh.*, 8 (1873): 42–55.

Moerenhout, J.A. *Voyages aux Iles du Grand Océan*. Paris 1837.

Newbury, C.W., ed. *The History of the Tahitian Mission, 1799–1830, by John Davies*. Cambridge 1961.

Nicholas, J.L. *Narrative of a Voyage to New Zealand*. London 1817.

Novosil'skii, P.M. *Iuzhnyi polius: iz zapisok byavshego morskago ofitsera*. St. P. 1853.

Palmer, J. Linton. "Observations on the Inhabitants and the Antiquities of Easter Island." *Ethnological Society Journal* (1869): 371–77.

————"A Visit to Easter Island, or Rapa Nui, in 1868." *Royal Geographical Society Journal*, 40 (1870): 167–81; also that Society's *Proceedings*, 14 (1870): 108–19.

Pamiatniki diplomaticheskikh snoshenii Drevnei Rossii s Derzhavami inostrannymi, vol. 8. St. P. 1867.

Parkinson, S. *A Journal of a Voyage to the South Seas in His Majesty's Ship "Endeavour."* London 1784.

Penrose, C. Vinicombe. *A Memoir of James Trevenen, 1760–1790*. Ed. R.C. Anderson and C. Lloyd. London 1959.

Pis'ma i bumagi Imperatora Petra Velikogo. St. P. 1887–1917; L. 1922–52.

Polack, J.S. *Manners and Customs of the New Zealanders, with Notes Corroborative . . .* London 1840.

Purdy, J. *The Oriental Navigator*. London 1816.

Ratmanov, M.I. "Vyderzhki iz dnevnika krugosvetnogo puteshestiviia na korable 'Nadezhda'." *Iakhta* (1876): no. 16, pp. 902–5; no. 24, pp. 1326–27.

Registers of the Church Missionary Society, from 1816 to 1840. London 1816–1841, 1844.

Rezanov, N.P. "Pervoe puteshestvie Rossiian vokrug sveta, opisannoe N. Riazanovym." *Otechestvennye Zapiski*, 25 (1825): 246–53.

Roggeveen, J. *Extracts from the Official Log of Mynheer J. Roggeveen, 1721–1722.* London 1908.

Rozen, A.E. *Zapiski dekabrista.* 3d ed. St. P. 1907.

Saint-Simon, Duc de. *Mémoires.* Ed. Boislisle. Paris 1920.

Samarov, A.A., ed. *Russkie flotovodtsy: M.P. Lazarev.* M. 1952.

Sarychev, G.A. *Pravila, prinadlezhashchie k morskoi geodezii.* St. P. 1804.

Sauer, Martin. *An Account of a Geographical and Astronomical Expedition.* 2 vols. London 1802.

Savage, J. *Some Account of New Zealand.* London 1807.

Sbornik materialov dlia istorii Rumiantsevskago Muzeia. M. 1882.

Scheltema, I. *Peter de Groote, Keizer van Rusland in Holland en te Zaandam in 1697 en 1717.* Amsterdam 1814.

Schumacher, J.-D. *Palaty Sanktpeterburgskoi Akademii Nauk: biblioteki i Kunstkamery.* St. P. 1744.

Sementovskii, V.N., ed. *Russkie otkrytiia v Antarktike v 1819–21 godakh.* M. 1951. Contains extracts from the writings of E. Kiselev and P. Novosil'skii, as well as I.M. Simonov's "Slovo o uspekhakh puteshestviia shliupov 'Vostok' i 'Mirnyi'" and passages from his unfinished work, "Shliupy 'Vostok' i 'Mirnyi,' ili plavanie Rossiian v Iuzhnom ledovitom okeane i vokrug sveta."

Severgin, M.V. "Instruktsiia dlia puteshestviia okolo sveta." *Severnyi vestnik* (1804): nos. 2–3.

Shemelin, F.I. "Istoricheskoe izvestie o pervom puteshestvii Rossiian krugom sveta." *Russkii invalid: literaturnye pribavleniia* (1823): nos. 247, 249–52, 256–57, etc.

———*Zhurnal pervogo puteshestviia Rossiian vokrug zemnago shara.* 2 vols. St. P. 1816–18.

Shortland, E. *The Southern Districts of New Zealand: A Journal, with Passing Notices . . .* London 1851.

———*Traditions and Superstitions of the New Zealanders.* London 1854.

Shubert, F.I. "O sushchestvovanii Devisovoi zemli." *Tekhnologicheskii Zhurnal*, 2 (1805): pt. 2.

Simonov, I.M. "Plavanie shliupa Vostoka v Iuzhnom ledovitom more, iz zhurnala ekstraordinarnogo professora Simonova." *Kazanskii vestnik* (1822): pts. 4–5.

———"Izvestiia o puteshestvii kapitana, nyne kapitan-komandora Bellinsgauzena, v 1819, 1820, i 1821 godakh." *Severnyi arkhiv* (1824): pt. 12.

———"Précis du Voyage de découvertes, fait par ordre du gouvernement russe, en 1819, 1820, et 1821, par le Capitaine Bellingshausen." *Journal des Voyages* 23 (1824), No. 69:12–15.

———"Opredelenie geograficheskogo polozheniia mest iakornogo stoianiia shliupov 'Vostok' i 'Mirnyi'." *ZMNP*, (1828): pt. 22, pp. 44–68.

————"Kratkii istoricheskii vzgliad na puteshestviia znameniteishikh moreplavatelei do nachala XIX veka." *ZMNP* (1844): pt. 42, pp. 92–115. See also Sementovskii, above.

Skelton, R.A., ed. *The Voyages of Captain Cook: Charts and Views Drawn by Cook and His Officers.* Cambridge 1955.

Sopikov, V. *Opyt Rossiiskoi bibliografii.* Ed. Rogozhin. St. P. 1813; reprint, London 1962.

Sparrman, Anders. *A Voyage Round the World with Captain James Cook.* London 1944.

Thevenot, M. *Relations de Divers Voyages Curieux.* Paris 1696.

Turgenev, N.I. *Rossiia i Russkie.* 3d ed. M. 1915.

Unkovskii, S.Ia. "Istinnye zapiski moei zhizni." In A.A. Samarov, ed., *Russkie flotovodtsy: M.P. Lazarev.* M. 1952.

Valentijn, F. *Oud en Nieuw Oost-Indien, vervattende een naaukeurige en uitvoerige verhandelinge van Nederlands Mogentheyd.* Dordrecht & Amsterdam 1726.

Vancouver, G. *A Voyage of Discovery to the North Pacific Ocean and Round the World.* 3 vols. London 1798.

Vneshniaia politika Rossii: XIX i nachala XX veka. M. 1961–70.

Vosstanie dekabristov; materialy po istorii vosstaniia dekabristov: dela verkhovnogo ugolovnogo suda. Ed. M.N. Pokrovskii and M.V. Nechkina. 18 vols. M.-L. 1925–80.

Wafer, L. *A New Voyage and Description of the Isthmus of Panama*... London 1699.

Watrous, S.D., ed. *John Ledyard's Journey through Russia and Siberia, 1787–88.* Madison, WI 1966.

Witsen, N. *Aeloude en Hedendaegsche Scheepsbouw en Bestier*... Amsterdam 1671.

————*Noord en Oost Tartarye, ofte bondig ontwerp van eenige dier landen en volken* Amsterdam 1692; 2d ed., 1705.

Wright, O., ed. and trans. *New Zealand, 1826–1827: From the French of Dumont D'Urville.* Wellington 1950.

Zagorskii, P.A. "Vypiska iz zamechanii g. Tuenia o lene Novoi Zelandii." *Tekhnologicheskii Zhurnal*, 7 (1810): pt. 1, pp. 105–20.

Zavalishin, D.I. "Krugosvetnoe plavanie fregata 'Kreiser' v 1822–25 godakh, pod komandoiu Mikhaila Petrovicha Lazareva." *Drevniaia i novaia Rossia* (1877): nos. 6–7, 10–11, etc.

————*Zapiski dekabrista.* St. P. 1906.

Zimmermann, H. *Poslednee puteshestvie okolo sveta kapitana Kuka, slavnago nyneshniago veka morekhodtsa, s obstoiatel'stvami o ego smerti*... St. P. 1786.

Zubkov, S. *Kratkoe istoricheskoe obozrenie otkrytiia Ostrovov*... *lezhashchikh v prostranneishem okeane.* Kursk 1804.

Zumbohm, G. "Lettres du Père ... sur la mission de l'Ile de Pâques." *Annales de la Congrégation des Sacrés-Coeurs de Jésus et de Marie*, 5–6 (1879–80).

Secondary Printed Material

Aitken, R.T. *Ethnology of Tubuai.* (Honolulu) Bernice P. Bishop Museum Bulletin No. 70. 1930.

Aleksandrenko, V. *Russkie diplomaticheskie agenty v Londone v XVIII veke.* Warsaw 1897.

Aleksandrov, I.N. "Professor I.M. Simonov: uchastnik antarkticheskoi ekspeditsii F.F. Bellinsgauzena i M.P. Lazareva." *Uchennye Zapiski Kazanskogo Pedagogicheskogo Instituta* (1950): pt. 9.

Alekseev, A.I. *"Russkaia morskaia gidrograficheskaia nauka v xix-nachale xx vekov."* *TIIE*, 42 (L., 1962), 3:86–89.

Andersen, J.C. *Maori Music, with Its Polynesian Background.* New Plymouth, NZ 1934.

Anderson, M.S. "Great Britain and the Growth of the Russian Navy in the Eighteenth Century." *MM*, 42 (1956): no. 1, pp. 132–46.

————"Great Britain and the Russian Fleet, 1769–70." *SEER*, 21 (1952): 148–64.

Anderson, R.C. "British and American Officers in the Russian Navy." *MM*, 33 (1947): 17–27.

Armstrong, T. "Cook's Reputation in Russia." In R.H. Fisher and H. Johnston, eds., *Captain James Cook and His Times.* Vancouver 1979.

Artem'ev, S.A. "Sledstvie i sud nad dekabristami." *Voprosy istorii* (1970): no. 3, pp. 115–17.

Balfour, H. *"Some Ethnological Suggestions in Regard to Easter Island, or Rapanui."* *Folklore,* 28 (1917): 356–81.

Bantysh-Kamenskii, N.D. *Slovar' dostoprimechatel'nykh liudei russkoi zemli.* 5 vols. M. 1836.

Barratt, G.R. *Voices in Exile: The Decembrist Memoirs.* Montreal and London 1974.

————"Russian Warships in Van Diemen's Land: The *Kreyser* and *Ladoga* by Hobart Town, 1823." *SEER*, 53 (1975): no . 133, p. 566–78.

————"The Enemy That Never Was: The New Zealand Russian Scares, 1870–1885." *NZSJ* (1976): no. 1, pp. 13–33.

————"The Visit of the Russian Cruiser *Afrika* to Auckland, 1881," *NZSJ* (1978), no. 1:1–13.

————"The Russian Navy and New Holland: Part I, 1705–1814," *JRAHS*, 64 (1979): no. 4, pp. 217–34.

————*Bellingshausen: A Visit to New Zealand, 1820.* Palmerston North, NZ 1979.

————*The Russians at Port Jackson, 1814–1822.* Canberra 1980.

————*Russia in Pacific Waters, 1715–1825: A Survey of the Origins of Russia's Naval Presence in the North and South Pacific.* Vancouver 1981.

————*Russophobia in New Zealand, 1838–1908.* Palmerston North, NZ 1981.

————*Russian Exploration in the Mariana Islands, 1816–1828.* Micronesian Archaeological Series, No. 17. Saipan 1985.

————*The Russian Discovery of Hawaii, 1804: The Journals of Eight Russian Explorers.* Honolulu 1987.

————, ed. *Queen Charlotte Sound, New Zealand: Traditional and European Records.* Ottawa 1987.

Barsukov, N.P. *Zhizn' i trudy M.P. Pogodina.* M. 1896.

Bax, A.E. "Australian Merchant Shipping, 1783–1849." *JRAHS*, 38 (1952): pt. 3.

Beaglehole, J.C. "The Colonial Office (1782–1854)." *Historical Studies, Australia and New Zealand,* 1 (1963): no. 3.

Beddie, M.K., ed. *A Bibliography of Captain James Cook*. 2d ed. Sydney 1970.

Begg, A.C., and N.C. Begg. *James Cook and New Zealand*. Wellington 1969.

Bellier-Auvray, E. *Dictionnaire général des artistes de l'école française*. 2 vols. Paris 1882–85.

Bénézit, E. *Dictionnaire critique et documentaire des peintres*. Paris 1948–55.

Berezhnoi, A.S. "Krugosvetnyi moreplavatel' L.A. Gagemeister." *Izvestiia Akademii Nauk Latviiskogo SSR* (Riga), (1984): no. 8, pp. 48–59.

Berg, L.S. "Bellinsgauzen i Pal'mer." *IVGO*, 83 (1951).

——"Russkie otkrytiia v Antarktike i sovremennyi interes k nei." *IVGO*, 81 (1949): no. 2 .

——*Geschichte der russischen geographischen Entdeckungen*. Trans. R. Ulbricht. Leipzig 1954.

Best, Elsdon. *The Stone Implements of the Maori*. Dominion Museum Bulletin No. 4. Wellington 1912.

——*The Maori*. 2 vols. Wellington 1924.

——*The Maori Canoe*. Dominion Museum Bulletin No. 7. Wellington 1925.

——*Maori Agriculture*. Dominion Museum Bulletin No. 9. Wellington 1925.

——*The Pa Maori*. Dominion Museum Bulletin No. 16. Wellington 1927.

Binney, J. *The Legacy of Guilt*. Auckland 1968.

Bolkhovitinov, N.N. *Rossiia i SShA: stanovlenie otnoshenii, 1765–1815*. M. 1980.

Bradley, H.W. *The American Frontier in Hawaii: The Pioneers, 1789–1843*. Gloucester, MA 1968.

Branchi, E.C. *L'Isola de Pasqua*. Santiago de Chile 1934.

Braunholtz, H.J. "Ethnography Since Sloane." In *Sir Hans Sloane and Ethnography*. London 1970.

Brun, X. *Adelbert de Chamisso de Boncourt*. Lyon 1896.

Buck, Peter (Te Rangi Hiroa). *On the Maori Art of Weaving Cloaks, Capes, and Kilts*. Dominion Museum Bulletin No. 3. Wellington 1911.

——"A Visit to Rapa Island in Southern Polynesia." *Natural History*, 22 (1922): 71–81.

——*The Evolution of Maori Clothing*. Wellington 1926.

——*Ethnology of Tongareva*. Bernice P. Bishop Museum Bulletin No. 92. Honolulu 1932.

——*Vikings of the Sunrise*. New York 1938.

——*The Coming of the Maori*. 2d ed. Wellington 1949.

Buick, T.L. *Old Marlborough*. Palmerston North, NZ 1900.

Butinov, N.A. "Korotkoukhie i Dlinnoukhie na ostrove Paskhi." *Sovetskaia Etnografiia* (1960): no. 1, pp. 72–82.

——and L.G. Rozina. "Nekotorye cherty samobytnoi kul'tury Maori." *SMAE*, 21 (1963).

Butinov, N.A. and Rozina, L.G. "Kollektsiia s ostrova Paskhi v sobraniiakh Muzeia Antropologii i Etnografii, *SMAE*, 18 (1958): 305–23.

Caillet, X. "Note sur Rapa. *Bulletin de la Société Bretonne de Géographie*, 5 (1886): no. 26, pp. 207–19.

Caillot, A.-C.E. *Les Polynésiens Orientaux au contact de la civilisation*. Paris 1909.

——*Histoire de la Polynésie orientale*. Paris 1910.

————*Histoire de l'Ile Oparo ou Rapa.* Paris 1932.

Charlot, J. *Choris and Kamehameha.* Honolulu 1956.

Chauvet, S. *L'Ile de Pâques et ses mystères.* Paris 1936.

Christensen, C. *Den danske Botaniks Historie.* Copenhagen 1926.

Christie, E.W. Hunter. *The Antarctic Problem: An Historical and Political Study.* London 1951.

Churchill, W. *Easter Island: The Rapanui Speech and the Peopling of Southeast Polynesia.* Washington, DC 1912.

Colenso, W. "On the Maori Races of New Zealand." *TNZI*, (1868): 97–122.

Cook, W.L. *Flood Tide of Empire: Spain and the Pacific Northwest, 1543–1819.* London & New Haven 1973.

Cooke, G.H. *Te Pito te Henua, known as Rapa Nui.* U.S. National Museum Report, Pt. 1. Washington, DC 1899.

Cross, A.G. "Samuel Greig, Catherine the Great's Scottish Admiral." *MM*, 60 (1974): 251–66.

————*By the Banks of the Thames: Russians in Eighteenth-Century Britain.* Newtonville, MA 1980.

Cruise, R.A. *Journal of Ten Months' Residence in New Zealand.* London 1824.

Danckerts, D. *Afbeelfing van 't Stadt huys van Amsterdam.* Amsterdam 1661.

Davis, C.O. *The Life and Times of Patuone, the Celebrated Ngapuhi Chief.* Auckland 1876.

Day, A.S. *The Admiralty Hydrographic Service, 1795–1919.* London 1967.

Dening, G. "Ethnohistory in Polynesia: The Value of Ethnohistorical Evidence." *Journal of Pacific History*, (1966): 22–43.

Desmedt, M. "Les funérailles et l'exposition des morts à Mangareva (Gambier)." *Société des Américanistes de Belgique: Bulletin* (1931): pp. 128–36.

Destombes, M. *Cartes Hollandaises.* Saigon 1941.

Dieffenbach, E. *New Zealand and Its Native Population.* London 1841.

Dixon, R.B. *The Building of Cultures.* New York 1928.

Dodge, E.S. *The New Zealand Maori Collection in the Peabody Museum of Salem.* Salem, MA 1941.

————"Austral Islands Tapa," *JPS*, 50 (1941): 107–13.

Duff, R., ed. *No Sort of Iron: The Culture of Cook's Polynesians.* Auckland 1969.

Dumitrashko, N.V. "Iu.F. Lisianskii i russkie krugosvetnye plavaniia." In *Iu.F. Lisianskii: Puteshestvie vokrug sveta v 1803, 1804, 1805 i 1806 godakh na korable "Neva."* M. 1947.

Dunbabin, T. *Slavers of the South Seas.* Sydney 1935.

Elder, J.R. *Marsden's Lieutenants.* Dunedin, NZ 1934.

Emory, K.P. *Hawaiian Tattooing.* Bernice P. Bishop Museum Occasional Paper No. 17. Honolulu 1946.

Edge-Partington, J., and C. Heape. *An Ethnographical Album of the Pacific Islanders.* 3 vols. Manchester 1890–98.

Englert, S. *La Tierra de Hotu Matu'a.* Padre las Casas, Chile 1948.

Escher, E. *Hörner's Leben und Wirken.* Zurich 1834.

Fedorov-Davydov, A.A. *Russkii peizazh XVIII-nachalaXIX veka.* M. 1953.

Fedorova, I.K. "Areoi na ostrove Paskhi." *Sovet. Etnografiia* (1966): no. 4, pp. 66–82.

Ferdon, E.N. "A Reconnaissance Survey of Three Fortified Hilltop Villages." In T. Heyerdahl and E.N. Ferdon, eds., *Reports of the Norwegian Archaeological Expedition to Easter Island and the East Pacific: Volume 2, Miscellaneous Papers*. Monographs of the School of American Research and the Kon Tiki Museum, No. 24.

Fisher, R.H., ed. *Captain James Cook and His Times*. Vancouver 1979.

Fitzhardinge, V. "Russian Ships in Australian Waters, 1807–35." *JRAHS*, 51 (1962): no. 2, pp. 113–47.

———"Russian Naval Visitors to Australia, 1862–1888." *JRAHS*, 52 (1966): no. 2, pp. 129–58.

Force, R.W., and M. Force. *The Art and Artifacts of the Eighteenth Century: Objects in the Leverian Museum as Painted by Sarah Stone*. Honolulu 1968.

Friis, H.R., ed. *The Pacific Basin: A History of its Geographical Exploration*. New York 1967.

Gartvig, V. *Chelovek i priroda na ostrovakh Velikogo okeana*. M. 1877.

Gebhard, J.F. *Het leven van Mr. Nicolaas Corneliusz. Witsen*. 2 vols. Utrecht 1881–82.

Geiseler, A. *Die Oster-Insel*. Berlin 1883.

Gennadi, G.N. *Spravochnyi slovar' o russkikh pisateliakh i spisok russkikh knig s 1725 po 1825 god*. Berlin 1876–80.

Gibson, J.R. *Imperial Russia in Frontier America: The Changing Geography of Supply of Russian America, 1784–1867*. New York 1976.

Gigioli, E.H. *La Collezione etnografica del Prof. Enrico Hillyer Gigioli: Parte I, Australasia*. Firenze 1911.

Gleason, J. *The Genesis of Russophobia in Great Britain*. Cambridge, MA 1950.

Golder, F.A. *Bering's Voyages*. 2 vols. New York 1922.

Goncourt, E., and J. Goncourt. *L'Art du XVIIIe siècle*. Paris 1882.

Goodliffe, J. "The Image of New Zealand in Russia." *NZSJ*, Old Series (1973): no. 12, pp. 142–52.

Gough, B., ed. *To the Pacific and Arctic with Beechey*. Cambridge 1973.

Green, J.L. "Austral Islands: Visit of the Rev. J.L. Green." *Missionary Magazine and Chronicle*. (1864): pp. 264–67.

Greenwood, G. "Contact of American Whalers, Sealers and Adventurers with New South Wales Settlement." *JRAHS*, 29 (1935): no. 3.

Gudger, E.W. "Wooden Hooks Used for Catching Sharks and Revettus in the South Seas." *Anthropological Papers of the American Museum of Natural History*, 28 (1927): pt. 3, pp. 233–36.

Gvozdetskii, N.A. "Pervoe morskoe puteshestvie Rossiian vokrug sveta." *Priroda* (1947): no. 1, pp. 85–88.

Haddon, A.C., and J. Hornell. *Canoes of Oceania*. Bernice P. Bishop Museum Special Publications Nos. 27–29 (printed as one volume). Honolulu 1975.

Hall, Vine. "On the Island of Rapa." *TNZI*, 1 (1868): 75–83.

Hamilton, A. *Fishing and Sea Foods of the Ancient Maori*. Dominion Museum Bulletin No. 2. Wellington 1908.

Hanson, F.A. *Rapan Lifeways: Society and History on a Polynesian Island*. Boston 1970.

Healy, T. *New Zealand and the New Zealand Company*. London 1842.

Henry, Teuira. *Ancient Tahiti*. Bernice P. Bishop Museum Bulletin No. 48. Honolulu 1928.

Heyerdahl. T. *Aku-Aku: the Secret of Easter Island*. London 1958.

Heyerdahl, T. & E.N. Ferdon, eds. *Reports of the Norwegian Archaeological Expedition to Easter Island . . . Volume 1: Archaeology of Easter Island*. Monographs of the School of American Research and the Museum of New Mexico, No. 24. New Mexico 1961.

Hoare, M.E. *The Tactless Philosopher: Johann Reinhold Forster (1729–1798)*. Melbourne 1976.

Hocken, T.M. *The Early History of New Zealand*. Wellington 1914.

Hotimsky, C.M. "A Bibliography of Captain James Cook in Russian, 1772–1810." *Biblionews and Australian Notes and Queries*, 5 (1971): no. 2, pp. 3–12.

Howay, F.W. *List of Trading Vessels in the Maritime Fur Trade, 1785–1825*. Ed. R.A. Pierce, Kingston, Ont. 1973.

Ivashintsev, N.A. *Russkie krugosvetnye puteshestviia s 1803 po 1849 god*. St. P. 1872. Trans. G. Barratt as *Russian-Round-the-World Voyages from 1803–1849*. Kingston, Ont. 1980.

James, W. *A Naval History of Great Britain from the Declaration of War by France*. London 1822–26.

Jaussen, T. "Destruction d'une Chrétienté." *Les Missions Catholiques*, 6 (1874): 382–86.

Kabo, V.R., and N.M. Bondarev. "Okeaniiskaia kollektsiia I.M. Simonova." *SMAE*, 30 (1973): 101–11.

Kaeppler, A. *"Artificial Curiosities": Being an Exposition of Native Manufactures Collected on the Three Pacific Voyages of Captain James Cook, RN*. Bishop Museum Special Publication 65. Honolulu 1978.

———*Cook Voyage Artifacts in Leningrad, Berne, and Florence Museums*. Bishop Museum Special Publication 66. Honolulu 1978.

Keesing, F.M. *The South Seas in the Modern World*. New York 1941.

Kelly, L.G. *Marion du Fresne at the Bay of Islands*. Wellington 1951.

Khmyrev, M.D. "Svedeniia o Vasilii Kiprianove, bibliotekare." *Russkii arkhiv*, 9 (1865): 1298ff.

Kirwan, L.P. *The White Road: A Survey of Polar Exploration*. London 1960.

Knoche, W. *Die Österinsel*. Concepcion de Chile 1925.

Komissarov, B.N. *Grigorii Ivanovich Langsdorf, 1774–1852*. L. 1975.

Kondakov, S.N., ed. *Iubileinyi spravochnik Imp. Akademii Khudozhestv*. St. P. 1914.

Kuznetsova, V.V. "Novye dokumenty o russkoi ekspeditsii k severnomu poliusu." *IVGO*, (1968): no. 3, pp. 237–45.

Laird Clowes, W. *History of the Royal Navy*. London 1899–1904.

Larionov, A.L. "Korabli pervoi russkoi antarkticheskoi ekspeditsii—shliupy 'Vostok' i 'Mirnyi'." In M.I. Belov, ed., *Pervaia russkaia antarkticheskaia ekspeditsiia 1819–1821 godov . . .* L. 1963.

Lavachéry, H. *L'Ile de Pâques*. Paris 1935.

Lebedev, D.M. *Geografiia v Rossii petrovskogo vremeni*. M.-L. 1950.

Lebedev, V.L. "Geograficheskie nabliudeniia v Antarktike." *Antarktika: doklady komisssii 1960 goda* (1961).

Lensen, G.A. *The Russian Push Toward Japan: Russo-Japanese Relations, 1697–1875.* Princeton 1959.

Likhtenberg, Iu. M. "Gavaiskie kollektsii v sobraniiakh Muzeia Antropologii i Etnografii." *SMAE,* 19 (1960): 168–205.

Ling Roth, H. *The Maori Mantle.* Halifax 1923.

Lipshits, V.A. "Etnograficheskie issledovaniia v russkikh krugosvetnykh ekspeditsiiakh." In *Ocherki istorii russkoi etnografii, fol'kloristiki, i antropologii,* 1 (1956): 298–321.

Loti, Pierre (J. Viaud). "Expedition der Fregatte 'La Flore' nach der Osterinsel, 1872." *Globus,* 23 (1873): no. 5, pp. 65–68.

————*Reflets sur la sombre route.* Paris, n.d.

Lukina, T.A. *Iogann Fridrikh Eshchol'ts.* Leningrad 1980.

Lupach, V.S., ed. "Ivan Fedorovich Kruzenshtern i Iurii Fedorovich Lisianskii." In *Russkie moreplavateli.* M. 1953.

Lysaght, A. "Banks' Artists and His Endeavour Collection." In T. Mitchell, ed., *British Museum Yearbook,* 3 (1979): 9–80.

Machowski, J. *Island of Secrets.* Trans. M. Michael. London 1975.

MacCallum, D. "The Alleged Russian Plans for the Invasion of Australia, 1864." *JRAHS,* 44 (1959): pt. 52: 301–22.

Mahr, A.C. *The Visit of the "Rurik" to San Francisco in 1816.* Stanford 1932.

Maireau, J. "Notes sur Rapa." *Journal de la Société des Etudes Océaniennes* (Papeete), 5 (1936): 561–67.

Major, R.H. *Early Voyages to Terra Australis.* London 1869.

Malakhovskii, K.V. *Bor'ba imperialisticheskikh derzhav za tikhookeanskie ostrova.* M. 1966.

————*Istoriia kolonializma v Okeanii.* M. 1979.

————, and N.P. Nikolaev. *Okeaniia: spravochnik.* M. 1982.

Marsden, J.B., ed. *Memoirs of the Life and Labours of Rev. Samuel Marsden.* Christchurch 1913.

Marshall, D. *Ra'ivavae: An expedition.* Garden City, NY 1961.

McLintock, A.H. *History of Otago.* Dunedin, NZ 1949.

————*Crown Colony Government in New Zealand.* Wellington 1958.

McCormick, E.H. *Tasman and New Zealand: A Bibliographical Study.* Alexander Turnbull Library Bulletin 14. Wellington 1959.

McNab, R. *Murihiku and the Southern Islands, from 1770–1829.* Invercargill, NZ 1907.

————*Old Whaling Days.* Christchurch 1913.

————*From Tasman to Marsden.* Dunedin, NZ 1914.

Mead, S.M. *Traditional Maori Clothing.* Wellington 1969.

Mel'nitskii, P. *Admiral Rikord i ego sovremenniki.* St. P. 1856.

Menza, G. *Adelbert von Chamissos Reise um die Welt mit der Romanzoffischen Entdeckungs-Expedition in den Jahren 1815–1818.* Lang Verlag: Deutsche Literatur, Reihe 1, No. 251. Frankfurt am Main 1970.

Métraux, A. "Easter Island Sanctuaries." *Ethnological Studies,* 5 (1937): 104–53.

————"Relief Carving on Stone in Polynesia." *Ethnos,* 2 (1937): 340–44.

————*The Ethnology of Easter Island*. . . Bernice P. Bishop Museum Bulletin No. 160. Honolulu 1940.

————*Easter Island*. . . Trans. M. Bullock. London 1957.

Miller, E. *That Noble Cabinet*. London 1973.

Moshkovskaia, Iu.A. *Georg Forster—nemetskii prosvetitel' i revoliutsioner XVIII veka*. M. 1961.

Murray, J. *An Account of the Phormium Tenax*. London 1838.

Nevskii, V.V. *Pervoe puteshestvie Rossiian vokrug sveta*. M. 1951.

Novakovskii, S. *Iaponiia i Rossiia*. Tokyo 1918.

Okun', S.B. *Rossiisko-Amerikanskaia Kompaniia*. M. 1930. Trans. C. Ginsburg as *The Russian-American Company*. Cambridge, MA 1951.

Pasetskii, V.M. *Geograficheskie issledovaniia dekabristov*. M. 1977.

Paszkowski, L. *Polacy w Australii i Oceanii, 1790–1840*. London 1962.

Pavlovskii, E.N., ed. *Antarktika: sbornik materialov po istorii issledovaniia*, M. 1958.

Pekarskii, P. *Nauka i literatura v Rossii pri Petre Velikom*, St. P. 1862.

Pierce, R.A. *Russia's Hawaiian Adventure, 1815–1817*. Berkeley 1965.

Pinart, A. "Voyage à l'Ile de Pâques." *Le Tour du Monde*, 36 (1878): 225–40.

Plischke, H. *Johann Friedrich Blumenbachs Einfluss auf die Entdeckungsreisenden seiner Zeit*. Göttingen 1937.

Porter, K.W. "The Cruise of the 'Forester'." *Washington Historical Quarterly*, 23 (1932): 261–85.

Reymond, E. du Bois. *Adelbert von Chamisso als Naturforscher*. Leipzig 1889.

Roussel, H. "Ile de Pâques." *Annales des Sacrés-Coeurs* (1926): nos. 305–9, 355–60, 423–30, 462–66.

Routledge, C.S. "The Bird Cult of Easter Island." *Folklore*, 28 (1917): 337–81.

————*The Mystery of Easter Island*. London 1919.

————"Survey of the Village and Carved Rocks of Orongo, Easter Island, by the Mana Expedition." *Royal Anthropolgical Institute of Great Britain and Ireland Journal*, 50 (1920): 425–51.

Rozina, L.G. "Kollektsiia Muzeia Antropologii i Etnografii po Markizskim ostrovam." *SMAE*, 21 (1963): 110–19.

————"Kollektsiia Dzhemsa Kuka v sobraniiakh Muzeia Antropologii i Etnografii." *SMAE*, 23 (1966): pp. 78–91.

————"V.V. Sviatlovskii—sobiratel' kollektsii iz Okeanii." *SMAE*, 30 (1974): 127–39.

Russov, F. "Beiträge zur Geschichte der etnographischen und anthropologischen Sammlungen der Kaiserlichen Akademie der Wissenschaften zu St Petersburg." In *Sbornik Muzeia po Antropologii i Etnografii pri Imp. Akademii Nauk*, vol. 1 St. P. 1900.

Ryden, S. *The Banks Collection: An Episode in Eighteenth-Century Anglo-Swedish Relations*. Ethnological Museum Monograph Series, No. 8. Stockholm 1965.

Schumacher, W.W. "On the Linguistic Aspect of Thor Heyerdahl's Theory: The So-called Non-Polynesian Number Names from Easter Island." *Anthropos*, 71 (1976): 806–47.

Shafranovskaia, T.K., and B.N. Komissarov. "Materialy po etnografii Polinezii v dnevnike E.E.. Levenshterna." *Sov. Etnografiia* (1980): no. 6: 99–105.

————, and A.I. Azarov. "Katalog kollektsii otdela Avstralii i Okeanii MAE." *SMAE*, 39 (1984).

Shapiro, A.L. *Admiral D.N. Seniavin*. M. 1958.

Shapiro, H.L. "Mystery Island of the Pacific." *Natural History*, 35 (1935): no. 5, pp. 365–77.

Sharp, A. *The Discovery of the Pacific Islands*. Oxford 1960.

————*The Voyages of Abel Janszoon Tasman*. Oxford 1968.

————*Duperrey's Visit to New Zealand in 1824*. Wellington 1971.

————, ed. *The Journal of Jacob Roggeveen*. Oxford 1970.

Sherrin, R.A., and J.H. Wallace. *Early History of New Zealand: to 1845*. Auckland 1890.

Sheshin, A.B. *Dekabrist K.P. Torson*. Ulan-Ude 1980.

Shokal'skii, Iu. M. "Stoletie so vremeni otpravleniia russkoi antarkticheskoi ekspeditsii pod komandoi F. Bellinsgauzena i M. Lazareva." *IVGO*, 60 (1928): bk. 2.

Shteinberg, E.L. *Zhizneopisanie russkogo moreplavatelia Iuriia Lisianskogo*. L. 1950.

Shur, L..A. "Dnevniki i zapiski russkikh puteshestvennikov kak istochnik po istorii i etnografii stran Tikhogo okeana." In *Avstraliia i Okeaniia*. M. 1970.

Simmons, D.R. "Little Papanui and Otago Prehistory." *Records of the Otago Museum of Anthropology*, 4 (1967): 1–63.

————"The Lake Hauroko Burial and the Evolution of Maori Clothing." *Records of the Otago Museum of Anthropology*, 5 (1968): 1–40.

————"Cyclical Aspects of Early Maori Agriculture." *Records of the Auckland Institute and Museum*, 12 (1975): 83–90.

————*The Great New Zealand Myth*. Wellington 1976.

————, and H.D. Skinner. *The Maori Hei Tiki*. Dunedin, NZ 1966.

Skinner, H.D. "Murdering Beach Collecting and Excavating: The First Phase, 1850–1950." *JPS* 68 (1959): 219–35.

————*Comparatively Speaking*. Dunedin 1974.

Smith, B.W. *European Vision and the South Pacific, 1768–1850*. Oxford 1960.

Smith, S. Percy. *Maori Wars of the Nineteenth Century*. 2d ed. Christchurch 1910.

Sokolov, A.P. "Prigotovlenie krugosvetnoi ekspeditsii 1787 goda pod nachal'stvom kapitana Mulovskogo." *ZGDMM* 6 (1848): 168–87.

————, ed. *Russkaia morskaia biblioteka: period chetvertyi*. St. P. 1883.

Staniukovich, T.V. *Etnograficheskaia nauka i muzei*. L. 1978.

Stolpe, H. "Ueber die Tatowierung der Öster-Insulaner," *Königl. Zoolog. und Anthropol.-Ethnographisches Museum zu Dresden: Festschrift No. 6*. Dresden 1899.

Svet, Ia. M. *Istoriia otkrytiia i issledovaniia Avstralii i Okeanii*. M. 1966.

Tapp, E.J. *Early New Zealand*. Melbourne 1958.

Thomson, W.J. *Te Pito te Henua, or Easter Island*. U.S. National Museum Annual Report. Washington, DC 1889.

Tikotin, M.A. *P.A. Zagorskii i pervaia russkaia anatomicheskaia shkola*. M. 1950.

Tikhmenev, P. *Istoricheskoe obozrenie obrazovaniia Rossiisko-Amerikanskoi Kompanii i deistvii eio do nastoiashchego vremeni*. 2 vols. St. P., 1861–63. Trans. D. Krenov as *Historical Review of the Formation of the Russian-American Company*. Seattle 1939–40. Imperfect and incomplete translation.

Tooley, R.V. *Maps and Map-makers.* London 1970.

Treshnikov, A.F. *Istoriia otkrytiia i issledovaniia Antarktidy.* M. 1963.

Ustrialov, N. *Istoriia tsarstvovaniia Petra Velikogo.* St. P. 1858.

Vayda, A.P. *Maori Warfare.* Wellington 1960.

Venevitinov, A. *Russkie v Gollandii: velikoe posol'stvo 1697–98 godov.* M 1897.

Veselago, F.F. *Ocherki istorii morskago kadetskago korpusa.* St. P. 1852.

————*Admiral I.F. Kruzenshtern.* St. P. 1869.

————*Kratkaia istoriia russkogo flota.* L. 1939.

Vives Solar, J.I. *Rapa Nui: cuentos Pascuences.* Santiago de Chile 1920.

Voenskii, K. "Russkoe posol'stvo v Iaponiiu v nachale xix veka." *Russkaia starina*, 96 (July–October 1895).

Vorob'ev, N.I., et al. "Etnograficheskie nabliudeniia I.M. Simonova na ostrovakh Tikhogo okeana." *IVGO*, 81 (1949): bk. 5, pp. 497–504.

Vorontsov-Vel'iaminov, B.A. *Ocherki istorii astronomii v Rossii.* M. 1956.

Vucinich, A.S. *Science in Russian Culture: A History to 1860.* London 1965.

Ward, J.M. *British Policy in the South Pacific, 1786–1893.* Sydney 1948.

Ward, R.G., ed. *American Activities in the Central Pacific, 1790–1870.* 8 vols. Ridgewood, NJ 1966–67.

Watson, J.H. "Early Shipbuilding in Australia." *JRAHS*, 6 (1912): pt. 2.

Wheeler, M.E. "Empires in Conflict and Cooperation: The Bostonians and the Russian-American Company." *PHR*, 40 (1971): 419–41.

White, J. *The Ancient History of the Maori.* 6 vols. Wellington 1888.

Wieder, F.C., ed. *Monumenta Cartographica.* The Hague 1929.

Williams, G. *The British Search for the Northwest Passage in the Eighteenth Century.* London 1962.

Wolff, W. *Island of Death.* New York 1973.

Zdobnov, N.V. *Istoriia russkoi bibliografii.* M. 1951.

Zubov, V.P. *Istoriografiia estestvennykh nauk v Rossii, XVIII-pervaia polovina XIX veka.* M. 1956.

Name Index

Place Index

Ship Index